# Undergraduate Topics in Computer Science

'Undergraduate Topics in Computer Science' (UTiCS) delivers high-quality instructional content for undergraduates studying in all areas of computing and information science. From core foundational and theoretical material to final-year topics and applications, UTiCS books take a fresh, concise, and modern approach and are ideal for self-study or for a one- or two-semester course. The texts are authored by established experts in their fields, reviewed by an international advisory board, and contain numerous examples and problems, many of which include fully worked solutions.

The UTiCS concept centers on high-quality, ideally and generally quite concise books in softback format. For advanced undergraduate textbooks that are likely to be longer and more expository, Springer continues to offer the highly regarded *Texts in Computer Science* series, to which we refer potential authors.

Gerard O'Regan

# Philosophical and Cultural Aspects of Computing

## A Companion Guide to Ethical and Historical Elements

Springer

Gerard O'Regan
Mallow, Ireland

ISSN 1863-7310 ISSN 2197-1781 (electronic)
Undergraduate Topics in Computer Science
ISBN 978-3-032-29283-4 ISBN 978-3-032-29284-1 (eBook)
https://doi.org/10.1007/978-3-032-29284-1



This Springer imprint is published by the registered company Springer Nature Switzerland AG
The registered company address is: Gewerbestrasse 11, 6330 Cham, Switzerland

*In memory of my friend*
*Dr. Seán O. Nualláin (John Nolan)*
*Requiescat in pace*

# Preface

## Overview

The objective of this book is to give the reader an overview of philosophical and cultural aspects of the computing field. The book is written from the point of view of a non-specialist (a software engineer who is interested in philosophy and its applications to the computing field). A professional philosopher examines issues in forensic detail, whereas this book has been written at a lighter level. The author hopes that his broad coverage will be both interesting and insightful to the reader.

## Organization and Features

The introduction of modern computer technology has led to immense changes in society, with new technologies impacting everyone in society. There has been an extraordinary growth in the use of the Internet and World Wide Web, and personal devices such as smartphones and tablets are ubiquitous. Users are monitored online for commercial purposes (surveillance capitalism), and while many of these new technologies are useful and serve the interests of society, there are also negative affects to consider. These include an erosion (or invasion) of privacy, the dangers of addiction on social media and other sites, as well as the dangers of scams, viruses, and cybercrime. This means that users need to exercise caution to ensure that they remain in control of the technology, and do not become victims of crime.

The author has worked both as a software engineer and as an international academic. His interests include software engineering (especially software quality and software process improvement), formal methods, mathematics in computing, the history of computing, as well as philosophical, ethical, cultural and legal aspects of computing.

A professional philosopher performs a painstaking and forensic analysis of the underlying philosophical issues, whereas the author's goals are more modest, and instead important areas are introduced (including the historical background), and some of the fundamental questions and philosophical issues are discussed (at a lighter level from that of the professional philosopher). And so, it is hoped that the broad coverage will provide a nice introduction to some of the key philosophical and ethical topics in computing.

The early chapters focus on the philosophical side of computing with chapters on an introduction to philosophy, followed by chapters that explore the philosophy of science, engineering and technology; an examination of what exactly a computer is, as well as understanding the difference between hardware and software. We then examine computer science and the nature of a computer program, and proceed to a study of algorithms and computability. We then discuss the philosophy of Artificial Intelligence.

We then focus on ethics (an important sub-field of philosophy) including a short history of ethics and proceed to examine professional responsibilities of computer professionals. We then discuss ethical software engineering and proceed to examining the ethics of data science, and then consider ethical social media and ethical AI. We then examine contemporary issues in the philosophy of computing.

The final two chapters are specific to cultural aspects of computing, where we consider the social and cultural impacts of the industrial revolution, the IBM System 360 and the World Wide Web. We then consider how computing technology has impacted various sectors in society such as health, education, politics, the media, religion and so on.

Chapter 1 introduces philosophical and cultural aspects of computing, and we discuss various philosophical and ethical problems that arise in the computer field. Chapter 2 presents a brief history of philosophy including important areas and leading figures throughout its history. We start with a discussion of Greek philosophy, move on to the scholastic philosophy of St. Augustine and St. Thomas, to the rationalist philosophy of Descartes, to British empiricism with the work of Locke, Berkley and Hume, and the response of Kant (which he regarded as a Copernican revolution in philosophy). We proceed to the philosophy of language with contributions by Russell, Frege and Wittgenstein, and finally we consider the field of existentialism. We briefly discuss eastern philosophy, and conclude with some important philosophical questions in computing.

Chapter 3 discusses the philosophy of science, engineering and technology, and we explore the nature of science, engineering and technology, and investigate the extent to which computer science is 'science' and the extent to which it is 'engineering'. The philosophy of science is concerned with the nature and foundations of science, and uses the scientific method, which helps in distinguishing science from pseudo science. Engineering involves the application of science to build safe and useful products for the public, whereas the philosophy of engineering is concerned with philosophical issues that arise in engineering, including ethical issues that may arise, as well as the aesthetics of the engineered products.

Chapter 4 discusses the nature of a computer, and we note that Boole's symbolic logic was the perfect mathematical model for the design of digital circuits. A Turing machine gives a precise definition of the process of computing.

Chapter 5 discusses the nature of computer science, which consists of a body of knowledge that is used by computer professionals in their work. Computer science has become intertwined with many other disciplines that in many ways it is really about everything. It studies computers and the algorithms that run on them, and it is, in a way, both science and engineering.

Chapter 6 discusses the nature of computer programs, where a computer program provides the instructions to a computer to implement some algorithm to solve a particular problem. We discuss the specification of a program, the nature of a programming language, syntax and semantics, and the implementation and verification of a computer program.

Chapter 7 discusses the nature of algorithms and computation, and we investigate computability. The intuitive meaning of computability is in terms of an algorithm (or effective procedure) that specifies a set of instructions to be followed to solve the problem. The concept of computability is made precise in several equivalent ways such as Church's lambda calculus, recursive function theory or by the theoretical Turing machines. We discuss the halting problem, which is not computable, and its applicability to showing that mathematics is not decidable.

Chapter 8 discusses the philosophy of AI and we examine Descartes mind-body distinction, in that he states that there are two substances in the universe: mental substances and bodily substances. The mind-body distinction is relevant in AI, with the analogy of the human mind and brain given by software running on a computer. We consider the Turing test of machine intelligence as well as Searle's "Chinese Room" rebuttal, which argues that even if a computer passed the Turing Test that it would still not be intelligent, as it would have no understanding (i.e., syntax is not semantics).

Chapter 9 presents a short history of ethics, and we discuss ethics in ancient civilisations as well as ethics in several religious traditions. We discuss utilitarian and deontological ethics, and consider the question of what it means to be ethical in a complex world.

Chapter 10 discusses the professional responsibilities of computer professionals, and we discuss the code of ethics of the Association for Computing Machinery, the Institute of Electrical and Electronic Engineers and the British Computer Society. We discuss the role of the whistle blower and its importance.

Chapter 11 discusses ethical software engineering, and we discuss notable incidents such as the space shuttle disaster and the defective Therac-25 radiotherapy machine. We discuss the Volkswagen emissions scandal, where engineers designed a "defeat device" that would allow Volkswagen cars to pass their emission tests in the United States.

Chapter 12 discusses the ethics of data science. There has been a phenomenal growth in the use of digital data with vast amounts of data collected, processed and used, and we investigate what is fair and ethical in data science, and what should or should not be done with data. We discuss ethical problems of privacy that arise in social media, the Internet of Things, AI and facial recognition.

Chapter 13 discusses social media and ethics, where social media is designed to have individuals share as much information as possible about themselves, and to continue to do so while they are on the site. Social media sites are designed to be addictive and pose risks to the privacy of an individual. We discuss the Facebook revolution and its impact during the Arab spring, as well as the Cambridge

Analytica affair, and its impact in influencing voters in the 2016 election in the United States.

Chapter 14 discusses ethics and AI, and we discuss Weizenbaum's Eliza program and the challenge that AI poses to human dignity. We discuss the ethics of self-driving cars, where there is a need to encode a moral compass in the vehicle to deal with situations where ethical decisions need to be made. We discuss ethical problems that arise with AI and surveillance.

Chapter 15 discusses contemporary issues in the philosophy of computing, and we examine explainability, which considers the extent to which AI systems can explain their decision making process, as well as emerging technologies such as AR/VR which pose philosophical questions on perception, reality and truth. Finally, we discuss the progress in quantum computing, which raises philosophical questions on computation.

Chapter 16 discusses cultural issues in computing, where the relationship between culture and computing is like a two-way feedback loop. On the one hand computing shapes culture, and on the other hand cultural values influence the development of new computing technology.

Chapter 17 explores the impact of computing on wider society, including health, education, politics, law, media, government, family, and religion. Computer technology has shaped how people interact and communicate, and reflects and reinforces the social values in society, with the design of digital technology (e.g., computers, apps, algorithms) reflecting the social values of their creators.

Chapter 18 is the concluding chapter in which we summarize the journey travelled in this book.

## Audience

The main audience of this book are computer science students who are interested in learning about philosophical and cultural issues in the computing field. It will also be of interest to the general reader.

Cork, Ireland Gerard O'Regan

**Acknowledgments** I am deeply indebted to family and friends who supported my efforts in this endeavour, and my thanks, as always, to the team at Springer.

This book is dedicated to my late friend, Dr. Seán O'Nualláin (John Nolan), who was a gifted academic and musician. I first met Dr. O'Nualláin (John) during my first job as a lecturer at what was then called Carlow RTC (it is now called South East Technological University). John was a highly competent professional, and I was highly impressed by his intellectual honesty and commitment to truth, as well as his determination to do the right thing, irrespective of whether it had any negative consequences on him personally. He was also an excellent squash player (we were about the same level during the Carlow period, but when we played again at Trinity College Dublin it was a struggle to get even a point). He was active in research and made many contributions to cognitive science, and he ran the successful *Foundations of Mind* conference that adopted a multi-disciplinary (e.g., linguistics, physics, neuroscience) approach to explore the nature of consciousness and cognition. I was deeply saddened to hear the news of his passing. *Requiescat in pace.*

Cork, Ireland Gerard O'Regan

**Competing Interests** The author has no competing interests to declare that are relevant to the content of this manuscript.

# Contents

# List of Figures

# List of Tables

# Introduction to Philosophical and Cultural Aspects of Computing 1

## 1.1 Introduction

The objective of this book is to give the reader an overview of philosophical and cultural issues that arise in the computing field, and the book was influenced by the author's experience in working in academia and industry over many years. The author became conscious of these issues in computing during his career, and this motivated him to explore these disciplines in more detail, especially in their applications to computer science. And so while the author is not a specialist in these fields (i.e., the book is written from the point of view of a software engineer who is a non-specialist in philosophy, culture and ethics), he hopes that that the reader will find the coverage to be both interesting and insightful.

The early chapters focus on philosophical aspects of computing with chapters on an introduction to philosophy, followed by chapters that explore the philosophy of science and engineering, an examination of what exactly a computer is, as well as the nature of computer science (i.e., whether it is a science or engineering). We explore the nature of programs as well as implementation and correctness of programs with respect to their specification, as well as the study of algorithms and computability, and the nature of Artificial Intelligence.

The focus then moves on an important sub field of philosophy (i.e., ethics) with chapters on the history of ethics; the professional responsibility of computer professionals; ethical software engineering; the ethics of data science; ethical social media; and ethical AI. We then examine some contemporary issues in the philosophy of computing, and the final chapters are concerned with cultural aspects of computing, and the cultural impacts of computing technology on various areas of society.

Philosophical aspects of computing are concerned with the study of fundamental concepts and assumptions in the computing field. This includes fundamental questions such as "what is a computer?", what is an algorithm?", "what is computability?", "what is computation?", "what is a computer program?", "how can

 
G. O'Regan, *Philosophical and Cultural Aspects of Computing*, Undergraduate Topics in Computer Science, https://doi.org/10.1007/978-3-032-29284-1_1

we verify the correctness of a computer program?", and "what exactly is computer science?"

It is difficult to come up with one sentence that characterises the entire discipline of the field, as any such definition tends to focus on one aspect of the field. Computer science is connected with many other disciplines, and so it is difficult to think of it as a field in its own right, as it has become an integral part of other fields. This means that in many ways the field of computer science is really about everything, and the discipline is an integral part of the evolution of many other fields, as computers are tools that enhance reasoning in any discipline.

Computer science is a science since it consists of a body of knowledge and scientific principles that are used by computer professionals in their work. On the other hand computer scientists build things and use engineering principles in their work, and so it is reasonable to ask if computer science is engineering? Is it is both science and engineering? Is it neither?

Computer science emerged from the field of mathematics, and theoretical computer science is quite mathematical. And so, another view is that computer science is that it is mathematics, as it emerged from the theoretical work of Boole in the nineteenth century, and theoretical work on the foundation of mathematics in the early twentieth century. That is, Boole's theoretical and foundational work on symbolic logic in the mid-nineteenth century was important, and while Boole was a theoretician (i.e., he did not build things and never built a computer), although Charles Babbage, who was a contemporary of Boole, designed the Difference Engine, which was a calculator for evaluating polynomials, and the Analytic Engine, which was the design of a mechanical computer. It was Claude Shannon who realised in the late 1920s that Boole's symbolic logic was the perfect model for digital computing (as recorded in his famous Masters thesis).

The early twentieth century saw important work on the foundations of mathematics, and several of its theoretical results (on computability, decidability, and completeness) are relevant to the computer field today. The work on the foundations of mathematics led to the fields of logicism (as developed by Frege and Russell), formalism (as developed by Hilbert and others) and intuitionism (as proposed by L.E.J. Brouwer).

Kurt Godel showed in 1931 that the formal axiomatic system of arithmetic is incomplete (i.e., it cannot determine the truth or falsity of all statements about numbers). Turing and Church did important work on computability and decidability in the 1930s, and they showed that the halting problem for Turing Machines was not computable, and that the formal axiomatic system of mathematics is undecidable.

Ethics explore what actions are right or wrong within a specific context or society, and seek to find satisfactory answers to moral questions. It is a search for moral principles to guide the behaviour of individuals or groups, and ethical issues occur when a conflict arises between an individual's moral compass, and the values or moral principles held by the society or organisation that the individual belongs to. We discuss the Space Shuttle Challenger disaster (an important case study in workplace safety and ethics) back in the mid-1980s, where the decision making process that led to the launch was deeply flawed.

The book concludes with chapters on the cultural side of computing, and we discuss cultural aspects of technology, including the industrial revolution, the System 360, and the World Wide Web, as well as the cultural impacts of computing technology on wider society.

## 1.2 What Is Philosophy?

Philosophy is a systematic enquiry into fundamental questions, and it proceeds by reflection on important areas where exact knowledge has not been established or is not yet possible. There is a contrast between the work of the professional philosopher and that of the scientist who studies the world of science and what we can know about the world. That is, the scientist proceeds with empirical observation and uses the scientific method, whereas philosophy uses logic and critically reasoning to fundamentally enquire into the foundations and theories of a particular discipline, and it investigates the extent to which the foundations of a theory can be defended, and whether the answers that the theory gives are tenable. That is, the philosopher is searching for truth, and any theory that has gaps or is not tenable is rejected.

Philosophy examines many fundamental questions that science cannot deal with at this time. For example, it considers questions such as "What does it mean to be human?", "What is beauty?", and "What is the nature of knowledge?". These are questions that arise naturally as part of the human condition, but science cannot assist, at this time, in answering them.

Philosophy is, in a sense, something intermediate between science and theology, where theology consists of dogma that may arise from revelation or traditional beliefs, whereas scientific knowledge comes from the use of the scientific method and rational argument.

Philosophy is a subject with many branches and deals with many fundamental questions such as questions about existence, knowledge, values, mind and language. Often, there is no consensus on the answer to a particular question in philosophy, and philosophers critically examine a particular answer to see if is a tenable explanation. Few answers survive the forensic analysis of professional philosophers, and, in many ways, there has been little progress in philosophy over the millennia.

Some philosophical questions are related to free will; some relate to how one should live in order to lead a good and happy life; some are questions as to how society and government should be organised; some are questions related to being, some are questions relating to how knowledge of the world is obtained, and some are questions as to whether the belief in a deity and organised religion is justified.

Philosophy may involve an enquiry into areas that are not yet amenable to scientific knowledge, and it may show us that things that we thought to be true are not actually so. Science has been extremely successful in determining knowledge, but it has limitations when dealing with questions of values such as what is good or what is bad as an end (rather than as a means). Philosophy does not provide certainty, as there is always some element of doubt regarding the particular situation. That is, there is always some degree of uncertainty as to how one should act or proceed in a particular situation, and so one should reflect carefully, and act in a way such that there is a high probability that the course of action that one takes is correct.

Philosophy proceeds by a coherent enquiry into the matter of concern, and arguments are usually made in natural language (or in rarer situations using formal logic). Philosophers proceed from premises to conclusions using logical arguments, and they examine their arguments closely with the goal of avoiding fallacies in reasoning. The study of philosophy is invaluable in developing critical thinking skills, and helps to prevent "woolly" arguments in everyday life.

The writing of a philosopher may be an attempt to answer a particular philosophical question, and despite the many philosophical theories or systems that have been developed over the millennia, most have been shown to be incorrect. And so, in many ways there has been little progress in philosophy over the last 2500 years from Classical Greece to the modern age, with the English mathematician and philosopher, Alfred North Whitehead (the co-author of the three-volume *Principia Mathematica* with Bertrand Russell), describing the European philosophical tradition as a series of footnotes to Plato.

### 1.2.1 Philosophical Aspects of Computing

Computer science is the study of both computers (i.e., the physical devices that compute) and computing (i.e., the algorithms that run on computers). The field emerged from the development of the earliest digital computer in the early 1940s, and the term "*computer science*" first appeared in a 1959 article by Louis Fein in Communications of the ACM [Fei:59]. The 1959 article described the role of the university in computers, data processing and related fields.

A digital computer is a sequential device that generally operates on data one step at a time, and the data are represented in binary format. A single transistor (initially a bulky vacuum tube) is used to represent a binary digit, whereas several transistors are required to store larger numbers.

We mentioned that computer science has become so intertwined with many other disciplines, that is, it is difficult, in a sense, to think of it as a field in its own right, as it enhances reasoning in most fields, and so computer science is really about everything. It consists of a body of knowledge that is used by computer professionals, and as it involves building things it uses engineering principles as well. Further, there is a mathematical dimension to the field as it arose from mathematics. And so, it is very difficult to come up with one sentence that characterises the entire discipline.

Computer science differs from natural science in many fundamental ways, and it deals with artificial rather than natural objects. The objects of study are computers, algorithms, and the processing of information. In a way, programs running on a computer are like experiments, but they differ from the experiments carried out in natural science. In many ways, computer science is almost like a new kind of science that studies computers and algorithms.

Computer scientists are like engineers in that they build things, and so engineering principles are an integral part of the computer scientist's work. That is, the modern computer scientist needs to follow sound engineering practices to ensure that products are properly designed and implemented, and are safe for the public to use. Computer scientists (as engineers) have professional responsibilities in their work, and need to behave ethically at all times.

Theoretical Computer science is quite mathematical, and includes areas such as formal specification that aims to give a precise mathematical description of what a program is to do, and program verification that aims to prove that a program satisfies its specification. Other mathematical areas include the semantics of programming languages using axiomatic or denotational semantics; the field of cryptography is concerned with enciphering messages so that any unauthorised access by an eavesdropper is meaningless, and the field of error-correcting codes as in coding theory aims to identify and correct any errors in data transmission. Other areas include Turing machines and lambda calculus which are used in the study of computability, and complexity theory that is concerned with whether a computationally complex problem can be solved in a reasonable period of time (polynomial time).

Dijkstra [Dij:73] argued that parts of computer science such as programming, computability and complexity theory are mathematical activities, where mathematics is a "formal" science that proceeds from premises to conclusions via deductive reasoning.

Perhaps, a more inclusive answer to what computer science is that it is a STEM discipline: i.e., a discipline that involves Science, Technology, Engineering, and Mathematics. It involves the study of many areas including computers, algorithms, information, processes and procedures, problem solving, the way of thinking about algorithms and computation, the art of computer programming, artificial intelligence, and complexity.

Computer science studies many areas such as computers and algorithms, with programming employed to implement algorithms; program specification (either in natural language or a formal specification language) is a formal statement of what the program is to do; program verification is used to verify the correctness of programs and algorithms with respect to the specification; computability theory is related to the existence of an algorithm to solve a particular problem; operating systems provide important software on the computer that manage the computer hardware as well as providing common services for software programs. Software engineering deals with how high-quality software is designed and developed to satisfy the customer requirements; and AI is concerned with software that simulates human intelligence and problem solving.

A computer is essentially a computing or calculating device with software running on the machine. Computer science intersects many fields such as science, engineering, mathematics, and logic, and deals with computers and algorithms. Software is essentially a set of instructions that a computer can follow to implement an algorithm, and is for a particular machine architecture and operating system. A computer program may need to work on different computers and operating systems, and if so it will need to be customised for each machine/ operating system. This means that the set of instructions may vary depending on the customisation required.

An algorithm takes symbols as inputs and produces symbols as output, and is implemented by some computer program. The Church-Turing Thesis was formulated in the 1930s, and states that every effective computation may be carried out by the theoretical Turing machine (see [ORg:23]). *Computers and programs are symbiotic in that computers require programs to do anything, and programs require computers in order for the programs to actually do anything.* That is, computation processes arise only from the union of a computer with a program.

The earliest calculating machines were developed in the seventeenth century with Pascal's mechanical calculator, the Pascaline, developed in 1642, and Leibniz's more advanced calculator, the Step Reckoner was built in 1673. The study of algorithms goes back, at least, to Euclid, and Turing's theoretical study of algorithms in the 1930s led to his theoretical Turing machine. Turing analysed how humans compute and he devised a theoretical machine that would do the same. He showed that computation could be described in terms of a machine changing through a finite set of states in response to a sequence of symbols read and written one at a time on a potentially infinite tape.

A key question in computer science is "what is computable?", or another words is there a computational solution to a particular problem, and if so, how should the solution be implemented? Church and Turing investigated the question of "which mathematical functions are computable?" in the 1930s, with the answer given by the Church-Turing thesis. This thesis states that a function is computable if and only if it is computable by a Turing machine (or equivalent formalism such as lambda calculus). There are non-computable functions such as the halting problem, where there is no general algorithm that solves the halting problem for all possible program—input pairs. The halting problem is the problem of determining from a description of an arbitrary computer program and an input whether the program will halt or continue to run forever.

The intuitive meaning of computability is in terms of an algorithm (or effective procedure) that specifies a set of instructions to be followed to complete the task. Another words, a function $f$ is *computable* if there exists an algorithm that produces the value of $f$ correctly for each possible argument of $f$. The computation of $f$ for a particular argument $x$ just involves following the instructions in the algorithm, and it produces the result $f(x)$ in a finite number of steps if $x$ is in the domain of $f$. If $x$ is not in the domain of $f$ then the algorithm may produce an answer saying so, or it might run forever never halting. A computer program implements an algorithm.

The fact that the problem is computable is the first step, and the next question is how it is computable: i.e., it requires a constructive answer in the form of an algorithm to solve the problem. Further, the constructive solution needs to be efficient in solving the problem: e.g., if the proposed solution requires 5000 years to solve the problem then this is not a practical solution, and so other solutions to solve the problem within an acceptable timeframe will be sought (and if no solution exists in an acceptable timeframe a heuristic will be sought). This leads to the area of computational complexity theory, which includes problems that can be solved in polynomial (P) time, as well as those that can be solved in non-deterministic polynomial (NP) time.

A computer program is an expression of an algorithm in some programming language. That is, a program is written in some programming language (e.g., C, Java, etc.) and is a set of instructions to implement an algorithm. Computers are essentially calculating devices with a computer program being a set of instructions to run on the physical machine to implement the algorithm.

The progress in computer science has been the result of the success of engineering better and better calculating machines as well as a more detailed understanding of algorithmic computation.

### 1.2.2 Recent Trends in the Philosophy of Computing

The philosophy of computing continues to expand its boundaries and among the recent trends in the field is a greater focus on AI Ethics and Safety, which is concerned with developing AI that is trustworthy, accountable and fair. This area studies the area of bias mitigation (techniques that aim to deal with bias in the data), as well as the area of explainability (that examines the extent to which AI systems can explain their decision making process, which is essential for accountability and trust). It also studies the systemic risk of advanced AI development.

Other areas studied include emerging technologies relevant to the AI field, including the study of quantum computers, which are a paradigm shift in computer technology (they use the principles of quantum mechanics and qubits are used instead of bits). The area of augmented/virtual reality (AR/VR) is also studied including its impact on experience and identity. Another technology examined is blockchain technology, with philosophical analysis of decentralisation on trust and security.

Other areas include the energy consumption and environmental impact of AI technologies (especially with the development of energy hungry data centres around the world), and the extent to which more efficient algorithms and architectures can address the problem.

## 1.3 Philosophy and Ethics

Philosophy is a broad discipline and includes many branches such as metaphysics, epistemology, ontology, the philosophy of science, the philosophy of mathematics and logic, the philosophy of art and aesthetics, as well as ethics. Philosophy proceeds by rational argument and attempts to answer fundamental questions, and the philosophical method involves formulating a theory or explanation of some aspect of the world, and then subjecting the theory to critical analysis.

That is, philosophy is, in a sense, a subject with many branches in that it has many objects of study rather than one. Some philosophical questions are related to human nature and free will, some are questions as to how one should live in order to lead a good and happy life; some are questions as to how one should live morally and ethically (moral philosophy or ethics); some are questions related to what knowledge is (epistemology); some are questions related to the nature of being (ontology); some are questions as to how society and government should be organised (political philosophy); and some are questions as to the belief in a deity and organised religion (the philosophy of religion). Often there is no consensus on the answer to a particular question, and any answers are subjected to a forensic examination to determine their truth or falsity.

Ethics is a practical branch of philosophy that studies moral principles and values, to determine what is morally right or wrong, and how we should live. For example, should we pursue our own happiness or the happiness of others? Is it right that some individuals have extreme wealth (e.g., the billionaire class) whereas many people in the world live in extreme poverty? What obligations do we, as humans, have to future generations, given that our actions today are adversely affecting the planet (leading to devastating climate change around the world) thereby impacting future generations, as well as the long-term survival of the planet?

That is, ethics deals with questions such as what is right or wrong, and explores what actions are right or wrong within a specific context, or within a certain society. It searches for moral principles to guide individuals and groups to find satisfactory answers to moral questions. An ethical issue occurs when a conflict arises between an individual's moral values, and the values or moral principles held by the society or organisation that the individual belongs to.

Ethics is considered to be a branch of philosophy (i.e., moral philosophy), but it also has links to other areas of knowledge such as anthropology, politics, sociology and theology.

### 1.3.1 Philosophy and Ethics in Computing

The philosophical aspects of computing are concerned with the nature of computing, and considers fundament questions such as what exactly a computer is as well as what exactly is computer science? Ethical aspects of computing are concerned with problems (often unforeseen or unintended) that arise from the use of computing technology.

Philosophical aspects of computing are concerned with fundamental questions that arise in the computing field. We consider questions such as what exactly a computer is as well as what exactly is computer science? We consider the extent to which computer science is a "science" and the extent to which it is "engineering", and we briefly explore the philosophy of science, engineering and technology.

We examine the nature of a computer program including the language aspects of a computer program, as well as its semantics and implementation. A programming language is defined by its syntax and semantics, where the syntax is the grammar of a language and the semantics give its meaning. There are several approaches to the definition of the semantics of a programming language, including axiomatic semantics, denotational semantics and operational semantics. The compiler preserves the semantics of a programming language rather than giving the semantics.

We discuss the specification of a computer program, as well as examining how we can be confident that a program satisfies its specification. This leads to the concept of program verification, which is a mathematical approach to show that the program satisfies its specification (however, it is essential that the specification is correct). That is, the correctness of a computer program can, in principle, be demonstrated mathematically, as in the demonstration of a proof in mathematics. However, in practice, given the effort involved in program verification, it is generally only employed in the safety critical sector, whereas extensive testing (rather than program verification) is generally employed in the verification of commercial software. We examine the nature of algorithms and computability and whether a computational solution exists for a particular problem.

The philosophy of AI considers questions such as what exactly is mind and consciousness? It examines the nature of knowledge and intelligence as well as discussing the mind-body problem. There has been remarkable progress in recent times in simulating intelligent behaviour (e.g., ChatGPT and robot technology), but the development of real artificial intelligence is a long-term goal.

Software engineers have professional responsibilities as engineers in developing products that are safe for the public to use. Thus they need to be educated as engineers and to employ engineering principles in their work. Many professional bodies and corporations have formulated codes of conduct for their members or employees, and these codes stipulate the required behaviour of members or employees.

Ethical software design and development is concerned with having an appropriate and professional software engineering environment in place. The environment enables software engineers to create high quality and safe products that are fit for purpose and safe for the public to use. Ethical outsourcing is concerned the selection and management of a software supplier, and an ethical organisation will ensure that employees in the particular country are not exploited (e.g., excessive hours, low pay, poor accommodation as in the Apple/Foxconn controversy back in 2006). It requires much more than just complying with the laws of the particular country (as these laws may not be fit for purpose).

Social media has become very popular but it has led to problems such as trolling and harassment of individuals from the deliberate posting of provocative or insulting content designed to upset others. Other problems include disinformation and fake news, where false information is deliberately spread on line. The new field of surveillance capitalism tracks the online activities of users with a view to the commercial exploitation of their personal data. It is essential that users have some control over their personal data, and that inaccurate data may be corrected, and their personal data should not be abused.

The growth of AI has led to further problems as AI models are trained using data, and if the data is biased it potentially leads to biased algorithms (for example, the predicting police algorithms and Amazon hiring algorithms discussed in Chap. 14). Computer technology has become highly addictive with many users spending hours on their smart phones everyday, checking and posting messages leading to social media addiction, as well as addiction to online games. Deepfake technology is an AI technology that allows videos to be created that appear to show an individual performing or saying something inappropriate. The technology is mainly used for comedy, but it may potentially be used for sinister purposes in the future.

## 1.4 What Is Ethics?

Ethics is a practical branch of philosophy that deals with moral questions such as what is right or wrong, and how should a person respond when presented with a situation that requires ethical decision making? Ethics explore what actions are right or wrong within a specific context or within a certain society, and seek to find satisfactory answers to moral questions. It is a search for the appropriate principles to guide the behaviour of individuals or groups, and ethical issues occur when a conflict arises between an individual's moral values, and the values or moral principles held by the society or organisation that the individual belongs to (e.g., the clash between an individual's conscience and the laws of the state as in Sophocles' *Antigone*). The origin of the word "ethics" is from the Greek word ἠθικός, which means habit or custom.

There are various schools of ethics such as the *relativist* position (as defined by the sophist philosopher, Protagoras), which argues that each person decides on what is right or wrong for himself or herself, and that there is no objective grounding of truth and reality; *cultural relativism* argues that the particular society determines what is right or wrong based upon its cultural values; *deontological ethics* (as defined by Kant) argues that there are moral laws to guide people in deciding what is right or wrong and individuals have a duty to follow the moral law; and *utilitarianism* (as defined by Bentham and refined by Mills) which argues that an action is right if its overall affect is to produce more happiness than unhappiness in society.

*Professional ethics* are a code of conduct that governs how members of a profession deal with each other and with third parties. A professional code of ethics expresses ideals of human behaviour, and it defines the fundamental principles of the organisation, and is an indication of its professionalism. Several organisations such as the Association Computing Machinery (ACM), the Institute of Electrical and Electronic Engineers (IEEE) and the British Computer Society (BCS) have developed a code of conduct for their members, and violations of the code by members are taken seriously and are subject to investigations and disciplinary procedures (see Chap. 3). Groucho Marx[1] had a humorous quote on principles (or lack of principles)

> Those are my principles, and if you don't like them … well, I have others

Business ethics define the core values of the business, and are used to guide employee behaviour. Should an employee accept gifts from a supplier to a company (as this could influence the employee's decision making) leading to a conflict of interest? A company may face ethical questions on the use of technology. For example, should the use of a new technology be restricted because people can use it for illegal or harmful actions as well as beneficial ones?

For example, consider mobile phone technology, which has transformed communication between people, and thus is highly beneficial to society. What about mobile phones with cameras? On the one hand, they provide useful functionality in combining a phone and a camera. On the other hand, they may be employed to take indiscreet and inappropriate photos of others without their permission, and then placed on inappropriate sites causing distress and harm to others. In other words, how can the benefits of technology be balanced with unintended consequences, and how can individuals be protected from inappropriate use of technology?

Ethics does not directly tell us what we should or shouldn't do, and it is in a sense a set of standards to evaluate good or bad behaviour. An individual needs to be conscious of ethical situations that arise in human existence, and to use their moral compass and values to decide on the appropriate response, and to do the right thing. Moral standards are important for the proper functioning of society.

The influential Canadian philosopher and theologian, Fr. Bernard Lonergan, outlined four key steps on being human his influential book "*Insight: A study on human understanding*" [Lon:78]. These steps are based on four levels of conscious

[1] The Marx brothers (Groucho, Chico, Harpo, and Zeppo) were a famous American family comedy act in the 1930s, and they made hilarious movies such as "Duck Soup" and "A Night at the Opera". Groucho was renounced for his quick wit and his extremely funny one-liners, and his quote on principles essentially indicates that his character does not live by any principles.

functioning namely experience, understanding, judgment and decision. Lonergan summarises the demands of the human spirit by "*Be attentive, be intelligent, be reasonable, and be responsible*".

## 1.5 Business Ethics

Business ethics (also called corporate ethics) is concerned with ethical principles and moral problems that arise in a business environment. They refer to the core principles and values of the organization, and apply throughout the organization. They guide individual employees in carrying out their daily roles, and they include the rights and duties of a company, its employees, customers and suppliers.

Many corporation and professional organizations have a written "*code of ethics*" that defines the professional standards expected of all employees in the company. Unfortunately, sometimes the code of ethics of an organisation is just *window dressing*, where it gives the impression that these are the core values of the organisation. However, the reality on the ground may be quite different, with values neither properly implemented, or not being rigorously followed by employees in their day-to-day work practices. That is, the code of ethics needs to be ingrained in organisation culture to be effective.

All employees are expected to adhere to the core values of the code of ethics in the daily performance of their duties and whenever they represent the company. The human resource function in a company plays an important role in promoting ethics, and in putting internal HR policies in place relating to the ethical conduct of the employees, as well as addressing discrimination, sexual harassment and ensuring that employees are treated appropriately (including cultural sensitivities in a multi-cultural business environment). HR has a responsibility to provide training and awareness to staff on its core values (including its code of ethics), and it needs to investigate any alleged violations of the code by employees, and discipline employees (including possible termination of employment) for serious violations of the code.

Companies are expected to behave ethically and not to exploit their workers. There was an infamous case of employee exploitation at the Foxconn plant (an Apple supplier of the *i*Phone) in Shenzhen in China in 2006, where conditions at the plant were so dreadful (long hours, low pay, unreasonable workload, and crammed accommodation) that several employees committed suicide. The scandal raised questions on the extent to which a large corporation such as Apple should protect the health and safety of the factory workers of its suppliers. Further, given the immense profits that Apple makes from the *i*Phone, is it ethical for Apple to allow such workers to be exploited?

Today, the area of *corporate social responsibility* (CSR) has become applicable to the corporate world, and it requires the corporation to be an ethical and responsible citizen in the communities in which it operates (even at a cost to its profits). It is therefore reasonable to expect a responsible corporation to pay its fair share of tax, and to refrain from exploiting tax loopholes to avoid paying billions in taxes on international sales. Today, environmental ethics has become topical, and it is concerned with the responsibility of business in protecting the environment in which it operates. It is reasonable to expect a responsible corporation to make the protection of the environment and sustainability part of its business practices, even if this has an impact on its profitability.

Unethical business practices refer to those business actions that don't meet the standard of acceptable business operations, and they give the company a bad name. It may be that the entire business culture is corrupt or it may result from the unethical actions of an employee. It is important that such practices be exposed, and this may place an employee in an ethical dilemma (i.e., the loyalty of the employee to the employer who pays her salary, versus doing the right thing, such as becoming a *whistleblower* to expose the unethical or unsafe business practices). There are dangers that a whistleblower could suffer career suicide as a result of exposing unsafe or unethical practices, and so organisations need to create an effective structure or mechanism, where employees can raise serious issues that may then be discussed and resolved without fear of negative consequences to their career (Fig. 1.1).

Some accepted business practices in the workplace might cause ethical concerns. For example, in many companies it is normal for the employer to monitor email and Internet use to ensure that employees do not abuse them, and so employees may have grounds for privacy concerns. On the one hand, the employer is paying the employee's salary, and has a reasonable expectation that the employee

**Fig. 1.1** Corrupt legislation. 1896. Public domain

will be professional and will not abuse email and the Internet. On the other hand, the employee has reasonable rights of privacy provided that computer resources are not abused.

The nature of privacy is relevant in the business models of several technology companies. For example, Google specializes in Internet based services and products, and its many products include *Google Search* (the world's largest search engine); *Gmail* for email; and *Google Maps* (a web mapping application that offers satellite images and street views). Google's products gather a lot of personal data about its users that is used to create revealing profiles of the users, which can then be exploited for commercial purposes.

A Google search leaves traces on both the computer and in records kept by Google, which has raised privacy concerns as such information may be obtained by a forensic examination of the computer, or in records obtained from Google or the Internet Service Providers (ISP). Gmail automatically scans the contents of emails to add context sensitive advertisements to them and to filter Spam, which raises privacy concerns, as it means that all emails sent or received are scanned and read by some computer.

Google has argued that the automated scanning of emails is done to enhance the user experience, as it provides customized search results, tailored advertisements, and the prevention of Spam and viruses. Google maps provides location information which may be used for targeted advertisements, and smartphones with Google maps have a location tracking feature that may be used for the electronic surveillance of users by recording the places that they visit as well as the times and duration of the visit.

The surveillance practices of many technology companies have led to the new field of *surveillance capitalism*, where the personal data of individuals is gathered and exploited for commercial purposes. The ethics of data science is discussed in Chap. 12.

## 1.6 What Are Computer Ethics?

Computer ethics is a set of principles that guide the behaviour of individuals when using computer resources. Several ethical issues that may arise include privacy concerns, intellectual property rights, as well as the impacts of computer technology on wider society. The more awareness and knowledge that computer professionals and the general public has on the ethical implications of computer technology, the better they will be able to navigate through these issues in a thoughtful and considered manner.

The Computer Ethics Institute (CEI) is an American organisation that examines ethical issues that arise in the information technology field. It published the *ten commandments on computer ethics* in the early 1990s [Bar:92], which attempted to outline principles and standards of behaviour to guide people in the ethical use of computers (Table 1.1).

**Table 1.1** Ten commandments on computer ethics

| No. | Description |
|---|---|
| 1 | Thou shalt not use a computer to harm other people |
| 2 | Thou shalt not interfere with other people's computer work |
| 3 | Thou shalt not snoop around in other people's computer files |
| 4 | Thou shalt not use a computer to steal |
| 5 | Thou shalt not use a computer to bear false witness |
| 6 | Thou shalt not copy or use proprietary software for which you have not paid |
| 7 | Thou shalt not use other people's computer resources without authorization or proper compensation |
| 8 | Thou shalt not appropriate other people's intellectual output |
| 9 | Thou shalt think about the social consequences of the program you are writing or the system you are designing |
| 10 | Thou shalt always use a computer in ways that ensure consideration and respect for your fellow humans |

The first commandment says that it is unethical to use a computer to harm another user (e.g., destroy their files or steal their personal data), or to write a program that on execution does so. That is, activities such as spamming, malware, spyware, phishing, ransomware, and cyberbullying are unethical.

The second commandment is related and may be interpreted that malicious software and viruses that disrupt the functioning of computer systems are unethical. The third commandment says that it is unethical (with some exceptions such as dealing with cybercrime and international terrorism) to read another person's emails, files and personal data, as this is an invasion of their privacy.

The fourth commandment states that cybercrime and the theft or leaking of confidential electronic personal information is unethical (computer technology has made it easier to commit fraud from the theft of personal information). The fifth commandment states that it is unethical to spread false or incorrect information (e.g., the spreading of fake news or misinformation via email or via a social media platform).

The sixth commandment states that it is unethical to obtain illegal copies of copyrighted software, as software is considered an artistic or literary work that is subject to copyright law or license. All copies should be obtained legally. The seventh commandment states that it is unethical to break in to a computer system with another user's id and password (without their permission), or to gain unauthorised access to the data on another computer by hacking into the computer system.

The eight commandment states that it is unethical to claim ownership of an intellectual creation written by another, and so it would be unethical to claim ownership of a program that was written by another as in copyright violation, or to use an invention that is protected by a patent without proper authorisation. The ninth commandment states that it is important for companies and individuals to think about the social impacts of the software that is being created, and to create software only if it is beneficial to society (i.e., it is unethical to create malicious software or addictive software that may harm others). That is, individual and companies need to consider the common good as well as profitability.

The tenth commandment states that communication over computers and the Internet should be courteous, and should show courtesy and respect for others (e.g., there should be no use of abusive language or spreading of false or misleading information).

### 1.6.1 Ethical Problems in Computing

The ten commandments of computer ethics describe various principles to guide ethical behaviour in the information technology field. The computing field has introduced a unique set of ethical problems such as the unauthorized use of computer resources, the problem of privacy with the gathering of personal data, the development of addictive technology, the problem of hacking and theft of personal data, and the problem of computer viruses.

Computer professionals have a professional responsibility to develop software to the highest standards, and to object to any compromise of these standards. Organizations may monitor employee use of computer resources in the workplace to ensure that they are not abused, and there is a need to protect personal data and privacy. Several ethical problems that arise in the computing field are listed in Table 1.2.

### 1.6.2 The Digital Divide

The Digital Divide refers to the unequal access to digital technology around the world, including access to hardware devices such as smartphones, laptops, and tablets, as well as access to the resources on the Internet and World Wide Web. This means that there is a gap and deep inequalities between people who have access to modern communications technologies and those that don't, as well as a gap between highly developed countries and less developed countries. People without access to modern digital technology are disadvantaged, as they are unable to search for and apply for jobs online, purchase goods or services on line, as well as participating in on-line activities such as social media, obtaining news or researching information via search engines, participating in online conference calls, and so on.

Inequality of access to the state of the art in technology is not a new phenomenon in society, as, for example, those with visual impairment were unable to access the printed media until the publication of the Braille system (as developed by Louis Braille in France in the 1820s). The Braille system allows the visually impaired to read the news using their sense of touch, with collections of raised dots in a $3 \times 2$ matrix format representing characters. Access to televisions for the hearing impaired was initially non-existent, but it has been improved with the

**Table 1.2** A selection of ethical problems in computing

| Type | Description |
|---|---|
| Privacy | The use of computer technology raises concerns on data protection and privacy, as sensitive data may be compromised |
| Computer crime | This may involve the theft of funds using a computer, or the theft of confidential information through unauthorised access of computer resources |
| Viruses | A virus is malicious code that an individual places on a network, and it is designed to spread and infect other machines. The virus may have destructive behaviour such as destroying data |
| Hacking | This is where a hacker who uses his (or her) computer skills to gain unauthorised access to computer files or networks (to cause damage or steal confidential information) |
| On line monitoring of staff/users | This is where employers monitor the online use of the internet by staff to ensure that it is not abused, or where companies monitor the online behaviour of users to build up user profiles that may be sold on to advertisers |
| Fake news | This is where false or misleading information is spread online with the intention of influencing user behaviour or outcomes |
| Cyberbullying | This is where an individual is bullied online, and it may lead to deep emotional distress (or worse) to the individual |
| Facial recognition/surveillance | AI technologies allow faces to be recognised at mass demonstrations, and combined with GPS technology it allows for mass surveillance of individuals |
| Deepfakes | AI technologies allow videos to be created that appear to show an individual performing/saying something inappropriate. They have been mainly used (up to now) for comedy/satire, but the technology may potentially be used for more sinister purposes in the future |

(continued)

**Table 1.2** (continued)

| Type | Description |
|---|---|
| Addictive technology | Technology addictions may potentially be dangerous leading to psychological problems and adversely affecting an individual's mental well being, as well as their education or career. This includes gaming addiction, social media addiction, mobile phone addiction, on line gambling addiction, pornography addiction, and so on |
| Professional responsibility of software engineers | The development of a software product is a professional activity, and software engineers have a professional responsibility to ensure that the software product is properly designed and implemented correctly, as well as adhering to the highest possible standards. Software engineers must be accountable for their decisions and actions, and must ensure that the software is safe to use and that the public is not endangered in any way |

support for sign language and sub-titles on the screen, and lip reading may be possible in their native language. Monastic communities used early forms of sign languages in Europe from the tenth century, and sign languages have been used in England since the sixteenth century. The visually and hearing impaired communities have suffered inequalities in their access to education to education throughout history.

The Covid-19 pandemic demonstrated the importance of digital technology, and highlighted the digital divide around the world. The pandemic led to the rapid spread of infection, and so governments around the world were required to impose lockdowns of their population in line with World Health Organisation (WHO) guidelines. This led to major disruptions of everyday life, and meant that non-essential workers could no longer attend the workplace to carry out their employment, and that children and students could not attend school or university to be educated.

It meant that there was a radical need to find alternative approaches to conduct every day life, and the use of the Internet played an essential role in adjusting to this brave new world. It led to the introduction of virtual classrooms for children and students, on-line shopping to purchase groceries and goods, and remote working for non-essential employees. All of these required high-speed broadband, and the digital divide between children from affluent backgrounds and those from lower socio-economic groups was very evident. Often, those from poorer backgrounds had unreliable Internet access in the home, or lacked a computer to complete their assignments.

There are several perspectives by which the digital divide between those that have access to the appropriate digital environment and those that don't may be measured including:

- Digital Infrastructure and participation
- Digital Skills
- Digital Accessibility in Location

*Digital infrastructure* refers to the technology that individuals and businesses use to connect to the Internet including computers, laptops and smartphones, as well as the way in which the Internet is accessed such as by fixed or mobile broadband, digital subscriber lines (DSL), and satellites. *Digital skills* refer to the skills required to make use of the information once the individual has the required technology to access the Internet, and includes skills such as the ability to use electronic mail and search engines, as well as knowledge of how to use Microsoft Office packages such as Word, Excel and Powerpoint. *Digital accessibility* refers to where the Internet is accessed such as at the library, in schools, in offices and in the home.

The inequality in the accessibility of the Internet around the world is evident, as approximately 35% of the world's population does not have access to the Internet in the early 2020s. Further the speed of connection to the Internet is problematic, as in some parts of the world the upload and download speeds to the Internet are not fit for purpose.

## 1.7 Ethics Examples from Software Engineering

Software engineering involves multi-person construction of multi-version programs. It requires the engineer to state precisely the requirements that the software product is to satisfy, and to produce designs that will meet these requirements. It involves starting with a precise description of the problem to be solved; producing a design to solve the problem and validating the correctness of the design; finally, the design is implemented in some programming language, and testing is performed to verify its correctness.

The eminent computer scientist, David Parnas, has argued that computer scientists need the right education to apply scientific and mathematical principles in their work. Software engineers need the right engineering education on creating specifications and designs, turning designs into programs, software inspections and testing. The appropriate engineering knowledge should enable the software engineer to produce well-structured programs using module decomposition and information hiding.

Further, Parnas argues that *"software engineers have individual responsibilities as professionals"*.[2] They are responsible for designing and implementing high-quality and reliable software that is safe to use. They are also accountable for their

[2] The concept of accountability for actions dates back thousands of years. The ancient Babylonians employed a code of laws c. 1750 B.C. known as 'The Hammarabi Code'. This included a law that if a house collapsed and killed the owner then the builder of the house would be executed.

own decisions and actions, and have a responsibility to object to decisions that violate professional standards.

Professional engineers have a duty to their clients to ensure that they are solving the real problem of the client. They need to precisely state the problem before working on its solution. Engineers need to be honest about current capabilities when asked to work on problems that have no appropriate technical solution, rather than accepting a contract for something that cannot be done.[3] Ethical software engineering is described in more detail in Chap. 11.

### 1.7.1 The Ethical Software Engineer

Software engineers have a professional responsibility and are required to behave ethically with their clients, and they may be members of professional bodies such as IEEE, ACM or BCS. The membership of the professional engineering body requires the member to adhere to the code of ethics of the profession. The code of ethics[4] will detail the responsibilities and expected ethical behaviour of the employee including:

- Honesty and fairness in dealings with clients
- Responsibility for actions.
- Continuous learning to ensure appropriate knowledge to serve the client effectively.

The *licensing of a professional engineer* provides confidence that the engineer has the right education, experience to build safe and reliable products. Otherwise, the profession gets a bad name because of poor work carried out by unqualified people. Professional engineers are required to follow rules of good practice and to object when rules are violated. The licensing of an engineer requires that the engineer completes an accepted engineering course, and understands the professional responsibility of an engineer. The professional body is responsible for enforcing standards and certification. The term '*engineer*' is a title that is awarded on merit, but *it also places responsibilities on its holder.*

[3] Parnas applied this professional responsibility faithfully when he argued against the Strategic Defence Initiative (SDI), as he believed that the public (i.e., taxpayers) were being misled and that the goals of the project were not achievable.

[4] These are core values of most mature software companies and many companies today have a code of ethics that employees are required to adhere to. Sometimes the code of ethics of an organisation is just window dressing (see Volkswagen emissions scandal).

### 1.7.2 The Ethical Software Tester

Software testers are professionals and need to behave ethically at all times during the development and testing of the software. The ISTQB Code of Ethics is based on the IEEE and ACM code of ethics, and it states that software testers should act in the public interest and in the best interest of their client and employer. They should ensure that their deliverables meet the highest standards, and that they are independent in their professional judgments. They are required to be ethical and to be supportive of their colleagues, and to work closely with software developers. Software testers need to keep their knowledge up to date and so they have a professional responsibility to participate in continuous and lifelong learning.

It is impossible to test everything due to time constraints, and so the testers need to focus their testing on the areas of greatest risk. It is essential that the testers have the appropriate expertise, that the right test environment is set up, that they have prepared appropriate test plans and test specifications to test the software, and that they have all the required hardware and software to conduct high quality testing.

Ethical issues could arise during the testing when the project is behind schedule, and when pressure is applied to the testing team to stay with the original schedule. This could lead to compression of the time available for testing (especially in traditional software engineering), resulting in quality being compromised. Therefore, the test manager needs to be firm and proactive in resisting any pressure that poses risks to the quality and safety of the software.

### 1.7.3 The Ethical Project Manager

Project managers need to behave professionally and ethically at all times during the project, and the core values of an ethical project manager includes:

- Professional responsibility
- Respect
- Fairness
- Honesty

Project management is concerned with the effective management of software projects to ensure the successful delivery of a high-quality product, on time and on budget, to the customer. The project manager is accountable for the success of the project, and larger projects have more opportunities for ethics being compromised than smaller projects. Project managers endeavour to balance budget, schedule, effort and quality, which may potentially lead to ethical dilemmas when the project manager is tempted to cut corners to enable the project to be delivered on time and on budget. This could potentially result in quality being compromised, health and safety being compromised, privacy being compromised, and so on.

The selection of a subcontractor could pose a conflict of interest to the project manager, where one of the candidate subcontractors is known to the PM from a previous working relationship or family relationships. It is therefore important that in such a situation that the project manager excludes herself from the supplier selection to ensure that there is no conflict of interest.

Project management involves ethical decision-making, and good project governance is a good enabler of ethical project management. It enables the key project stakeholders to be kept informed of the key project status and the key decisions being made regularly during the project. Any unethical or illegal conduct should be reported to management, and project management professionals should be aware of the regulations and laws that govern their work.

## 1.8 What Is Culture?

The origin of the word "*culture*" is derived from the Latin word "cultura" meaning "to till the land" or "cultivate", and the word was originally employed to describe the cultivation of crops. It has expanded over time to include the cultivation of mind and taste, and today, the word "culture" refers to the characteristic features of everyday existence shared by a group of people, a community, an organisation or corporation, or a region or country at a particulate date and time.

Culture is the integration of human behaviour that includes ideas, beliefs and norms, language, values, knowledge, works of art and music, morals, rituals and ceremonies, law, customs, tools and techniques, communications of various groups (e.g., ethnic groups, religious groups and social groups) within society. The culture of a particular society or organisation determines what is acceptable behaviour within the culture, and this may or be codified (*cultural norm*) as in an organisation's code of conduct, or implicit in the society. Some aspects of culture are presented in Fig. 1.2.

An individual who joins a new organisation or corporation learns about the culture through a process of induction, where the individual is presented with various policies and procedures to be followed in the work environment. That is, organisation or corporate culture refers to the way that things are done within the organisation, and an employee who does not follow the defined work practices may be subjected to disciplinary procedures. In society, individuals learn about

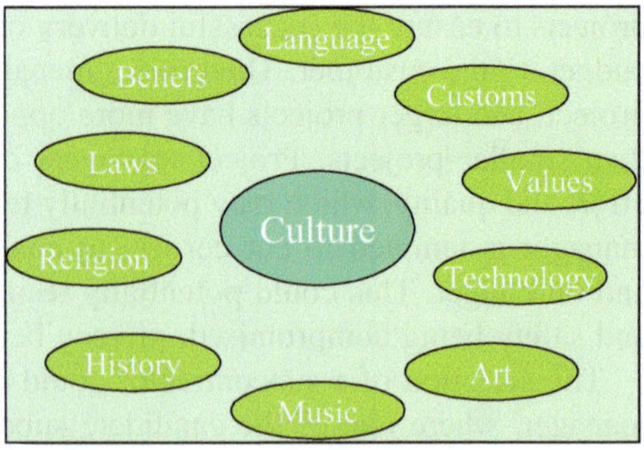


**Fig. 1.2** Some aspects of culture

acceptable/unacceptable behaviour within their culture through instruction from their parents, schools and wider society.

Culture is not static as such given that societies change, beliefs change, laws change, and attitudes to religion changes, customs change, and technology changes. Often, there can be a conflict in society between those who embrace change and those who resist change, and this also applies also to change within organisations and corporations. An organisation needs to carefully consider cultural issues in change management when embarking on a change programme (e.g., the introduction of new technology or changes in work practices) to ensure that the change programme will be successful, and to ensure that there will be a "buy in" for change within the organisation.

Technology and society are highly integrated with the development of new technologies impacting culture within society and organisations (and vice versa), with advances in technology leading to changes in the way that things are done in society or the organisation. For example, human communication has evolved from letter writing, to telegrams, to land phones, to email and the Internet, to smart phones, and so on. The vast changes in communication today can be seen in the evolution of human language (over tens of thousands of years), to the development of the alphabet and writing (from Mesopotamia and Egypt c. 5–6000 years ago), to printing (early printing techniques developed in China in the seventh century and later work by Gutenberg in Germany in the fifteenth century), etc.

Clearly, these foundational tools had immense consequences for society and acted, in a sense, as a cultural revolution, and so, in general, there are cultural consequences from the introduction of new technology, and vice versa, cultures influence the development of new technology with technologies developed and adapted based on cultural needs and norms. That is, there is a cyclical interplay where technology reshapes culture, and culture shapes technology.

## 1.9 Cultural Aspects of Computing

Cultural aspects of computing explores how computer technology and culture influence each other, and examines the impact of technology on daily life, the digital divide, and the role of computing in cultural preservation and globalization. That is, it is, in a sense, the integration of computing technology with culture, and it considers the impact of computing technology on culture and everyday life. Computing technology has revolutionalised and affected the daily lives of many in the modern world, and technology has many positive impacts. However, the introduction of computing technology has highlighted issues concerning privacy, as well as raising cultural, legal, ethical and environmental concerns.

It has become very difficult to "switch off" from all this computer technology, with social media sites addictive with dangers lurking in the shadows (such as cyberbullying). Online shopping sites allow individuals to shop 24 h a day but potentially affect the survival of stores in cities. Further, the increase in delivery vehicles leads to environmental pollution. The growth of Online entertainment and streaming poses challenges to the survival of cinemas.

Culture has shaped the development of computing technologies as well as the people that create it in many ways. Culture influences what technologies are built, how they are built, who builds them, the values that are part of them, and how they are used. For example, the second world war and its aftermath led to the need for new for faster computation, and led to the development of early computing machines such as ENIAC, EDVAC, and SAGE, and later the Internet (see [ORg:26]).

The early computers reflected Western culture with English characters employed, with multilingual support added much later. The idea of a computer for individual use, as well as a phone that contacted a person rather than a place reflected cultural philosophies. That is, computing technology is not just a technical product as it is also a cultural product.

## 1.10 Review Questions

1. What is ethics?
2. Explain computer ethics
3. How can a software company demonstrate that it took all reasonable steps to deliver a high-quality software product?
4. Describe the behaviours of the ethical software engineer.
5. Explain and give examples of ethical problems in computing.
6. Explain the digital divide.
7. What philosophical problems arise in computing?
8. What is computer science?
9. Explain the differences between a computer, a computer program and an algorithm.
10. What is culture?

## 1.11 Summary

This book aims to give the reader an overview of philosophical and cultural aspects of the computing field. Philosophical aspects of computing are concerned with the study of fundamental concepts and assumptions in the computing field. This includes fundamental questions such as "what is an algorithm?", "what is computability?", "what is computation?", "what is a program?", and "what is computer science?"

Ethics explore what actions are right or wrong within a specific context or within a certain society, and seek to find satisfactory answers to moral questions. It is a search for principles to guide the behaviour of individuals or groups, and ethical issues occur when a conflict arises between an individual's belief system, and the values held by the society or organisation that the individual belongs to. An individual may need to take a moral stand and become a whistle blower to expose unsafe practices in the country.

Cultural aspects of computing explore how computer technology and culture influence each other, with technologies influencing culture, and vice versa. Culture influences the development of computing technologies such as what technologies are built, who builds them, the values that are part of them, and how they are used.

## References

[Bar:92] In Pursuit of a 'Ten Commandments' for Computer Ethics. Ramon C. Barquin. Computer Ethics Institute. 1992.

[Dij:73] Programming as a discipline of Mathematical Nature. Edsger W. Dijkstra. EWD 361. Technological University of Eindhoven. 1973.

[Fei:59] The Role of the University in Computers, Data Processing and Related Fields. Louis Fine. *Communications of the ACM*. **2** (9): 7–14. 1959.

[Lon:78] Insight. A Study of Human Understanding. Bernard J. Lonergan. Harper Collins. 1978.

[ORg:23] Mathematical Foundations of Software Engineering. Gerard O' Regan. Springer. 2023.

[ORg:26] A Brief History of Computing. Fourth Edition. Gerard O' Regan. Springer. 2026.

# A Brief History of Philosophy

# 2

## 2.1 Introduction

Philosophy is, in a sense, an attempt to understand the world, and although science has been very successful in explaining the natural world, there remain many important fundamental questions that science cannot deal with at this time. For example, consider questions such as "What does it mean to be human?", "What is beauty?", "What can I know?", "What should I do?", and "What is the nature of reality?". These are questions that arise naturally as part of the human condition, but science cannot assist, at this time, in answering them.

Philosophy is a systematic enquiry into matters where exact knowledge has not been established or is not yet possible, and the work of the philosopher may be contrasted with that of the scientist who studies the world of science and what we can know about the world. Philosophy is, in a sense, something intermediate between science and theology, where theology consists of dogma that may arise from revelation or traditional beliefs, whereas scientific knowledge comes from the use of the scientific method and rational argument. The beliefs that arise from theology may give the impression of knowledge, but often there is just ignorance and uncertainty in the world.

Philosophy is, in a sense, a subject with many branches in that it has many objects of study rather than one. Some philosophical questions are related to human nature and free will, some are questions as to how one should live in order to lead a good and happy life; some are questions as to how one should live morally and ethically; some are questions as to how society and government should be organised; and some are questions as to the belief in a deity and organised religion. Philosophical questions are fundamental and often there is no consensus on the answer to a particular question.

Philosophy may involve speculation about things that are not yet amenable to scientific knowledge, and it may show us that things that we thought to be true are not actually so. Science has been extremely successful in determining knowledge,



G. O'Regan, *Philosophical and Cultural Aspects of Computing*, Undergraduate Topics in Computer Science, https://doi.org/10.1007/978-3-032-29284-1_2

but there are limitations to the knowledge that it can provide, especially when dealing with questions of values such as what is good or what is bad as an end (rather than as a means). Philosophy does not provide certainty in how one should act, as there is always some element of doubt regarding the particular situation. That is, there is always some degree of uncertainty as to how one should proceed, and so one should reflect upon the situation, and act in a way such that there is a high probability that the course of action that one takes is correct.

Philosophy proceeds by a rational enquiry into matter of concern, and arguments are generally made in natural language. Philosophers tend to be coherent thinkers who proceed from premises to conclusions using logical arguments, and they aim to avoid fallacies in reasoning. The study of philosophy is invaluable in developing critical thinking skills, and helps to prevent "woolly" arguments. The writing of a philosopher may be an attempt to answer a particular philosophical question, and despite the many philosophical theories or systems that have been developed over millennia, most have been shown to be incorrect. And so, in many ways there has been little progress in philosophy over the last 2500 years from Classical Greece to the modern age, with Whitehead describing the European philosophical tradition as a series of footnotes to Plato.

## 2.2 Concise History of Western Philosophy

The origin of the term "philosophy" is from the classical Greek words "φίλός" (*philos* meaning love or that which is loved), and "σόφός" (*sophos* meaning wisdom), and so the traditional meaning is thus given by "love of wisdom". However, this definition does not get us very far, and a more informative definition of philosophy is that it is an attempt to understand the world, where the philosopher is a thinker (or seeker of wisdom) who asks fundamental and profound questions on human existence in an attempt to understand the world.

In philosophy, the questions are, in a sense, more important than the answers that various philosophers have given over the millennia, as many of the answers given have been shown to be false. However, the philosophical questions discussed by many of the great philosophers remain fundamental, and philosophy, in a sense, teaches us to examine our lives and the world around us, as well as teaching us to live with uncertainty.

Western philosophy arose in various parts of the Ancient Greek world of the sixth century B.C., with the work of the pre-Socratics (i.e., the Miletians, Heraclitus, Parmenides and Pythagoras).[1] The Athenian city-state became the centre of learning of the Greek world in the fifth century (B.C.), and its important contributions to philosophy include the moral philosophy developed by Socrates followed by the major contributions of Plato and Aristotle.

[1] There may have been earlier philosophy in Mesopotamia that influenced the pre-Socratic philosophers.

Socrates wrote nothing on philosophy, but a clear picture on his views and approach to philosophy may be seen in, Plato's early dialogues, which involve his former mentor Socrates. Plato's later dialogues use Socrates as a mouthpiece to reflect the views of the more mature Plato.

Socrates himself claimed a total lack of knowledge (Socratic ignorance), and he often engaged in dialogue with the citizens of Athens with the goal of clarifying and clearly defining key concepts. Often, his interaction with the citizens of Athens demonstrated that those considered wise were really not that wise after all. That is, Socrates showed that they knew even less about the object of enquiry than he did, where he himself claimed no knowledge whatsoever. His approach involved forensically examining his opponent's argument, and showing that it led to contradictions, and this inevitably made his opponents look silly (whether intended to or not), and so this hardly made him popular in Athenian society.

Plato made major contributions to philosophy and also to education (he founded Plato's Academy which was a school/early university). He contributed to political philosophy in The Republic, where he advocated for rule by "philosopher-kings", who have been educated on philosophy (Plato became disillusioned with Greek democracy after it condemned the moral philosopher, Socrates, to death). The Republic also presents the Allegory of the Cave, which is used to show the difference between the world of appearances (i.e., the shadows that the prisoners see on the wall), and the ultimate reality of the world of ideas (the real world that an escaped prisoner would see) [Pla:12].

Plato argues that the world of appearances is deceptive (it is not the real world), whereas reality is the world of forms (also called ideas). Plato argues that ultimate reality consists of abstract and unchanging ideas (or forms) such as "Beauty" or "Good", rather than physical instantiations of them (as in a beautiful picture as given in the world of appearances or a good person). Plato's dialogue "Theatetus" is concerned with the question of what knowledge is (epistemology), and he explores various answers such as knowledge as perception, knowledge as true belief, and knowledge as true belief with rational justification. However, following a discussion of each answer, he rejects all of these definitions [Pla:14].

Plato's dialogue "Symposium" is concerned with the question of love, and he explores the physical love of a beautiful person, the love of a morally beautiful person, to the love of wisdom, divine love and Platonic love. That is, for Plato love is like a ladder that starts with physical attraction, to appreciating beauty in all bodies, to the pursuit of inner beauty, knowledge and virtue, and so is much more than the possessing of a beautiful physical body [Pla:08].

Aristotle became a student of Plato at Plato's academy in Athens, and he later founded his own school (known as the Lyceum) in Athens. His starting point to knowledge acquisition was the senses, as he believed that these were essential to acquire knowledge. His position is the opposite of Plato who argued that the senses deceive and should not be relied upon, and that knowledge is more than just sense perception. Instead, for Plato knowledge is eternal and unchanging, and consists of truths (or Platonic ideas or forms) that are not objects of perception.

Aristotle emphasised observation, classification and logical reasoning, and his starting point for knowledge was sense perception. He separated knowledge into distinct sciences such as Biology, Physics, etc., and argued that it was essential to understand the four causes (material, formal, efficient, and final) to give an account of explanation. *For Aristotle, the nature of a thing is given by its end* (i.e., the purpose for which it exists), and so for Aristotle, nature acts for an end with everything having some purpose or final cause (i.e., everything has a teleological explanation).

*Aristotle's emphasis on a teleological approach to explanation and science acted as an impediment to the development of science* (in many ways *it led science down a blind alley*, with Aristotle's ideas dominating science up to the time of Galileo). Aristotle's investigation of motion was influenced by the motion of animals, and the movement of heavenly bodies (celestial motion is circular and eternal, whereas earth motion is linear and temporary). Further, *he argued that everything in motion must be moved by something* (i.e., there is some agent pushing it).

Aristotle believed that an object moves towards its natural place based on its composition (air/fire rise whereas earth/water sink), and that an object in motion was changing from a potential state to an actual. He believed that heavier objects fell faster than lighter objects (i.e., he believed that the speed of a falling object is proportional to its weight), and Galileo disproved this theory in the seventeenth century.

Aristotle formulated a geocentric model of the universe, where the earth was at the centre, surrounded by concentric spheres of the four elements (earth, air, wind and fire), and then celestial spheres. He emphasised common-sense observations rather than experimentation (where modern science formulates hypotheses or theories that are then tested with experiments), and instead he over-relied on his deductive logic (syllogistic logic) to derive causal explanations (which he believed to be rigorous and necessary) from he what he believed were true primary premises.

Finally, Aristotle was "Christianised" by St. Thomas Acquinus (St. Thomas refers to Aristotle as "The philosopher"), which led to his philosophy becoming official church doctrine, and so it became an integral part of the Christian Church (an authoritarian body that sanctioned any individual who challenged its beliefs). That is, to question the philosophy of Aristotle (and his philosophy of science) was, in a sense, to challenge the church and its teachings, which meant that the church persecuted any thinkers who challenged Aristotle's position on science as well as his geocentric model of the universe. It was roughly 2000 years before Galileo showed that the Aristotelian view of the world was false.

Further progress in philosophy was made in the later Greek schools such as the works of the Cynics (who focused on gaining happiness through living simply), and the Stoics (who were focused on morality and endured hardship or pain without complaining), and these became popular in the Greco Roman world. Following the collapse of the Western Roman Empire in the late fifth century, philosophy became subservient to Christian theology (i.e., philosophy became the handmaiden of theology), with Christianity becoming an all-powerful organisation led by the pope that gained more and more power over bishops, abbots and the clergy, and eventually over nobles and the monarchy. Power was viewed as delegated by God to the pope in sacred matters, and to the emperor in secular matters.

The contributions of thinkers from the early Christian period to the late medieval period include the work of philosopher/theologians such as St. Augustine and St. Thomas, where philosophy was, in a sense, employed during this period to defend the Christian faith and revelation using reason. St. Augustine of Hippo was originally a Manichaean (a now extinct competitor religion to Christianity) but he converted to Christianity. He was influenced by Greek philosophy (especially Plato), and among his influential works are "*De civitate Dei*" (The City of God, with the Church representing the spiritual city of God where spiritual power and the love of God reigns, as distinct from an earthly material city that is concerned with secular power and earthly pleasures).

Another of his works is "*Confessions*", which is an autobiography that describes his sinful youth and conversion to Christianity, and it, in a sense, is a confession to God of his sins, as well as praising God's mercy. St. Thomas was an Italian priest who was influenced by Aristotle, and he produced a comprehensive synthesis of Christian theology and Aristotelian philosophy. His most influential work is "*Sumna Theologica*", which is a compendium of the main theological teachings of Christianity, and includes several proofs of the existence of God (with God the ultimate explanation of causation, motion, and order).

The Renaissance of the fifteenth and sixteenth centuries saw a renewed interest in ancient Greek philosophy, and it led to new knowledge and learning, as well an erosion of the power of the papacy in countries such as France and England. The Reformation led a split between those who regarded the church as a vehicle of revelation (Catholics), and those who rejected the interpretation of an intermediary (i.e., the church) between God and individual belief (Protestants). The latter regarded the individual's interpretation of the bible as the way to achieve spiritual truth.

Descartes was a seventeenth century French mathematician who invented Cartesian geometry, and he is considered the father of modern philosophy. The philosophy that he developed is termed Rationalism, and his goal was to answer the question as to how we can know with certainty anything about the world around us. That is, Descartes aimed to defeat the sceptics by showing that certain knowledge can be developed that cannot be questioned by the sceptics, and his goal was to defeat the strongest formulation of the argument of the sceptics. Descartes demonstrates the existence of himself and his thoughts, as well as the existence of a benevolent creator, and from this the external world is inferred (Fig. 2.1).

His approach in the *Meditations on First Philosophy* [Des:99] was to doubt everything that could be doubted (Cartesian Doubt). For example, the senses deceive and cannot be trusted, and so one must doubt all knowledge gained from the senses. He continued in this way until he eventually reached some elementary knowledge that could not doubted. He deduced that the only knowledge that he could be certain of was that of his own existence as a thinking thing: i.e., "*cogito ergo sum*"—I think therefore I am. This, for Descartes, is the first philosophical

**Fig. 2.1** René Descartes

principle, and it acts as a firm foundation for his new philosophy. From this basic principle he then argues that he has an idea of a benevolent God who does not deceive, and he then proceeds to demonstrate the existence of God and the soul (using the ontological argument).

He argued that since God is benevolent that he can have some trust in the reality that his senses provide. He thus argues that he can, in general, trust his senses, and from this he reconstructs the edifice of knowledge that he had earlier demolished. For Descartes, mind is more certain than matter, and his mind is more certain (to him) than the minds of others, and so there is a tendency towards subjectivism in his philosophy.

God has provided him with a thinking mind and does not wish to deceive him. He argues that knowledge of the external world can be obtained by both perception and deduction, and that reason (or rationalism) is the only reliable method of obtaining knowledge. Descartes founded what would become known as the Rationalist school of philosophy, where knowledge is derived solely by human reasoning.

Descartes was a *dualist* and he makes a clear *mind-body* distinction. He states that there are two substances in the universe: mental substances and bodily substances. This thinking thing (*res cogitans* or mind/soul) is distinct from the rest of nature (*res extensa*), and interacts with the world through the senses to gain knowledge. Knowledge is gained by mental operations using the deductive method, where starting from the premises that are known to be true, further truths may be logically deduced.

Descartes' Rationalism used reason or the intellect to gain knowledge, and this position was rejected by British empiricism that argued that knowledge is gained via the senses. The empiricists stressed the importance of empirical data in gaining knowledge about the world, and argued that all knowledge is derived from sense experience. *For empiricists, there is no idea in the mind that cannot be traced back to some particular experience*, and so according to empiricists humans do not possess innate ideas or knowledge as held by the Rationalists.

British empiricism included philosophers such as John Locke, George Berkeley[2] and David Hume. Locke's essay "*An Essay Concerning Human Understanding*" [Loc:1690] was a starting point for the British Empiricist tradition. Locke argued that a child's mind is a blank slate (*tabula rasa*) at birth, and that all knowledge is gained by sense experience. That is, Locke rejects innate ideas and argues that all knowledge can be traced back to sense perception and reflection. The mind in all its thoughts and reasoning has no other object other than its own ideas, and so there is a tendency towards subjectivity in British Empiricism. Locke also made important contributions to political philosophy, including social contract theory and liberalism.

Berkeley argued that the ideas in a man's mind have no existence outside of his mind [Ber:1710], and his (slightly bizarre) philosophical position rejects materialism, and is known as "Immaterialism" or "Idealism".[3] For Berkeley, "*esse est percipi aut percipere*" or "To be is to be perceived or to perceive".[4] That is, the existence of an idea consists in it being perceived, and the objects of the external world are ideas or collections of ideas.

David Hume (Fig. 2.2) formulated the standard empiricist philosophical position in "An Enquiry concerning Human Understanding" [Hum:1740]. Hume argued that all objects of human knowledge may be divided into two kinds: *matters of fact* propositions that are based entirely on experience, or *relation of ideas* propositions that may be demonstrated via deduction reasoning in the operations of the mind.

---

[2] Berkeley was an Irish philosopher and he was born in Dysart castle in Thomastown, Kilkenny, Ireland. He was educated at Trinity College, Dublin, and served as bishop of Cloyne in Co. Cork. Ireland. He planned to establish an education seminary in Bermuda for the sons of colonists in America, but the project failed due to lack of funding from the British government. Berkeley University in San Francisco is named after him, as was Berkeley Library at Trinity College Dublin (until it was de-named in 2023 due to a politically correct controversy over Berkeley's purchase of several slaves to work on his Rhode Island estate).

[3] That is, Berkeley rejected the existence of material objects.

[4] Berkeley's theory of Ontology is that for an entity to exist it must be perceived: i.e., "*Esse est percipi*". He argues that "It is an opinion strangely prevailing amongst men, that houses, mountains, rivers, and in a world all sensible objects have an existence natural or real, distinct from being perceived". This led to a famous Limerick that poked fun at Berkeley's theory. "There once was a man who said God; Must think it exceedingly odd; To find that this tree, continues to be; When there is no one around in the Quad". The reply to this Limerick was appropriately: "Dear sir, your astonishments odd; I am always around in the Quad; and that's why this tree will continue to be; Since observed by, yours faithfully, God".

**Fig. 2.2** David Hume

He argued that any subject[5] proclaiming knowledge that does not adhere to these empiricist principles should be committed to the flames. "When we run over libraries persuaded of these principles what havoc must we make? If we take in our hand any volume of divinity or school metaphysics, for instance, let us ask. Does it contain any abstract reasoning concerning quantity or number? No. Does it contain any experimental reasoning containing matter of fact and existence? No. *Commit it then to the flames: For it can contain nothing but sophistry and illusion*" [Hum:1740].

Hume's account of *causation* has been influential, and he argues that reasoning alone cannot establish the grounds of causation, and that causal relations are not something that we experience in the world. Instead, Hume argues that the concept of causation is formed in our mind as a result of repeated experiences of 'causes' preceding 'effects' i.e., the link between cause and effect is the observation of a '*constant conjunction*' in one's sensory experience. That is, we do not experience causation as such, and so cannot know with certainty that two things are necessarily connected—the best that we have is probable knowledge.

Hume also identified problems with justifying the *principle of induction* as part of his study of cause and effect, and this principle is fundamental in formulating empirical laws using the scientific method. Hume asks on what grounds do we come to our beliefs on the unobserved on the basis of inductive inferences. Induction involves generalising from events that have always occurred in the past to state that they will always occur in the future. However, the only evidence for

[5] Hume argues that these principles apply to subjects such as Theology as its foundations are in faith and divine revelation, which are neither matters of fact nor relations of ideas.

this is in the past, and we are assuming that the future will be like the past, but the only evidence for this is in the past.

For example, a chicken may receive a regular hearty meal every day (and so may have grounds for assuming that the future will always be like this) until one day its owner decides to have a chicken casserole. Another words, we cannot apply a definite conclusion about a particular set of observations to a general set of observations, and all that we infer is a probable conclusion. That is, deductive reasoning leads to certain conclusions, whereas inductive reasoning leads to probable conclusions. And so, if we proceed to the logical conclusion of empiricism, it leads, in a sense, to the abolishment of science, as the foundations of inductive reasoning in science cannot be established.

Hume argues that reason alone is not the source of our moral principles and instead, he argues that we sense the rightness or wrongness of an action immediately prior to making a rational judgment. Hume notes that *the self,* insofar as it is accessible through inner experience *consists of nothing but perceptions,* and therefore any *knowledge of the nature of mind that go beyond the "bundle of perceptions"* cannot be justified.

Immanuel Kant is the founder of German Idealism and is regarded as one of the greatest modern philosophers. He spent his whole life in Königsberg (now called Kaliningrad) in East Prussia (now a Russian enclave north east of Gdansk, Poland and west of Lithuania). Hume's criticism of the theory of causality and his refutation of metaphysics awakened Kant from his dogmatic slumbers,[6] and he set out to refute Hume's theory of empiricism which resulted in scepticism with respect to causation, induction, the scientific method and metaphysics. Kant's most famous work is '*The Critique of Pure Reason*' [Kan:1787], which was originally published in 1781. It is a response to Hume's theory of empiricism, and Kant's goal was to provide a bridge between the two opposing epistemological standpoints of Rationalism and Empiricism, and he advocated a blend of Rationalist and Empiricism theories. He described the Critique as a Copernican revolution in philosophy (Fig. 2.3).

Kant argued that there is a third force in human knowledge that provides concepts that can't be inferred from experience. Such concepts include the laws of logic (e.g., modus ponens), causality, and so on, and Kant argued that the third force is the manner in which the human mind structures its experiences. Kant argues that some of our knowledge is *a priori* and not inferred inductively from experience. He distinguishes between "*analytic*" and "*synthetic*" propositions, and between "*a priori*" and "*a posteriori*" propositions.

An *analytic* proposition is a proposition that is true in virtue of the meaning of its words alone, and a denial of its truth would be self-contradictory (the predicate is generally part of the subject). We can determine the truth of an analytic proposition by a mere examination of its meaning. For example, "an equilateral

[6] Russell (who was not a fan) joked that the awakening was temporary, and that Kant soon invented a soporific (a substance inducing sleep) that enabled him to sleep again.

**Fig. 2.3** Immanuel Kant

triangle is a triangle" and "all bachelors are unmarried men" are analytic propositions. A proposition that is not analytic is termed *synthetic*, and the truth of a synthetic proposition depends on its meaning as well as certain facts about the world. That is, a synthetic proposition is known to be true only through experience (e.g., 'Today is Wednesday' is true if it is Wednesday and false otherwise).

Synthetic judgements are made on the basis of sense experience, whereas analytic judgments are a *priori.* Analytic judgments do not extend our knowledge, in any way, whereas synthetic judgments do, since the predicate is not contained in the subject, and so it expresses a connection or synthesis between two elements that were not previously joined. The principle of contradiction can be used to determine the truth of analytic judgments but not synthetic judgments.

An "*a posteriori*" (or "*empirical*") proposition depends on empirical evidence, and so its truth is unknown without sense perception. These include facts of history as well as scientific knowledge, whose truth depends on observation data. The truth of an "*a priori*" proposition is independent of any experience, and this includes all of the propositions of pure mathematics, tautologies, and deduction from pure reason.

Kant believed that arithmetic and geometry are *synthetic* but *a priori*, and he also maintained that causation is *synthetic* but *a priori.* His fundamental question was how *synthetic a priori* knowledge is possible, and the answer to this question and its consequences is the subject matter of The Critique of Pure Reason. Kant argues that the outer world causes only the matter of sensation, whereas our own mental apparatus orders this in terms of space and time, and supplies the concepts by which we understand experience. The idea of *synthetic a priori* was controversial, and it was highly criticized and rejected by the logical positivists in the twentieth century. Further, the later discovery of geometries such as Riemannian geometry of the sphere as well as hyperbolic geometry as developed by Bolyai and Lobachevsky (which were developed by replacing the parallel postulate in traditional Euclidean geometry) showed that there were several possibly geometries for the world, and so *Euclidean geometry could not be apriori.*

For Kant, things in themselves (*noumena*), which are the causes of our sensations, are unknowable, in contrast to the object of our senses (*phenomena*). Things in themselves are not in space or time and are not substances or categories. Space and time are part of our apparatus of perception and are subjective, and so whatever we experience will exhibit the characteristics of geometry and science of time (e.g., an analogy is if you always wear green spectacles then everything that you will see will be green, and similarly if you always wear spatial spectacles then everything that you will see will be spatial). Thus geometry is *a priori* in the sense that it must be true of everything experienced, but we cannot say this of things in themselves, which we do not experience.

Kant argues that human understanding is structured by concepts of understanding (or categories of understanding) that are present in the mind prior to experience, and which make outer experience possible. A person would not experience the world as an orderly place unless space, time and causality were determinant functions of our perception apparatus. There are twelve categories that are *a priori* concepts, and these include quantity, quality, cause and effect, and these are subjective in that they are applicable to whatever we experience, but there is no reason to believe that they are applicable to things-in-themselves.

The most important part of the Critique is the doctrine of space and time, where Kant argues that the *phenomena* of perception are due to both the external things-in-themselves (*noumena*) and our own subjective perceptive apparatus. Kant argues that space and time are *a priori* from the nature of space and time and mathematics.

Thomas Hobbes was a seventeenth century philosopher who is regarded as one of the founders of modern political philosophy. His political philosophy was influenced by the destruction of the English civil war between Royalists and Parliamentarians in the mid-seventeenth century, which led him to advocate for rule by an absolute monarch, and a formulation of the *social contract theory* as described in *Leviathan* [Hob:1691].

Hobbes outlines a "science of politics" in *Leviathan* that would enable a government to establish and maintain a peaceful state for its people. He employed deductive reasoning to human activities to ensure the validity of his conclusions, as deductive reasoning is invaluable in preserving truth in mathematics and science. His approach was to establish certain basic facts about human nature from which he could then deduce the way that humans would behave in certain circumstances. In this way, he could determine causes that lead to peaceful existence, as well as causes that lead to strife. This allowed him to outline a form of government that would infallibly establish and maintain peace.

Hobbes maintains that the only way to secure perpetual peace is for people to covenant together to place themselves under an absolute or all powerful sovereign, who is authorised to act to preserve the lives of those who submit to him, and who has sufficient power to restrain the natural warlike passion of his subjects. That is, Hobbes social contract is that each person enters a '*contract*', and agrees to hand over freedom in return for protection from an all-powerful state. For Hobbes, *the right to rule depends on the power of the sovereign to protect and preserve perpetual peace.*

Hegel was an eighteenth/nineteenth century German philosopher who believed that Mind or Spirit is the ultimate reality (universal spirit), and he was a monist in that he viewed everything as interrelated within one vast complex system, which he called the Absolute. He was an idealist but did not reject the existence of material objects (as distinct from Berkeley). In Hegel's philosophy, knowledge proceeds by way of the Hegelian dialectic, where a thesis is proposed for some particular view or position; next this is countered by an antithesis, which is the opposite or contrary position. Finally, there is a synthesis reconciling the two previous positions, and becoming the basis for a new thesis.

Karl Marx was a nineteenth century German philosopher who was influenced by Hegel. Marx's view of history (historic materialism) was influenced by Hegel's claim that reality and history should be viewed dialectically. However, as Marx was a materialist (matter is the fundamental substance in nature and mental properties are in some way an aspect of matter) in contrast to Hegel's idealism (all reality is in some way mental), Marx rewrote dialectics in materialist terms, and he rejected the Hegelian concepts of Absolute and Mind as true reality, and instead placed human beings and human consciousness at the centre of his philosophy.

Jeremy Bentham was a nineteenth century English philosopher, and is one of the founders of *utilitarianism.* This philosophy involves measuring the consequences of an action against one value (such as benefit or happiness). The sole moral criterion for good or bad lies in the *utility principle*, which is the greatest happiness of the greatest number of a community. That is, the *right action in a given situation is the action that produces the most benefit or happiness to society*, and so if a particular law or action doesn't do any good then it isn't any good.

Bentham argued that utilitarianism allows (in a sense) a moral balance sheet to be drawn up with the costs and benefits of each action recorded, and it thereby allows the action with the best consequences to be chosen. The process to determine the action that leads to the greatest happiness for the greatest number of people involves a summation of the pleasure/pain for all individuals.

Bentham argued that utilitarianism should become the standard to determine the right action to be taken by the government and individuals, and the nineteenth century philosopher, John Stuart Mills, later promoted his ideas. Utilitarianism argues that the consequences of one's action are the ultimate basis for a judgment as to whether the action is right or wrong. That is, an action in itself is neither right nor wrong in itself: rather, it is the consequence of the action that is morally relevant.

**Fig. 2.4** J. S. Mill

One of the key criticisms of utilitarianism is that the individual is not protected when the utility calculation yields that the pleasure of the majority outweighs the unhappiness of a small number of people. This could result in the abuse of individuals and minorities, and John Stuart Mill introduced the "*no harm principle*", where one is free to do as one wishes provided that no harm is done to others. However, this principle is difficult to apply in full as moral problems often include the risk of harm to others (Fig. 2.4).

Edmund Husserl was a nineteenth/twentieth century German/Austrian philosopher and mathematician, and is the founder of the school of *phenomenology*, which aims to study phenomena as they appear to a subject as well as investigating universal features of consciousness. Other important figures in the field include Heidegger, Sartre and Merleau Ponty.

Martin Heidegger was a twentieth century German philosopher who made important contributions to ontology, phenomenology and existentialism. In his influential work, *Being and Time*, he attempted to access being (*sein*) by means of a phenomenological analysis of human existence (*dasein*). In his later work, he changed his approach and placed the emphasis on language as the vehicle to which the question of being can be explained.

Maurice Merleau-Ponty was a twentieth century French philosopher of phenomenology, and was influenced by Husserl and Heidegger. He was interested in the constitution of meaning in human experience, and especially the foundation role of perception in human experience of the world. For Merleau-Ponty, perception is an ongoing dialogue between one's body and the world it perceives, in which perceivers strive to express the world jointly with others. He argued that *the perceiving body and the perceived world may not be disentangled from each other*.

Gottlob Frege was a nineteenth/twentieth century mathematician and logician, who (along with Bertrand Russell) laid the foundation of modern logic and the philosophy of language. Frege regarded logic as the foundation of philosophy, and his work, *Foundations of Arithmetic*, he asked "what are numbers?" and "what is arithmetical truth?", and he aimed to demonstrate that logic can fully account for mathematics. In the work, Frege demonstrated how arithmetic may be derived from logic, but Kurt Godel's results in the late 1920s showed that certain logical systems of mathematics are *incomplete* (some truths are unprovable in the logical system), and that consistency cannot be proved of the logical system of arithmetic. Frege also did important work in the philosophy of language.

Bertrand Russell was a highly influential twentieth century English mathematician and philosopher, and his most important contributions were to mathematical logic and the philosophy of logic. He also made contributions to several other areas of philosophy, and he was active in social and political issues (especially on nuclear disarmament). Russell and Whitehead wrote *Principia Mathematica* in the early twentieth century, in which they put forward a system of logic that generates mathematics, and has the effect of reducing mathematics to logic. He also tackled philosophical problems relating to truth, belief and meaning, identified in Russell's paradox) and he developed *The Theory of Types* (as a way to deal with Russell's Paradox) and the *Theory of Descriptions* (which is a contribution to the philosophy of language, and gives meaning (via logic) to phrases such as "The present king of France is bald") (Fig. 2.5).

Russell was the founder of the philosophy of *logical atomism*, which maintains that all complex entities are, upon analysis, reducible to simple particulars

**Fig. 2.5** Bertrand Russell

that can be denoted by logically proper names. Wittgenstein was Russell's student at Cambridge, and Wittgenstein's early philosophy (as in the *Tractatus*) is based on logical atomism, whereas the later Wittgenstein (as in the *Philosophical Investigations*) rejected this approach.

The early Wittgenstein took the view that the structure of reality determines the structure of language, and he saw logic as copying reality precisely and completely (Russell and Frege regarded logic as the science of the laws of thought). *What can be said can be said clearly; what cannot be said clearly is not in the world, and one must be silent about it.* The later Wittgenstein rejects the position outlined in the Tractatus, and instead explores the opposite *view that language gives us our conception of reality*. Both of his philosophies are concerned with language and its limits, and his early work is written in a very orderly and precise (if somewhat cryptic) style, whereas the later Wittgenstein writes in a discursive style with no obvious structure (Fig. 2.6).

The early Wittgenstein believed that the Tractatus contained truths that are 'unassailable' and 'definitive', and that he had found the solution to the problems in philosophy. The goal of the Tractatus is to reveal the *relationship between language and the world, including what can be said about it, and what can only be shown*. It presents the *picture theory* of meaning, where language presents a picture of reality through propositions. *Each proposition is a picture that corresponds to a possible state of affairs or atomic fact*, and a statement is meaningful if and only if it can be defined or pictured in the real world. He claims that there is an

**Fig. 2.6** Ludwig Wittgenstein

unbridgeable gap between what can be expressed in language, and what can only be expressed in non-verbal ways.

The later Wittgenstein rejected and replaced his picture-based theory with a *use theory of meaning*. He argues that philosophical problems arise due to a disease (or myth) of language, where we are caught up in the idea that words are names, and that the meaning of a word corresponds to what it stands for, and we then start an investigation as to what that thing can be. Wittgenstein argues that this view of meaning is incorrect, and that instead *words do jobs and are tools of many different kinds, and that words participate in a language game*, where meaning is given by grammar and the way in which the language works in the language games that we play [Wit:99].

Moritz Schlick was a German physicist and philosopher and a founder member of the *Vienna circle*, which was a group of twentieth century scientists and philosophers. Its members included Rudolf Carnap, Otto Neurath, Kurt Gödel and others, and the group met in Vienna with the broad goal of cleaning up science and philosophy. The Vienna circle formulated the philosophy of *logical positivism* (also called logical empiricism, which was a more extreme form of Hume's empiricism). Schlick and others in the circle formulated and refined the famous *verification principle*, which states that the meaning of a proposition is the method of its verification. The method of verification is empirical: i.e., it is grounded in experience and observation, and so we understand the meaning of a statement if we know what observations are needed to verify it.

A statement has no meaning if it has no method of verification, and so metaphysical statements, religious statements, ethical and aesthetic statements for which there are no empirical observations to establish their truth or falsity are meaningless. And so, in a sense, logical positivists aimed to overhaul philosophy with the verification principle, with verified statements viewed as being scientific and meaningful, whereas unverifiable statements are considered unscientific and meaningless.

One of the goals of the logical positivists was to remove metaphysics from philosophy, as they regarded such statements as factually meaningless. The logical positivists maintained that mathematics is derived from logic, and so the statements of mathematics are necessarily true in that they are tautologies that say nothing about how things are in the world. It was clear that ethical, religious and aesthetic statements are meaningless when assessed by the verification principle. However, logical positivism ultimately failed as a philosophy, and Karl Popper showed that the *empirical verification of the induction principle in science is logically impossible*, and so just about everything in science was meaningless as well (as induction is a basic scientific principle). Popper later formulated the *falsification principle* as a way to clearly distinguish science from non-science, and he argued that for a theory to be considered scientific it must be testable and conceivably proven false [Pop:59].

The *existentialist* movement emerged in France following the horrors of the Second World War, the devastating holocaust and the atomic bombing of

**Fig. 2.7** Jean-Paul Sartre

Hiroshima and Nagasaki. A whole generation was forced to confront the challenges of the human condition, including freedom, death, and the meaninglessness of life. The roots of the movement go back to the nineteenth century in the work of Kierkegaard, and work by Heidegger in the 1920s and 1930s.

Jean-Paul Sartre was one of the leading figures in the philosophy of existentialism. He was influenced by Heidgger's *Sein und Zeit*, and he argued that "*humans are condemned to be free*" in that their "being" is not determined, and so each person has to determine his or her own existence, for which they are then responsible. His influential works include "*Being and Nothingness*" and "*Existentialism is a Humanism*". Another leading figure in the existentialist movement was Simone De Beauvoir, who was a feminist and philosopher, as well as being Sartre's life long companion (Fig. 2.7).

Albert Camus was a French/Algerian philosopher and writer who made important contributions to the existentialist movement. One of his earliest works is "*The Outsider*", which is concerned with the meaninglessness and absurdness of life (i.e., there is no inherent meaning in life), and the indifference of the universe. The story is set in Algeria (then a French colony which received independence in 1962). It is concerned with Mersault, who is a French Algerian individual, but cast as an outsider and alienated from society, as he does not conform to the emotional expectations of society. The story opens with his response to the death and funeral of his mother, where he does not view the body and he remains emotionally detached. He later kills an Arab on a sun-soaked beach near Algiers, and the trial focuses on his response to his mother's death, where his apathy is seen as proof of his guilt, and he is sentenced to death [Cam:13].

## 2.3 What Are Some Important Areas of Philosophy?

Table 2.1 lists some of the important areas in philosophy, and gives a flavour of some of the areas studied.

## 2.4 Some Famous Philosophers

Table 2.2 provides a brief summary of some well-known philosophers (the selection reflects the bias of the author).

## 2.5 Eastern Philosophy

Eastern philosophy is a general label that includes philosophies originating in countries such as India, China and Japan, and includes philosophies such as Hinduism, Jainism, Buddhism, Confucianism, Taoism and the Yin-Yang school.

### 2.5.1 Hinduism

Hinduism is a polytheistic religion with the three main gods being Brahma the creator, Vishnu the protector and Siva the destroyer. There are other incarnations of Vishnu in Krishna and Rama. The religion is characterized by its belief in re-incarnation and the caste system, and the source of early Hinduism is in the four Vedas (the word Veda means knowledge). These ancient Sanskrit scriptures were composed between 1500 and 500 B.C., and include hymns, chants, rituals, and spells). The Brahmanas are explanations or commentaries on the sacred text of the Vedas, and the ritualism performed by the Brahmin priests. The forest treatises (*Aranyakas*) as recited by hermits were a reaction against the rise of the Brahmins, and this culminated with the *Upanishads*, (a Sanskrit text from the late Vedic period that included philosophy and meditation) which contains the fundamentals of Hindu philosophy.

The philosophy in the Upanishads is concerned with the relationship between the rituals, gods, and the human body or person. It identifies *Brahman* as the supreme divinity, and *Atman* as the eternal portion of the Brahman that abides in every living human being (another meaning for Atman is a life force or ultimate reality). Other Hinduism writings include the Sutras and the Hindu epics, e.g., the *Ramayana*, and the *Bhagavad Gita* (song of the Blessed One) has been called "India's favourite bible". The latter forms part of a larger epic, the *Mahabharata.*

Hinduism includes belief in re-incarnation and the caste system. The Hindu castes include the *Brahmins* (priestly caste) that perform the religious ceremonies; the *Kshatriyas* (the warrior caste) generally perform deeds of valour; the *Vaisyas*, (the merchant caste) performs business; the *Sudras* include farm workers and the

**Table 2.1** Some areas in philosophy

| Area | Description |
|---|---|
| Metaphysics (the nature of reality) | Metaphysics is one of oldest branches of philosophy, and it examines the basic structure of reality including existence, objects and their properties, possibility and necessity, space and time, causation, and the relation between mind and matter. It examines the nature of existence, as well as the nature of space, time and change. It examines possibility and necessity, free will, the contrast between universals and particulars, as well as causality and its relation to the laws of nature. It differs from the sciences in that it studies very general and abstract aspects of reality |
| Ontology (the nature of being) | Ontology (from the Greek words οντος and λογος meaning an account of being) is an area in metaphysics that is concerned with the nature of existence or being, and Aristotle regarded it as "first" philosophy when he considered the question of "being *qua* being". Ontology concerns claims about existence and being, and asks the meaning of questions such as "what is being?", as well as "what it means for something to exist?" it may also be concerned with questions such as "what exists?" or "what sort of things exist?" |
| Epistemology (the theory of knowledge) | Epistemology (from the Greek επιστημη meaning knowledge or skill and λογος meaning account/theory) is the branch of philosophy concerned with knowledge. It is concerned with the sources of knowledge such as sense perception and reason, as well the relationship between belief and truth, and philosophical scepticism which questions whether knowledge is possible, and whether it is possible to refute scepticism. Epistemology considers questions such as "what do people know? And "how are beliefs justified? |

(continued)

**Table 2.1** (continued)

| Area | Description |
|---|---|
| Ethics (study of human conduct) | Ethics (ἠθικός) is a practical branch of philosophy that deals with moral questions such as what is the right thing to do in a particular situation?, and in dealing with conflicts between individual moral values and the values of an organisation or society. How should one live a good life? How should a person behave in a given situation in a complex world? Ethics explores what actions are right or wrong within a specific context or within a particular society, and attempts to find satisfactory answers to moral questions. It provides a framework to think critically about moral problems and moral values, and assist in forming a judgment on the most appropriate way to proceed in a situation where there is a conflict between values, and where the individual is trying to do the right thing |
| Logic (the study of valid reasoning) | The philosophy of logic (based on the Greek λογος) is concerned with the nature of logic, and it investigates the philosophical problems raised by logic, as well as the relation of logic to other disciplines. It is, in a sense, the study of the laws of thought, and it investigates correct reasoning, valid inference and logical truth. Logic is concerned with how a valid conclusion may be drawn from a set of premises, and it focuses on deductive inference. Formal logic is expressed in a formal language, whereas natural language may include deductive and inductive reasoning |
| Political philosophy (study of political theory) | Political philosophy is concerned with the philosophical study of the practices and institutions of government, and it studies questions such as politics, justice, liberty, law, property, the rights of citizens, the enforcement of laws by the state, and the justification and limits of political authority. It considers questions such as "why should we obey the laws of the state?", "do freedom and equality exist?", and "what is a fair distribution of wealth and goods in society?" |

(continued)

**Table 2.1** (continued)

| Area | Description |
|---|---|
| Philosophy of religion | The philosophy of religion is concerned with the philosophical study of religious traditions and matters of religious significance. It investigates the nature of religion itself, as well as the religious significance of the cosmos and laws of nature. Its scope has been mainly limited to the theistic religions, but alternatives to religious viewpoints as well as atheistic religions are also studied. The philosophy of religion examines the relationship between faith and reason, whereas theology studies faith and revelation |
| Philosophy of language | The philosophy of language studies the nature of language, and the relationship between language, users and the world. It inquires into the nature of meaning, learning and thought, and Frege, Russell, and Wittgenstein have made important contributions |
| Philosophy of mind | The philosophy of mind studies the nature of mind, and its relationship to the body and external world. It studies the nature of mental states and consciousness, as well as the mind-body problem |
| Philosophy of science | The philosophy of science studies the nature of science, which is a distinctive form of human inquiry. Scientists in the various sciences use the scientific method, which distinguishes science from pseudo science. The philosophy of science studies the foundations, methods and implications of science. Among the philosophical problems studied is the problem of induction, and whether inductive reasoning can be justified |
| Philosophy of mathematics | The philosophy of mathematics studies the nature of mathematics, and considers questions such as mathematical rigour, the use of mathematical logic, the nature of mathematical truth, and whether mathematics is solely a product of the human mind or whether it has some reality by itself. There were several schools in the twentieth century that aimed to develop a solid foundation for mathematics, and these include logicism, formalism and intuitionism |

(continued)

**Table 2.1** (continued)

| Area | Description |
|---|---|
| Science and religion | This is a study of the relationship between religion and science, and the extent to which science and religion are compatible. It considers questions such as "do religious beliefs support or pose obstacles to scientific inquiry?" |
| Existentialism | Existentialism is a philosophical movement that became popular in France after the calamity of the second world war, where challenges of the human condition including freedom, death, and meaninglessness of life were key concerns. Its adherents included Jean-Paul Sartre, Albert Camus and Simone de Beauvoir, but its roots go back to the nineteenth century with the work of Kierkegaard |
| Aesthetics (philosophy of beauty) | The philosophy of aesthetics is concerned with the philosophical study of beauty and taste. It is closely related to the philosophy of art (it is broader in scope), which is concerned with the nature of art and the way in which works of art are interpreted and evaluated. We experience works that are beautiful, ugly, sublime and elegant, and, in a sense, these terms are vague and subjective, as someone might see almost anything as beautiful from some point of view. There are several philosophical approaches to aesthetics, including the analysis of the "language of criticism", a philosophical study of certain states of mind, and the philosophical study of the aesthetic object |

servant class. Finally, there are the untouchable *Dalits* (pariahs) that include street sweepers and dead body handlers.

The principle of *karma* is important in Indian religions, and operates, in a sense, like cause and effect. Another words, an individual's actions in this life (cause) influence their future rebirth. A person is born into a particular caste based on actions performed in previous existences, and if exceptional deeds are performed in this life then the person may be reborn in a higher caste, and vice versa. For more detailed information on Hinduism see [Hin:91].

### 2.5.2 Buddhism

Buddhism is centred on the teachings of the Buddha, which arose as a breakaway religion from Hinduism. It is an atheist religion (i.e., a religion without God), and

**Table 2.2** Some famous philosophers

| Philosopher | Description |
|---|---|
| Socrates | Socrates was a fifth century B.C. moral philosopher, and a clear picture on his approach to philosophy may be seen in Plato's early dialogues (he himself wrote nothing). Socrates claimed a total lack of knowledge (Socratic ignorance), and he often engaged in dialogue with the citizens of Athens with the goal of clarifying and clearly defining key concepts |
| Plato | Plato (a fourth/fifth century B.C. philosopher) is a central figure in the history of philosophy, and he has made contributions to just about every area in philosophy. His writings are in dialogues involving his former mentor Socrates. The early dialogues reflect the views of the historical Socrates, and the later dialogues reflect the reviews of the older and more mature Plato |
| Aristotle | Aristotle (a fourth century B.C. philosopher) was a pupil of Plato and tutor of Alexander the great. He made contributions to biology, logic, politics, ethics and metaphysics. His starting point to knowledge acquisition was the senses, as he believed that these were essential to acquire knowledge |
| St. Augustine | St. Augustine was a fourth/fifth century theologian and philosopher, and his most popular works are the "City of god" and "confessions". His theological teachings include original sin, the doctrines of grace and predestination. His other works include writing on the just war, free will, natural law, and the nature of time and slavery |
| St. Thomas Aquinas | St. Thomas was a Dominican priest and influential thirteenth century theologian and philosopher. Aristotle influenced him, and his most famous work is Sumna Theologica, which is a synthesis of Christian theology and Aristotelian philosophy |
| Hobbes | Thomas Hobbes (a seventeenth century English philosopher) was one of the founders of modern political philosophy, and he presents an account of social contract theory in his influential book, *leviathan* |
| Descartes | Descartes (a seventeenth century French mathematician and philosopher) is considered the father of modern philosophy. He developed rationalist philosophy, and his goal was to develop knowledge that is certain, so that it is not open to attack from the sceptics |
| Locke | John Locke (a seventeenth century English philosopher and physician), made important contributions to philosophy (especially to British empiricism). He also contributed to political philosophy with his work on social contract theory and liberalism. He argued that the mind is a blank slate at birth, and he rejected that a newly born child has innate ideas at birth (as proposed by Descartes) |
| Berkeley | George Berkeley (an eighteenth century Irish philosopher and bishop of Cloyne) made important contributions to British empiricism. His theory denies the existence of material substances, and states that the objects that we perceive in our mind have no existence outside of our mind. This philosophical position is known as immaterialism or idealism |

(continued)

**Table 2.2** (continued)

| Philosopher | Description |
|---|---|
| Hume | David Hume (an eighteenth century Scottish philosopher) formulated the standard empiricist philosophical position. He argued that all objects of human knowledge may be divided into two kinds: *Matters of fact* propositions that are based entirely on experience, or *relation of ideas* propositions that may be demonstrated via deduction reasoning in the operations of the mind. His investigations identified problems with justifying the principle of induction and causation |
| Kant | Kant (an eighteenth century German philosopher) aimed to provide a bridge between the opposing philosophies of rationalism and empiricism. He described the critique of pure reason as a Copernican revolution in philosophy. Kant argued that there is a third force in human knowledge that provides concepts that can't be inferred from experience, and this force is the manner in which the human mind structures its experiences |
| Hegel | Hegel (an eighteenth/nineteenth century German philosopher) contributed to several areas in philosophy including ontology, epistemology and political philosophy |
| Marx | Karl Marx (a nineteenth century German philosopher) was influenced by Hegel. Marx's view of history is influenced by Hegel's claim that reality and history should be viewed dialectically |
| Husserl | Edmund Husserl (a nineteenth/twentieth century German/Austrian philosopher and mathematician) founded the field of phenomenology |
| Frege | Gottlob Frege (a nineteenth/twentieth century mathematician and logician) did important work on the foundations of modern logic and the philosophy of language |
| Russell | Bertrand Russell (an influential twentieth century philosopher) made important contributions to mathematical logic and the philosophy of language |
| Wittgenstein | Wittgenstein was an influential twentieth century logician and philosopher. He studied under Russell at Cambridge in England, and produced two distinct (diametrically opposed) and influential philosophies as recorded in the Tratatus and philosophical investigations respectively |
| Heidegger | Martin Heidegger (a twentieth century German philosopher) made important contributions to phenomenology and existentialism |
| Schlick | Schlick was a founder member of the Vienna circle, which formulated the philosophy of *logical positivism* |
| Sartre | Jean-Paul Sartre (a French philosopher), and along with his life long companion, Simone de Beauvoir (who was a feminist and noted philosopher in her own right), was one of the leading figures in the philosophy of existentialism. He was influenced by Heidgger's *sein und Zeit*. His influential works include "being and nothingness" and "existentialism is a humanism" |

the Buddha's teachings are preserved in the *Pali canon* (the foundational collection of early Buddhist scriptures representing its core teachings), which was handed down in an oral tradition, until they were written down in the first century A.D. (it is composed in the Pali language). The Pali Canon consists of the *Vinayana* (Discipline for the monks), *Sutta* (Discourses or basic teachings of the Buddha), and *Abhidhamma* (a more detailed systematisation of the doctrine). At the core of the Buddha's teaching is the doctrine of the *four noble truths*:

- Existence of suffering (*dukkha*)
- Origin/cause of suffering (*samudaya/trsna*)
- Cessation of suffering (*nirodha*)
- Eightfold path to end suffering (*magga*)

The four noble truths are outlined in the form of a medical diagnosis, where there is an illness; the causes of the illness are identified; a solution is proposed; and the steps to implement the solution are identified. The Buddha specified an *eight-fold path* to reach Nirvana, which involves self-discipline and asceticism. The earliest Buddhist tradition is called *Theravada* (also called *Himayana* or Small Vehicle), and is close to the teachings of the historical Buddha. The other major tradition of Buddhism developed in the first century B.C is called *Mahayana* (Great Vehicle), and it spread to China, Mongolia and Tibet.

Buddhism is concerned with leading a good life, practicing virtues and following meditation exercises. Meditation plays a role for being in the moment and concentrating to avoid distracting thoughts, and rational analysis and argument plays an important role in Buddhism. At the heart of Buddhism is the concept of *dukkha* which includes suffering, pain, sickness and essentially all the undesirable things that are part of the human condition. The Buddhist teaching on egolessness (*anatta*) and impermanence (*anicca*) involves a denial of the sense of self that humans' possess. The world of things is impermanent: i.e., things come into existence and go out of existence, and so everything passes in time.

The Buddha stressed that wisdom (*prajna*) and compassion (*karunā*) go hand in hand, and are essential to achieving enlightenment. For more information on Buddhism see [Rin:98].

### 2.5.3 Jainism

Jainism is an Indian religion that teaches the importance of non-violence, and reducing harm to living things as much as possible. This includes plants and animals, as Jains believe that animals and plants have souls. Jains are strict vegetarians, and only eat vegetables that grow above the ground, as eating root vegetables would kill the plant. Jains avoid swatting mosquitoes and stepping on ants, and Jains share many of the beliefs and values of Hinduism and Buddhism. For more detailed information on Jainism see [Hin:91].

### 2.5.4 Confucianism

Confucianism is a way of life that was proposed by Confucius in the sixth century B.C., and it is a system of thought and behaviour for a person and society.

Other systems of Chinese thought such as Taoism and the Legalist school of Chinese philosophy have influenced it. Confucianism shaped Chinese society for over 2000 years, and it is a hierarchical system with benevolence (仁 or *ren*) at its core, where people know their place in society, and the *expectation is that those in superior positions will take care of those in inferior positions in the hierarchy.* The ruling class can live happier and more fulfilling lives by observing the right conduct in accordance with a moral code that results in effective and just government.

Confucianism believes that humans are fundamentally good and understand the difference between right and wrong, and generally choose what is right. People generally choose wrong over right due to ignorance of what is right due to a lack of understanding of a moral code. *In general, people are teachable, improvable and perfectible through personal and community development*, and people will choose right over wrong when they are educated in right action and have a proper understanding of the world and their place in it. The way to understand one's place in the world is to recognise the existence of *Tian* (天 or Heaven), and the constant flux of the opposite forces of *Yin* (陰) and *Yan* (陽) (these opposite but complementary forces interact and coexist to create a balanced whole—i.e., harmony rather than conflict is promoted as everything in the universe contains the seed of its opposite).

Ethics are concerned with practical problems, such as how one should live as well as one's duties to families, strangers and wider society. It integrates the personal, social and the political, and the process of behaving ethically is achieved in the context of the social relationships of family and wider society, and especially to those to whom one has responsibilities (e.g., such as parent, daughter, sibling, friend, neighbour, and so on).

That is, there is an emphasis on the family and social context in making the right ethical choices and taking the appropriate action. It advocates a strict code of ethics to adhere to or maintain the middle way, including *Ren* (benevolence), *Yi* (righteousness), *Zhi* (knowledge) and *Xiao* (filial piety). People are encouraged to honour and respect their parents and observe a hierarchy of authority. The right behaviour involves more than instructions or a code, as the instructions need to be interpreted to the particular situation, and a person's duties are duties of their station towards other socially described persons or things.

Confucius coined the *Silver Rule* (an earlier version of the Golden Rule in Christianity). It is expressed in a negative "*whatsoever you do not want done to you, do not do to another*".

### 2.5.5 Taoism

*Taoism* (or Daoism) is an ancient Chinese philosophy that emphasises living in harmony with the *Tao* (which means way or path) of the universe. The Tao is a system of guidance and is not God, nor is it worshipped. It is the ultimate creative principle of the universe, and covers concepts such as creation, the natural universe, and the way of nature as a whole. Taoism includes the concepts of *yin* and *yang*, which represent matching pairs of opposites (e.g., hot and cold, wet and dry, light and dark, and so on) that work together towards a universal whole. *Yin Yang* is the principle of natural and complementary forces, and the opposites fit together to work in perfect harmony, and show that everything in the universe is connected. The body is a miniature of the universe filled with the Tao.

Taoism has many deities that are worshipped, and it promotes the achievement of harmony with nature as well as spiritual immortality. Its practice includes meditation and feng shui, and it promotes self-development and being virtuous. The *One* is the essence of Tao and enables things to be truly themselves; the terms *Wu* and *Yu* indicate being and non-being; *Te* refers to virtue and awareness/following of the Tao; *Wu Wei* is the method of following the Tao; *Ch'i* or *qi* refers to the cosmic energy that enables beings to survive and links them to the universe as a whole.

Taoism notes that as the universe is always changing that knowledge is always changing, and human knowledge is always partial. Ethics in Taoism is concerned with becoming a good person who lives in harmony with all things and people, and taking decisions in the context of the Tao. Lao Tzu (Laozi) is the traditional founder of Taoism but he is not believed to be a historical person, with the book attributed to him, The *Tao Te Ching*, likely to have been written by several authors.

## 2.6 Some Philosophical Questions in Computing

We will be discussing various philosophical questions that arise in computing such as those in Table 2.3.

## 2.7 Review Questions

1. What is philosophy?
2. What is knowledge?
3. What is metaphysics?
4. What is rationalism?
5. What is British empiricism?
6. What is the difference between noumena and phenomena according to Kant's theory?
7. What is the difference between Eastern and Western philosophy?
8. Explain the difference between the early and later Wittgenstein.
9. What is Artificial Intelligence?
10. Compare/contrast the contributions of Plato and Aristotle.

**Table 2.3** Philosophical questions in computing

| Question | Initial Answer |
|---|---|
| What is science? | The philosophy of science is concerned with the study of scientific enquiry, including philosophical questions that arise from reflections on the nature of science |
| What is a computer? | A computer is a tool that enhances the reasoning capability and productivity of humans, and it is a programmable electronic device that can process, store and retrieve data |
| What is an algorithm? | An algorithm is the procedure (or set of instructions) for solving a problem (e.g., computing the value of a function), and it transforms the input into the output |
| What is a computer program? | A computer program is a set of instructions to implement some algorithm, and the execution of the program carries out the algorithm |
| What is engineering? | Engineering involves the design, development and manufacturing, and maintenance of technology products |
| What is computer science? | The discipline of computer science studies computers and the algorithms that run on them |
| What is mathematics? | Mathematics is concerned with logical reasoning from accepted axioms and premises to conclusions. It employs deductive reasoning, which is truth, preserving: i.e., if the premises are true then the conclusion must be true |
| What is a number? | One view is that numbers are just numerals. Another view is that numbers are ideas in our mind. Another view is that numbers are just abstractions of physical magnitudes |
| What is computability? | A function *f* is computable if there is an algorithm that computes *f* |
| What is mind? | This is an enquiry into the nature of mental phenomena, including the relation of mind to body and the external world. It explores what a mind is and how we can know anything about it |
| What is artificial intelligence? | Artificial intelligence is the ability of computer/robot to perform tasks that are considered intelligent |

## 2.8 Summary

Philosophy is an attempt to understand the world, and it asks fundamental questions on the nature of reality, or on the fundamental assumptions underlying any discipline. It is a systematic enquiry into the subject under discussion, where the professional philosopher subjects the discipline to a forensic analysis with penetrating questions to examine its foundations, and to assess the extent to which its foundations are secure. Philosophy inquires into matters where exact knowledge has not been established or is not yet possible, and the work of the philosopher may be contrasted with that of the scientist who studies the world of science and what we can know about the world.

Philosophy may show us that things that we thought to be true are not actually so. Philosophy proceeds by a rational enquiry into matter of concern, and arguments are generally presented in natural language. Philosophers tend to be coherent thinkers who proceed from premises to conclusions using logical arguments, and they aim to avoid fallacies in reasoning.

Many philosophical theories or systems that have been developed over the millennia, but most have been shown to be incorrect. In many ways, there has been little progress in philosophy over the last 2500 years, from the dawn of philosophy in Classical Greece to the modern age, and so the questions are, in a sense, more important than the answers.

## References


[Ber:1710] Treatise concerning the Principles of Human Knowledge. George Berkeley. 1710.

[Cam:13] The Outsider. Albert Camus. Penguin Classics. 2013. (Originally published in 1942).

[Des:99] Discourse on Method and Meditations on First Philosophy, 4th Edition. Rene Descartes. Translated by Donald Cress. Hackett Publishing Company. 1999.

[Hin:91] A Handbook of Living Religions. Edited by John R. Hinnells. Penguin. 1991.

[Hob:1691] Leviathan. Thomas Hobbes. 1691.

[Hum:1740] An Enquiry Concerning Human Understanding. David Hume. 1740.

[Kan:1787] Critique of Pure Reason. 2nd Edition. Immanuel Kant. 1787.

[Loc:1690] An Essay Concerning Human Understanding. John Locke. 1690.

[Pla:08] Symposium. Plato. Oxford University Press. 2008.

[Pla:12] The Republic. Plato. Penguin Classics. 2012.

[Pla:14] Theaetetus. Plato. Oxford University Press. 2014.

[Pop:59] The Logic of Scientific Discovery. Karl Popper. 1959.

[Rin:98] The Tibetan Book of Living and Dying. Sogyal Rinpoche. Random House Ltd. UK. 1998.

[Wit:99] Philosophical Investigations. 3rd Edition. Ludwig Wittgenstein (Translated by G.E.M Anscombe). Blackwell Publishers. 1999.

# 3 Philosophy of Science, Engineering and Technology

## 3.1 Introduction

Computer science involves both science and engineering, where science is concerned with understanding the world, and engineering is concerned with modifying the world with the creation of useful products to serve society. The objective of this chapter is to introduce both the philosophy of science and the philosophy of engineering, and to understand the differences between them.

The philosophy of science is concerned with the nature and foundations of science, and philosophical questions that arise from these reflections. It uses the scientific method, which helps in distinguishing science from pseudo science. The *scientific method* is the process by which science is carried out, and it involves formulating hypotheses (the discovery of a hypothesis and its justification), deriving predictions from the hypotheses, and carrying out experiments to test the hypotheses and verify the predictions. Often, the *principle of parsimony* (*Occam's razor*) is employed to choose a scientific theory with the smallest set of elements.

The philosophy of science studies the foundations, methods and implications of science. It examines what can be qualified as science, as well as the reliability of scientific theories. It considers questions such as "What is a scientific theory?" and "What is scientific explanation?". Among the philosophical problems studied in science is the problem of induction, and whether inductive reasoning can be justified (especially given Hume's criticism as discussed in Chap. 2).

Engineers build useful artefacts for the public and wider society, and so engineering involves the application of science to build safe and useful products for the public to use. Engineering involves the design, development and manufacturing, and maintenance of technology products, and it provides, in a sense, a rational solution to technical problems that arise during the various activities. And so, engineering may be considered a process of effecting change in the world through its design (which may be creative) and manufacture of useful artefacts such as planes, computers, buildings and so on. The philosophy of engineering is concerned with



G. O'Regan, *Philosophical and Cultural Aspects of Computing*, Undergraduate Topics in Computer Science, https://doi.org/10.1007/978-3-032-29284-1_3

philosophical issues that arise in engineering, including ethical issues that may arise, as well as the aesthetics of the engineered products.

Engineers have a professional responsibility and are required to behave professionally and ethically at all times with their clients. They may be members of professional engineering bodies, where the professional body requires the member to adhere to the code of ethics of the profession.

Technology refers to the application of tools and processes as well as state of the art knowledge and innovation in science and engineering to create products and services to serve humanity. Technology has evolved over the millennia from primitive technology of hunter-gatherer and agrarian societies, to the industrial revolution that led to mass production and urbanisation, to the computer technology information age with global connectivity, and to the emerging technology age of Artificial Intelligence and Biotechnology. The philosophy of technology is concerned with the nature of technology and its social effects, and is discussed in Sect. 3.4.

## 3.2 Philosophy of Science

Science is a body of knowledge about the natural world that aims to describe the world as it is, as well as developing scientific theories that explain the physical world. Scientific theories enable predictions of future behaviour to be made and tested, and the accuracy of the predictions is used to judge the adequacy of the theory. Science involves observation of the world, analysis and reflection, formulation of a hypothesis or theory, experiments and testing of the hypothesis, and acceptance or rejection of the hypothesis.

The process of scientific discovery leads to new facts about the world, and it is a distinctive form of human inquiry, where scientists in the various sciences use the scientific method to obtain new knowledge. The scientific method is the process by which science is carried out, and it involves observing the world; discovering and formulating a hypothesis about the world; deriving predictions from the hypothesis, making observations and gathering data by carrying out experiments to test the hypothesis and to verify the predictions; analysing the data and evidence; and finally, accepting or rejecting the hypothesis. The scientific method helps in distinguishing science from pseudo science.

The philosophy of science studies the foundations, methods and implications of science. It is concerned with the study of scientific enquiry, and is concerned with philosophical questions that arise from reflections on the nature of science. It is concerned with considering how science differs from other human activities, as well as the nature of science itself. It examines how science differs from pseudo science, as well as how scientific hypotheses are formulated (discovered) and justified (grounded). It examines scientific inquiry and the reliability of scientific theories, and whether scientific knowledge gained by induction can be regarded as definite knowledge. The choice of a particular theory where there is more than one theory available to explain the physical reality is important, and Occam's razor is often employed to choose a scientific theory with the smallest set of elements.

The goal of the philosophy of science is not to answer specific scientific questions as such, but instead to answer questions about the nature of science and the scientific method. Among the philosophical problems studied in science is the problem of induction, and whether inductive reasoning can be justified. Hume had demonstrated that the principle of induction cannot be demonstrated, and attempts by logical positivism to use their verification principle also failed in dealing with the problem of induction, and so logical positivism failed as a way of distinguishing science from pseudo science.

Aristotle made important contributions to the development of ancient Greek science, and one of the earliest attempts at a philosophy of science is described in the *Posterior Analytics* of Aristotle's *Organon*, which was written in the fourth century B. C. He claimed that science, like geometry, has certain necessary starting points or axioms, and that scientific knowledge (truths) are demonstrated from these axioms (or necessary premises) using syllogistic logic (i.e., Aristotle's deductive logic) to produce conclusions or theorems.

Aristotle's starting point to knowledge acquisition was the senses, as he believed that these were essential in knowledge acquisition. He emphasised observation, classification and logical reasoning, and he separated knowledge into distinct sciences such as Biology, Physics, etc. He argued that everything has a teleological explanation in science, and *his teleological approach led science down a blind alley for roughly 2000 years*, until the time of Galileo.

Aristotle identified four causes (material, formal, efficient, and final) to give an account of explanation, and he argued that everything in motion must be moved by something (i.e., there is a mover), where an object in motion is changing from a potential state to an actual state. He believed that heavier objects fell faster than lighter objects (Galileo disproved this theory in the seventeenth century). Aristotle formulated a geocentric model of the universe, where the earth was at the centre, surrounded by concentric spheres of the four elements, and then the celestial spheres.

He emphasised common sense observations rather than experimentation (where modern science formulates hypotheses or theories that are then tested with experiments), and his over-reliance on deductive logic (syllogistic logic) from what he believed to be true primary premises, to yield causal explanations (which he believed to be rigorous and necessary) was deeply flawed. That is, for Aristotle, the premises must give the real explanation of the fact mentioned in the conclusion, and Aristotle's empirical method begins with observation of the physical world to gather observable data, and then use syllogistic reasoning to reach conclusions. He states that different sciences need different starting points due to the fact that they are dealing with different subject matter, and that one must use premises and methods appropriate to the question under discussion.

Acquinus was deeply influenced by Aristotle and his analysis made Aristotle's philosophy compatible with the Church, and so the Aristotelian view of science became an integral part of church teaching. This meant (given the authoritarian nature of the church) that anyone who criticised Aristotelian science was seen as criticising the church (an infallible entity), and so any dissent against the prevailing wisdom was subject to sanction (persecution).

Francis Bacon criticized Aristotelian philosophy, and he outlined his *Baconian Method*, which was an early formulation of the scientific method, as a means of observation and induction in his *Novum Organum* [Bac:1620]. Bacon is considered to be the father of science and empiricism, and he believed that all learning and knowledge comes from sense experience, with inductive reasoning to interpret the observations. He argued for empirical studies, as knowledge is always supported by the observed facts, and so scientific knowledge comes from the careful observation of nature combined with inductive reasoning. Inductive generalisation may take place from a set of facts, and so in this way an essential base of knowledge is slowly built up. Bacon's philosophy of science was influential (Fig. 3.1).

Hume demonstrated (see Chap. 2) that experience shows us very little about cause and effect, as if we have two events A and B we say that A causes B if they both occur together (i.e., they are *constantly co-joined* in that whenever we find A we find B, and we have a certainty that this conjunction will continue to happen). That is, according to Hume pure reason alone cannot prove causation, and the human mind is unable to perceive causal relations directly. The notion of necessity in causation is weak in that we are psychologically certain that B will follow A.

The weak notion of necessity in causation leads to the problem with induction, in that we are not justified in making any inductive inference about the world. Induction involves generalising from events that have always occurred in the past to state that they will always occur in the future. However, the only evidence for

**Fig. 3.1** Francis Bacon

this is in the past, and we are assuming that the future will be like the past, but the only evidence we have for this is in the past.

The Vienna circle was formed in the 1920s in Austria with the goal of cleaning up science and philosophy, and especially in distinguishing science from pseudo science. The members of the Vienna circle (the logical positivists) formulated the *verification principle* as a way to distinguish science from pseudo-science, and a statement is considered meaningful only if it is empirically verifiable or true from the meaning of its terms (i.e., a logical tautology as in logic or mathematics).

Another words, every meaningful statement is either verifiable or analytic, and so for logical positivists metaphysical statements, as well as statements about religion and ethics are meaningless, as they may not be empirically verified, neither are they logical tautologies. The implication of this, if the logical positivists are correct, is that metaphysical statements as well as statements on religion, ethics, and metaphysics are meaningless. However, the verification principle was quite vague and was never quite properly formulated (it left in too little or too much), and ultimately logical positivism and the verification principle failed.

The members of the circle met regularly to discuss problems in philosophy, logic, language, mathematics and science, and its members included scientists and philosophers such as Moritz Schlick, Otto Neurath, Rudolf Carnap, Kurt Gödel and others. Ludwig Wittgenstein was in Vienna at the time but he was not a member of the group, although he met Schlick on a number of occasions. Similarly, Karl Popper was in Vienna at the time but he too was not a member. A. J. Ayer spent a year in Vienna at the time becoming familiar with the work of the Vienna Circle, and he later promoted logical positivism in England (especially with his book *Language, Truth and Logic*) which was published in the mid-1930s (when he was just in his mid-20 s) [Ayr:36].

Popper has been influential in the philosophy of science, and he has argued that scientific theories cannot be proved to be true as such, but can be proven false through empirical testing. He formulated the *falsification principle* as a way to test and evaluate scientific theories and hypotheses, and this principle may be employed to demarcate science from non-science. A theory is falsifiable if it can be logically disproved by an empirical test, and theories that rely on un-testable assumptions or where empirical testing is not possible are classified as *pseudo science*, as they lack the rigour of scientific theories (Fig. 3.2).

Popper emphasised critical thinking in science, and he argued that science is an *open system* in that it is open to being criticised and challenged. Science is built on the falsification principle, where scientific theories are subject to rigorous testing, and open to rejection based on empirical evidence. That is, according to Popper, scientists are active in criticising and replacing defective theories (including their own), and Popper has been highly influential in the philosophy of science [Pop:59].

Thomas Kuhn has also been influential in the philosophy of science, and he has provided a coherent account of how scientific change happens. His analysis suggests that scientists are not quite as open as Popper suggests, as they work within a prevailing paradigm that provides the scientific community with an associated set of problems to solve, and that scientists are generally reluctant to change

**Fig. 3.2** Karl Popper

paradigm. He argued in "*The Structure of Scientific Revolutions*" [Kuh:70] that the development of science is governed by adherence to a paradigm, where the paradigm refers to a prevailing theory and associated set of problems for the scientists to solve. However, a crisis in science occurs when the paradigm is unable to deal with anomalies, and the crisis is followed by a revolution where the prevailing theory is replaced with a new paradigm that can deal with the anomalies (Fig. 3.3).

Kuhn noted that paradigm shifts and scientific revolutions take place in science, and he coined the term '*normal science*' to refer to the theoretical framework or paradigm in which scientists are working prior to a scientific revolution. A scientific revolution, according to Kuhn, leads to a *paradigm shift*, where there is a noticeable change in the scientific discipline, and the previous approach is replaced with a newer theory that provides a better explanation and more accurate predictions.

Kuhn noted that normal science provides a framework for scientists with a clearly defined set of problems to be solved, and often there is often a resistance to a change of paradigm from scientists. This may result in some scientists staying with the old paradigm rather than moving to the new paradigm (they may have spent their entire career working on problems related to the old paradigm). Kuhn suggests that the new paradigm becomes dominant as adherents of the old scientific paradigm die off. And so, scientists according to Kuhn are not as open as Popper suggests.

Kuhn argued that adherence to the *status quo* is a characteristic of normal science, and that scientists work in a community with other scientists and are subject

**Fig. 3.3** Thomas Kuhn. Creative commons

to social-cultural factors that influence the acceptance or rejection of new scientific theories.

Imre Lakatos and Paul Feyerabend initially accepted Popper's philosophy of science, but later reacted against it. Lakatos sought to reconcile Kuhn and Popper, by characterising science as a process of competing research programmes. Feyerabend initially emphasised the need to develop rival theories to facilitate empirical testing of accepted theories, but he later came to the view that theories that are incompatible with one another cannot be compared empirically. Feyerabend came to reject method in science and became a critic of the philosophy of science, and especially of attempts to lay down rules of the scientific method. An imaginary debate between Lakatos and Feyerabend on the philosophy of science is presented in "*For and Against Method*" [LF:99].

### 3.2.1 Is Computer Science a Science?

Computer science involves both science and engineering, and in this section we consider in what ways computer science may be regarded as science. There are, in a sense, two types of sciences namely pure and applied science. Empirical science is an applied science that refers to those sciences that require empirical evidence from observations and experiments to explain the natural world, and they include fields such as physics, chemistry, biology, and so on. The non-empirical sciences (or pure sciences) do not rely on empirical evidence as such, and they include the fields of mathematics and logic.

Computer science arose from the fields of mathematics and logic, and so it is, in a sense, a non-empirical science of computers or a science of algorithms. George Boole developed his symbolic logic in the mid-nineteenth century, and

Claude Shannon recognised that it was the perfect mathematical model for switching theory and for the design of digital circuits. Boole's symbolic logic is the basic concept that underlies all electronic digital computers.

Theoretical computer science is abstract and mathematical, and covers topics such as language theory, automata theory, complexity theory, graph theory, computability, cryptography, and coding theory. It studies algorithms including the efficiency of algorithms, and numerical analysis that determines approximate solutions where the exact solution may be difficult or impossible to determine. Other areas include information theory that was founded by Claude Shannon, and the area of formal methods that is a mathematical approach to the specification and verification of software for the safety critical field.

There is also an empirical side to computer science where, for example, in the AI field researchers formulate hypotheses on how intelligent behaviour may occur, and they then develop systems to test these hypotheses. Machine learning involves spotting patterns in datasets to generate a hypothesis that best describes the pattern (this is the opposite approach to hypothesis testing in statistics where a hypothesis is proposed and then tested against the data and either accepted or rejected). Another example is the software reliability field in software engineering, where researchers use these mathematical models to predict the reliability of the software.

The development of a new software system or program is like an experiment, and the test cases prepared to evaluate the program are based on the program specification, with each test case including the expected (or predicted) result from running each test case. Test execution involves observation and analysis to determine the extent to which the software exhibits the predicted behaviour of its specification, and the software is accepted if all tests pass (i.e., the program satisfies its specification).

That is, software engineering is an empirical activity (especially peer reviews and software testing to evaluate the correctness of a program). Similarly, several other areas of computer science such as Artificial Intelligence (AI) and Machine Learning (ML) are empirical, as they use real world data to train algorithms, as well as evaluating their performance and making predictions. Data Science and Analytics is empirical since it involves analysing large data sets to find patterns and derive insights; Human–Computer Interaction (HCI) assesses how humans interact with machines and so is empirical; Computer Vision and Image Processing involves analysing and developing algorithms for image data and so is empirical. Finally, the fields of Computer Graphics and Cybersecurity are empirical.

## 3.3 Philosophy of Engineering

The field of engineering has been around for millennia (without being formally defined as a discipline or profession as such), with engineers (or skilled builders and labourers) creating remarkable structures in the ancient world such as the Hanging Garden of Babylon, the Colossus of Rhodes, the Pyramids of Egypt, the statue of Zeus at Olympia, the Mausoleum at Halicarnassus, the temple of Artemis at Ephesus, and the Lighthouse in Alexandria.[1]

The constructions of the pyramids at Giza required tens of thousands of skilled workers, with huge blocks of stone carved out from quarries, and then dragged and lifted into position. The Romans were great builders with the ruins of Roman roads, Roman baths, aqueducts, amphitheatres, temples and theatres still visible in parts of the former Roman World. The Greco-Roman period considered the aesthetics of buildings as well as their functionality, and this is very evident in the Parthenon on the Acropolis in Athens, and especially the frieze of the Parthenon, which may be seen in the Elgin marbles at the British Museum in London.

Engineering is more concerned with the application of existing knowledge rather than the creation of new knowledge as in science. An engineer is a builder who applies his/her knowledge to build useful artefacts to transform the world and create a better society, and so it is essential that the engineer has the right body of knowledge to build quality products that are safe for the public to use. Engineering involves the application of science and mathematics, and its activities include the design, development, manufacturing, and maintenance of technology products. Engineering education needs to include a solid foundation in science and mathematics, as well as education in mathematical modelling, creating the design, turning the design into specifications and implementation, as well as the professional and ethical responsibilities of their profession. Engineers are required to stay up to date with current knowledge to ensure that they are competent for their assignments.

That is, engineers need the right education to apply scientific and mathematical principles in their work, and they need education on creating specifications and designs, modelling, turning designs into products, and testing. The appropriate engineering knowledge should enable the engineer to produce high-quality and well-structured products that are safe for the public to use.

The engineer is required to state precisely the requirements that the product is to satisfy, and to produce designs that will satisfy these requirements. It involves starting with a precise description of the problem to be solved; producing an appropriate design to solve the problem and validating the correctness of the design; finally, the design is implemented and manufactured (where applicable), and testing is performed to verify its correctness.

There is always a creative step in identifying the most appropriate design for a product, and engineers may employ mathematical modelling to test the design to determine whether it is adequate in meeting the user requirements. Inadequate designs are rejected and replaced (e.g., a model of a bridge may be developed and tested to determine if can deal with all of the expected stresses on the bridge such as traffic, gravity, wind, storms). A model is a mathematical representation of the physical world, and is a simplification of the underlying reality. The adequacy of the model is a key concern, and this indicates the extent to which the model is

[1] The pyramids of Egypt are the only remaining wonder of the ancient world.

a good representation of the underlying reality, or whether an alternative model should be sought. This means that it is important for the engineer to explore the model and its predictions to determine the extent that they reflect the required behaviour in the real world.

We discuss the professional responsibilities of computer professionals in Chap. 10, and similarly engineers have individual responsibilities as professionals in that they are responsible for designing and implementing high-quality and reliable products that are safe for the public to use. They are also accountable for their own decisions and actions, and have a responsibility to object to decisions that violate professional standards. Professional engineers have a duty to their clients to ensure that they are solving the real problem of the client. They need to precisely state the problem before working on its solution. The term "engineer" is a title that is awarded on merit: however, it places responsibilities on its holder to behave professionally and ethically. Finally, professional engineers are required to follow the code of ethics of the engineering bodies to which they belong.

The philosophy of engineering is an enquiry into the discipline of engineering, and is concerned with philosophical issues that arise in engineering, including answering questions such as what exactly is engineering? Is engineering all about design? Is design creative? What role does aesthetics play in engineering? What role do ethics play in engineering? What values should an engineer have? What does it mean to be an ethical engineer? Should engineers consider the ultimate purpose for which the technology is used? Should engineers develop a certain technology if it has negative impacts on society? Who should be held accountable when engineered technology fails and causes damage or loss to the public? What is the relationship between engineering and other disciplines such as science, technology and ethics?

The philosophy of engineering is an emerging discipline, and whereas engineering is a practical discipline focused on building products, and problem solving to resolve issues that arise, the philosophy of engineering is more abstract and focused on understanding what being an engineer means, and what an engineer should strive to achieve? There are relevant philosophical questions that need to be considered specifically for engineering as well as for general philosophy, and these include questions concerning ethics, epistemology, ontology and aesthetics.

The *engineering method* is a systematic approach to providing the desired solution to a problem, and it is employed by engineers and the project team. There is no strict formulation of the method as such, but it basically starts with a set of requirements, followed by analysis and then design, followed by an evaluation of the design, and then development and concludes with the output of the solution to the problem.

There are several phases (or steps) starting from the initial *idea* (identifying the problem); to formulating the *concept* (modelling and refining the concept to find a solution that best meets customer's needs and constraints); *planning*, which is concerned with the preparation of the project plan, including the people involved as well as their roles and responsibilities; *design*, where the customer requirements are translated into engineering specifications, *development* often involves an iterative cycle of design, test, debug and re-design to create a working prototype that provides a solution to the problem; and finally launch is concerned with releasing the design and documentation to manufacturing for production.

*The choice of the particular design from the various available options is a key engineering decision.* There will often be several different choices for the design, with each option having advantages and disadvantages. The choice of design will generally require tradeoffs for technical and non-technical reasons (e.g., budget constraints, legal restrictions and so on). The technical and non-technical tradeoffs are at the heart of the design process, where the engineer needs sound judgment (good analysis and intuition) to make the right decision on the appropriate design of the product.

How does the engineer go about choosing the best option? One approach that the engineer could adopt is to list all of the desired criteria for the design (including weightings to highlight the importance of each criterion), and evaluate the extent that each design option satisfies each criterion. The criteria could include quality, usability, aesthetics, etc. The engineer could then choose the design that scored highest in the evaluation. Good engineering judgment plays an essential role in avoiding expensive or catastrophic design errors, and choosing the design in a methodical way increases confidence in the decision. Table 3.1 shows one approach to choosing the best design from several candidate designs.

The sample design evaluation process in Table 3.1 lists all of the requirements vertically that the design is to satisfy, and the candidate designs that are to be evaluated and rated against each requirement are listed horizontally. Various rating schemes may be employed, and a simple numeric mechanism is employed above, and the design evaluation criteria are used to rate the effectiveness of each candidate design, and indicate the extent to which the design satisfies the defined requirements. The chosen design in this example is design *k* as it is the most highly rated of the evaluated designs.

There are differences in the education that engineers and computer scientists receive in their degree programmes. Engineers generally receive a solid foundation in engineering design and mathematics, which enables them to build products safely and tackle real world problems. The education of the computer scientist

**Table 3.1** Design evaluation table

| | Design 1 | Design 2 | … | Design *k* |
|---|---|---|---|---|
| Requirement 1 | 8 | 7 | | 9 |
| Requirement 2 | 4 | 6 | | 8 |
| ……….. | | | | |
| ……….. | | | | |
| Requirement *n* | 3 | 6 | | 8 |
| Total | 35 | 38 | … | 45 |

tends to include many areas such as programming, algorithms, software engineering, the latest technologies, and so on, and so while computer scientists receive education in mathematics, it is often not as substantial as that of the classical engineer.

Often, the day-to-day knowledge used by engineers is knowledge that is based on their experience rather than formal education, where formal education tends to provide knowledge for the novice engineer. Experienced engineers develop conscious and unconscious ways to solve problems based on what has worked for them in the past, and where this competence is in specific domains.

Classical engineers are generally certified as "engineers" by professional engineering bodies, where these bodies verify that the engineer has the right education and competence to be called an "engineer", as otherwise the engineering body would get a bad name with unqualified people practicing as engineers. That is, the title of "engineer" is a title that is awarded on merit: its title places duties and responsibilities on its holder to behave professionally and ethically, and to adhere to the code of conduct of the professional engineering body.

The vast majority of qualified computer scientists do not become members of professional bodies as such, although in recent years some computer scientists have joined professional bodies such as the ACM, BCS, and IEEE.

### 3.3.1 Aesthetics in Engineering

The origin of the word "aesthetics" is from the ancient Greek αισθητικος (*aisthetikos*) meaning sensory perception, and so aesthetics has something to do with human perception. It is the branch of philosophy that deals with the nature of beauty as well as the nature of taste, and it includes the philosophy of art, music, drama and poetry. Aesthetics is a type of emotional response or judgment that we experience when we view an object of beauty (or an object that is hideous), and the field provides critical reflection on art and culture (Fig. 3.4).

Plato believed that beauty (καλος or kalos) exists in an abstract Platonic Form, and he seemed to believe in some absolute beauty that resided in the Platonic world of ideas (Forms). True beauty, according to Plato, may not be discovered as an attribute of a beautiful thing, as these are beautiful things, and not the absolute beauty in itself.

Aristotle developed some principles on beauty and art in his *Metaphysics*, and he saw universal elements of beauty to be order, symmetry, harmonious and being of a certain magnitude. He believed that mathematics especially demonstrates these forms of beauty, and he also analysed beauty in both natural organisms and in artistic works (e.g., a play). He distinguishes between the good and the beautiful, saying that the former is always in action, but that the latter may be motionless.

Edmund Burke was an eighteenth century parliamentarian and writer, who was born in Ireland, and served as a member of parliament in the U.K. He wrote an influential work on aesthetics (*A Philosophical Enquiry into the Origin of Our*

**Fig. 3.4** Forth bridge, Scotland. Creative commons

*Ideas of the Sublime and Beautiful*) published in 1759 [Bur:1759]. The "beautiful", according to Burke, is well formed and aesthetically pleasing, whereas the "sublime" is that which has the power to compel and destroy us (i.e., the sublime is something of such excellence that it inspires great admiration, but is connected more with pain than pleasure). According to Burke, the elements of beauty include smallness, smoothness, gentle curves, delicacy and brightness. Burke explains beauty and the sublime in terms of Aristotle's account of causation (i.e., formal, material, efficient and final causes).

Kant's views on aesthetics are discussed in the *Critique of Judgment* [Kan:1790]. He discusses aesthetical experience and judgment in relation to the beautiful and sublime, and he argues that it is our faculty of judgment that allows us to have experience of beauty. Kant believed that an aesthetic judgment was similar to moral judgement, and that a judgment had four key features (disinterested, universal, necessary and purposive without purpose). *For Kant, beauty does not reside inside the object but results from a subjective response to the object*, and an aesthetic judgment is always an individual one (e.g., "this rose is beautiful"). Kant explores in the Critique how aesthetical judgments are possible and what such judgments mean using these four unique features of aesthetic judgments.

Hume argued that in order to be able to judge between different tastes (in the aesthetic sense) that we need a standard of taste, and he makes a distinction between judgments on the one hand and sentiment or feeling on the other hand. Hume argues that judgments are objective as they have reference objects that are out there in the world, whereas sentiments are subjective and so have reference to nothing beyond themselves. And so, we cannot have a distinction between a false and true sentiment in the way that we can have a distinction between a false and a true judgment. And so, if taste is about sentiment and subjective, then we cannot argue about taste as it is subjective.

However, there are universal principles of taste and beauty that are nearly the same for everyone, and Hume argues that we can refine our sense of taste with delicacy to make better judgments (e.g., consider the art of developing expertise in wine tasting and becoming more effective over time in identifying the flavours). He emphasises the importance of good sense, delicacy, practice, comparison and avoiding prejudice in developing a better sense of taste.

Aesthetics plays an important role in the field of engineering in that aesthetical considerations arise during the design, and their resolution will determine how a product looks and feels. That is, a good design brings aesthetical and functional elements together to create a product that is greater than the sum of its parts. Good design includes both good functionality and aesthetics, and so good design engineering involves a blending of both the aesthetic and the functional, which results in the functionality of the product being expressed by its aesthetic appearance.

Often, the first impression that we have of a product is its visual appearance, and so its aesthetics and its look and feel are very important. There is an overlap between usability engineering and aesthetics, where usability engineering is concerned with designing products that are easy to use, and considers human-product interaction. There are several other factors that could influence a user's opinion of a product such as colour, sound, taste, and smell, as well as its quality. There may be commercial factors (e.g., budget) with respect to the level of aesthetics employed in product design, as the aesthetics budget of a high-quality car such as a "Mercedes" will be at a different level from that of a low-quality vehicle such as a "Lada". A good design will be aesthetically pleasing to the eye and have good functionality.

The combination of aesthetics with technical design in engineering involves integrating artistic principles with engineering principles, and the goal is to create products that are both functionally and visually appealing. That is, an interdisciplinary approach plays a key role in the creation of innovative and visually appealing products in the modern world, and so aesthetics potentially plays an important part of the creative design process.

This means that aesthetics needs to become an integral part of the design and development process (to ensure that it is embedded in the artefacts created during development). Another words, aesthetics needs to become part of engineering design curricula, and engineers need to be educated on how aesthetics is relevant to their work, as well as learning about the technical activities in engineering.

### 3.3.2 Ethics in Engineering

Chapter 9 provides a brief history of ethics, and we discuss the professional responsibilities of engineers in Chap. 10. Engineers are professionals and need to behave professionally and ethically at all times, and they should carry out their work to the highest standards, as well as using sound judgment in the exercise of their duties. Engineers have individual responsibilities as professionals in that they are accountable for their own decisions and actions, and they should object to decisions that violate professional standards.

Engineers are accountable to themselves and others for their actions, and they must be willing to accept professional responsibility when performance does not meet professional standards. They should participate only in assignments where they have the appropriate competence, and they have a duty to their clients to ensure that they are solving the real problem of the client. They are responsible for designing and implementing a high-quality and reliable product that is safe for the public to use. They should follow the codes of the engineering profession and behave ethically at all times.

### 3.3.3 Is Computer Science Engineering?

Computer science is both a theoretical and practical discipline, with theoretical aspects concerned with areas such as computability, algorithms and their efficiency, complexity theory, automata theory, language theory, formal methods and program verification, graph theory, cryptography, and coding theory. There are several areas in computer science (e.g., software engineering) that are practical, and which apply the theory of computer science as well as engineering principles to build products (hardware and software) for society. That is, computer science may also be viewed as a part of engineering (or intersecting with engineering), as well as being a scientific discipline. Several areas of computer science that emphasise engineering principles include, software engineering, computer engineering and Artificial Intelligence.

Computer scientists are engineers in the sense that they build things (i.e., they build computer systems or application software for their clients), and they employ scientific and engineering principles in their work. For example, a computer scientist who is developing a software system for a client will apply software engineering principles to design and develop high-quality and reliable software that will be fit for purpose, and satisfy the customer requirements.

A software engineering project needs to be managed as a project, and is subject to schedule and budget constraints. It may require a dedicated project manager to ensure that the project is delivered on time/budget and with the right quality. This means that engineering activities such as project management, requirements engineering, software design and development, testing, quality management, and software release and maintenance all need to be employed in the project, and software engineers need to follow sound engineering principles to enable high-quality software to be produced that will be safe for the public.

The area of computer engineering is concerned with the integration of electronic engineering with computer science, and the field designs and develops computer systems for areas such as the automotive or medical device fields. Engineering principles are employed to ensure that the computer systems developed are of high quality, and satisfy safety and regulatory requirements.

The area of Artificial Intelligence is concerned with building technology that simulates intelligence or behaves intelligently. It involves developing technologies for vision, speech recognition and articulation, and other sensory inputs, as well as technologies for robots, including sensors where the response to the sensory data being action to change the position of its effectors (e.g., leg, wheel, arm). Clearly, it is essential that all AI technologies and systems are properly engineered, and work as expected when deployed outside of the laboratory.

There are many areas in AI that involve engineering, including machine-learning, deep learning, natural language processing, development of neural networks, decision-making systems, security, robotics, self-driving cars, and so on.

## 3.4 Philosophy of Technology

Technology refers to the application of tools and processes as well as state of the art of knowledge (and innovation) to create products and services to serve humanity. Technology has evolved over the millennia from the primitive technology of hunter-gatherer and agrarian societies, to the industrial revolution that led to mass production and urbanisation, to the computer technology of the modern information age with global connectivity, and to the emerging technology age of Artificial Intelligence and Biotechnology (Fig. 3.5).

**Fig. 3.5** Siemens steam turbine. Creative commons

There are many positive impacts of technology such as improvements in the quality of life of people around the world, as, for example, in medical care, communication with friends and family, and so on. However, there are also negative impacts of technology such as job displacement due to automation, or concerns over the impact of technologies on the environment, the violation of privacy from the use of modern technologies, and the dangers of addiction from technologies such as social media.

The origin of the term "technology" is from the Greek τεχνη (*techne*), which means craft knowledge, and λογος (logos), which means an account of, and so the historic meaning of the word "technology" is an account of craft knowledge.

The early Greek philosophers viewed technology arising as an imitation of nature, with Aristotle arguing that this is often the case, but that *techne* can also go beyond this, and completes what nature cannot bring to a finish or it may produce things that nature cannot (e.g., tools). Aristotle argues that natural things have an inner principle of generation and final cause, whereas *techne* is shaped by an outside cause and end. That is, for Aristotle, technology acts as an instrument to achieve human ends (it serves human goals and is controlled by humans), and it is grounded in reason (which causes it to be developed), and it has a specific purpose (or final end).

The philosophy of technology is concerned with the nature of technology and its social effects. The industrial revolution in the nineteenth century led to immense changes to society with mass urbanisation and mechanisation (see Chap. 16). Among the questions that the philosophy of technology asks are:

- Is technology a tool that humans control?
- Does technology shape society and culture?
- To what extent does society influence how technology develops and is used?

Aristotle saw technology as a form of practical wisdom, where he viewed *techne* as a productive skill or craft that imitates nature, and completes what nature cannot finish. We discussed the contributions of Bacon to science earlier in this chapter (*Baconian Method* was an early formulation of the scientific method). Bacon reflected on the impact of technology on society, and his views on technology were optimistic, in that he saw technology as extending human power over nature for the betterment of society, through work to improve living conditions.

One of the earliest formulations of a philosophy of technology was by the German-American philosopher, Ernst Kapp, in the late nineteenth century. Kapp argued in his book "Elements of a Philosophy of Technology" [Kap:1877] that technology expands and extends human bodily and mental capabilities (e.g., consider a simple tool like the axe that extends and expands the human arm).

Marx provided a scientific analysis of the capitalist system in Das Kapital with the goal of understanding its inner workings. He argued that technology was capitalist, and that capitalism does not work to develop technology as such, but instead it develops only those machines that serve its interests (e.g., economic, political and social). Further, it inhibits the developments of technologies that do not advance its interests [Marx:1867].

That is, for Marx, technology is a tool for exploitation under capitalism, with technology used to increase productivity and profit, and so, for Marx, technology does not serve humanity as such—rather it serves the interests of the capitalist class. He predicted that increasing automation under capitalism could undermine the system itself, and could lead eventually to a society where technology serves humanity.

Heidegger saw technology as a powerful but potentially dangerous way of revealing the world that may potentially obscure other truths. He suggests that thinking in society may become dominated by its view of technology that sees everything as a resource. Instead, he suggests a more holistic approach, and highlights the historic connection between the older views of technology in the world of the ancient Greeks. He does this by linking technology back to the ancient word "*techne*", which meant not just skill or craft as such, but also the arts. Heidegger suggests that this leads to a more holistic view of technology, which includes craftsmanship and art.

Heidegger's philosophy of technology suggests that technology plays a role in bringing about a decline in the human condition by constricting our experience of things as they are. The implications of this according to Heidegger are that we view nature and to an extent other human beings only technologically: i.e., nature and other humans are raw materials to be used in technology.

Heidegger sees his role as highlighting this phenomenon, as well as seeking a way of thinking to save modern civilisation, which has been shackled throughout the world (irrespective of their political structures) from the controlling power of technology. Heidegger is not urging a rejection of technology as such, but instead urging society to be aware of the danger of bondage from technology, and to ensure that such dangers are appropriately managed.

Heidegger's views on technology are described in "*The Question Concerning Technology*", where Heidegger explores the essence of modern technology. He argues that technology is a way of revealing the world (*enframing*), and that this may become a dominant, all-encompassing view. He criticises the prevailing views of technology as a neutral means to human ends, and urges a more free and questioning relationship with technology to reveal its true essence [Hei:54].

Mumford argues that the development of technology is shaped by human choices and cultural values, and is not a predetermined path. He views technology as deeply integrated with, but not the sole determinant of civilisation, with technological development shaped by human choices. He discusses the "*Myth of the Machine*", which describes the dominant philosophy in society that elevates technological and organisational power to the supreme good, with humans viewed as exchangeable parts of the "*mega machine*" that is designed for maximum efficiency. Mumford contrasts this approach with the field of *biotechnics* (biotechnology) that advocates a holistic approach that emphasises human flourishing along side material progress.

He distinguishes between two types of technology namely *authoritarian* versus *democratic*, with authoritarian referring to large, powerful and centralised technologies that concentrate power and threaten personal autonomy. On the other hand, democratic technologies are small scale and human-centred that promote democratic values such as individual responsibility.

Mumford was critical of the prevailing technological trend that emphasised constant growth and expansion, which he saw as detrimental to the human condition. He issued warnings that the "mega machine" could lead to the situation where technology reduces or eliminates alternatives to itself, thereby reducing or eliminating choice in the world.

Mumford explains his views on technology and civilisation in his book "*Technics and Civilisation*", which presents the history of technology (starting from the development of mechanical clocks in the fourteenth century up to the mid-twentieth century), and its role in shaping and being shaped by civilisations. Mumford argues that it is the choices that we make rather than the machines that we use that have created a capitalist machine-oriented industrial economy. Another words, *the human race has the ability to shape the world of technology, and should therefore consider its options in the face of threats that it faces such as industrial warfare or environmental catastrophe, and decide rationally the best way forward for humanity* [Mum:34].

Ellul highlighted threats to human freedom and religion from modern technology, and he sought to change the perception of technology in society to that of a tool rather than as a regulator of society. He highlights the dangers of emergence of a technological tyranny over humanity, and his most important work on technology is "*The Technological Society*" [Ell:67]. Next, we consider some philosophical questions that arise in the philosophy of technology.

### 3.4.1 Questions in Philosophy of Technology

There are several philosophical questions that arise in the philosophy of technology such as those in Table 3.2.

## 3.5 Review Questions

1. Explain the difference between engineers and computer scientists.
2. What is computer science?
3. What is engineering?
4. Is computer science engineering?
5. Is computer science just science?
6. Explain the difference between the Popper view of science and Kuhn's view.

**Table 3.2** Philosophical questions in philosophy of technology

| Question | Initial answer |
|---|---|
| What is technology? | Technology is the application of scientific and engineering knowledge to create machines and tools to serve humanity |
| How does technology differ from science and engineering? | Technology refers to the practical tools or products created from the application of science and engineering, where science is a body of knowledge about the world, and engineering is more the application of science to build products that are safe for the public to use |
| Do humans control technology? | Humans create technology and so the way that it operates is within the limits of human design. However, the design of a technology can influence human behaviour, as can be seen with addictive technologies such as social media sites and smart phones. Humans have free will in that they may make a choice to use or not to use the technology |
| Does technology control humans (shape human behaviour)? | Once technology exists it exerts an influence on human behaviour, as may be seen in the invention of a smart phone and how it has transformed the world in social interactions between people using social media sites such as Facebook and twitter/X. Further, some of these technologies have led to the field of surveillance capitalism, where the online behaviour of users is monitored and exploited for monetary purposes. Users have become addicted to their smart phones checking their phones many times throughout the day |
| What is the relationship between technology and society/culture? | Technology shapes society in many ways such as transport, energy, electricity, TV, radio, internet, automation, and social media. That is, technology acts as a driver of change in society, and it is natural to ask whether technology promotes progress or deepens inequalities, and, in a sense, it does both (e.g., improvements in education with new technologies and inequalities from the digital divide around the world) |

(continued)

**Table 3.2** (continued)

| Question | Initial answer |
|---|---|
| What are the risks of emerging technologies? | Emerging technologies offer many opportunities for society, but they also pose major risks. For example, there has been substantial progress in the AI field in recent years, leading to risks of massive job losses in traditional roles (especially job entry roles). There are also risks of biased algorithms that may harm individuals, as well as an invasion of privacy, misuse of autonomous weapon systems and a loss of control. There are dangers of misuse of bioengineering to engineer and spread viruses, as well as the dangers of accidents and leaks at nuclear power plants |
| What are the ethical responsibilities of the designers of technology? | This question is related to the ethical responsibilities of engineers discussed in Chap. 10, and include protecting the public with safe and reliable products, as well as designing products to be accessible by different categories of users, protecting privacy of personal data, as well as transparency and accountability |
| How do we balance the benefits of technologies with the harm that may be caused? | The public needs to be educated and informed on the benefits/risks of new technologies so that they can make better choices, and political decision makers should be active in protecting the public. That is, it is important to identify, articulate and clearly understand the benefits versus the risks, and it is essential to have regulation of new technologies, with an external board providing governance to oversee their implementation, with the board providing transparency and accountability |

7. What is technology?
8. Explain the differences between science, engineering and technology.
9. Do humans control technology?
10. Does technology control humans?

## 3.6 Summary

Computer science involves both science and engineering, and so it is important to discuss both the philosophy of science and the philosophy of engineering, and to understand the differences between them.

The philosophy of science is concerned with concerned with the nature and foundations of science, and philosophical questions that arise from these reflections. It uses the scientific method, which helps in distinguishing science from pseudo science. It considers questions such as "What is a scientific theory?" and "What is scientific explanation?".

Engineers build useful artefacts for the public and wider society, and so engineering involves the application of science to build safe and useful products for the public to use. Engineering involves the design, development and manufacturing, and maintenance of technology products. The philosophy of engineering is concerned with philosophical issues that arise in engineering, including ethical issues that may arise, as well as the aesthetics of the engineered products.

Technology refers to the application of tools and processes as well as the state of the art of knowledge to create products and services to serve humanity. The philosophy of technology is concerned with the nature of technology and its social effects.

## References

[Ayr:36] Language, Truth and Logic. A.J. Ayer. 1936.

[Bac:1620] *Novum Organum.* Francis Bacon. 1620.

[Bur:1759] A Philosophical Enquiry into the Origin of Our Ideas of the Sublime and Beautiful. Edmund Burke. 2nd Edition. 1759. England.

[Ell:67] The Technological Society. Jacques Ellul. Random House. 1967.

[Hei:54] The Question Concerning Technology and Other Essays. Martin Heidegger. Harper Perennial. 2013. (Originally published in 1954).

[Kan:1790] The Critique of Judgment. Immanuel Kant. 1790.

[Kap:1877] Elements of a Philosophy of Technology: On the Evolutionary History of Culture. Ernst Kapp. Univ. of Minnesota Press. 2018. (originally published 1877).

[Kuh:70] The Structure of Scientific Revolutions. Thomas Kuhn. 1970

[LF:99] For and Against Method. Imre Lakatos and Paul Feyerabend. University of Chicago Press. Edited by Matteo Motterlini. 1999.

[Marx:1867] Das Kapital. A Critique of Political Economy. Fingerprint Publishing. 2018. Originally published in 1867.

[Mum:34] Technics and Civilisation. Lewis Mumford. Routledge (UK). 1934.

[Pop:59] The Logic of Scientific Discovery. Karl Popper. 1959.

# 4 What Is a Computer?

## 4.1 Introduction

Computers are an integral part of modern society and new technology has transformed the modern world into a global village. Communication today may be conducted using text messaging; WhatsApp; mobile phones; video calls over the Internet; email; and social media sites such as Facebook, Twitter/X and Instagram. New technology allows people to keep in touch with friends and family around the world, and the World Wide Web allows business to be conducted in a global market.

A computer is a programmable electronic device that can process, store and retrieve data. It processes data according to a set of instructions (a program) that is stored in the computer's memory. All computers consist of two basic parts namely *hardware* and *software*. The hardware is the physical part of the machine, and the components of a digital computer include memory for short-term storage of data or instructions; an arithmetic/logic unit for carrying out arithmetic and logical operations; a control unit responsible for the execution of computer instructions in memory; and peripherals that handle the input and output operations. Software is a set of instructions that tells the computer what to do.

The original meaning of the word "*computer*" referred to someone who carried out calculations rather than an actual machine: i.e., *a computer is a human who computes*. This remained the definition of a computer until the early 1940s when the earliest digital computers were developed. These early digital computers were enormous machines consisting of thousands of vacuum tubes, and were built in the 1940s and 1950s. However, their computational power was a fraction of the personal computers or smartphones used today.

Von Neumann emphasised that the computer code should be binary, and his definition of a digital computer is given in his "First Draft Report on EDVAC" [VN:45].



G. O'Regan, *Philosophical and Cultural Aspects of Computing*, Undergraduate Topics in Computer Science, https://doi.org/10.1007/978-3-032-29284-1_4

DEFINITION 10.1 (COMPUTER)

An automatic computing system is a (usually highly composite) device, which can carry out instructions to perform calculations of a considerable order of complexity. The instructions must be given to the device in absolutely exhaustive detail. They include all numerical information, which is required to solve the problem under consideration. All these procedures require the use of some code to express the problem, as well as the necessary numerical material. The device must be able to carry them out completely and without any need for further intelligent human intervention. At the end of the required operations the device must record the results again in one of the forms referred to above.

There are two distinct families of computing devices namely *digital computers* and the historical *analog computer*. These two types of computer operate on quite different principles, and the earliest computers were analog machines and not digital.

The representation of data in an analog computer reflects the properties of the data that are being modelled. For example, data and numbers may be represented by physical quantities such as electric voltage in an analog computer, whereas a stream of binary digits represents them in a digital computer. That is, an analog computer operates in a completely different way to a digital computer.

Arithmetic has traditionally been done using the decimal notation,[1] and Leibniz was one of the first to recognize the potential of the binary number system. This system uses just two digits namely "0" and "1", with the number two represented by 10; the number four by 100; and so on. Leibniz described the binary system in *Explication de l'Arithmétique Binaire* [Lei:1703].

A digital computer is a sequential device that generally operates on data one step at a time. The computation in a digital computer is based on binary digits: i.e., "0" and "1", where electronic circuits are used to represent binary numbers, with the state of an electrical switch (i.e., "on" or "off") representing a binary digit internally within a computer. That is, a single transistor acts as a switch and is used to represent a binary digit, whereas several transistors are required to store larger numbers.

## 4.2 Early Computers

A computer is a tool that enhances the reasoning capability and productivity of humans, and it is a programmable electronic device that can process, store and retrieve data. Early attempts at developing calculating devices include the slide rule developed by William Oughtred and others in the seventeenth century. Pascal introduced his Pascaline calculator in the seventeenth century, and Leibniz developed a more sophisticated machine (the Step Reckoner) in the late seventeenth century.

[1] The segadecimal (or base-60) system was employed by the Babylonians c. 2000 BC. Indian and Arabic mathematicians developed the decimal system between 800 and 900 AD.

Babbage provided a vision of the modern computer with his design of a general-purpose problem-solving machine (the Analytic Engine) in the nineteenth century, which was a significant advance over his earlier machine (the Difference Engine) that was used to evaluate polynomials (this was useful as many functions may be approximated by polynomials). The Difference engine is similar to a mechanical calculator, and it could produce and print mathematical tables mechanically.

Babbage's design of the Analytic engine envisioned that programming of the machine would be done by punched cards (this was based on the Jacquard Loom that was used for manufacturing textiles, with each card representing one row on the design). Lady Ada Lovelace (the daughter of Lord Byron) collaborated with Babbage on applications of the analytic engine, and she wrote what is considered the first computer program, with her step-by-step description of the computation of Bernouilli numbers with the machine. This involved moving numbers from the store, to the mill and back again according to the instructions on the cards.

The Harvard Mark I was developed by Howard Aiken with contributions from IBM in 1944. This was a large electromechanical calculator that could perform the basic arithmetic operations as well as having the ability to refer to previous results. It was designed to assist with the numerical computation of differential equations.

John Atanasoff and his student, Clifford Berry, developed the Atanasoff Berry Computer (ABC) from 1939 to 1942. This machine pioneered important developments in modern computing, including binary arithmetic and Boolean logic, the separation of memory and computation, as well as calculations performed electronically rather than by mechanical switches. Several of its concepts were later used in the development of ENIAC (an important milestone in the history of computing) (Fig. 4.1).

**Fig. 4.1** Setting the switches on ENIAC's function tables

John Mauchly and Presper Eckert developed the ENIAC computer at the University of Pennsylvania in the mid-1940s, and this vast fixed program computer used thousands of vacuum tubes. ENIAC was a fixed-program computer (it had to be physically rewired to solved a different problem), but, its successor, the EDVAC, was a stored program (program stored in memory) computer. EDVAC did not need to be physically rewired to solve a new task (all that was required was to place a new program in memory).

Tommy Flowers and others at Bletchley Park, England developed the Colossus computer during the Second World War, and it played an important part in confirming that the disinformation and deception tactics carried out as part of the D-Day Normandy landings were successful.

Konrad Zuse is considered *the father of the computer* in Germany, as he built the world's first programmable machine (the Z3) in 1941. Zuse developed several early computers in the late 1930s/early 1940s. He was unaware of computer-related developments in Germany or in other countries, and he implemented the principles of modern digital computers independently of others (in isolation). The Z3 was developed in 1941 and is considered the world's first functional tape-stored program controlled digital computer.

The Manchester Mark I was designed and developed in the late 1940s.by Frederic Williams, Tom Kilburn, Geoff Tootill, and others at the University of Manchester in England. It was the *first stored program computer* (developed just before EDVAC), and so it did not need to be physically rewired to solve a different problem. Instead, all that was required was to load a new program into memory (as described in Von Neumann's draft report on EDVAC).

For more details on early computers and the history of the computing field see [ORg:26].

### 4.2.1 Von Neumann Architecture

The earliest computers were fixed programs machines that were designed to do a specific task. However, this proved to be a major limitation on the machine, as it meant that a complex manual rewiring process was required to enable the machine to solve a different problem.

The computers used today are general purpose machines designed to allow a variety of programs to be run on the machine. Von Neumann and others [VN:45] described the fundamental architecture underlying computers in the late 1940s, and it became known as Von Neumann architecture (Fig. 4.2).

Von Neumann architecture arose on work done by von Neumann, Eckhert, Mauchy and others on the design of the EDVAC computer, which was the successor to ENIAC computer. Von Neumann's draft report on EDVAC described the new architecture [VN:45].

The von Neumann architecture led to the birth of stored program computers (the first stored program computers were EDVAC and the Manchester Baby), where a

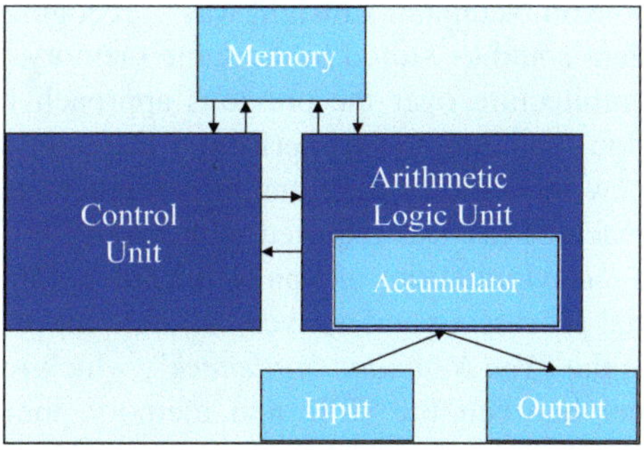


**Fig. 4.2** von Neumann architecture

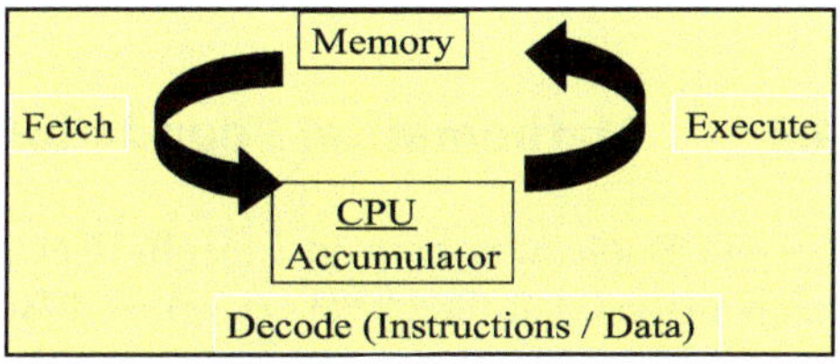


**Fig. 4.3** Fetch/execute cycle

single store is used for both machine instructions and data. The key components of the architecture is described in Table 4.1.

The key approach to building a general-purpose device according to von Neumann was in its ability to store not only its data and the intermediate results of computation, but also to store the instructions, or commands for the computation. The computer instructions can be part of the hardware for specialized machines, but for general purpose machines the computer instructions must be as changeable as the data that is acted upon by the instructions.

**Table 4.1** Von Neumann architecture

| Component | Description |
|---|---|
| Arithmetic unit | The arithmetic unit is capable of performing basic arithmetic operations |
| Control unit | The program counter contains the address of the next instruction to be executed. This instruction is fetched from memory and executed. This is the basic fetch and execute cycle (Fig. 4.3)@the control unit contains a built in set of machine instructions |
| Input–output unit | The input and output unit allows the computer to interact with the outside world |
| Memory | The one-dimensional memory stores all of the program instructions and data. These are usually kept in different areas of memory@@the memory may be written to or read from: i.e., it is random access memory (RAM)@@the program instructions are binary values, and the control unit decodes the binary value to determine the particular instruction to execute |

Von Neumann's insight was to recognize that both the machine instructions and data could be stored in the same memory. The key advantage of the von Neumann architecture over the previous approach was that it was much simpler to reconfigure a computer to perform a different task. All that was required was to enter new machine instructions in computer memory rather than physically rewiring a machine (as was required with ENIAC).

The limitations of Von Neumann architecture include that it is limited to sequential processing and not very suitable for parallel processing. Another key limitation is the "*Von Neumann bottleneck*", which refers to the shared communication channel between the CPU and memory, meaning that instruction fetches and data operations cannot occur simultaneously. This means that the CPU is often idle while waiting for data to be transferred from memory.

## 4.3 Mathematical Foundations of Computers

George Boole was born in Lincoln, England in 1815, and he was self-taught in mathematics and Greek. He developed Boolean algebra, which is the foundation for modern computing, and he is considered (along with Babbage) to be one of the grandfathers of computing. His work was theoretical, and he never actually built a computer or calculating machine. *However, Boole's symbolic logic was the perfect mathematical model for switching theory and for the design of digital circuits* (Fig. 4.4).

His paper on logic [Boo:48] introduced two quantities "0" and "1". He used the quantity 1 to represent the universe of thinkable objects (i.e., the universal set), and the quantity 0 represents the absence of any objects (i.e., the empty set). He then employed symbols such as *x*, *y*, *z*, etc., to represent collections or classes of objects given by the meaning attached to adjectives and nouns. Next, he introduced three operators (+, −, and ×) that combined classes of objects.

**Fig. 4.4** George Boole

Boole's symbolic logic played a key role in the development of the modern computer, with his logic acting as the basic concept that underlies all electronic digital computers. Claude Shannon's Master's Thesis showed that Boole's algebra was the perfect mathematical model for switching theory and for the design of digital circuits. Further, Boole's algebra may be used to optimise the design of systems of electromechanical relays, and circuits with relays solve Boolean algebra problems.

The use of switches to represent binary values is the foundation of modern computing, and the properties of electrical switches to process logic is the basic concept that underlies all modern electronic digital computers. Boolean logical operations may be implemented by electronic AND, OR and NOT gates, and more complex circuits (e.g., arithmetic) may be designed from these fundamental building blocks. Boole's logic led to the birth of the digital age.

Modern electronic computers use billions of transistors that act as switches and can change state rapidly. A high voltage generally represents the binary value 1 with low voltage representing the binary value 0. A silicon chip may contain billions of tiny electronic switches arranged into logical gates. The basic logic gates are AND, OR and NOT. These gates may be combined in various ways to allow the computer to perform more complex tasks such as binary arithmetic. Each gate has binary inputs and outputs.

Claude Shannon was the first person[2] to see the applicability of Boole's algebra to simplify the design of circuits and telephone routing switches. He showed that Boole's symbolic logic was the perfect mathematical model for switching theory and for the subsequent design of digital circuits and computers (Fig. 4.5).

His influential *Master's Thesis is a key milestone in computing*, and it shows how to lay out circuits according to Boolean principles. It provides the theoretical foundation of switching circuits, and *his insight of using the properties of electrical switches to do Boolean logic is the basic concept that underlies all electronic digital computers*.

Shannon realized that you could combine switches in circuits in such a manner as to carry out symbolic logic operations. This allowed binary arithmetic and more complex mathematical operations to be performed by relay circuits. He designed a circuit, which could add binary numbers, and he later designed circuits that could make comparisons and thus be capable of performing a conditional statement. *This was the birth of digital logic and the digital computing age.*

His Master's thesis "*A Symbolic Analysis of Relay and Switching Circuits*" [Sha:37] showed that the binary digits can be represented by electrical switches. This allowed binary arithmetic and more complex mathematical operations to be performed by relay circuits, and provided electronics engineers with the mathematical tool to design digital electronic circuits.

[2] Victor Shestakov at Moscow State University also proposed a theory of electric switches based on Boolean algebra (published in Russian in 1941 whereas Shannon's were published in 1937).

**Fig. 4.5** Claude Shannon

The design of circuits and telephone routing switches may be simplified with Boole's symbolic algebra. Shannon's Master's thesis became the foundation for the practical design of digital circuits. These circuits are fundamental to the operation of modern computers and telecommunication systems, and Shannon's insight of using the properties of electrical switches to do Boolean logic is the basic concept that underlies all electronic digital computers.

## 4.4 Philosophical Study of a Computer

A computer is more than just a machine in that it is an information processing system that manipulates symbols according to rules, processes information, and executes algorithms. It takes input, stores data and produces output based on its instructions (i.e., the software), and its behaviour is defined functionally by what it does (i.e., in the transformation of input into output), rather than its physical constituents (i.e., the underlying hardware). That is, a computer integrates its physical hardware with abstract algorithms and logic to create a system that is defined by what it does, rather than just its underlying physical hardware, and so a computer has a dual nature both as a physical system and as a functional system.

A naïve and circular definition of a computer is "*a computer is a machine that computes*". And so, the question of what a computer is then becomes what does it mean "*to compute*", and this leads on to the separate field of *computation* and *computability* (as discussed in Chap. 7). Another approach might be to define a computer in terms of its constituent parts, but given the extraordinary pace of change in the information technology field, any such definition would not work, as it would rapidly go out of date, as well as inadequately capturing the functional side of a computer.

Does a computer have to be an engineered physical device or could a biological entity (e.g., the human brain) be considered a computer? In many ways, a biological system is similar to a computer, in that both are information processing systems. For computers, processing is done by non-living hardware (i.e., silicon), whereas living processors do the processing in biological systems. Biological system perform information processing in a similar way to computers, in that they use receptors that act as input sensors, which they then process to produce output.

Does a computer have to be physical or may an abstract mathematical machine also be considered a computer? We will discuss the theoretical Turing Machine later in this section, and this theoretical device (i.e., the universal Turing Machine rather than the standard hardwired Turing Machine that computes a single function) may be programmed to solve any problem for which there is an algorithm. This shows that a computer does not need to be a physical device as such, but given the very slow speed of computation on a Turing Machine, there is a need for more practical solutions (as was given with the development of von Neumann architecture, which acts as a physical implementation of a Turing Machine as a digital computer).

A computer is *automatic* in that there is no human intervention after the program is run (apart from any input required). It is *general-purpose* in that it is capable of solving any problem (with a program) that has an algorithm (subject to space and time constraints). A computer is generally *digital* (using binary digits) but earlier computers were analog, whereas the fundamental unit in quantum computers is the qubit (this exists in a state called superposition—i.e., a linear combination of 0 and 1).

The question of what a computer is may be looked at from several philosophical perspectives including:

- Historical View
- Symbol Manipulation System
- Calculator view
- Turing Machine view
- Von Neumann Architecture view

The historical view of a computer is that it referred to someone who carried out calculations rather than an actual machine: i.e., a computer is a human who computes. This remained the definition of a computer until the development of the earliest digital computers in the 1940s, where a digital computer had similarities to a human computer performing computation, in that it is essentially an executor of logical, procedural instructions.

A computer may also be viewed as a symbol manipulation system that manipulates, rearranges, and transforms symbols based on formal, syntactic rules. That is, a computer operates on symbols (*syntax*) without understanding their meaning (*semantics*). It is a purely syntactic engine that follows rules of logic or arithmetic. This view of computation defines syntactic rules that operate on symbols (0, 1, letters, etc.) rather than their meanings. The machine manipulates these patterns without understanding what they represent, with meaning being derived only by an external observer or through interpretation. A purely symbolic system lacks a way to convert its internal symbols to the real world objects they represent (i.e., syntax is not sufficient for semantics).

A computer may be viewed as a calculator in that both calculators and computers perform calculations through input, processing, storage and output. That is, a computer is a type of calculating device that executes computer algorithms: i.e., they are machines that take input data; process it according to the instructions in the computer program, and return output data. This perspective treats computers not merely as fast calculators for numbers, but as general-purpose systems that process, store, and reason about information structured as symbols.

The operation of a computer is automatic in that there is no human intervention beyond writing the program to perform the desired processing. Computers may be applied to a wide variety of problems (i.e., they are general purpose machines), and they are usually digital machines (but they could also be Analog or Quantum computers).

Computers interact with other physical devices in the world, and they manipulate symbols into other symbols according to algorithms. They are physical implementations of the Turing machine in that they exhibit the same input-output behaviour (even though the details of the processing may differ).

Alan Turing proposed the Turing machine (TM) as an abstract model for computation in the 1930s, and the Church-Turing Thesis states that anything that is computable is computable by a Turing Machine or equivalent formalism (e.g., Lambda Calculus). The TM is a theoretical "paper and pencil" machine that captures the step-by-step logic of any algorithm, and it consists of an infinite tape, a read/write head, and a finite state machine).

The TM is a formal mathematical model of a human computer, and a human calculator, who is provided with pencil and paper as well as explicit instructions, may be regarded as a kind of Turing machine. A computer is a machine that computes, and so it is natural to ask what exactly is the relationship between a Turing machine and a computer? A Turing machine gives a precise definition of the process of computing, and the behaviour of a computer is logically equivalent to a Turing machine, in that they compute the same set of functions (although they may compute them in different ways).

The Turing machine may be programmed to solve any problem for which there is an algorithm, and it computes one function only. Turing showed that the universal Turing machine (UTM) could do the work of all other machines, in that it can compute any computable function. And so, in a sense, a standard Turing machine is like a *hardwired computer*, whereas the universal Turing machine is like a *programmable general-purpose machine.*

Turing Machines are theoretical and minimalist models of computation, and as they are not physical machines, their speed are measured in computational steps rather than in physical time. They can simulate any algorithm but are typically too slow for computation in practice, and the von Neumann architecture was an improvement of the Turing Machine model for computation.

We discussed the von Neumann architecture in Sect. 4.2.1, where the architecture consists of an arithmetic unit (for performing basic arithmetic and logical operations), a control unit (it is like the brain of the computer, and consists of a program counter pointing to the next instruction in memory, which is fetched, decoded and executed), an input-output unit (which allows the computer to interact with the outside world), and memory (the RAM memory consists of data and instructions).

Von Neumann's insight was to recognize that both the machine instructions and data could be stored in the same memory (stored program), which made it simpler to reconfigure a computer to perform a different task. All that was required was to enter new machine instructions in computer memory rather than physically rewiring a machine.

### 4.4.1 Philosophical Questions on Computers

There are different types of computers including the historical Analog computers; digital computers that are the dominant paradigm today; and there is emerging interest in quantum computers (that operate on *qubits*), which is likely to become more important in the future. However, there may also be other possibilities (e.g., the brain may be regarded as a type of computer, and so, in a sense, a computer may also be a biological entity). Therefore, a computer is some entity (usually a physical device but perhaps a biological entity) that performs computation, where computation involves the manipulation of symbols according to rules.

A computer may be described by the function that it performs (i.e., its input, the instructions for processing the input data, and the output that is produced). However, it may also be defined by its physical make up (i.e., its structural properties), and this leads to the question as to which kinds of structures can perform computation.

Another words, the question of what a computer really is therefore more complex, and the question is whether a computer needs to be an artificial entity (i.e., a physical machine that needs to be engineered) or are there other possibilities (such as the evolution of a biological entity such as the brain)? That is, does a computer need to be a physical device or may a biological (natural) entity also be considered a computer?

Further, what is the relationship between a real physical computer and the abstract model of a computer (as given in the theoretical Turing machine)? A physical computer may perform any computation that an abstract Turing Machine may perform and vice versa, and so, in a sense, a physical computer does not add value in the sense of solving new problems, but it does, of course, solve problems in a much more time efficient manner than the theoretical Turing Machine.

It is reasonable to ask whether the Turing Machine is the fundamental concept of a computer (with the real computer just a physical instantiation of the underlying theoretical machine), or whether it is the real physical computer that is the fundamental underlying concept, with the Turing Machine just providing a model for computation.

Another view may be to define a computer as a valid implementation of the Universal Turing Machine, in that they compute the same set of functions. Several philosophical questions with respect to a computer are presented in Table 4.2 below, and we discuss some of these in more detail in the remainder of the chapter.

### 4.4.2 What Is the Difference Between Hardware and Software?

At first there appears to be no problems with the standard concepts of hardware and software. The standard view is that hardware is the physical part of the computer (e.g., screen, keyboard, mouse, etc.), and software is the intangible or abstract part of the computer consisting of various computer programs that contain instructions to make the machine perform different activities to solve particular problems. That is, there is a clear distinction between the hardware (the physical part of the machine) and the software (the set of instructions to be carried out to solve the problem).

However, there are philosophical difficulties with this distinction, and the difference between hardware and software is an ongoing topic in the philosophy of computer science. There are various positions regarding the ontological[3] nature of hardware and software. Does the distinction apply only to computers or to all machines? Do we call anything a computer if it appears to take instructions? In the early days of computing and especially with ENIAC and other hard wired computers, the distinction between hardware and software was blurred in that programming consisted of setting switches and wiring the machine to perform certain operations, and so, in a sense, the software was part of the hardware.

However, this changed in a fundamental way with the introduction of the first stored program computer (on the Manchester Baby machine at the University of Manchester and on EDVAC, the successor to ENIAC) in the late 1940s. This meant that the software was now separate from the machine, and in order to change the task performed by the computer all that was required was to load a new program into the computer memory, rather than physically rewiring the machine.

Moor [Moor:78] has argued that there is essentially no significant ontological difference between hardware and software, with Suber [Sub:88] going further arguing that hardware is software. Colburn argued that software has both an abstract

[3] Ontological refers to the branch of metaphysics that deals with the nature of being (ontology which is derived from the Greek words οντως and λογος).

**Table 4.2** Philosophical questions on computers

| Question | Initial answer |
|---|---|
| What is a computer | An entity that performs computation (involving the manipulation of symbols according to rules), and is equivalent to a Turing machine |
| Is everything a computer | Searle states that while a brain's operations may be computationally simulated, the brain itself is not a digital computer. The brain has causal powers, and his Chinese room argument shows that symbol manipulation is not understanding |
| Is the universe a computer? | This is an enquiry into whether the universe operates as a gigantic quantum computer processing data |
| What is computation | A computation is any well-defined calculation that is performed by humans or machine |
| What is hardware | Hardware is the physical part of the computer (e.g., screen, keyboard, mouse, etc.) |
| What is software | Software is the intangible or abstract part of the computer consisting of computer programs to solve particular problems |
| What is a specification | This is a statement of the required behaviour of the program or computer system (usually written in a natural language) |
| Can a computer be conscious | This is an enquiry into the possibility of a computer/program being conscious |
| Does a computer have a mind? | This is an enquiry into whether machines and the programs running on them can act as a mind |
| Can a computer think? | This is an enquiry into whether machines and the programs running on them can think |
| Does a computer truly understand what it processes? | This is an enquiry into whether machines have a human level of understanding and comprehension |
| Is intelligence just computation? | Intelligence seems to involve more than the application of an algorithm to solve a problem (we also need experience, social context, consciousness, etc.) |
| Ethical responsibilities and accountability | Who should be held accountable if a computer makes a poor decision that results in harm (designer? Programmer? User? System)? |
| What knowledge can a computer have? | Can computers know things? What is the difference between data, knowledge and understanding? |
| Can a computer understand natural language? | Computers use AI techniques to process and interpret language, and their analysis of syntax and semantics is very different way from the ways that humans understand language |

and a concrete nature, and is best understood in what he calls a "concrete abstraction" [Col:99]. Turner argues that it is the abstract nature of specifications that are crucial in determining whether something is hardware or software [Tur:10].

The views of Moor and Suber are difficult for the computer scientist to accept, especially given that most individuals would be of the belief that there are some basic intrinsic differences between hardware and software. These include the fact that software is portable and easy to modify, whereas hardware is generally not. Further, hardware executes the instructions of the software, rather than vice versa.

Tanenbaum has argued that hardware and software are logically equivalent, in that any operation performed by software can also be built directly into the hardware, and vice versa, as the software can also simulate any instruction executed by the hardware. That is, he argues that the boundary between software and hardware is arbitrary, and that it is constantly changing [Tan:90].

Duncan accepts that hardware and software are logically equivalent, but he rejects that the boundary is arbitrary and constantly changing. Instead, he argues that there are distinctions between hardware and software from his definition of these terms. He defines a *software program* as "a specification that consists of one or more programming language instructions, and whose concretisation is embodied by an artefact that is designed so that a physical machine may read the concretised instructions", whereas *hardware* is defined as "an artefact whose functions are realized in processes that directly or indirectly bring about the result of some calculation" [Dun:17].

### 4.4.3 Is the Brain a Digital Computer?

It is common in the AI field to regard the brain as a kind of computer, with the mind representing software running on the computer. This is often referred to as Cartesian Dualism, where the brain represents the hardware of the computational system, and the mind represents the program that is running on the hardware (i.e., *the mind is to the brain as the program is to the hardware*). This view of the world is controversial, but if it is correct then the brain is a computer that is programmed by the mind.

Human brains are biological and analog, whereas computers are binary and rigid. Human cognition appears to be implemented by neuron firings in the brain (the brain is a complex interconnected structure consisting of roughly $10^{15}$ synapses—i.e., junctions between two neuron that allow nerve signals to be transmitted), and so the brain's cognitive functioning is not achieved by computation, as employed on a digital computer. However, if cognitive functions are computable then there are algorithms that compute cognition, even if the brain does not do it that way.

Computers operate by algorithms and lack the subjective experience of a human mind. That is, computers are programmable things, whereas the brain does not appear to be programmable or to run algorithms. However, the brain does appear to compute, as may be seen, for example, in the transformation of acoustic signals into neural activity that leads to the appropriate behaviour. That is, brain computation seems to transform sensory signals into some mental activity.

There are many open questions to consider including: What is thinking? Can thinking be reproduced by hardware running software? Are neural patterns software? Is the brain hardware? Which software makes us intelligent? How can thought and intelligence arise from the complex interaction of unthinking and unintelligent parts? How is human consciousness created? How can a computer be conscious?

Searle rejects the idea that a brain is a computer, and he argues instead that while the operations in the brain may be computationally simulated, simulation is not the real thing, and the brain itself is not a digital computer. He states that the brain has causal powers to create consciousness and intentionality through neurobiological processes (i.e., for Searle mental states such as consciousness are biological phenomena, and not just a result of formal symbol manipulation as done by a computer program).

That is, a computer/program deals with syntactic entities (i.e., computers deal with 0 and 1 s), and processes symbols and follows rules, but symbol manipulation is not the same as genuine meaning or understanding. This is described in his Chinese room thought experiment, which shows that syntax by itself is neither constitutive of nor sufficient for semantics: i.e., programs are neither constitutive of nor sufficient for semantics (see Chap. 8).

### 4.4.4 Can a Computer Be Conscious?

The question as to whether a computer can be conscious is controversial (with strong views on both sides of the argument), and the debate is currently unresolved. Computers today lack the structure of the human brain needed for conscious subjective experience, but many experts believe that future advanced AI systems (with fundamentally different architectures) could potentially develop consciousness. Other experts believe that no matter how advanced computers become that they will always just simulate human-behaviour, and that digital binary systems can never replicate the analog biological processes necessary for subjective inner experience of the world and consciousness.

Computers today are binary-driven machines that process information sequentially, whereas the brain is a vast system of parallel and analog connections. Further, the architecture of the brain is that of a vast neural network, which is totally different from the traditional von Neumann architecture, and so computers today just simulate intelligence, rather than being intelligent conscious entities.

It also depends on what exactly consciousness is, as traditional digital computers deal with computation, and so if consciousness is more than computation it may not be achievable. For example, is consciousness just information processing? or is it self-awareness?, or does it mean having a subjective, inner "experience" of the world? What distinguishes human intelligence and consciousness from AI?

(Does understanding require consciousness? Can a machine truly understand? Can a machine be conscious?).

Searle's Chinese Room argument is a rebuttal of functionalism and strong AI, and his position is that while the operations in the brain may be computationally simulated, simulation is not the same as the real thing. For Searle, mental states such as consciousness are biological phenomena, and not just a result of formal symbol manipulation as done by a computer program.

Faggin has proposed a theory of consciousness where consciousness is a purely quantum phenomenon unique to each individual. He states that a pure quantum state is not reproducible (i.e., it is private knowledge that is knowable within the system that is in that state, and only minimally knowable from outside). He argues that a classical machine can never be conscious, as a classical state is reproducible (where the program and data can be perfectly copied, whereas a quantum state remains private). For Faggin, consciousness is not linked to the functioning of the human body [Fagg:24].

### 4.4.5 Can a Computer Have a Mind?

It is common in the AI field to regard the brain as a kind of computer, with the mind representing the software running on the computer. The question as to whether a computer can have a mind is controversial (with strong views on both sides of the argument), and the debate remains unresolved. Current AI systems lack true consciousness, self-awareness, empathy and understanding, and while current systems may simulate human intelligence, most experts agree that current binary-based systems cannot act as a human mind.

The simulation of intelligence is hardly the same thing as the actual phenomenon (e.g., a model is not the reality), and Searle's Chinese room highlights that an entity can appear to exhibit intelligence yet possess no understanding. Computers operate by algorithms and lack the subjective experience of a human mind, and Searle's argument shows that the processing of rules does not lead to understanding. Finally, human brains are biological, analog and organic, whereas computers are binary and rigid, and so one wonders how an inanimate physical object could exhibit a mind, intelligence, and empathy.

However, some experts believe that if a computer can emulate the complex interconnected structure of the human brain (with approx. 100 billion or $10^{11}$ neurons and $10^{15}$ synapses) that it might develop consciousness. Functionalism (which Searle's Chinese Room argument appears to demolish) suggests that if a machine can perform the same functions as a brain (e.g., processing information, learning, etc.), then it is functionally equivalent to a mind (irrespective of its physical makeup).

Dennett argued that machines, in principle, could have minds, given that human brains are complex physical systems that have evolved to form complex machines. He rejects the view that the human mind is special as such, and instead argues that it is a physical, computational and evolutionary process. For Dennett, consciousness is an illusion as such, produced by the billions of neurons in the brain (i.e., he calls this "robots made of robots"). He argued that humans and machines may demonstrate high-level intelligence without needing to understand what they are doing. He rejects Cartesian dualism including the idea that there is a central place in the brain where consciousness happens (the Cartesian Theatre), and suggested instead that various competing streams of sensory input (including revised interpretations of the input) compete for dominance in the brain.

### 4.4.6 Is the Universe a Computer?

There is no consensus at this time on the question as to whether the universe is a computer, but it is subject to an ongoing debate in physics and philosophy. Some of its proponents argue that the universe operates as a gigantic quantum computer processing information; others suggest that the universe is a computational system or the output of a program; and others suggest that gravity might be some informational force.

Some of their opponents argue that the universe contains non-computable quantities (the fundamental reality is non-algorithmic), which means that computers cannot perfectly simulate it. Others argue that the fundamental laws of physics cannot be fully contained in a simulation, as they are necessary to create the space and time in which the simulation would exist. Others argue that the universe is not a simulation, as it may be measured to discover truths that algorithms cannot predict.

And so, whereas models may describe specific physical processes, they do not prove that the entire universe is a computer.

### 4.4.7 Does a Computer Understand What it Processes?

Digital computers operate on binary code (0 and 1 s), where the binary code represents data and instructions. A computer blindly follows rules in the manipulation of the data (i.e., the CPU fetches an instruction from computer memory, and then executes the instruction), and so they do not understand in the sense of human comprehension. Computers just understand binary data (implemented by an electrical switch in a transistor), and all text, data, images and videos are translated into a collection of bits that are then manipulated by some program (which contains the instructions to carry out the manipulation). A computer has no semantic understanding, in that it does not realise what a photo, spreadsheet, document or video is, and all it knows is the binary code instruction to manipulate the object.

## 4.5 Review Questions

1. What is a computer?
2. Explain the significance of Boole in the computing field.
3. What is the von Neumann architecture?
4. What is the difference between hardware and software?
5. Explain the significance of Shannon's contribution to computing.
6. Discuss the relationship between fixed/stored program computer and a Turing machine/Universal Turing machine.
7. Is the brain a computer?
8. What is the relationship between a Turing Machine and an actual computer?
9. Can a computer be intelligent and conscious?
10. Is the brain a computer?

## 4.6 Summary

A computer is a programmable electronic device that can process, store and retrieve data. It processes data according to a set of instructions or program. All computers consist of hardware and software, where the hardware is the physical part of the machine, and software is a set of instructions that tells the computer what to do. The hardware includes memory for short-term storage of data or instructions; an arithmetic/logic unit for carrying out arithmetic and logical operations; a control unit responsible for the execution of computer instructions in memory; and peripherals that handle the input and output operations.

We discussed Boole's symbolic logic that was the perfect mathematical model for switching theory and for the design of digital circuits. Shannon's insight of using the properties of electrical switches to do Boolean logic is the basic concept that underlies all electronic digital computers.

A Turing machine gives a precise definition of the process of computing, and the behaviour of a real physical computer is logically equivalent to a Turing machine, in that they compute the same set of functions (although they may compute them in different ways). A Turing machine may be programmed to solve any problem for which there is an algorithm, and it computes one function only. The universal Turing machine can do the work of all other machines, in that it can compute any computable function.

There are different types of computers such as analog, digital, and quantum computers. A computer is some entity (usually a physical device but perhaps a biological entity) that performs computation, where computation involves the manipulation of symbols according to rules.

## References


[Boo:48] The Calculus of Logic. George Boole. Cambridge and Dublin Mathematical Journal. Vol. III (1848), pp. 183–198.

[Col:99] Software, abstraction, and ontology. T.R. Colburn The Monist, 3–19. 1999.

[Dun:17] Using ontological dependence to distinguish between hardware and software. William D. Duncan. *Applied Ontology*. 2017;12(1):5-32.

[Fagg:24] Irreducible: Consciousness, Life, Computers and Human Nature. Federico Faggin. Essentia Books. 2024.

[Lei:1703] *Explication de l'Arithmétique Binaire* Wilhelm Gottfried Leibniz. *Memoires de l'Academie Royale des Sciences.* 1703.

[Moor:78] Three Myths of Computer Science, *The British Journal for the Philosophy of Science*, 29(3): 213–222. James H. Moor, 1978.

[ORg:26] A Brief History of Computing. Fourth Edition. Gerard O' Regan. Springer. 2026.

[Sha:37] A Symbolic Analysis of Relay and Switching Circuits. Claude Shannon. Masters Thesis. Massachusetts Institute of Technology. 1937.

[Sub:88] What is Software. Peter Suber. Journal of Speculative Philosophy. 2 (2):89–119 (1988).

[Tan:90] *Structured Computer Organization* (3rd ed.). A.S. Tanenbaum, Englewood Cliffs, NJ: Prentice-Hall. 1990.

[Tur:10] Programming languages as mathematical theories. R. Turner. In J. Vallverdú (Ed.), *Thinking Machines and the Philosophy of Computer Science: Concepts and Principles* (pp. 66–82). Hershey, PA: Information Science. 2010.

[VN:45] First Draft of a Report on the EDVAC. John von Neumann. University of Pennsylvania. 1945.

# The Nature and Philosophy of Computer Science

# 5

## 5.1 Introduction

The discipline of computer science studies computers (i.e., the physical devices that compute) and computing (i.e., the algorithms that run on computers), and the field emerged from the development of the earliest digital computer in the early 1940s. Today, it is of an interdisciplinary nature and intersects with many other fields, providing tools and methods for them. The term "*computer science*" first appeared in a 1959 article in Communications of the ACM, where Louis Fein argued for the creation of a Graduate School in Computer Sciences [Fei:59].

A digital computer is a sequential device that generally operates on data one step at a time, and the data are represented in binary format. A single transistor (initially a bulky vacuum tube) is used to represent a binary digit, whereas several transistors are required to store larger numbers.

We briefly discussed the nature of computer science in Chap. 3, and noted that it has become intertwined with so many other disciplines that it is, in a sense, difficult to think of it as a field on its own, as it plays such an important role in the natural evolution of other disciplines. It intersects many fields such as science, engineering, mathematics, and logic, and deals with computers and algorithms. That is, computers are tools that enhance reasoning in most fields, and so computer science is really about everything.

Computer science consists of a body of knowledge that is used by computer professionals in their work. On the other hand, computer scientists build things and use engineering principles in their work (especially in software engineering). And so, it is natural to ask whether computer is science? Is it engineering? Is it both science and engineering? Is it neither? Is it mathematics? It is very difficult to come up with one sentence that characterises the entire discipline of computer science, as any such definition tends to focus on one aspect of the field.

Computer science differs from natural science in many fundamental ways, and it deals with artificial rather than natural objects. The objects of study are computers,



G. O'Regan, *Philosophical and Cultural Aspects of Computing*, Undergraduate Topics in Computer Science, https://doi.org/10.1007/978-3-032-29284-1_5

algorithms, and the processing of information. In a way, programs running on a computer are like experiments, but they differ from the experiments carried out in natural science. In many ways, computer science is almost like a new kind of science that studies computers and algorithms.

In other ways, computer science is not really a science at all in that computer scientists are like engineers in that they build things, and so engineering principles are an integral part of the computer scientist's work. That is, the modern computer scientist needs to follow sound engineering practices to ensure that products are properly designed and implemented, and are safe for the public to use. Computer scientists (as engineers) have professional responsibilities in their work, and need to behave ethically at all times. Another words, computer science is both an engineering activity and a science.

Computer science studies computers and algorithms, with programming employed to implement algorithms; program verification is used to verify the correctness of programs and algorithms; computability theory is related to the existence of an algorithm to solve a particular problem; complexity theory is concerned with the limits of efficient computation; operating systems provide important software on the computer that manages the computer hardware, as well as providing common services for software programs; software engineering deals with how high-quality software is designed and developed to satisfy the customer requirements; and AI is concerned with software that simulates human intelligence and problem solving.

An algorithm takes symbols as inputs and produces symbols as output, and is implemented by some computer program. The *Church-Turing Thesis* was formulated in the 1930s, and states that every effective computation may be carried out by the theoretical Turing machine or equivalent formalism (see Chap. 7).

Computers and programs are symbiotic in that computers require programs to do anything, and programs require computers in order for the programs to actually do anything. That is, computation processes arises only from the union of a computer with a program.

Dijkstra argued that parts of computer science such as programming are mathematical activities, where mathematics is a "formal" science that proceeds from premises to conclusions via deductive reasoning [Dij:73]. However, this is not to say that computer science is part of mathematics, as they are very distinct fields. However, computer science emerged from the field of mathematics with Boole's symbolic logic, which was developed in the mid nineteenth century. Boole's logic provided the foundation for digital computing, and Claude Shannon recognised that it was the perfect model for digital computing in the 1930s. Further, the theoretical work on the foundations of mathematics in the early twentieth century by leading figures such as Frege, Russell, Whitehead, Hilbert, Godel, Turing, Church and Brouwer, led to a close examination of fundamental concepts such as computability, consistency, completeness, incompleteness, and decidability [ORg:23].

Perhaps, a more inclusive answer to what computer science is that it is a STEM discipline: i.e., a discipline that involves Science, Technology, Engineering, and Mathematics. It involves the study of many areas including computers, algorithms, information, processes and procedures, problem solving, the way of thinking about algorithms and computation, the art of computer programming, artificial intelligence, and complexity.

The study of algorithms goes back, at least, to Euclid, and Turing's theoretical study of algorithms in the 1930s led to his theoretical Turing machine. The progress in computer science has been the result of the success of engineering better and better calculating machines, as well as a more detailed understanding of algorithmic computation.

### 5.1.1 Philosophical Questions in Computer Science

Several philosophical questions arise naturally in computer science such as what exactly is a computer, as well as what is computation, and what are the limits of computation? Other questions that arise include what does it mean for a program to be correct, and what exactly is miscomputation? The area of ethics is important, and so questions such as what are the ethical responsibilities of computer scientists as well as how can we be sure that an algorithm is not biased (i.e., causes harm) are important. The AI field leads to several questions such as what exactly is consciousness, and whether a computer can ever be conscious, as well as whether a computer can think and have intentionality? Table 5.1 lists some philosophical questions related to computer science.

## 5.2 Computer Science as Science

We discussed the philosophy of science in Chap. 3, and noted that science consists of a body of knowledge that is concerned with the pursuit of knowledge and understanding of the world. The *scientific method* is the process by which science is carried out, and it involves observation of the world, formulating hypotheses about the world, deriving predictions from the hypotheses, and carrying out experiments to test the hypotheses and verify their predictions. Often, the *principle of parsimony* (*Occam's razor*) is employed to choose a scientific theory with the smallest set of elements (Fig. 5.1).

The philosophy of science is concerned with the study of scientific enquiry, and is concerned with philosophical questions that arise from reflections on the foundations, methods and nature of science (e.g., justifying causation and induction, and whether science can infer truth about non-observable entities). Scientific enquiry is a distinctive form of human inquiry, where scientists in the various sciences use the scientific method, which distinguishes science from pseudo science (the demarcation problem).

**Table 5.1** Some philosophical questions in computer science

| Question | Initial answer |
|---|---|
| What is computation? | A computation is any well-defined calculation that is performed by humans or machine. It has a semantic side as it involves meaning and correctness |
| What are the limits of computation? | The limits of computation are the limits of what may be computed (as given by a Turing machine or Church's lambda calculus), as well as limits from complexity theory (e.g., some problems may not be solved in polynomial time) |
| Can machines think? | This is an enquiry into whether machines (or the programs running on them) can think |
| Can machines be conscious? | This is an enquiry into whether machines (or the programs running on them) can be conscious |
| What is machine intelligence? | Machine intelligence is the ability of machines to exhibit cognitive functions such as learning, reasoning, problem solving, and decision-making |
| What is machine learning? | Machine learning refers to the ability of machines to learn and adapt without being explicitly instructed, where algorithms and statistical models are used to draw inferences from patterns in the underlying data |
| What does it mean for a program to be correct? | The behaviour of a machine is judged against its specification, and so if its behaviour corresponds to the specification then it is performing correctly (but, the specification may be incorrect) |
| What is a miscomputation? | Miscomputation is where the implemented system produces an incorrect output due to errors in specification, design, algorithm, or physical hardware (i.e., the input/output does not satisfy the specification or the specification may be incorrect) |
| What are the ethical responsibilities of computer scientists? | Computer scientists are, in a sense, engineers, and so have a professional responsibility for their work. This includes questions such as accountability should the system make an incorrect decision that leads to harm. Other problems include biased algorithms, deepfakes, etc. |
| Should harmful technologies be developed | This is a complex ethical debate that includes balancing the benefits of technologies with the associated risks (e.g., environment, military, economic, etc.) |

**Fig. 5.1** Very large array radio telescope in New Mexico. Creative commons

We mentioned that Hume demonstrated that experience shows us very little about causation, and that the human mind is unable to perceive causal relations directly. The notion of necessity in causation is weak in that we are psychologically certain that B will follow A. The weak notion of necessity in causation leads to the problem with induction, in that we are not justified in making any inductive inference about the world (where induction involves generalising from events that have always occurred in the past to state that they will always occur in the future).

The logical positivists attempted to deal with the problems raised by Hume using their verification principle, but it too failed, and logical positivism was unable to distinguish science from pseudo science. Their *verification principle* aimed to distinguish science from non-science, where a proposition is considered meaningful only if it is empirically verifiable or true from the meaning of its terms (i.e., a logical tautology as in mathematics or logic). However, the verification principle was quite vague and was never quite properly formulated (it left in too little or too much), and ultimately logical positivism and the verification principle failed.

That is, the logical positivists goal of cleaning up science (to ensure clarity and avoid wooliness) to put philosophy on a new road failed, and so logical positivism failed, and it is of historical interest only.

Karl Popper has been influential in the philosophy of science, and he argued that scientific theories cannot be proved to be true, but can be proven false through empirical testing. His *falsification principle* is a way to test and evaluate scientific theories and hypotheses, and it may be used as the criterion to demarcate science from non-science. That is, every genuine scientific claim is falsifiable (capable of being proven false), at least in principle [Pop:59].

Popper argued that science is an open system in that is open to being criticised and challenged, and scientific theories are subject to rigorous testing, and open to rejection based on empirical evidence. Theories that rely on un-testable assumptions or where empirical testing is not possible are classified as *pseudo science*, as they lack the rigour of scientific theories.

Thomas Kuhn noted that scientific progress does not always proceed in a linear and continuous way, and that sometimes there is an abrupt transformation in the nature of scientific enquiry. These paradigm shifts or *scientific revolutions* often open up a totally new approach to understanding, and the new paradigm is often irreconcilable to the previous paradigm that provided a competing account of reality. Kuhn noted that scientists are often not as open as Popper suggests (as they may have worked for years on the framework defined by the older paradigm, and that the new paradigm becomes dominant as the adherents to the old paradigm die off).

This means that scientific truth cannot be totally determined by objective criteria, and instead there is a need for consensus of the scientific community on the nature of truth, and on a replacement of the existing paradigm. The term '*normal science*' refers to the theoretical framework or paradigm in which scientists are working prior to a scientific revolution, and it provides a framework with a clearly defined set of problems to be solved, and often there is a *resistance to a change of paradigm* from scientists, with some scientists staying with the old paradigm, and the new paradigm becomes dominant as adherents of the old paradigm die off [Kuh:70].

### 5.2.1 Is Computer Science a Science?

Computer science is both a theoretical and applied discipline that arose, in a sense, as a science of algorithms from the theoretical fields of mathematics and logic in nineteenth/twentieth century. George Boole developed his theoretical symbolic logic in the mid-nineteenth century, and Claude Shannon recognised in the mid 1930s that Boole's logic was the right mathematical model for switching theory and for the design of digital circuits.

Theoretical computer science is abstract and mathematical, and covers topics such as language theory, automata theory, complexity theory, graph theory, computability, cryptography, and coding theory. It studies algorithms including the efficiency of algorithms, and the area of formal methods that is a mathematical approach to the specification and verification of software (used mainly in the safety critical field).

Computer science is also an empirical discipline with fields such as Software Engineering, Artificial Intelligence (AI), Machine Learning (ML), Human-Computer Interaction (HCI), Computer Vision and Image Processing all empirical. Further, the development of a new software system (or program) is like an experiment, with test cases prepared to evaluate the program, with each test case including the expected (or predicted) result from running each test case. Test execution involves observation and analysis to determine the extent to which the software exhibits the predicted behaviour of its specification, and the testing is complete when all tests pass (i.e., the program satisfies its specification). Empirical data is then used to make a judgment as to whether the software is of high quality, fit for purpose, and ready to be released to customers.

There is an empirical side to the AI field where researchers formulate hypotheses on how intelligent behaviour may occur, and they then develop systems to test these hypotheses. Machine learning involves spotting patterns in datasets to generate a hypothesis that best describes the pattern. Another example is the software reliability field in software engineering, where researchers use these mathematical models to predict the reliability of the software.

## 5.3 Computer Science as Engineering

We discussed the philosophy of engineering in Chap. 3, and engineering involves the design, development and manufacturing, and maintenance of technology products to serve society. Engineering is concerned with modifying the natural world with the development of useful technology for the public (Fig. 5.2).

The philosophy of engineering is concerned with philosophical issues that arise in the engineering field, and considers what engineering is as a discipline, including what engineers do, how engineering is done, why it is done the way that it is done, and how engineering affects and benefits society. The philosophy of engineering also considers aesthetics and engineering ethics.

**Fig. 5.2** Pont du Gard. Creative commons

The engineer builds things and so modifies the natural environment, and so the management of change is an important part of engineering. It starts with a precise description of the problem to be solved (problem definition); produces a design to solve the problem, and then validates the correctness of the design; finally, the design is implemented, and testing is performed to verify its correctness. Engineers may employ mathematical modelling to test the adequacy of the design.

Engineers have professional responsibilities and are responsible for designing and implementing high-quality and reliable products that are safe for the public to use. They are required to behave ethically with their clients and are accountable for their own decisions and actions, and have a responsibility to object to decisions that violate professional standards. The term '*engineer*' is a title that is awarded on merit, but *it also places responsibilities on its holder.*

There are several areas in computer science that involve the application of engineering including software engineering, computer engineering, networking, robotics and embedded systems. For example, software engineering applies engineering principles in the development of software, and computer engineering combines electronic engineering and computer science to build microprocessors and hardware for computer systems and embedded systems.

## 5.4 Computer Science as Mathematics

Mathematics is a theoretical science that differs from the natural sciences in the objects that it studies and also in its method of investigation. It studies abstract entities and proceeds from axioms and premises to conclusions via deductive reasoning. Deductive reasoning is truth preserving, in that if the premises are true then the conclusions must be true. This leads to a high level of confidence in the truth of mathematical knowledge, especially since the proofs of mathematical theorems are subject to peer review by independent professional mathematicians, which increases the confidence in their correctness.

However, while mathematical proof provides the most certain knowledge that may be obtained in an uncertain world, it would be inappropriate to regard mathematical proof as infallible, as errors may still be present in a proof that may be missed in a peer review. And so, one should always maintain a healthy "*Lakatosian suspicion*" [Lak:76].

In contrast, the natural sciences are empirical and proceed via inductive reasoning to yield scientific knowledge. This involves using the scientific method, where observations of the world lead to the formulation of a hypothesis, and experiments are then performed to confirm or reject the hypothesis. This means that the theories in the natural sciences are somewhat uncertain, and therefore subject to revision and change, whereas mathematics tends to provide a more certain kind of truth. The influential mathematician and philosopher, Bertrand Russell, made some interesting remarks on the nature of mathematics in [Rus:07].

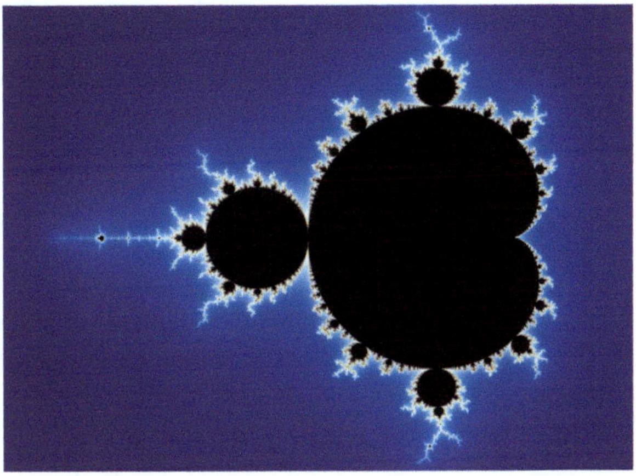

**Fig. 5.3** Mandlebrot set. Creative commons

> Mathematics, rightly viewed, possesses not only truth, but supreme beauty—a beauty cold and austere, like that of sculpture, without appeal to any part of our weaker nature, without the gorgeous trappings of painting or music, yet sublimely pure, and capable of a stern perfection such as only the greatest art can show. (
> Fig. 5.3)

We mentioned that Mathematics is in many areas of computer science (e.g., cryptography, coding theory, language theory and semantics, networks and graph theory, formal specification and verification, automata theory, computability, computational complexity and data science).

Cryptography consists of mathematical techniques that provide secrecy in the transmission of messages between computers, and its goal is to solve security problems such as privacy and authentication over a communications channel. It involves enciphering and deciphering messages, and uses theoretical results from number theory to convert the original message (or plaintext) into cipher text that is then transmitted over a secure channel to the intended recipient. The cipher text is meaningless to anyone other than the intended recipient, and the recipient uses a key to decrypt the received cipher text and to read the original message.

Coding theory is a practical branch of mathematics that is concerned with the reliable transmission of information over communication channels. It allows errors to be detected and corrected, which is essential when messages are transmitted through a noisy communication channel. The channel could be a telephone line, radio link or satellite link, and coding theory is applicable to mobile communications, and satellite communications.

Formal methods refer to various mathematical techniques used for the formal specification and development of software, and program verification to verify its correctness. They consist of a formal specification language, and employ a collection of tools to support the syntax checking of the specification, as well as the proof of properties of the specification. They allow questions to be asked about what the system does independently of the implementation. The use of formal methods generally leads to more robust software and increased confidence in its correctness.

The formal specification may be used as the reference point for the requirements; program implementation; testing and program documentation. It thus promotes a common understanding for all those concerned with the system. Formal methods may be employed at a number of levels such as the formal specification only with the program developed informally; formal specification, refinement, and verification with some proofs; and formal specification, refinement, and verification with extensive theorem proving.

The specification is written in a mathematical language, and the implementation may be derived from the specification via step-wise refinement. The refinement step makes the specification more concrete and closer to the actual implementation. There is an associated proof obligation to demonstrate that the refinement is valid, and that the concrete state preserves the properties of the abstract state. Thus, assuming that the original specification is correct and the proof of correctness of each refinement step is valid, then there is a very high degree of confidence in the correctness of the implemented software.

There are several schools in the philosophy of mathematics including Logicism, Intuitionism and Formalism. Gottlob Frege founded the *Logicism school* in the late nineteenth century, and his goal was show that mathematics could be reduced to logic (i.e., All mathematics may be derived from logic). Frege extended Boole's work to create first order predicate calculus.

Unfortunately, Frege's system contained a contradiction (due to his definition of a set) that was pointed out by Bertrand Russell. This is known as *Russell's paradox*, and it considered the set of all sets that do not contain themselves as members, and showed that this led to contradiction. Russell introduced the theory of types as a way to deal with the paradox, but while his typed system was an improvement, he had to introduce another basic principle (not a logical one) in order to deduce the basic laws of arithmetic. Russell and Whitehead wrote the *Principi Mathematica* with the goal of showing that all of mathematics is reducible to logic.

L. E. J. Brouwer founded the *Intuitionist school* that argued that mathematics is essentially an activity of construction. Intuitionists reject the actual infinite, as a human cannot construct it in a finite period of time, but accept the potentially infinite as being part of the activity of construction. They reject non-constructive proofs as such, and argue that an existence proof must be accompanied by an associated method of construction of the entity. Finally, they rejected the law of the excluded middle in logic ($P \vee \neg P$) or equivalently ($\neg\neg P \rightarrow P$), and insisted on an explicit construction of the mathematical object. Intuitionism never became mainstream as a foundation for mathematics, as its acceptance would have led to a rejection of large parts of mathematics.

*Formalism* was proposed in the early twentieth century by David Hilbert as a way to provide a secure foundation for mathematics. It is a formal system that contains meaningless symbols, together with rules for manipulating them. The individual formulas are certain finite sequences of symbols obeying the syntactic rules of the formal language.

Hilbert's programme was concerned with the formalization of mathematics (i.e., the axiomatization of mathematics), and one goal was to demonstrate (with a mathematical proof) that the axiomatization is *consistent* (i.e., there is no formula $A$ such that both $A$ and $\neg A$ are deducible in the calculus). Another goal was to show that the axiomization was *complete* in that all mathematical truths could be proved within the system, and a final goal was that the axiomaization was *decidable* in that there is an algorithm to determine the truth or falsity of any mathematical statement.

Hilbert believed that the formalism of mathematics would allow a mechanical procedure (or algorithm) to determine whether a particular statement was true or false (i.e., he believed that the formal system of mathematics was decidable). Church and Turing independently showed this to be impossible in 1936, with Turing developing a theoretical machine (Turing Machine) and Church developing the Lambda Calculus formalism to show that the formal system of mathematics is undecidable. The Church-Turing thesis states that anything that is computable is computable by a Turing machine or equivalent formalism (see Chap. 7).

There are first-order theories that are decidable. However, first-order logic that includes Peano's axioms of arithmetic (or any formal system that includes addition and multiplication) cannot be decided by an algorithm. That is, there is no algorithm to determine whether an arbitrary mathematical proposition is true or false. Propositional logic is decidable as there is a procedure (e.g., using a truth table) to determine whether an arbitrary formula is valid in the calculus.

*Gödel proved that first order predicate calculus is complete. i.e., all truths in the predicate calculus can be proved in the language of the calculus.* Gödel's *first incompleteness theorem showed that the formal system of arithmetic is incomplete: i.e., there are truths within the formal system that cannot be proved as such.* Gödel's *second incompleteness theorem showed that the consistency of arithmetic cannot be proved within the formal system of arithmetic. Hilbert's program was ambitious but ultimately failed.*

## 5.5 Nature of a Computer

We discussed the nature of a computer in Chap. 4, and the study of computers is the study of physical machines and the software running on them. A computer is a tool that enhances the reasoning capability and productivity of humans, and is a programmable electronic device that can process, store and retrieve data. It processes data according to a set of instructions or program (Fig. 5.4).

All computers consist of hardware and software, where the hardware is the physical part of the machine, and includes memory for short-term storage of data or instructions; an arithmetic/logic unit for carrying out arithmetic and logical operations; a control unit responsible for the execution of computer instructions in memory; and peripherals that handle the input and output operations. Software is a set of instructions that tells the computer what to do.

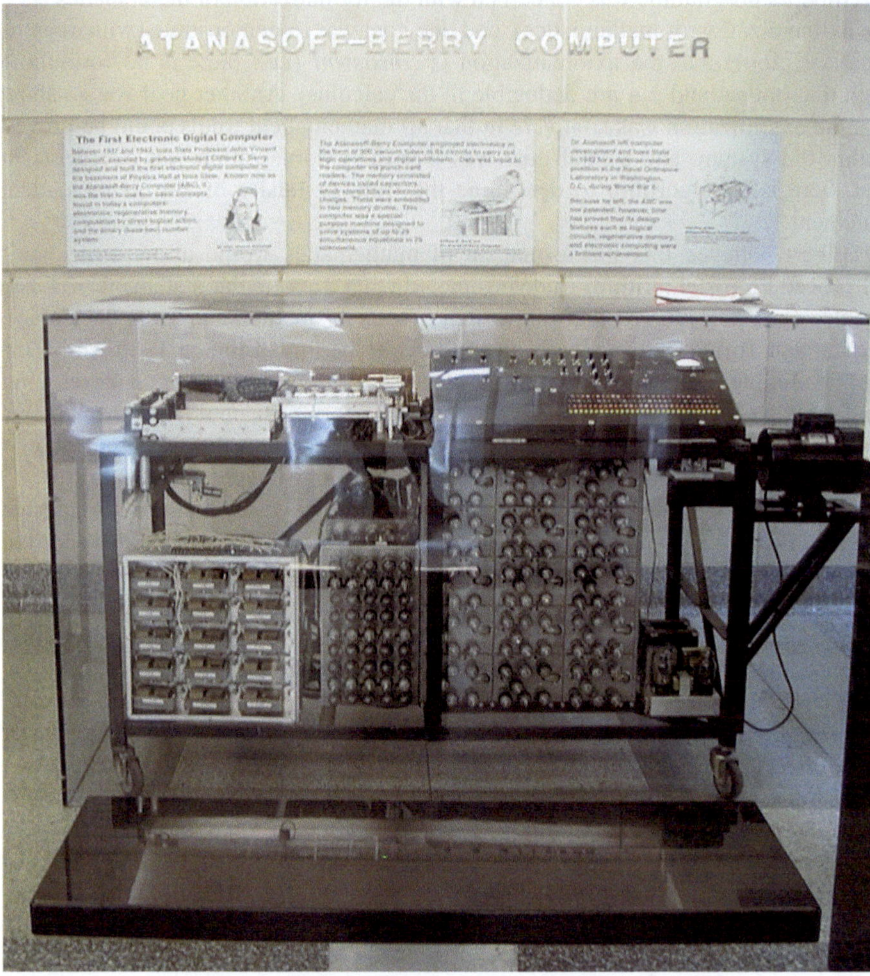


**Fig. 5.4** The Atanasoff-Berry computer (ABC)

We mentioned that the original meaning of the word "*computer*" referred to someone who carried out calculations rather than an actual machine: i.e., "a computer is a human who computes". The early computers of the 1940s and 1950s were enormous machines consisting of several thousand vacuum tubes, and typically filled a large room.

A *computer program* is a set of instructions for the computer to solve some problem (e.g., to implement an algorithm or specification), and it is written in some programming language. The programming language has an associated syntax and semantics, with syntax being the grammar of the language whereas semantics gives the meaning of the language. Computers and programs are symbiotic in that they both need each other, with a computer needing a program to do anything useful, and a program needing a computer to execute.

The *formal semantics* of a language is given by a mathematical model that describes the possible computations described by the language. There are three main approaches to programming language semantics namely axiomatic semantics, operational semantics and denotational semantics (these are discussed in more detail in Chap. 6).

The implementation (computer program) is a solution to a particular problem, and the problem to be solved needs to be clearly stated, so that those who are to implement the solution are clear on what needs to be done, and those who verify the correctness of the implementation can do so effectively. And so, it is essential to specify the requirements of the particular problem, and this may be done in natural language (care is always required in a natural language description of a system due to the ambiguities inherent in natural language), or in more precise mathematical notation such as logic or a formal specification language such as VDM or Z (for the safety critical field).

In general, the entity doing the implementation is a physical thing, whereas the entity that is being implemented is an abstract thing. For example, the thing doing the implementation may be a computer; with the thing being implemented may be a specification or an algorithm (the procedure to solve the problem). It is essential that the software program is a correct implementation of its specification, where the specification defines the input-output behaviour to be satisfied, and it may be written in a natural language or in a formal specification language.

*Program verification* is concerned with verifying that the program is correct and satisfies its specification, where the specification defines the input-output behaviour to be satisfied. Program verification is often limited to peer reviews and testing (when the specification is written in natural language), but extra rigour may be provided in the safety critical field when formal specification and verification may be employed. Software testing is quite rigorous in current software engineering, and testers define and execute test cases, which provides confidence that the software satisfies its specification.

*Intellectual property law* deals with the rules that apply in protecting inventions, designs and artistic work, and in enforcing such rights. Intangible assets such as software designs or inventions may be protected in a similar way to the protection of private property, and an inventor is generally granted exclusive rights to the invention for a defined period of time. This gives the inventor the incentive to develop creative works that may benefit society, as it allows the owner of the invention to profit from their work without fear of misappropriation by others.

A computer program is the expression in some programming language of the implementation of an algorithm (or some invention or idea), and so computer programs are protected under *copyright law*. An algorithm is a procedure for solving a particular problem, and so is potentially a novel invention or solution to the problem. It may be possible (subject to the specifics of patent law such as the invention is novel, not disclosed to public, first filed, etc.) to obtain a *patent* for the algorithm. For a detailed explanation of Intellectual Property Law and especially how it applies to the computing field see [ORg:24].

### 5.5.1 Nature of an Algorithm

Algorithms are fundamental in computing as they define the procedure by which a problem is solved. That is, the algorithm is the procedure that transforms the input into the output, and it explicitly shows how to get to the output from the input. That is, an algorithm is a set of instructions for computing the value of a function, where the value is computed by executing the instructions. A computer program implements the algorithm, and the execution of the program instructions carries out the algorithm (Fig. 5.5).

It is essential that the algorithm is correct and that it is an efficient way to solve the problem. This requires careful analysis to ensure both its correctness and computational efficiency. Further, the implementation of an algorithm must be correct in that both the program and the algorithm yield the same result for a given value.

Algorithms are relevant in several fields, and there are algorithms for sorting and machine learning in computer science and artificial intelligence; algorithms for

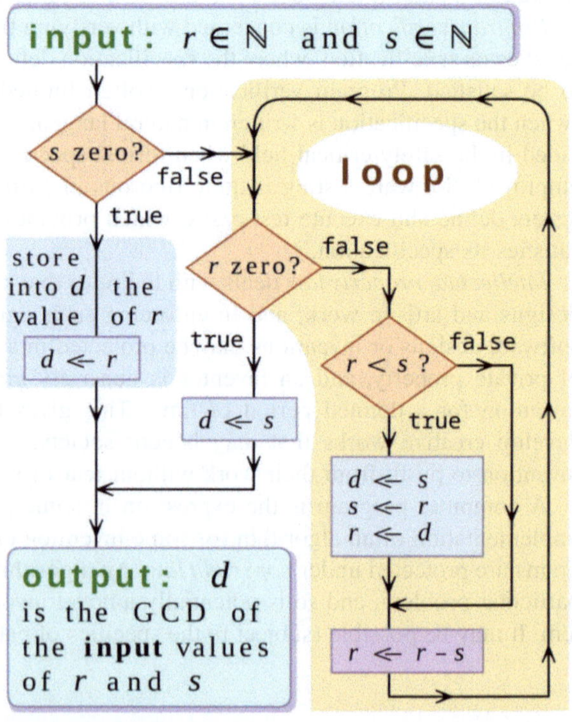


**Fig. 5.5** The GCD algorithm. Creative commons

finding shortest or longest paths in discrete mathematics; algorithms for decision-making and optimisation in operations research; and algorithms to generate insight from large amounts of data as in machine learning.

A computer program implements the algorithm in some programming language. The term "computing" includes just about everything that can be done with computers, and so it is more than just numerical calculation, as it potentially includes all of the algorithms that may be run on the computer.

The behaviour of the algorithm may be studied empirically by examining the software running on the machine. Another approach is to study the algorithm mathematically rather than executing a program on a computer.

Church introduced the *lambda calculus* in the 1930s as a way of providing an abstract definition and application of a function, and any function computed in lambda calculus is effectively computable. Turing developed an alternate but equivalent approach to computability with his formal mathematical model of a human computer, which became known as the *Turing machine* (TM). We discuss algorithms and computability in more detail in Chap. 7.

## 5.6 Nature of Computability and Complexity

A key question in computer science is "what is computable?", or another words is there a computational solution to a particular problem, and if so, how should the solution be implemented? Church and Turing investigated the question of "which mathematical functions are computable?" in the 1930s, with the answer given by the Church-Turing thesis. This thesis states that *a function is computable if and only if it is computable by a Turing machine* (or equivalent formalism).

There are non-computable functions such as the halting problem, where there is no general algorithm that solves the halting problem for all possible program-input pairs (The halting problem aims to determine from a description of an arbitrary computer program and an arbitrary input whether the program will halt or continue to run forever).

The intuitive meaning of computability is in terms of an algorithm (or effective procedure) that specifies a set of instructions to be followed to complete the task. Another words, a function $f$ is *computable* if there exists an algorithm that produces the value of $f$ correctly for each possible argument of $f$. The computation of $f$ for a particular argument $x$ just involves following the instructions in the algorithm, and it produces the result $f(x)$ in a finite number of steps if $x$ is in the domain of $f$. If $x$ is not in the domain of $f$ then the algorithm may produce an answer saying so or it might run forever never halting. A computer program implements an algorithm.

The concept of computability is made more precise in several equivalent ways such as Church's *lambda calculus*, *recursive function theory* or by the theoretical *Turing machines*. These are all equivalent, and the Turing machine is a mathematical machine in which basic operations can be carried out. The set of functions that are computable are those that are computable by a Turing machine.

The fact that the problem is computable is the first step, and the next question is to determine whether it is feasible to perform the computation within an acceptable time period: i.e., an efficient algorithm is required that solves the problem in a reasonable timeframe. For example, if the proposed solution requires 5000 years to solve the problem then this is not a practical solution, and so other solutions (including heuristics) will be sought. This leads to the area of *complexity theory*, which includes problems that can be solved in polynomial (*P*) time, as well as those that can be solved in non-deterministic polynomial (*NP*) time.

Many practical problems can be solved in polynomial time, and so if the initial algorithm can only be solved in *NP* time then an algorithm that solves the problem in polynomial time will be sought. If no such algorithm may be devised, then it may be possible to find a heuristic for the problem, where an algorithm exists for a closely related problem that may be solved in polynomial time, and where this solution is good enough to be used for the original problem.

## 5.7 Review Questions

1. What is science?
2. What is engineering?
3. What is computer science?
4. What is mathematics?
5. What is a computer?
6. What is an algorithm?
7. What is computation?
8. What is computability?
9. What is decidability?
10. Explain the terms polynomial time and non-polynomial time in complexity theory.

## 5.8 Summary

The discipline of computer science studies computers and the algorithms that run on them, and the field emerged from the development of the earliest digital computer in the early 1940s. The term "computer science" was coined in an ACM article in the late 1950s.

Computer science plays an important role in the development of many other disciplines, where computers are tools that enhance reasoning in most fields. It is difficult to come up with a definition of computer science that covers all its applications. In some ways, it is a science since it consists of a body of knowledge that is used by computer professionals in their work.

On the other hand computer scientists build things and use engineering principles in their work, and so computer science is, in a sense, engineering. Further, it arose from work done in mathematics in the nineteenth and twentieth century, and so computer science is, in a sense, mathematics.

And so, perhaps the best definition is that it is a STEM discipline, that has been applied to most disciplines.

## References


[Dij:73] Programming as a discipline of Mathematical Nature. Edsger W. Dijkstra. EWD 361. Technological University of Eindhoven. 1973.

[Fei:59] The Role of the University in Computers, Data Processing and Related Fields. Louis Fine. *Communications of the ACM*. **2** (9): 7–14. 1959.

[Kuh:70] The Structure of Scientific Revolutions. Thomas Kuhn. 1970

[Lak:76] Proof and Refutations. The Logic of Mathematical Discovery. Imre Lakatos. Cambridge University Press. 1976.

[ORg:23] Mathematical Foundations of Software Engineering. Gerard O' Regan. Springer. 2023.

[ORg:24] Ethical and Legal Aspects of Computing. Gerard O' Regan. Springer. 2024.

[Pop:59] The Logic of Scientific Discovery. Karl Popper. 1959.

[Rus:07] The Study of Mathematics. The New Quarterly 1. Bertrand Russell, 1907.

# What Is a Computer Program? 6

## 6.1 Introduction

A computer program provides the instructions to a computer to solve a particular problem. The earliest computers were "*fixed program*" computers, and this limitation led to the development of "*stored program*" computers as described in von Neumann's draft report on EDVAC. That is, the earliest computers were hardwired, in that the computer was wired to solve a specific problem, and it was necessary to re-wire the computer to solve a new problem. EDVAC led to the introduction of a stored-program computer, where the computer program was loaded into memory, rather than physically wiring the machine. Its advantage was that it was no longer necessary to rewire the computer to change the program, and all that was required was to move a new program into the computer memory (as discussed in Chap. 4).

A computer program is written in some programming language such as C++ or Java, and a program implements some algorithm. The execution time of the computer program depends on several factors such as the efficiency of the algorithm employed, the input value(s), how the algorithm has been implemented in the programming language, whether a compiler or interpreter is employed for the language, the operating system, and the computer hardware.

A programming language is a language, and so has a clearly defined syntax (rules or grammar for the language) and semantics (meaning of the language). A compiler checks the program for syntactic validity, and converts it into the equivalent machine code that can be understood by the computer. The executable code is equivalent to the source code in the sense that they exhibit the same input-output behaviour.

The starting point is the specification of the program, and this involves specifying the input-output behaviour required of the program. The specification will often be in a natural language but formal specification languages are sometimes used (especially in the safety critical sector). It is essential that the program developed satisfies its specification, and that the specification of the program is correct.



G. O'Regan, *Philosophical and Cultural Aspects of Computing*, Undergraduate Topics in Computer Science, https://doi.org/10.1007/978-3-032-29284-1_6

```javascript

const LOCALE = globalThis.navigator.language

const div = document.body.appendChild(document.createElement('div'))
const list = div.appendChild(document.createElement('ol'))

const dayNames = new Map()

for (let i = 0; i < 7; ++i) {
    const d = Temporal.PlainDate.from({
        year: Temporal.Now.plainDateISO().year,
        month: 1,
        day: i + 1,
    })

    dayNames.set(d.dayOfWeek, d.toLocaleString(LOCALE, { weekday: 'long' }))
}

for (const num of [...dayNames.keys()].sort((a, b) => a - b)) {
    list.appendChild(Object.assign(
        document.createElement('li'),
        { textContent: dayNames.get(num) },
    ))
}

```

**Fig. 6.1** Javascript program

A computer is a calculating device with software running on the machine. The software refers to the various computer programs that run on the computer, where a computer program consists of a set of instructions that a computer can follow to implement an algorithm. The software is for a particular machine architecture and operating system, but it may also be adapted to other machines and operating systems. That is, the computer programs may be customised for each machine/operating system, and so the set of instructions may vary depending on the customisation required (Fig. 6.1).

A programming language has a clearly defined syntax and semantics, with the syntax being the grammar of the language with an associated set of rules that determine whether the program is syntactically valid. The semantics of the language is deeper and is concerned with the actual meaning of the program or program construct.

The set of instructions may be written in a high-level language such as C or Java that is then compiled into the object code of the native computer and operating system. The *compiler preserves the semantics* of the programming language, in that each construct of the programming language has a precise meaning (using axiomatic, denotational or operational semantics), and so the compiler preserves (rather than giving) the semantics of the language during the code generation.

That is, the programmer creates a program to implement some algorithm (i.e., the program is semantically equivalent to the algorithm in that they exhibit the same input-output behaviour), and the program is then compiled and converted into the equivalent machine code (same input-output behaviour) that may be executed on the physical computer.

The term "software" refers to the instructions in the computer program that are run on the computer, whereas "hardware" refers to the physical parts of the machine (we discussed the difference between hardware and software in Chap. 4). The programmer writes a computer program to run on a particular computer and operating system, but the computer programmer generally does not change the physical hardware of the computer. That is, software is intangible and changeable, whereas hardware is physical and tends to be unchanging, and so it seems that there is a clear distinction between hardware and software.

However, it has also been argued that hardware and software are logically equivalent, in that any operation performed by software can also be built directly into the hardware, and the software can also simulate any instruction executed by the hardware. That is, *the boundary between software and hardware is fuzzy* (we discussed the difference between hardware and software in Chap. 4).

The earliest computer programs used the machine code of the particular machine, where a machine instruction consisted of a string of binary code. The introduction of assembly languages where a mnemonic stood for binary code helped to reduce errors and improved productivity. The introduction of high-level programming languages such as Fortran and Cobol, and procedural languages such as C, followed by object-oriented languages such as C++ and Java led to major improvements in quality and productivity. These were all compiled languages and the object code generated preserved the semantics of the programming language.

Most programming languages are imperative (i.e., they involve a change of state). However, functional programming languages such as Miranda or Haskell do not involve a change of state, and similarly for relational (or logic) programming languages such as Prolog. Functional programming languages use pure functions that do not affect the state, which makes it much easier to reason about them. That is, they have the property of referential transparency, where there are no side effects in a functional programming language, since there is no change of state in the language. That is, the value of $x$ at one part of the program is equal to the value of $x$ in another part of the program. Table 6.1 lists several aspects of a computer program.

### 6.1.1 Philosophical Questions on Computer Programs

A computer program provides the instructions to a computer to solve a particular problem. Table 6.2 lists some pertinent philosophical questions related to a computer program.

**Table 6.1** Aspects of a computer program

| Area | Description |
|---|---|
| Specification of a program | This is a statement of the required behaviour of the program written in either natural language or a formal specification language |
| Programming language | A programming language is a language that allows a human to communicate with a computer |
| Syntax | The syntax provides the rules or grammar of the language |
| Semantics | The semantics provides the meaning of the language |
| Compiler | The compiler converts a syntactically valid program into the equivalent machine code |
| Compiled versus source program | The compiled program is equivalent to the source code program in that they exhibit the same input-output behaviour |
| Program meets its specification | The program meets its specification if it is a valid implementation (faithful to) of the specification |
| Program verification | Program verification is concerned with verifying that the source code/executable code satisfies the specification |
| Legal aspects | A program is a "legal object" in that copyright law may protect it, and a patent may protect an algorithm |
| Miscomputation | Miscomputation is where the implemented system produces an incorrect output. This may be due to errors in design, algorithm, specification, or physical hardware (i.e., the program does not meet its specification) |

## 6.2 What Is the Specification of a Program?

It is, of course, essential that the problem to be solved is clearly stated and unambiguous, so that those who are to implement a solution are clear on what needs to be done, and that those who verify the correctness of the solution can do so effectively. This leads to the idea of the *specification* of the program, which defines the required behaviour of the program, and is used by both the programmers to implement the solution, and the testers to verify the correctness of the implementation. That is, a correct program must satisfy its specification, and it is the responsibility of the team of programmers to correctly implement the specification in some programming language, and for the testers to verify the correctness of the implementation with respect to its specification.

The specification may be in natural language (this is the usual approach, but it requires care, due to the ambiguities inherent in natural language). Other approaches (used mainly in the safety-critical sector) include a mathematical definition of the specification using logic, formal specification languages, pseudo code, and so on. Dijkstra and Hoare emphasised that a program and its proof of correctness should be developed hand-in-hand, but this approach is more the exception rather than the general rule in current software engineering (i.e., the standard approach in industry is to employ a natural language description with

**Table 6.2** Philosophical questions related to a computer program

| Question | Initial Answer |
|---|---|
| What is a program? | One answer is that it is a set of instructions for the computer to solve a problem. A computer program is a syntactic entity generated from a grammar (language aspect). In another sense, it is a legal entity (protected by copyright law). In another sense it is a mathematical object |
| What does it mean for a program to be correct? | One answer is that a correct program satisfies its specification (provided that the specification is correct). Another words, the program should exhibit the same input-output behaviour as the specification |
| What are the limits of computation? | The limits of computation are the limits of what can or cannot be computed (i.e., what are the fundamental limits of algorithms)? Is there an algorithm to solve the problem? Can the algorithm be carried out within a reasonable timeframe? Is there a heuristic? |
| Can a program/machine think? | This is an enquiry into the extent to which a program/machine can think and be conscious. Searle's Chinese room is a rebuttal of strong AI (and a rebuttal of functionalism). Syntax is not semantics |
| How are biased algorithms identified and prevented? | Errors often occur due to the training data that machine learning algorithms use (they often devise a hypothesis from the data, and so may, in a sense, be performing correctly except that the results do not correspond to expectations). Comprehensive testing needs to be done to provide confidence in its correctness |
| Who is responsible when a program errs leading to injury (or worse)? | Who is responsible if a self-driving car crashes (the car, owner, programmer)? The organisation that develops the car needs to demonstrate that it followed best practice in software engineering, with comprehensive testing performed to verify its correctness |

extensive testing to verify correctness, with mathematical definitions used mainly in the safety critical field).

We discuss formal methods (which offer a rigorous approach to formal specification) in the next section, and this approach is mainly used in the safety critical field.

### 6.2.1 Formal Methods

The term "*formal methods*" refer to various mathematical techniques used for the formal specification and development of software. They consist of a formal specification language, and employ a collection of tools to support the syntax checking of the specification, as well as the proof of properties of the specification. They allow questions to be asked about what the system does independently of the implementation.

The use of mathematical notation avoids speculation about the meaning of phrases in an imprecisely worded natural language description of a system. Natural language is inherently ambiguous, whereas mathematics employs a precise rigorous notation. Spivey [Spi:92] defines formal specification as:

**Definition 6.1 (*Formal Specification*)** Formal specification is the use of mathematical notation to describe in a precise way the properties that an information system must have, without unduly constraining the way in which these properties are achieved.

The formal specification becomes the key reference point for the different parties involved in the construction of the system. It may be used as the reference point for the requirements; program implementation; testing and program documentation. It thus promotes a common understanding for all those concerned with the system. The term "*formal methods*" is used to describe a formal specification language, and a method for the design and implementation of a computer system. Formal methods may be employed at a number0 of levels:

- Formal specification only (program developed informally)
- Formal specification, refinement and verification (some proofs)
- Formal specification, refinement and verification (with extensive theorem proving)

The specification is written in a mathematical language, and the implementation may be derived from the specification via step-wise refinement.[1] The refinement step makes the specification more concrete and closer to the actual implementation. There is an associated proof obligation to demonstrate that the refinement is valid, and that the concrete state preserves the properties of the abstract state. Thus, assuming that the original specification is correct and the proof of correctness of each refinement step is valid, then there is a very high degree of confidence in

[1] It is questionable whether step-wise refinement is cost effective in mainstream software engineering, as it involves re-writing a specification *ad nauseum*. It is time-consuming to proceed in refinement steps with significant time also required to prove that the refinement step is valid. It is more relevant to the safety-critical field. Others in the formal methods field may disagree with this position.

the correctness of the implemented software (i.e., there is high confidence that the system has been built right).

Step-wise refinement is illustrated as follows: the specification $S$ is the initial model $M_0$; it is then refined into the more concrete model $M_1$, and $M_1$ is then refined into $M_2$, and so on until the eventual implementation $M_n = E$ is produced.

$$S = M_0 \sqsubseteq M_1 \sqsubseteq M_2 \sqsubseteq M_3 \sqsubseteq \cdots \sqsubseteq M_n = \mathrm{E}$$

Requirements are the foundation of the system to be built, and irrespective of the best design and development practices, the product will be incorrect if the requirements are incorrect. The objective of *requirements validation* is to ensure that the requirements reflect what is actually required by the customer (in order to *build the right system*). Formal methods may be employed to model the requirements, and the model exploration yields further desirable or undesirable properties.

Formal methods provide the facility to prove that certain properties are true of the specification, and this is valuable, especially in safety critical and security critical applications. The properties are a logical consequence of the mathematical definition, and the requirements may be amended where appropriate. Thus, formal methods may be employed, in a sense, to debug the requirements during requirements validation.

The use of formal methods generally leads to more robust software and increased confidence in its correctness. Formal methods may be employed at different levels (e.g., just for specification with the program developed informally, etc). The challenges involved in the deployment of formal methods in an organization include the education of staff in formal specification, as the use of these mathematical techniques may be a culture shock to many staff.

Formal methods have been applied to a diverse range of applications, including the safety and security critical fields to develop reliable and dependable software. They have been applied to the railway sector, microprocessor verification, the specification of standards, and the specification and verification of programs. Parnas and others have criticized formal methods (Table 6.3):

However, formal methods are potentially quite useful and reasonably easy to use. The use of a formal method such as Z or VDM forces the software engineer to be precise, and helps to avoid ambiguities present in natural language. Clearly, a formal specification should be subject to peer review to provide confidence in its correctness. New formalisms need to be intuitive to be usable by practitioners, and an advantage of classical mathematics is that it is familiar to students.

## 6.3 What Is a Programming Language?

A programming language is a language with a clearly defined syntax and semantics that allows humans to communicate with computers. It provides a set of instructions for the computer to perform tasks, but computers understand only instructions

**Table 6.3** Criticisms of formal methods

| No. | Criticism |
|---|---|
| 1. | Often the formal specification is as difficult to read as the program[a] |
| 2. | Many formal specifications are wrong[b] |
| 3. | Formal methods are strong on syntax but provide little assistance in deciding on what technical information should be recorded using the syntax[c] |
| 4. | Formal specifications provide a model of the proposed system. However, a precise unambiguous mathematical statement of the requirements is what is needed[d] |
| 5. | Step-wise refinement is unrealistic.[e] It is like, for example, deriving a bridge from the description of a river and the expected traffic on the bridge. There is always a need for the creative step in design |
| 6. | Many unnecessary mathematical formalisms have been developed rather than using the available classical mathematics[f] |

[a]Of course, others might reply by saying that some of Parnas's tables are not exactly intuitive, and that the notation he employs in some of his tables is quite unfriendly. The usability of all of the mathematical approaches needs to be enhanced if they are to be taken seriously by industrialists

[b]Obviously, the formal specification must be analysed using mathematical reasoning and tools to provide confidence in its correctness. The validation of a formal specification can be carried out using mathematical proof of key properties of the specification; software inspections; or specification animation

[c]Approaches such as VDM include a method for software development as well as the specification language

[d]Models are extremely valuable as they allow simplification of the reality. A mathematical study of the model demonstrates whether it is a suitable representation of the system. Models allow properties of the proposed requirements to be studied prior to implementation e Step-wise refinement involves rewriting a specification with each refinement step producing a more concrete specification (that includes code and formal specification) until eventually the detailed code is produced. It is difficult and time consuming but, tool support may make refinement easier

[f]Approaches such as VDM or Z are useful in that they add greater rigour to the software development process. They are reasonably easy to learn, and there have been some good results obtained by their use. Classical mathematics is familiar to students and therefore it is desirable that new formalisms are introduced only where absolutely necessary

in binary code (i.e., 1 s or 0 s). This means that whatever is written by the programmer (i.e., the human who writes the program) needs to be converted into the equivalent binary code so that the computer can understand what needs to be done, and the conversion is done by a compiler.

The syntax is the grammar of the language and a program needs to be syntactically correct with respect to its grammar. That is, a programming language has a formal grammar that generates the formal language, and so the computer program must satisfy the rules of the grammar (i.e., it must be generated from the grammar). The semantics of the language determines the meaning of what has been written by the programmer, and determines what a syntactically valid program will compute.

A program's syntax[2] gives no information as to the meaning of the program, and therefore there is a need to supplement the syntactic description of the language with a formal unambiguous definition of its semantics. It is possible to write syntactically correct programs that behave in quite a different way from the intention of the programmer.

Compilers are programs that translate a syntactically correct program into the object code of the target machine and operating system, and the compiler preserves (i.e., it does not define) the semantics of the language. If the program is syntactically correct, then the compiler determines the meaning of what has been written (this may be different from the intentions of the programmer), and generates the corresponding machine code.

The formal semantics of a programming language defines the actual meaning of the language. Language semantics is deeper than syntax, and as mentioned the semantics are not defined by the compiler, but rather the function of the compiler is to preserve the semantics of the language.

The earliest computer programs were written in the machine language of the computer (*first generation languages*), and these programs were specific to the particular machine. They were error-prone as they consisted of sequences of 1 and 0 s, and programs needed to be rewritten for a new computer due to differences in machine architectures. Over time, low-level assembly languages were developed (*second generation languages*), and these used mnemonics to represent program instructions. An assembler was used to convert these programs to the machine code, and these languages are less error-prone that the machine languages. Often, they had to be rewritten for new computers, as the early computers had very distinct architectures, operating systems and machine code instructions.

Many programming languages have been developed since the birth of digital computing including Plankalkül which was developed by Zuse in the 1940s; Fortran developed by IBM in the late 1950s; COBOL was developed by the CODASYL committee in the late 1950s; Algol 60 and Algol 68 were developed by an international committee in the 1960s; Pascal was developed by Wirth in the early 1970s; Ada was developed for the US military in the late 1970s; the C language was developed by Richie and Thompson at Bell Labs in the early 1970s; C++ was developed by Stroustrup at Bell Labs in the early 1980s; and Java was developed by Gosling at Sun Microsystems in the mid-1990s. A short description of a selection of programming languages in use is in Chap. 15. of [ORg:26].

High-level languages are general-purpose languages that have been applied to business, scientific and general applications. A program written in a high-level language is compiled into the machine language of the target computer for execution. These *third-generation languages* are easier for humans to read, and include early *procedural* languages (such as Fortran and C) and later *object-oriented* languages

[2] There are attribute (or affix) grammars that extend the syntactic description of the language with supplementary elements covering the semantics. The process of adding semantics to the syntactic description is termed decoration.

(such as C++ and Java). They are machine independent and may be compiled for different platforms.

A programming language has a set of grammar rules that governs how the language works, and the syntax is more concerned with the sentence structure. The program needs to be syntactically correct with respect to its grammar (i.e., the program must be a valid derivation from the grammar). The semantics of the language determines the meaning of what has been written by the programmer.

The field of syntax, compilers and language semantics is relatively mature. Compilers are programs that translate a program that is written in some programming language into another form that may be directly executed by the physical computer. Compilation involves syntax analysis and parsing to check the syntactic validity of the program; semantic analysis to determine what the program should do; optimisation to improve the speed and performance; and code generation in some target language.

It may be that what the programmer has written is different from what the programmer intended. The semantics of the programming language determines what a syntactically valid program will compute, and semantic domains implement syntactic domains. A programming language is therefore given by:

$$\text{Programming Language} = \text{Syntax} + \text{Semantics}$$

A sentence (or program) may be syntactically correct but semantically meaningless. A compiler will not perform semantic analysis on a syntactically incorrect program, and so the first step is to write a program that adheres to the grammar of the language.

## 6.4 What Is Syntax?

A programming language has a set of grammar rules that governs how the language works, and the formal grammar generates a formal language, which is a set of finite length sequences of symbols created by applying the production rules of the grammar. The application of a production rule involves replacing symbols at the left hand side of the rule with the symbols on the right hand side of the rule. The formal language then consists of all words consisting of terminal symbols that are reached by a derivation (i.e., the application of production rules) starting from the start symbol of the grammar.

We distinguish between *concrete* and *abstract syntax*, where concrete syntax describes the external appearance of programs as seen by the programmer, whereas abstract syntax aims to describe the essential structure of programs rather than its external form. In other words, abstract syntax aims to give the components of each language structure while leaving out the representation details (e.g., syntactic sugar).

Backus Naur Form[3] (BNF) provides an elegant means of specifying the syntax of programming languages. It was originally employed to define the grammar for the Algol-60 programming language [Nau:60], and a variant was used by Wirth to specify the syntax of the Pascal programming language. BNF is widely used to specify the syntax of programming languages.

BNF specifications essentially describe the external appearance of programs as seen by the programmer. The grammar of a context free grammar may be input into a parser (e.g., Yacc), and the parser is used to determine if a program is syntactically correct or not.

A BNF specification consists of a set of production rules, with each production rule describing the form of a class of language elements such as expressions, statements, and so on. A production rule is of the form:

< symbol >::=< expression with symbols >

where <symbol> is a nonterminal, and the expression consists of a sequence of terminal and nonterminal symbols. A construct that has alternate forms appears more than once, and this is expressed by sequences separated by the vertical bar "|" (which indicates a choice). In other word, there is more than one possible substitution for the symbol on the left hand side of the rule. Symbols that never appear on the left hand side of a production rule are called terminals.

A grammar consists of

- A finite set of terminal symbols
- A finite set of nonterminal symbols
- A set of production rules
- A start symbol

A formal grammar generates a formal language, which is set of finite length sequences of symbols created by applying the production rules of the grammar. The application of a production rule involves replacing symbols at the left hand side of the rule with the symbols on the right hand side of the rule. The formal language then consists of all words consisting of terminal symbols that are reached by a derivation (i.e., the application of production rules) starting from the start symbol of the grammar.

A construct that appears on the left hand side of a production rule is termed a *non-terminal*, whereas a construct that only appears on the right hand side of a production rule is termed a *terminal*. The set of non-terminals $N$ is disjoint from the set of terminals $A$.

The theory of the syntax of programming languages is well established, and programming languages have a well-defined grammar that allows syntactically valid programs to be derived from the grammars.

---

[3] Backus Naur Form is named after John Backus and Peter Naur. It was created as part of the design of the Algol 60 programming language, and is used to define the syntax rules of the language.

**Fig. 6.2** Noah Chomsky. Public domain

Chomsky[4] (Fig. 6.2) is a famous linguist who classified a number of different types of grammar that occur. The Chomsky hierarchy consists of four levels including regular grammars; context free grammars; context sensitive grammars and unrestricted grammars. The grammars are distinguished by their production rules, which determine the type of language that is generated (Table 6.4).

Regular grammars are used to generate the words that may appear in a programming language. This includes the identifiers (e.g., names for variables, functions and procedures); special symbols (e.g., addition, multiplication, etc.); and the reserved words of the language.

A rewriting system for context free grammars is a finite relation between $N$ and $(A \cup N)^*$: i.e., a subset of $N \times (A \cup N)^*$: A production rule <N > → $w$ is one element of this relation, and is an ordered pair (<N>, $w$) where $w$ is a word consisting of zero or more terminal and non-terminal letters. This production rule means that <N > may be replaced by $w$.

[4] Chomsky made important contributions to linguistics and the theory of grammars. He is more widely known today as a critic of United States foreign policy.

**Table 6.4** Chomsky hierarchy of grammars

| Grammar Type | Description |
|---|---|
| Type 0 grammar | Type 0-grammars include all formal grammars. They have production rules of the form $\alpha \rightarrow \beta$ where $\alpha$ and $\beta$ are strings of terminals and non-terminals. They generate all languages that can be recognized by a Turing machine (see Chap. 7) |
| Type 1 grammar (context sensitive) | These grammars generate the context sensitive languages. They have production rules of the form $\alpha A \beta \rightarrow \alpha\gamma\beta$ where $A$ is a non-terminal and $\alpha$, $\beta$ and $\gamma$ are strings of terminals and non-terminals. They generate all languages that can be recognized by a linear bounded automaton[a] |
| Type 2 grammar (context free) | These grammars generate the context free languages. These are defined by rules of the form $A \rightarrow \gamma$ where $A$ is a non-terminal and $\gamma$ is a string of terminals and non-terminals. These languages are recognized by a pushdown automaton[b] and are used to define the syntax of most programming languages |
| Type 3 grammar (regular grammars) | These grammars generate the regular languages (or regular expressions). These are defined by rules of the form $A \rightarrow a$ or $A \rightarrow aB$ where $A$ and B are non-terminals and $a$ is a single terminal. A finite state automaton recognizes these languages, and regular expressions are used to define the lexical structure of programming languages |

[a]A linear bounded automaton is a restricted form of a non-deterministic Turing machine in which a limited finite portion of the tape (a function of the length of the input) may be accessed
[b]A pushdown automaton is a finite automaton that can make use of a stack containing data

## 6.5 What Is Semantics?

The formal semantics of a programming language is concerned with defining the actual meaning of a language (Language semantics is deeper than syntax). The theory of the syntax of programming languages is well established, and a programmer writes a program according to the rules of the language. The compiler first checks whether the program as written is valid according to the rules of the grammar of the language, and if so, the compiler then determines its meaning and generates the corresponding machine code.[5]

The purpose of the compiler is to preserve the semantics of the language, and so there is a need to have an unambiguous definition of the meaning of the language (independently of the compiler), with the meaning preserved during code generation.

The program's syntax provides no information as to its meaning, and thus there is a need to supplement the syntactic description of the language with a formal

[5] It is possible that what the programmer has written is not be what the programmer had intended.

**Table 6.5** Programming language semantics

| Approach | Description |
|---|---|
| Axiomatic semantics | This involves giving meaning to phrases of the language using logical axioms. It employs *pre* and *post condition assertions* to specify what happens when the statement executes. The relationship between the initial assertion and the final assertion essentially gives the semantics of the code |
| Operational semantics | This approach describes how a valid program is interpreted as sequences of computational steps. The sequences then define the meaning of the program<br>An abstract machine (SECD machine) may be defined to give meaning to phrases, with the semantics expressed by describing the transitions they induce on states of the machine |
| Denotational semantics | This approach provides meaning to programs in terms of mathematical objects such as integers, tuples and functions<br>Each phrase in the language is translated into a mathematical object that is the *denotation* of the phrase |

unambiguous definition of its semantics. It is possible to utter syntactically correct but semantically meaningless sentences in a natural language. Similarly, it is possible to write syntactically correct programs that behave in quite a different way from the intention of the programmer.

The formal semantics of a language is given by a mathematical model that describes the possible computations described by the language. There are three main approaches to programming language semantics namely axiomatic semantics (as developed by C.A.R Hoare), operational semantics (as developed by McCarthy and others), and denotational semantics (as developed by Scott and Strachey) (Table 6.5):

There are several applications of programming language semantics including language design, program verification, compiler writing and language standardization. The three main approaches to semantics are described in more detail below.

### 6.5.1 Axiomatic Semantics

Axiomatic semantics gives meaning to phrases of the language by describing the logical axioms that that apply to them. It was developed by C.A.R. Hoare[6] in a famous paper "*An axiomatic basis for computer programming*" [Hor:69]. His axiomatic theory consists of *syntactic elements, axioms* and *rules of inference.*

The well-formed formulae that are of interest in axiomatic semantics are pre-post assertion formulae of the form $P\{a\}Q$, where $a$ is an instruction in the

[6] Hoare was influenced by earlier work by Floyd on assigning meanings to programs using flowcharts [Flo:67].

language and $P$ and $Q$ are assertions: i.e., properties of the program objects that may be true or false.

An *assertion* is essentially a predicate that may be true in some states and false in other states. For example, the assertion ($x—y > 5$) is true in the state in which the values of $x$ and $y$ are 7 and 1 respectively, and false in the state where $x$ and $y$ have values 4 and 2.

The pre and post condition assertions are employed to specify what happens when the statement executes. The relationship between the initial assertion and the final assertion gives the semantics of the code statement. The *pre* and *post condition* assertions are of the form:

$$P\{a\}Q$$

The precondition $P$ is a predicate (input assertion), and the postcondition $Q$ is a predicate (output assertion). The braces separate the assertions from the program fragment. The well-formed formula $P\{a\}Q$ is itself a predicate that is either true or false.

This notation expresses the *partial correctness*[7] of $a$ with respect to $P$ and $Q$, and its meaning is that if statement $a$ is executed in a state in which the predicate $P$ is true and execution terminates, then it will result in a state in which assertion $Q$ is satisfied.

The axiomatic semantics approach is described in more detail in [ORg:06], and the axiomatic semantics of a selection of statements is presented below.

- **Skip**

The skip statement does nothing and whatever condition is true on entry to the command is true on exit from the command. It's meaning is given by:

$$P\{skip\}P$$

- **Assignment**

The meaning of the assignment statement is given by the axiom:

$$P^x_e\{x := e\}P$$

The meaning of the assignment statement is that $P$ will be true after execution of the assignment statement if and only if the predicate $P^x{}_e$ ($P$ with the value of

[7] Total correctness is expressed using $\{P\}a\{Q\}$ and program fragment $a$ is totally correct for precondition $P$ and postcondition $Q$ if and only if whenever $a$ is executed in any state in which $P$ is satisfied then execution terminates, and the resulting state satisfies $Q$.

$x$ replaced by $e$) is true before execution (since $x$ will contain the value of $e$ after execution).

The notation $P^x{}_e$ denotes the expression obtained by substituting $e$ for all free occurrences of $x$ in $P$.

- **Compound**

The meaning of the conditional command is:

$$\frac{P\{S_1\}Q,\ Q\{S_2\}R}{P\{S_1;\ S_2\}R}$$

The compound statement involves the execution of $S_1$ followed by the execution of $S_2$. The meaning of the compound statement is that $R$ will be true after the execution of the compound statement $S_1$; $S_2$ provided that $P$ is true, if it is established that $Q$ will be true after the execution of $S_1$ provided that $P$ is true, and that $R$ is true after the execution of $S_2$ provided $Q$ is true.

There needs to be at least one rule associated with every construct in the language in order to give its axiomatic semantics. The semantics of other programming language statements such as the "while" statement and the "if" statement are described in [ORg:06].

### 6.5.2 Operational Semantics

The operational semantics definition is similar to that of an interpreter, where the semantics of the programming language are expressed using a mechanism that makes it possible to determine the effect of any program written in the language. The meaning of a program is given by the evaluation history that an interpreter produces when it interprets the program. The interpreter may be close to an executable programming language or it may be a mathematical language.

The operational semantics for a programming language describes how a valid program is interpreted as sequences of computational steps. The evaluation history defines the meaning of the program, and this is a sequence of internal interpreter configurations.

John McCarthy did early work on operational semantics in the late 1950s with his work on the semantics of LISP in terms of the lambda calculus. The use of lambda calculus allows the meaning of a program to be expressed using a mathematical interpreter, which gives precision through the use of mathematics.

The meaning of a program may be given in terms of a hypothetical or virtual machine that performs the set of actions that corresponds to the program. An abstract machine (SECD machine[8]) may be defined to give meaning to phrases

[8] The SECD (Stack, Environment, Code, Dump) virtual stack based machine was originally designed by Peter Landin (a British computer scientist) to evaluate lambda calculus expressions,

in the language, and this is done by describing the transitions that they induce on states of the machine.

Operational semantics give an intuitive description of the programming language being studied, and its descriptions are close to real programs. It can play a useful role as a testing tool during the design of new languages, as it is relatively easy to design an interpreter to execute the description of sample programs. This allows the effects of new languages or new language features to be simulated and studied through actual execution of the semantic descriptions prior to writing a compiler for the language. Another words, operational semantics can play a role in rapid prototyping during language design, and to get early feedback on the suitability of the language.

One disadvantage of the operational approach is that the meaning of the language is understood in terms of execution: i.e., in terms of interpreter configurations, rather than in an explicit *machine independent specification.* Another disadvantage is that the interpreters for non-trivial languages often tend to be large and complex. A more detailed account of operational semantics is in [Plo:81, Mey:90].

### 6.5.3 Denotational Semantics

Denotational semantics expresses the semantics of a programming language by a translation schema that associates a meaning (*denotation*) with each program in the language [Mey:90]. It maps a program directly to its meaning, and it was originally called mathematical semantics, as it provides meaning to programs in terms of mathematical values such as integers, tuples and functions. That is, the meaning of a program is a mathematical object, and an interpreter is not employed. Instead, a meaning function is employed to map a program directly to its meaning, and the denotational description of a programming language is given by a set of *meaning functions M* associated with the constructs of the language (Fig. 6.3).

Each meaning function is of the form $M_T$: T → $D_T$ where T is some construct in the language and $D_T$ is some semantic domain. Many of the meaning functions will be "*higher-order*": i.e., functions that yield functions as results. The signature of the meaning function is from syntactic domains (i.e., T) to semantic domains

**Fig. 6.3** Denotational semantics

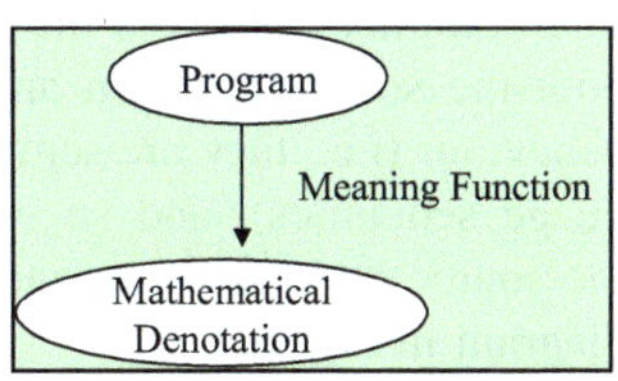


and it has since been used as a target for several compilers. Landin was influenced by McCarthy's LISP.

(i.e., $D_T$). A valuation map $V_T$: T $\rightarrow$ **B** may be employed to check the static semantics prior to giving a meaning of the language construct.[9]

A denotational definition is more abstract than an operational definition. It does not specify the computational steps and its exclusive focus is on the programs to the exclusion of the state and other data elements. The state is less visible in denotational specifications.

Denotational semantics provides a mathematical foundation for the semantics of programming languages, and it was developed by Christopher Strachey and Dana Scott at the Programming Research Group at Oxford University, England in the mid-1960s. It was initally known as the Scott-Strachey approach [Sto:77].

Dana Scott's contributions included the formulation of domain theory, which allows programs containing recursive functions and loops to be given a precise mathematical meaning. Each phrase in the language is translated into a mathematical object that is the *denotation* of the phrase. Denotational Semantics has been applied to language design and implementation.

## 6.6 What Is a Compiler?

A compiler is a program that converts syntactically valid programs into executable software that is understood by the targeted computer. That is, the compilation process translates the source code program into an executable file (i.e., a file in binary code specific to the architecture of the targeted computer and operating system), and the executable file may be directly executed on the targeted computer. Compilers provide several functions including:

- Detection of syntax errors in the source code
- Translation of the source code into equivalent machine code
- Full conversion of source code (interpreters operate line by line)
- Output of the compilation process is an executable file
- Platform dependent (computer/operating system)

### 6.6.1 Compiled Program Versus Source Code Program

The compiler preserves the underlying behaviour of the source program, in that both the source program and executable program exhibit the same input-output behaviour (i.e., they are semantically equivalent as the compiler preserves the language semantics), and so we wish to express the mathematical equivalence of the source code program and the compiled (executable) program, and we use the diagram in Fig. 6.4.

[9] This is similar to what a compiler does in that if errors are found during the compilation phase, the compiler halts and displays the errors and does not continue with code generation.

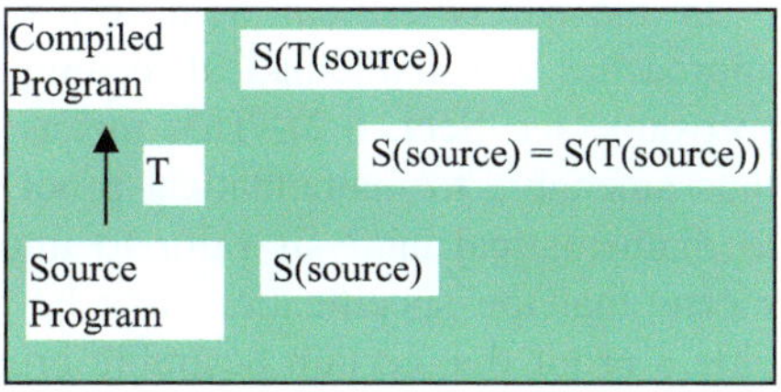


**Fig. 6.4** Compiled versus source program

The source program consists of a set of instructions in a high-level programming language that implements the specification. The compiler is a special program (T is a transformation function that preserves program semantics) that checks the syntactic validity of the source program, and then compiles the source program to produce the compiled (or executable) program that is semantically equivalent to the source code program. Thus we wish to express the mathematical equivalence of both representations (i.e., the compiled program and the source code program produce identical outputs for all possible inputs—i.e., they both exhibit the same input-output behaviour).

Figure 6.4 illustrates the equivalent relationship between the compiled program and source program. The mathematical equivalence is represented as a formal semantic preserving mapping (the compiler T is a transformation function which maps the source code into the targeted executable code), where both representations produce identical outputs for all possible inputs.

That is, we are assuming that there is a transformation function $T$ that converts the source code into the compiled code (i.e., $T(source)$ represents the compiled code). We assume that there is a semantic mapping $S$ that may be applied to both the source code (i.e., $S(source)$) and the compiled code (i.e., $S(T(source))$), and so the formal semantic equivalence of the source code and the compiled code is given by the equality of these:

$$S(source) = S(T(source))$$

## 6.7 Does the Program Satisfy its Specification?

The specification defines the required input-output behaviour of the program (or system), and acts as the blueprint (or foundation) for the development of the system. It may be a natural language description of the proposed system (the usual approach in industry), or it may be defined in a formal specification language such as VDM or $Z$ (especially in the safety critical field). The specification is a key project deliverable, and is used by the programmers to implement the solution, and by the testers to verify the correctness of the implementation. Another words, a correct program must satisfy its specification, and it is the responsibility of the team of programmers to correctly implement the specification in some programming language, and for the testers to verify its correctness.

In the safety critical field formal methods are often employed, and these approaches use mathematical techniques for the specification and verification of software (see Sect. 6.2). This means that the specification is mathematical and thus amenable to mathematical proof, and so the formal specification is subject to mathematical analysis prior to implementation. A mathematical specification means that the specification may be explored mathematically, and used to provide a proof that certain desirable properties are present in the specification, and that certain undesirable properties are absent in the specification. This increases confidence in the correctness of the specification.

Further, formal verification may be employed to demonstrate (increase confidence) that the implementation is valid with respect to the formal specification, where the implementation is derived from the formal specification by refinement steps, and where there is a proof of correctness of each refinement step. And so, formal specification and development leads to higher confidence in the correctness of the implementation.

Usually, in industry, the specification is written in a natural language, and so is not amenable to mathematical proof as such, and instead peer reviews of the specification may take place to ensure that all parties are confident that it is correct. The usual approach in industry to verify that a program satisfies its specification is to employ rigorous testing, and this generally involves the definition of the test cases, including inputs and expected outputs, conducting the testing, and verifying that all test cases pass during test execution.

### 6.7.1 Is Program Correctness the Same as Satisfying its Specification?

A program is correct if it satisfies its specification, but it is essential that the specification is correct. That is, the fact that a program satisfies its specification is not sufficient in itself to guarantee program correctness (i.e., it is a necessary but not a sufficient condition). Another words, if the specification of a program is incorrect, then irrespective of the best software development practices in the world, a faithful implementation of the specification (i.e., the program) will be incorrect. This means that the implemented software will not perform as required.

The specification of a program is usually written in a document using natural language (it's a little informal in the Agile world where the emphasis is on producing working code rather than producing documentation, and where the specification is more a collection of user stories to be implemented in the sprint). This means that the industrial approach to verifying the correctness of a specification generally includes processes such as peer reviews, prototyping and testing. In the Agile world, early feedback is provided on working software (testing and coding go hand-in-hand), and so any errors in the specification (an informal document or paragraph of text) are generally identified early, which reduces the cost of their correction. Errors are occasionally identified late in the software development for traditional waterfall development, and this potentially has major impacts on the project.

The use of formal methods as in the safety critical field allows the specification to be explored mathematically, including a proof of the presence of certain desirable properties and absence of certain undesirable properties, thereby increasing confidence in the correctness of the specification. However, if errors are missed in the mathematical analysis of the specification, then the implemented system will be incorrect.

## 6.8 What Is Program Implementation?

The starting point for program implementation is the program specification, and the programmer develops a program in some programming language to satisfy the specification. We mentioned that the specification defines the expected behaviour of the program, and is used by both the programmers to implement the solution, and the testers to verify its correctness. The specification is usually written in a natural language (supplemented with technical diagrams), or occasionally in precise mathematical notation such as VDM or Z, as extra precision is required in the safety and security critical fields.

That is, a computer program *P* is written in some programming language (e.g., C or Java), and the program must satisfy its specification *S*, where the specification may be a natural language description of what the program should do, or a precise mathematical description written in a formal specification language such as VDM or *Z*.

Implementation is like a bridge between an abstract entity and its concrete realisation as a physical system. That is, the implementation of a program is a physical realisation of an abstract entity into a concrete program that may be executed on the computer hardware, where the concrete realisation exhibits the same input-output behaviour as the abstract entity (i.e., the specification).

That is, the implementation must be faithful to the entity being implemented, and thus the program must satisfy its specification and exhibit the same input-output behaviour. The standard industrial approach is that the developers analyse the specification, and design a solution and write various programs to satisfy the specification (a more informal approach is adopted in the Agile world). Independent testers then verify the correctness of the implementation. However, this approach lacks the rigour of program verification using a mathematical specification, which offers mathematical proof of correctness of refinement steps.

A computer program runs on some computer, *C*, and the program *P* must be translated into the object language of the computer *C* and its operating system to execute. The first step is to write a program *P* that satisfies its specification *S*, and this may involve standard software engineering practices, or the use of formal specification and development as in the safety critical field (the latter involves a sequence of refinements of the specification until the eventual program is reached).

**Fig. 6.5** Commuting diagram property

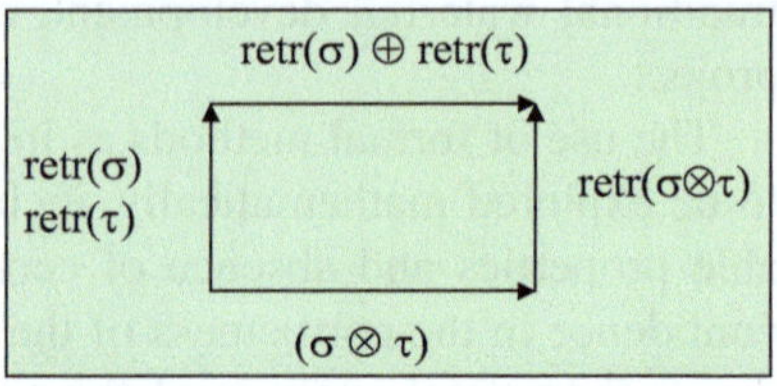


The second step is compilation of the program $P$ to produce the executable software $P_E$. The field of programming languages and semantics is quite mature, with compilers effective at preserving the semantics of programming languages.

The implementation must be faithful in that the compiled program should behave exactly as the source code program, and that they both satisfy their specification (i.e., see Sect. 6.6.1 where the diagram described in Fig. 6.4 should be satisfied). Another words, the compiled program must exhibit the same input-output behaviour as the abstract entity being implemented.

We can make the concept of the implementation satisfying its specification more precise if we examine the implementation with respect to a mathematical specification. That is, we can express what is required of the implementation to satisfy the specification in mathematical language. There is more than one way of implementing a specification (i.e., implementation is a relation), whereas each implementation satisfies one specification (i.e., the retrieval or mapping from a concrete implementation to less concrete or abstract representation is a function).

This is illustrated by the commuting diagram property where σ and τ represent the implementation of two entities, and *retr*(σ) and *retr* (τ) represent the entities before implementation (*retr* stands for a retrieval function that retrieves the abstract entity from the concrete implementation). The operation ⊕ refers to the abstract operation performed on the entity before implementation, whereas the concrete operation ⊗ refers to the equivalent operation performed post implementation[10] (Fig. 6.5).

For the implementation to be valid the commuting diagram property (which expresses the equivalent input-output behaviour of the abstract entity and the concrete implemented entity) must be satisfied: That is, we can proceed in either direction (either retrieval first and abstract operation or concrete operation first and then retrieval) and obtain the same answer: That is,

$$retr(\sigma \otimes \tau) = retr(\sigma) \ \oplus retr(\tau).$$

As mentioned, there are, in a sense, two parts to an implementation, with the first part concerned with constructing a program (s) written in a high-level language to satisfy the specification, and the second part being the compilation process of converting the source program (s) to the executable code of the target machine

[10] The commuting diagram property is similar to the concept of a homomorphism between two entities in pure mathematics.

architecture (where the compiler preserves the semantics of the programming language).

That is, what we have is a sequence of step-wise refinements starting from refinements of the initial specification until the program $P$ is reached, and then we have the compilation of $P$ to produce the executable implementation of $P$ (i.e., $P_E$) on a particular computer and operating system. This is illustrated as follows: the initial specification $S$ is successively refined into more concrete specifications $S_i$ until the concrete program $P$ is reached, and then $P$ is compiled to produce the executable software $P_E$. The program $P$ satisfies its specification and the final implementation $P_E$ satisfies its specification.

$$S = S_0 \sqsubseteq S_1 \sqsubseteq \cdots \sqsubseteq S_n = P \sqsubseteq P_E$$

Another words, we have a sequence of refinements starting from the abstract program (the specification), where each $S_i$ is more concrete than its predecessor $S_{i\text{-}1}$. The refinement step makes the refined specification more concrete and closer to the actual implementation ($P$). There is an associated proof obligation to demonstrate that the refinement is valid, and that the concrete specification observes the same input-output behaviour as the abstract specification (see the commuting diagram in Fig. 6.5).

Thus, assuming that the original abstract specification $S$ is correct, and the proof of correctness of each refinement step is valid, then there is a very high degree of confidence in the correctness of the implemented software $P_E$.

Suppose we have two different computers $C_1$ and $C_2$ then the implementation of $P$ on $C_1$ would differ from its implementation on $C_2$ (due to differences in their computer hardware and operating systems). However, both implementations would essentially be equivalent, in the sense that they would both exhibit the same input-output behaviour, as they both satisfy their specification.

## 6.9 What Is Program Verification?

It is essential that the executable software is a correct implementation of its specification, where the specification defines the input-output behaviour to be satisfied (irrespective of whether it is written in a natural language or in a formal specification language).

Program verification is a part of theoretical computer science concerned with verifying that the program is correct and satisfies its specification. The standard approach to specification is via a natural language description of the required behaviour, and so program verification in this case is limited to software reviews and testing. Software testing is quite rigorous, and is generally carried out by an independent test group. The testers define test cases that are traceable to the requirements (to ensure all requirements are covered by the testing), and the test execution provides confidence that the requirements have been correctly implemented.

Formal specification may be employed in the safety critical field to specify the required behaviour mathematically, and the program may be developed formally with mathematical proof employed (with tool support) for program verification (e.g., via step wise refinement with proof obligations resolved during each refinement step), until eventually the implementation is reached. This generally does not eliminate the need for software testing as such, but it adds an extra layer of rigour to the verification, and thus provides extra confidence in the correctness of the implementation. The consequences of a failure of a safety-critical system could be serious injury or loss of life, and so it is essential that such a system is subject to the most rigorous verification to ensure that all defects are identified and eliminated.

The formal specification is written in a mathematical language, and the implementation may be derived from the specification via step-wise refinement. That is, the program may be developed formally (e.g., via step wise refinement with proof obligations resolved during each refinement step), until eventually the implementation is reached. The refinement step makes the specification more concrete and closer to the actual implementation. There is an associated proof obligation to demonstrate that each refinement is valid, and that the concrete state preserves the properties of the abstract state. That is, program verification using mathematical techniques is a precise way to increase confidence in the correctness of the implementation.

Thus, assuming that the original specification is correct and the proof of correctness of each refinement step is valid, then there is a very high degree of confidence in the correctness of the implemented software. However, program verification using mathematical techniques is more the exception than the norm in software engineering. There is a steep learning curve with these mathematical techniques and theorem proving tools, and the use of formal methods for program verification is quite limited outside the safety and security critical fields.

Hoare [Hor:69] and Dijkstra [Dij:76] have argued that programs may be derived from their specifications through mathematical insight and simple algebraic laws, and that the program and its proof should be developed hand-in-hand. C.A.R Hoare argued that all of the properties of a program as well as all of the consequences of its execution can be determined from the text of the program using logical deduction. He argued that once the correctness of a program, its compiler, and the hardware of the computer have been established with mathematical certainty, it will be possible to have high confidence in the results of the program and its predicted properties.

Hoare sees the construction of programs as being a mathematical activity, and argues that programs may be derived from their specifications using insight, mathematical proof, and simple and elegant algebraic laws. Many computer scientists reject the view that programs are like mathematical proofs, and formal verification of programs is more the exception rather that the general rule in current software engineering (i.e., program verification using mathematical techniques is not common in mainstream software engineering).

*Fetzel has been critical of the philosophy of absolute correctness of program verification*, and he argues that while algorithms and programs that are intended for abstract machines can be absolutely verified (because there is nothing physical about such machines), *programs that are compiled and executed may only be relatively verified*. Another words, *a program may be proven correct but fail to do what was intended, due to the computer on which the program is run failing physically, or the connections of the computer failing* [Fet:88].

That is, there are inherent limitations to what can be proven about computers and computer programs. Smith notes that program verification is an important technology, and is potentially useful, but that it should definitely not be called verification, as *even if a program has been proved to be correct that one cannot still be sure that it will do what was intended* [Smi:85].

We discuss Smith's view on the relationship between a program and the world in Sect. 6.12 (computers only deal with their representation of abstract models in the real world).

It is essential that the software program is a correct implementation of its specification (irrespective of whether the specification is in a natural language or in a formal mathematical specification language). We mentioned that there are two parts to reaching the implementation, with the first step being to create the program from the specification, and the second step being the compilation and linking with libraries to produce the executable code, where the compiler preserves the semantics of the program. Often, these steps are combined together rather than being separated out.

Testing plays a key role in verifying the correctness of the software and confirming that the specification has been correctly implemented. It is a constructive and destructive activity in that while, on the one hand, it aims to verify the correctness of the software, and on the other hand, it aims to find as many defects as possible in the software. Testing is defined in [Tmap:04] as:

> Testing is a process of planning, preparing, executing, and analysing, aimed at establishing the characteristics of an information system and demonstrating the differences between the actual status and the required status.

Software testing involves defining the test conditions and designing the test cases and then executing the test cases. Modern testing is a solid software engineering discipline to verify the correctness of the implementation with respect to its specification, and while it cannot match the absolute rigor of mathematics, it nevertheless provides a very high degree of confidence in the correctness of the implementation.

## 6.10 What Is Miscomputation?

Miscomputation refers to a situation where the computational system produces an incorrect or unintended result (i.e., the computation goes wrong), or in other words the result produced does not correspond to the required input-output behaviour of the specification (i.e., the system fails to meet its specification). That is, miscomputation describes errors that occur in computation, and places an emphasis on understanding the reasons for the errors, whether hardware or software.

A miscomputation occurs when a program produces an incorrect output for a given input, which may be due to a software defect in the program (i.e., errors made by the programmer in the source code of the program leads to failure); it could be due to an error in the compilation process (i.e., the compiler makes an error in translating the source code to the executable code); it could be due to hardware errors (e.g., a computer component such as the hard drive, power supply, motherboard, faulty RAM, ROM, etc., malfunction), which may cause the computer to freeze or crash. Finally, it may be due to an incorrect specification, where the implementation of the specification is correct, but the specification itself is incorrect, meaning that whereas the computation satisfies the specification it does not correspond to user requirements.

Miscomputation often occurs due to programming errors such as incorrect algorithms or logic errors by the programmers, which leads to the incorrect performance of a computation by the program. Miscomputation requires semantics as it, in a sense, evaluates computation with respect to its intended goal (as defined in the specification), and whether the specification is satisfied by the implementation. That is, when we say that a program miscomputes, it means that we know what it was meant to compute (as defined in the specification), and that what it computes does not satisfy its specification.

The situation is more complex in the AI field where machine-learning algorithms may produce biases or errors, which often arise due to the training data that they employ or due to design errors. Often, these algorithms are just executing an enormous statistical process that lacks meaning, and the algorithms may devise a hypothesis from the data (the opposite of statistical inference which tests a hypothesis against the data), and so in a sense the algorithm is computing correctly, except that its results do not align with expectations. And so, AI errors are not computational failures as such, but are a semantic mismatch between human meaning and statistical meaning.

Where does miscomputation come from? Is it in the machine because its states diverge from a model, or in our interpretation because we assign meaning and interpretation to the system? This is the conflict between the physicalist view of computation (computation is a physical process on the machine), and the semantic view of computation (computation depends on the interpretation of the process).

## 6.11 What Is Software Engineering?

Software engineering involves the multi-person construction of multi-version programs. The IEEE 610.12 definition of Software Engineering is:

Software engineering is the application of a systematic, disciplined, quantifiable approach to the development, operation, and maintenance of software; that is, the application of engineering to software, and the study of such approaches.

Software engineering is not just programming. It requires the engineer to state precisely the requirements that the software product is to satisfy, and then to produce designs that will meet these requirements. The project needs to be planned and delivered on time and budget. The requirements must provide a precise description of the problem to be solved: i.e., *it should be evident from the requirements what is and what is not required.*

The requirements need to be rigorously reviewed to ensure that they are stated clearly and unambiguously and reflect the customer's needs. The next step is then to create the design that will solve the problem, and it is essential to validate the correctness of the design. Next, the software code to implement the design is written, and peer reviews and software testing are employed to verify and validate the correctness of the software.

The *verification* and *validation* of the design is rigorously performed for safety critical systems (possibly employing mathematical techniques). However, it will often be sufficient to employ peer reviews or software inspections and testing as these methodologies provide a high degree of rigour. This may include approaches such as Fagan inspections [Fag:76], Gilb inspections [Glb:94], or Prince 2's approach to quality reviews [OGC:04].

The term "*engineer*" is a title that is awarded on merit in classical engineering, and is generally applied only to people who have attained the necessary education and competence to be called engineers, and who base their practice on classical engineering principles. The title places responsibilities on its holder to behave professionally and ethically. Often in computer science the term "*software engineer*" is employed loosely to refer to anyone who builds things, rather than to an individual with a core set of knowledge, experience, and competence.

Parnas has argued that software engineers have responsibilities as professional engineers, in that they are responsible for designing and implementing high-quality and reliable software that is safe to use, and are also accountable for their decisions and actions, and have a responsibility to object to decisions that violate professional standards. Engineers are required to behave professionally and ethically with their clients. The membership of the professional engineering body requires the member to adhere to the code of ethics of the profession. Engineers in other professions are licensed, and Parnas argues that a similar licensing approach be adopted for professional software engineers.

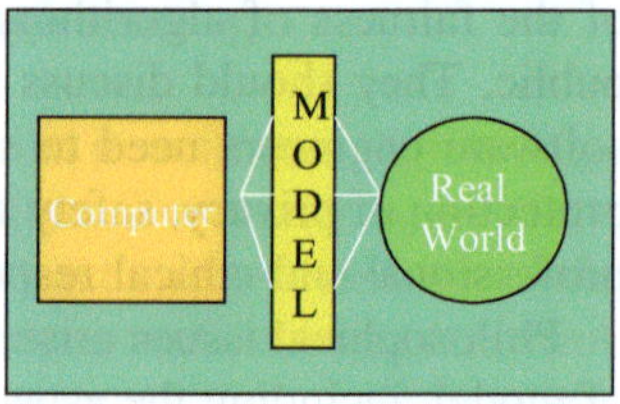


**Fig. 6.6** A computer model of the real world

the behaviour, its simplicity, and its elegance will be part of the criteria. The principle of "*Ockham's Razor*" (law of parsimony) is often used in modelling, and it suggests that the simplest model with the least number of assumptions required should be selected.

The adequacy of the model will determine its acceptability as a representation of the physical world. Ineffective models will be replaced with models that offer a better explanation (including more accurate predictions) of the manifested physical behaviour.

Modelling plays an important role in computer science, as computer systems tend to be highly complex, whereas a model allows simplification or an abstraction of the underlying complexity, and enables an understanding of the underlying reality to be gained. Further, whenever a computer is seeking to problem-solve in the real world then it needs to use an abstract model of the real world, and the abstract model is represented on the computer (Fig. 6.6).

The model is how the computer sees the world (i.e., the model is the world as seen by the computer), and so the computer performs actions in the world on the basis of the underlying model. *The problem is that the models may fail to correspond to the real world in appropriate ways, and therefore programs can fail due to failures in the model.* Program verification involves proving that the computer program (model) is correct with respect to its specification. However, even if a program has been proven correct with respect to its specification, it may fail in the real world due to inadequacies in the model.

Smith [Smi:85] argues that *computers deal only with their representation of abstract models of the real world, and thus they are twice removed from the underlying reality.* Perhaps, the real world situation may be directly represented in the computer, but even so the models will still be partial and incomplete, and there is no guarantee of their correctness (there is the well-known aphorism—all models are wrong, some are useful). *This means that action taken by the computer is based on partial and incomplete models, which means that decisions are made and actions taken with information that is incomplete or not fully accurate.*

## 6.13 Legal Aspects of a Computer Program

We briefly mentioned intellectual property in Sect. 5.5, and this branch of law deals with the rules that apply in protecting inventions, designs and artistic work, and in enforcing such rights. Intangible assets such as software designs or inventions may be protected in a similar way to the protection of private property, and an inventor is generally granted exclusive rights to the invention for a defined period of time. This gives the inventor the incentive to develop creative works that may benefit society, as it allows the owner of the invention to profit from their work without fear of misappropriation by others.

The main forms of intellectual property are patents, copyright and trademarks. A *patent* protects innovative ideas and concepts, and the invention itself must be novel and more than an obvious next step from existing technology. A *copyright* applies to original writing, music, motion pictures and other original intellectual and artistic expressions. It does not protect the underlying idea as such, and what is protected is the expression of the idea. Copyright law protects computer software source code from being copied by third parties without obtaining the required permission.

Patents are the strongest part of intellectual property and they provide much stronger protection than either copyrights or trademarks. A patent may be for an innovative idea for a product or a process for making something in a new way. There are several types of patents such as *utility patents* that are patents for a novel, useful and functional invention. These are the most common type of patent, and there is a variation termed the *utility model* for small useful functional innovations. *Design patents* protect the beauty or design of a manufactured product, and protect the appearance of the product but not its functionality.

Copyrights apply to original writing and to original intellectual and artistic expressions, and it protects the expression of the idea rather than facts or the idea itself. Copyright law protects literary, musical and artistic works such as poetry, songs, books, painting, dance, movies, music, information in news media and computer software. It provides exclusive rights to making copies of the expression (subject to copyright law and fair use), where the ways of expressing ideas is copyrightable.

A copyright gives the copyright owner rights to exclude others from using or copying the finished work, and most copyrights are valid for the creator's lifetime plus 70 years. The original reason of copyright was to motivate artists to produce more artistic work thereby encouraging creative art. Over time, the period of time for protection has increased in a major way, and today the purpose of copyright is more about protecting the artistic creations of business and large corporations.

The copyright holder has several rights including the right to *prevent others from making copies* of the work, as well as the rights to *stop others from making a derivative work*, i.e., something that is based upon the work. The copyright owners have the *right to distribute the work*, and to display the work anywhere and anytime they like. The owners of a copy have limited rights and may display the copy in one location only.

Computer software is protected by copyright with software code protected automatically without copyright registration in most countries, and software copyright law is part of global copyright law. A *copyright protects expression* (i.e., the way in which something is said), and a registered copyright is inexpensive and easy to get, although court cases for prosecuting copyright violation are expensive. Software *patents protect function* (not the expression of the function) and provide stronger protection, but they are costly and time consuming as well as being difficult to obtain.

The same function may be expressed in multiple ways by different programs, but if the function (or algorithm) is protected (as in a software patent) then nobody else can do that particular thing without permission or licensing from the patent holder. That is, copyright law protects one particular expression of the function, and as a different program could implement the same function in a different way, the function itself is not protected. Therefore, if it is important to protect the function (algorithm) itself rather than just one expression of the function, then it is necessary to protect it with a patent, as copyright law protects just one expression of the function.

*Stallman has argued against intellectual property such as patent law and copyright law.* He has argued against patenting software ideas, stating that a patent is an absolute monopoly on the use of an idea. He states that while twenty years may not seem like a long period of time, that in the software field it is essentially a generation, due to the pace at which technology changes in the world we live in. Further, *patents act a barrier to competition and lead to monopolies.* They make it difficult for new companies to enter a market place, due to the restrictions and costs associated with the licensing of patents.

Stallman argues that copyright law places Draconian restrictions on the general public, and takes away freedoms that they would otherwise have. They protect the copyright owner businesses, and he suggests that the digital era requires us to consider alternative approaches. For more detailed information on legal aspects of computing see [ORg:24].

## 6.14 Review Questions

1. What is a program?
2. Explain the difference between syntax and semantics.
3. What is a specification?
4. What is a compiler?
5. What is program implementation?
6. Discuss the difference between program correctness and miscomputation.
7. What is program verification?
8. Explain the relevance of copyright and patent law to the computer field.
9. Explain the relationship between a program and the real world.

## 6.15 Summary

A computer program provides the instructions to a computer to solve a particular problem. It is written in some programming language such as C++ or Java, and a program implements some algorithm. A programming language has a clearly defined syntax (rules or grammar for the language) and semantics (meaning of the language). A compiler checks the program for syntactic validity, and converts it into the equivalent machine code that can be understood by the computer. The executable code is equivalent to the source code in the sense that they exhibit the same input-output behaviour.

The starting point for program development is the specification of the program, and so the first step is to specify its required behaviour. The specification will often be in a natural language, but formal specification languages may be used in the safety critical field.

A computer program is written in some programming language, and the program must satisfy its specification. Program verification is concerned with proving the correctness of programs (i.e., showing that they satisfy their specification), and it may be done informally (via peer reviews and testing) in mainstream software engineering or mathematically in the safety critical field.

## References


[Dij:76] A Disciple of Programming. E.W. Dijkstra. Prentice Hall. 1976.

[Fag:76] Design and Code Inspections to Reduce Errors in Software Development. Michael Fagan. *IBM Systems Journal* 15(3). 1976.

[Fet:88] Program Verification: the very idea. James H. Fetzer. Communications of the ACM. 31 (9):1048—1063,1988.

[Glb:94] Software Inspections. Tom Gilb and Dorothy Graham. Addison Wesley. 1994.

[Hor:69] An Axiomatic Basis for Computer Programming. C.A.R. Hoare. Communications of the ACM. 12(10):576–585. 1969.

[Mey:90] Introduction to the Theory of Programming Languages. Bertrand Meyer. Prentice Hall. 1990.

[Nau:60] Report on the Algorithmic Language: ALGOL 60. P.Naur (eds) Communication of the ACM. 3(5). Pgs. 299–314. 1960.

[OGC:04] Managing Successful Projects with PRINCE 2. Office of Government Commerce. TSO, London. 2004.

[ORg:06] Mathematical Approaches to Software Quality. Gerard O' Regan. Springer. 2006.

[ORg:24] Ethical and Legal Aspects of Computing. Gerard O' Regan. Springer. 2024.

[ORg:26] A Brief History of Computing. Fourth Edition. Gerard O' Regan. Springer. 2026.

[Plo:81] A Structural Approach to Operational Semantics. Gordon Plotkin. Technical Report DAIM FN-19. Computer Science Department. Aarhus University, Denmark. 1981.

[Smi:85] Limits of Correctness in Computers. Brian Cantwell Smith, ACM SIGCAS Computers and Society, 1985.

[Spi:92] The Z Notation. A Reference Manual. J.M. Spivey. Prentice Hall International Series in Computer Science. 1992.

[Sto:77] Denotational Semantics. The Scott-Strachey Approach to Programming Language Theory. Joseph Stoy. MIT Press. 1977.

[Tmap:04] Tmaps (2004) TMap home pages. Sogeti Nederland B.V., Amersfoort. http://www.tmap.net

# 7 Algorithms and Computability

## 7.1 Introduction

A computer program is written in some programming language such as C++ or Java, and a program implements some algorithm. The execution time of the computer program depends on several factors such as the efficiency of the algorithm employed, the input value(s), how the algorithm has been implemented in the programming language, whether a compiler or interpreter is employed for the language, the operating system, and the computer hardware.

An algorithm is a procedure for solving a problem and consists of several steps that must be followed to compute the solution. The algorithm must terminate in a finite number of steps (as it hardly makes sense to wait for eternity), and there are mathematical problems for which there are no algorithmic solutions.

It is common to employ a natural language to describe an algorithm (care is needed to avoid the ambiguity inherent in natural language). However, it is also possible to use a more precise formalism for its description, with pseudo code, flow charts, programming languages themselves and formal specification languages used to describe the algorithm. *Pseudo code* is an informal high-level language description of an algorithm; flowcharts are diagrams that describe the algorithm; a programming language may be employed to describe the algorithm; or a formal specification language such as VDM or Z may be used when extra precision is required.

One of the earliest known algorithms is Euclid's GCD algorithm for determining the greatest common divisor of two natural numbers, and this algorithm finds the greatest common divisor of two numbers $a$ and $b$. The inputs of the algorithm are two natural numbers $a$ and $b$, and the output of the algorithm is $d$ (the greatest common divisor of.$a$ and $b$) (see Fig. 5.5).

$$\gcd(a,b) = \begin{cases} \text{Check if } b \text{ is zero.If so, then } a \text{ is the gcd} . \\ \textit{Otherwise, the } \gcd(a,b) \textit{isgivenby} \gcd(b, a \bmod b) \end{cases}$$

 
G. O'Regan, *Philosophical and Cultural Aspects of Computing*, Undergraduate Topics in Computer Science, https://doi.org/10.1007/978-3-032-29284-1_7

The mathematical analysis of an algorithm is used to demonstrate its correctness and its efficiency. It may be that the algorithm is inefficient in terms of the amount of time required to solve the problem, and it may be necessary to find (if one exists) a more efficient algorithm. The efficiency (or otherwise) of an algorithm is expressed in terms of polynomial or non-polynomial time as in complexity theory (discussed in Sect. 7.6).

A function is computable if there is an effective procedure or algorithm to compute $f$ for each value of its domain, and the concept of computability may be defined mathematically by Turing machines, recursive functions, and lambda calculus, all of which give equivalent definitions of computability (discussed in Sect. 7.5).

We briefly discussed the field of computability in Chap. 5, and noted that it emerged out of an attempt to find a secure foundation for mathematics in the early twentieth century, with early work done by individuals such as Frege, Russell, Hilbert, and Brouwer. Later work was done by Godel in the late 1920s/early 1930s with his famous incompleteness theorems (dealing a negative blow to Hilbert's program), and by Turing and Church in the mid-1930s (which gave a negative reply to the decidability of the formal system of mathematics as proposed in Hilbert's program, and giving a final blow to the program).

We give a short account of logicism, formalism and intuitionism in Sects. 7.2, which were different approaches to the foundations of mathematics. We discuss the nature of an algorithm in Sects. 7.3 and computation in Sects. 7.4, and then explore computability theory and the work of Turing and Church in Sect. 7.5. First, we discuss some philosophical questions that arise in computability theory.

### 7.1.1 Philosophical Questions in Computability Theory

Table 7.1 lists some philosophical questions that arise in computability theory.

## 7.2 Logicism, Formalism and Intuitionism

Gottlob Frege was a nineteenth century German mathematician and logician who invented a formal system which is the basis of modern predicate logic. It included axioms, definitions, universal and existential quantification, and formalization of proof. His objective was to show that mathematics was reducible to logic (*logicism*) but his project failed, as one of the axioms that he had added to his system led to inconsistency.

The inconsistency was pointed out by Bertrand Russell, and it is known as *Russell's paradox.*[1] Russell later introduced his theory of types as a way to deal

[1] Russell's paradox considers the question as to whether the set of all sets that contain themselves as members is a set. In either case there is a contradiction.

**Table 7.1** Philosophical aspects of computability theory

| Question | Initial answer |
|---|---|
| What is an algorithm? | An algorithm consists of steps to be followed to solve the problem (i.e., the procedure to solve the problem) |
| What are the limits of computability? | Is the answer given by the Church-Turing thesis, or could there be other forms of computation that go beyond Turing machines? |
| What are the limits of knowledge? | Does the undecidability of the halting problem suggest/ influence the limits of knowledge (i.e., are there limits as to what may be known) given that many mathematical statements are not computable? |
| Human computability | Can the human mind be mechanised? Can the human mind do something non-algorithmic? What distinguishes human reasoning? Creativity? Intuition? Free will? Consciousness? |
| Intelligence | Does intelligence involve something more than the execution of an algorithm? |
| Mathematics | Are mathematical truths discovered or constructed? Do non-computable numbers really exist? Is the set of real numbers meaningful since most are non-computable? |
| Mathematical intuition | Humans seem to possess intuition and appear able to see the truth of certain mathematical statements (beyond algorithms). What is mathematical intuition? Can a machine be intuitive? |
| Existence of mathematical objects | For Brouwer, to exist means constructive existence<br>For the formalists, to exist is just symbol manipulation<br>For Plato, to exist is to exist in the world of forms/ideas |

with the paradox, and he jointly published *Principia Mathematica* with Alfred North Whitehead as an attempt to derive the truths of arithmetic from a set of logical axioms and rules of inference.

The sentences of Frege's logical system denote the truth-values of true or false. The sentences may include expressions such as equality ($x = y$), and this returns true if $x$ is the same as $y$, and false otherwise. Similarly, a more complex expression such as $f(x,y,z) = w$ is true if $f(x, y, z)$ is identical with $w$, and false otherwise. Frege represented statements such as "5 is a prime" by "$P(5)$" where $P()$ is termed a concept. The statement $P(x)$ returns true if $x$ is prime and false otherwise. His approach was to represent a predicate as a function of one variable which returns a Boolean value of true or false.

Formalism was proposed by Hilbert (Fig. 7.1) as a foundation for mathematics in the early twentieth century. The motivation for the programme was to provide a secure foundations for mathematics, and to resolve the contradictions in the formalisation of set theory identified by Russell's paradox. The presence of a contradiction in a theory means the collapse of the whole theory, and so it was seen as essential that there be a proof of the consistency of the formal system.

**Table 7.2** Philosophical implications of halting problem

| Implication | Description |
|---|---|
| Limit of computation | The halting problem shows that there are fundamental limits to what may be computed, and that irresptive of the computational power of the computer it cannot solve every problem |
| Unsolvable problems | There are problems that may not be solved by any algorithm (e.g., the halting problem) |
| Limits of AI (intelligence) | The halting problem suggests that there are fundamental limits to how intelligent an artificial entity could be—i.e., there would be certain problems that it could not solve (i.e., it could not be a universal problem solver) |
| Limits of AI (algorithms) | Is human cognition a form of computation? Human-level intelligence cannot be achieved through computation alone—i.e., algorithms do not have human intuition and insight. Aspects of cognition such as consciousness, intuition, intentionality and mental states cannot be expressed with an algorithm |
| Limits of formal systems | It suggests limits to the usefulness of formal systems (i.e., the decidability of the formal system of mathematics was a key objective of Hilbert's program, and Turing/church showed that first order logic was undecidable) |
| Non algorithmic reasoning | The limits of computation show the importance of non-algorithmic reasoning such as insight and intuition |

The methods of proof in mathematics are formalised with axioms and rules of inference.

*Formalism* is a formal system that contains meaningless symbols together with rules for manipulating them. The individual formulas are certain finite sequences

**Fig. 7.1** David Hilbert

of symbols obeying the syntactic rules of the formal language. A formal system consists of:

- A formal language
- A set of axioms
- Rules of inference.

The expressions in a formal system are terms, and a term may be simple or complex. A simple term may be an object such as a number, and a complex term may be an arithmetic expression such as $4^3 + 1$. A complex term is formed via functions, and the expression above uses two functions namely the cube function with argument 4 and the plus function with two arguments.

A formal system is generally intended to represent some aspect of the real world. A rule of inference relates a set of formulas ($P_1$,$P_2$, ....$P_k$) called the premises to the consequence formula $P$ called the conclusion. For each rule of inference there is a finite procedure for determining whether a given formula $Q$ is an immediate consequence of the rule from the given formulas ($P_1$,$P_2$, ....$P_k$). A *proof* in a formal system consists of a finite sequence of formulae, where each formula is either an axiom or derived from one or more preceding formulae in the sequence by one of the rules of inference.

Hilbert's programme was concerned with the formalization of mathematics (i.e., the axiomatization of mathematics) together with a proof that the axiomatization is consistent (i.e., There is no formula $A$ such that both $A$ and $\neg A$ are deducible in the calculus). Its specific objectives were to:

- Provide a formalism of mathematics
- Show that the formalization of mathematics is *complete*: i.e., all mathematical truths can be proved in the formal system.
- Provide a proof that the formal system is *consistent* (i.e., that no contradictions may be derived).
- Show that mathematics is *decidable:* i.e., there is an algorithm to determine the truth of falsity of any mathematical statement

The formalist movement in mathematics led to the formalization of large parts of mathematics, where theorems could be proved using just a few mechanical rules. The two most comprehensive formal systems developed were *Principia Mathematica* by Russell and Whitehead, and the axiomatization of set theory by Zermelo-Fraenkel (subsequently developed further by von Neumann).

*Principia Mathematica* is a comprehensive three volume work on the logical foundations of mathematics written by Bertrand Russel and Alfred North Whitehead between 1910 and 1913. Its goal was to show that all of the concepts of mathematics can be expressed in logic, and that all of the theorems of mathematics can be proved using only the logical axioms and rules of inference of logic. It covered set theory, ordinal numbers and real numbers, and it showed that in principle that large parts of mathematics could be developed using *logicism.*

It avoided the problems with contradictions that arose with Frege's system by introducing the theory of types in the system. The theory of types meant that one could no longer speak of the set of all sets, as a set of elements is of a different type from that of each of its elements, and so Russell's paradox was avoided. It remained an open question at the time as to whether the *Principia* was consistent and complete. That is, is it possible to derive all the truths of arithmetic in the system and is it possible to derive a contradiction from the Principia's axioms? However, it was clear from the three volume work that the development of mathematics using the approach of the Principia was extremely lengthy and time consuming.

The controversial school of *Intuitionist mathematics* was founded by the Dutch mathematician, L. E. J. Brouwer, who was a famous topologist, and well known for his fixpoint theorem in topology. His constructive approach to mathematics proved to be highly controversial, as its acceptance as a foundation of mathematics would have led to the rejection of many accepted theorems in classical mathematics (including his own fixed point theorem in topology).

Brouwer was determined to provide a secure foundation for mathematics, and his view was that an existence theorem in mathematics has no validity, unless it was constructive and accompanied by a procedure to construct the object. He therefore rejected indirect proof and the law of the excluded middle ($P \vee \neg P$) or equivalently ($\neg\neg P \rightarrow P$), and he insisted that the existence of an entity was meaningless, unless accompanied by an explicit construction of the mathematical object.

The problem with the law of the excluded middle (LEM) arises in dealing with properties of infinite sets. For finite sets, one can decide if all elements of the set possess a certain property $P$ by testing each one. However, this procedure is no longer possible for infinite sets. We may know that a certain element of the infinite set does not possess the property, or it may be the actual method of construction of the set allows us to prove that every element has the property. However, the application of the law of the excluded middle is invalid for infinite sets, as we cannot conclude from the situation where not all elements of an infinite set possesses a property $P$ that there exists at least one element which does not have the property $P$. Another words, the law of the excluded middle may only be applied in cases where the conclusion can be reached in a finite number of steps.

Consequently, if the Brouwer view of the world were accepted then many of the classical theorems of mathematics (including his own well-known results in topology) could no longer be said to be true. His approach to the foundations of mathematics hardly made him popular with other contemporary mathematicians (the differences were so fundamental that it was more like a war between them), and intuitionism never became mainstream in mathematics. It led to deep and bitter divisions between Hilbert and Brouwer, with Hilbert accusing Brouwer (and Weyl) of trying to overthrow everything that did not suit them in mathematics, and that intuitionism was treason to science.

Hilbert argued that a suitable foundation for mathematics should aim to preserve most of mathematics. Brouwer described Hilbert's formalist program as a false theory that would produce nothing of mathematical value. For Brouwer, "to exist" is synonymous with "constructive existence", and constructive mathematics is relevant to computer science, as a program may be viewed as the result obtained from a constructive proof of its specification.

Brouwer developed one of the more unusual logics that have been invented (*intuitionist logic*), in which many of the results of classical mathematics were no longer true. Intuitionist logic may be considered the logical basis of constructive mathematics, and formal systems for intuitionist propositional and predicate logic were developed by Heyting and others [Hey:66].

Consider a hypothetical mathematical property $P(x)$ of which there is no known proof (i.e., it is unknown whether $P(x)$ is true or false for arbitrary $x$ where $x$ ranges over the natural numbers). Therefore, the statement $\forall x\ (P(x) \vee \neg\ P(x))$ cannot be asserted with the present state of knowledge, as neither $P(x)$ or $\neg P(x)$ has been proved. That is, unproved statements in intuitionist logic are not given an intermediate truth-value, and they remain of an unknown truth-value until they have been either proved or disproved.

The intuitionist interpretation of the logical connectives is different from that of classical propositional logic. A sentence of the form $A \vee B$ asserts that either a proof of $A$ or a proof of $B$ has been constructed, and $A \vee B$ is not equivalent to $\neg\ (\neg A \wedge \neg B)$. Similarly, a proof of $A \wedge B$ is a pair whose first component is a proof of $A$, and whose second component is a proof of $B$. The statement $\forall x\ \neg P(x)$ is not equivalent to $\exists x\ P(x)$ in intuitionist logic. Intuitionist logic was applied to Type Theory by Martin Löf in the 1970s [Lof:84].

## 7.3 What Is an Algorithm?

The origin of the word "*algorithm*" is from the name of the ninth century Persian mathematician, Mohammed Al Khwarizmi. An algorithm is a well-defined procedure for solving a problem, and it consists of a sequence of steps that takes a set of input values, and produces a set of output values. It is an exact specification of how to solve the problem, and a computer program implements the algorithm in some programming language.

It is essential that the algorithm is correct, and that it terminates in a reasonable period of time and does not consume an excessive amount of memory. There may be several algorithms for a problem, and so the choice of the best algorithm (e.g., fastest /most efficient) needs to be considered. For example, there are several well-known sorting algorithms (e.g., *merge sort* and *insertion sort*), and the merge sort algorithm is more efficient [$o(n \lg n)$] than the insertion sort algorithm [$o(n^2)$].

This may require mathematical analysis of the algorithm to demonstrate its correctness and efficiency, and to show that it terminates within an acceptable period of time and uses an acceptable amount of memory. A computer program implements the algorithm, and the speed of the program depends on the algorithm employed, the input value(s), whether a compiler or interpreter is employed, the speed of the CPU, and so on.

| | | | | | | | | | |
|---|---|---|---|---|---|---|---|---|---|
| | 2 | 3 | 4 | 5 | 6 | 7 | 8 | 9 | 10 |
| 11 | 12 | 13 | 14 | 15 | 16 | 17 | 18 | 19 | 20 |
| 21 | 22 | 23 | 24 | 25 | 26 | 27 | 28 | 29 | 30 |
| 31 | 32 | 33 | 34 | 35 | 36 | 37 | 38 | 39 | 40 |
| 41 | 42 | 43 | 44 | 45 | 46 | 47 | 48 | 49 | 50 |

**Fig. 7.2** Primes between 1 and 50

An algorithm may be described in natural language, or in a more common to use a more precise formalism. Its correctness may sometimes be seen by examination, but often it requires rigorous mathematical analysis. One advantage of the mathematical specification of an algorithm (as in a formal specification language) is that it is amenable to a proof of correctness, which is especially important in the safety critical field.

Eratosthenes was a Hellenistic mathematician who worked in the famous library in Alexandria. He developed the well-known *Sieve of Eratosthenes algorithm* for determining the prime numbers from 2 up to a given number $n$. The execution of the algorithm involves following the steps to completion, and it can be immediately seen that the algorithm will terminate, and that it is the desired solution to the problem.

The algorithm involves listing all numbers from 2 up to $n$. The first step is to remove all multiples of 2 up to $n$; the second step is to remove all multiples of 3 up to $n$; and so on (Fig. 7.2).

The $k$th step involves removing multiples of the $k$th prime $p_k$ up to $n$ and the steps in the algorithm continue while $p \leq \sqrt{n}$. The numbers remaining in the list are the prime numbers from 2 to $n$.

1. List the integers from 2 to $n$.
2. For each prime $p_k$ up to $\sqrt{n}$ remove all multiples of $p_k$.
3. The numbers remaining are the prime numbers between 2 and $n$.

The list of primes between 1 and 50 are then given by 2, 3, 5, 7, 11, 13, 17, 19, 23, 29, 31, 37, 41, 43, and 47.

## 7.4 What Is Computation?

*Computation* is the actual process of executing an algorithm to solve a problem, whereas *computability* is the study of whether a problem can be solved by an algorithm. That is, computation focuses on *how* to solve the problem (including its efficiency such as the time/resources required to solve it), whereas computability focuses on *whether* the problem can be solved.

A computation is any well-defined calculation that is performed by humans or machine, and examples include the solving of mathematical equations and the execution of computer programs. For example, the calculation could involve completing one's tax returns for the year, where the computation is with numbers representing full-time and part-time income.

The standard arithmetic operations such as addition, subtraction, multiplication and division are examples of basic computation, and may be carried out manually by a human with pencil and paper. More intensive computations are carried out by electronic computers, and we mentioned that the original meaning of the term "computer" was that of a human who performed calculations (or computations), whereas today the meaning is that of a machine that computes.

The roots of computation go back to the earliest civilisations where humans used their fingers for counting, and over time more sophisticated devices (such as the abacus) were developed to perform basic arithmetic operations. Over time, more sophisticated devices were introduced such as the *slide rule*. This was a hand-operated mechanical calculator for multiplication, division, calculation of roots, and scientific operations such as logarithms and trigonometry. It was invented by Oughtred in the seventeenth century (c. 1622), and built upon the discovery of logarithms by Napier. It remained in use up to the 1960s, until it was replaced by the pocket calculator.

And so, computation is essentially the process of performing mathematical operations on input data to produce output data. The input and output data may be in the form of numbers or text, and computation is more often performed today by electronic computers rather than by humans. These machines run computer programs that contain a set of instructions that implement an algorithm to solve the problem, and so they may implement sorting algorithms, encryption algorithms, and so on.

Computation is closely related to algorithms and computability, with computation refering to any process of performing calculation, whereas computability focusing on whether there is an algorithm to solve a problem that may be executed on a computer (or Turing machine).

Once an algorithm to solve a particular problem is known and the algorithm has been proved to be correct, the focus then moves to the efficiency of the algorithm and whether it solves the problem within acceptable time/memory constraints. Clearly, a correct algorithm serves little purpose if it takes hundreds of years or vast computer resources to solve the problem, and so the algorithm needs to be analysed to determine its computational complexity, and whether it may be solved in polynomial time or non-polynomial time (see Sect. 7.6).

It may be that a correct algorithm is not fit for purpose (e.g., in terms of time resources required), and that it may be necessary to find a better and more time/memory efficient algorithm (or an approximation or heuristic) to solve the problem.

### 7.4.1 What Are the Limits of Computation?

The limits of computation are governed by several factors such as physical limits to the computation or data storage. There are limits to the computation power of a computer in terms of the number of operations that may be performed per second (hardware limits), as well as the efficiency of the algorithms running on the machine (software limits).

The hardware speed is limited by the laws of physics, whereas software limits are due to the limitations of algorithms. The Church-Turing thesis (see Sect. 7.5) places limits on computation, and means that there are some problems that are impossible for computers to solve as there is no algorithm (e.g., the Halting problem). That is, the Halting problem (see Sect. 7.5.3) demonstrates that computation has inherent limits, and that not all problems may be solved by an algorithm.

Further, complexity theory (see Sect. 7.6) considers problems that are theoretically solvable, but in practice way beyond the power of the existing computers to solve (in terms of time and resources). These include computationally intractable problems that may not be solved in polynomial time, and that belong to the class of non-polynomial time (NP) problems.

*Hypercomputation* (or super-Turing computation) is an investigation into whether there is anything more powerful than a Turing machine. Another words, given that the Turing machine is the standard representation of a computing device, is it possible to replace it with another computational device that *can* solve problems that the Turing machine cannot solve?

It is theoretically possible to produce new computing devices by modifying the definition of the Turing machine (e.g., a Turing machine with an extra tape) to create an alternate computing device with different properties that can compute things that the Turing machine is unable to compute. However, such a machine would be unable to solve its own halting problem, but could solve the halting problem of other machines. It would be theoretically possible to build a ladder of such machines, with each machine solving the halting problem of the machine below it, and so the machine at the top would define the absolute limits of computability (see Sect. 7.7).

*Quantum computing* is a totally different paradigm from classical computing, and it has the potential to solve problems substantially faster than with classical computer technology. Anything that may be computed by a classical computer may be computed by a quantum computer, and vice versa. That is, quantum computing has no additional advantages over classical computers in terms of computability, but their advantage lies in their potential to revolutionise the computing field due to their turbo-charged computation.

Quantum computers are much more than the next generation of supercomputers. They have *quantum supremacy* in that they are believed to be capable of solving certain problems quickly that a classical computer is unable to solve in a feasible amount of time (see Chap. 15). The origins of quantum computing date back to the early 1980s, when a quantum mechanical model of the Turing machine was proposed [Ben:82].

## 7.5 What Is Computability?

The intuitive meaning of computability is in terms of an algorithm (or effective procedure) that specifies a set of instructions to be followed to complete the task. Another words, a function $f$ is *computable* if there exists an effective procedure or algorithm that produces the value of $f$ correctly for each possible argument of $f$. The algorithm is finite in length and sufficiently detailed so that a person can execute the instructions in the algorithm. The computation of $f$ for a particular argument $x$ just involves following the instructions in the algorithm, and it produces the result $f(x)$ in a finite number of steps if $x$ is in the domain of $f$. However, if $x$ is not in the domain of $f$ then the algorithm may produce an answer saying so, or it may get stuck, or it might run forever never halting. A computer program implements an algorithm.

The concept of computability may be made precise in several equivalent ways such as Church's *lambda calculus*, *recursive function theory* or by the theoretical *Turing machines.*[2] These are all equivalent and perhaps the most well known is the Turing machine (discussed later in the chapter). This is a mathematical machine with a potentially infinite tape divided into frames (or cells) in which very basic operations can be carried out. The set of functions that are computable are those that are computable by a Turing machine.

Functions are often described extensionally as a set of input-output pairs. A function $f{:}A \rightarrow B$ (i.e., a function $f$ from set $A$ to set $B$) is defined mathematically as a special type of relation (a relation is any subset of $A \times B$) such that no two of the input-output pairs have the same first element. If $(a,b)$ is an input pair of the function $f$ then this is written as $f(a) = b$. Functions may also be defined intensionally by a formula (e.g., $f(x) = 2x$).

A function $f$ is *computable* if there is an algorithm that computes $f$. There are *non-computable* functions that cannot be computed by an algorithm (i.e., some functions have no associated algorithm). For example, the halting problem is an example of a non-computable function, and a key question in computing is to determine *which functions have algorithms* to compute them? Many functions may be described in terms of the execution of software on a computer, where the software in the computer implements the algorithm to compute the function.

Algorithms have been in use for millennia with contributions by the Babylonians and the Greeks, and the term "algorithm" was made more precise in the twentieth century. It describes a procedure employing a finite set of rules and symbols that produces the answer in a finite amount of time. The emphasis is on finite since humans do not have infinite means at their disposal, as there is a limit on the number of computations that a human can perform in their lifetime. Several independent attempts were made to formalise the nature of computability in the 1930s, with work by Gödel, Church and Turing.

---

[2] The Church-Turing thesis states that anything that is computable is computable by a Turing Machine.

The *Church-Turing Thesis* states that *any computable function may be computed by a Turing machine.* This thesis about the nature of computable functions identifies the informal notion of effective computability with computability on a Turing machine. It states that any function that is computable is computable by a Turing machine (or equivalent formalism). There is overwhelming evidence in support in support of this thesis, including the fact that alternative formalizations of computability that have been proposed have been shown to be equivalent. That is, lambda calculus (as developed by Church), recursive function theory (as developed by Gödel), Markov algorithms (as developed by Markov), and Post production systems (as developed by Post) have all been shown to be equivalent to Turing machines.

**Definition 7.1 (*Algorithm*)** An algorithm (or effective procedure) is a finite set of unambiguous instructions to perform a specific task.

Alonzo Church developed the lambda calculus (λ-calculus) in the mid 1930s, as part of his work into the foundations of mathematics. Turing published a key paper on computability in 1936, which introduced the theoretical machine known as the Turing machine. This machine is computationally equivalent to the lambda calculus (but more intuitive), and is capable of performing any conceivable mathematical problem that has an algorithm (Fig. 7.3).

**Fig. 7.3** Alonzo church

### 7.5.1 Turing Machine

Turing analysed how humans compute and he devised a machine that would do the same. He showed that computation may be described in terms of a machine changing through a finite set of states in response to a sequence of symbols read and written to one at a time on a potentially infinite tape. A *Turing Machine* can compute one and only one function using the algorithm that is hardwired into it (i.e., it is hardwired to perform exactly one task as specified in its program), whereas the *Universal Turing Machine* is a single machine that can be used to compute anything that is computable.

A Turing machine consists of a head and a potentially infinite tape that is divided into cells. Each cell on the tape may be either blank or printed with a symbol from a finite alphabet of symbols. The input tape may initially be blank or have a finite number of cells containing symbols.

At any step, the head can read the contents of a frame. The head may erase a symbol on the tape, leave it unchanged, or replace it with another symbol. It may then move one position to the right, one position to the left, or not at all. If the frame is blank, the head can either leave the frame blank or print one of the symbols (Fig. 7.4).

Turing believed that a human with finite equipment and with an unlimited supply of paper could do every calculation. The unlimited supply of paper is formalized in the Turing machine by a potentially infinite tape marked off in cells.

The Turing machine is a simple theoretical machine, but it is equivalent to an actual physical computer in the sense that they both compute exactly the same set of functions. A Turing machine is easier to analyse and prove things about than a real computer. The formal definition of a Turing machine as *a* 7-tuple M = ($Q$, Γ, $b$, Σ, δ, $q_0$, $F$) is given in [ORg:23].

A Turing machine is essentially a finite state machine (FSM) with an unbounded tape. The machine may read from and write to the tape and the tape provides memory and acts as the store. The finite state machine is essentially the control unit of the machine, whereas the tape is a potentially infinite and unbounded store. A real computer has a large but finite store whereas the store in a Turing machine is potentially infinite. However, the store in a real computer may be extended with backing tapes and disks, and in a sense may be regarded as unbounded. The maximum amount of tape that may be read or written within $n$ steps is $n$.

A Turing machine has an associated set of rules that defines its behaviour. These rules are defined by the transition function that specify the actions that a machine

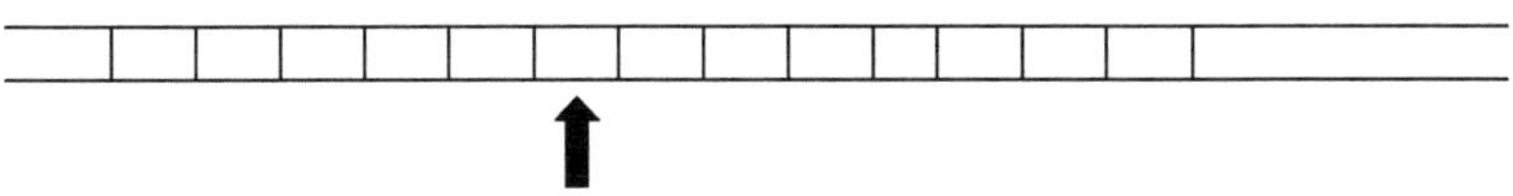

**Fig. 7.4** Tape of turing machine

will perform with respect to a particular input. The behaviour will depend on the current state of the machine and the contents of the tape.

A Turing machine may be programmed to solve any problem for which there is an algorithm. However, if the problem is unsolvable then the machine will either stop in a non-accepting state or compute forever. The solvability of a problem may not be determined beforehand, but, there is, of course, some answer (i.e., either the machine either halts or it computes forever).

Turing's 1936 paper on computability and the decision problem provided a clear mathematical analysis of computation, and it described the mathematical Turing Machine. Turing showed in the paper that there are some functions that are not computable, and the halting problem is one such function. That is, there is no general algorithm that can decide whether an arbitrary Turing machine halts or not (i.e., the halting problem is not computable). Turing also gave a negative answer to the decision problem in mathematics—The "*decision problem*" is concerned with whether there is a procedure that decides in a finite number of steps whether a given statement of first order logic is a theorem. That is, Turing showed that there is no general algorithm for deciding whether any given proposition is a theorem (which was one of the goals of the formalisation of mathematics as proposed by Hilbert). That is, he used this result to show that there is no solution to the decision problem (*entscheidungsproblem*) posed by Hilbert.

Hilbert believed that mathematics was decidable in that the truth or falsity of a mathematical problem may always be determined by a mechanical procedure, and he believed that first-order logic is decidable: i.e., there is a decision procedure to determine if an arbitrary formula is a theorem of the logical system. Turing gave a negative answer to the *entscheidungsproblem* by showing that decidability was related to the halting problem for Turing machines, and that if first-order logic were decidable then the halting problem for Turing machines could be solved. However, he had already proved that there was no general algorithm to determine whether an arbitrary Turing machine halts or not, and so if first-order logic is undecidable.

Turing also introduced the concept of a *Universal Turing Machine* (UTM), which is able to simulate any other Turing machine. The standard Turing machine runs only one program, whereas the universal Turing machine is a Turing machine that runs exactly one program (the fetch-execute cycle program), where it fetches another Turing machine and encodes it on the universal Turing machine tape, and then executes that Turing machine.

Turing's results on computability were proved independently of Church's lambda calculus equivalent results in computability. He studied at Princeton University in 1937 and 1938 and was awarded a PhD from the university in 1938. His research supervisor was Alonzo Church.[3]

[3] Alonzo Church was a famous American mathematician and logician who developed the lambda calculus. He also showed that Peano arithmetic and first order logic were undecidable. Lambda calculus is equivalent to Turing machines and whatever may be computed is computable by Lambda calculus or a Turing machine.

### 7.5.2 What Is Decidability?

Church and Turing independently showed in 1936 that the formal system of mathematics is not decidable. In other words, there is no mechanical procedure (i.e., algorithm) to determine whether an arbitrary mathematical proposition is true or false, and so the only way is to determine the truth or falsity of a statement is to try to solve the problem.

The decidability of the formal systems of mathematics was one of the goals of Hilbert's programme (discussed in Sect. 7.2), which was concerned with providing a secure foundations for mathematics.

The formalist movement in mathematics led to the formalization of large parts of mathematics, where theorems could be proved using just a few mechanical rules. The question remained whether these axioms and rules of inference are sufficient to decide the truth or falsity of any mathematical question that can be expressed in these systems. Hilbert believed that the formalism of mathematics would allow a mechanical procedure (or algorithm) to determine whether a particular statement was true or false. The problem of the decidability of mathematics is known as the decision problem (*Entscheidungsproblem*).

**Definition 7.2 (*Decidability*)** Mathematics is decidable if the truth or falsity of any mathematical proposition may be determined by an algorithm.

Turing showed that decidability was related to the halting problem for Turing machines, and that if first-order logic were decidable then the halting problem for Turing machines could be solved. However, he had already shown that there was no general algorithm to determine whether an arbitrary Turing machine halts or not, and therefore, first order logic is undecidable [Tur:36].

The question as to whether a given Turing machine halts or not can be formulated as a first-order statement. If a general decision procedure exists for first-order logic, then the statement of whether a given Turing machine halts or not is within the scope of the decision algorithm. However, Turing had already proved that the halting problem for Turing machines is not computable: i.e., it is not possible algorithmically to decide whether or not any given Turing machine will halt or not. Therefore, since there is no general algorithm that can decide whether an arbitrary Turing machine halts or not, there is no general decision procedure for first-order logic. The only way to determine whether a statement is true or false is to try to solve it. However, if one tries but does not succeed this does not prove that an answer does not exist (Fig. 7.5).

There are first-order theories that are decidable. However, first-order logic that includes Peano's axioms of arithmetic (or any formal system that includes addition and multiplication) cannot be decided by an algorithm. That is, there is no algorithm to determine whether an arbitrary mathematical proposition is true or false.

**Fig. 7.5** Alan Turing

Propositional logic is decidable as there is a procedure (e.g., using truth tables) to determine whether an arbitrary formula is valid[4] in the calculus.

**Definition 7.3 (*Completeness*)** A formal system is complete if all the truths in the system can be derived from the axioms and rules of inference.

Godel proved that first order predicate calculus is complete: i.e., all truths in the predicate calculus can be proved in the language of the calculus.

Gödel's *first incompleteness theorem* showed that first order arithmetic is incomplete; i.e., there are truths in first-order arithmetic that cannot be proved in the language of the axiomatization of first order arithmetic. Gödel's *second incompleteness theorem* showed that that any formal system extending basic arithmetic cannot prove its own consistency within the formal system.

[4] A well-formed formula is valid if it follows from the axioms of first-order logic. A formula is valid if and only if it is true in every interpretation of the formula in the model.

### 7.5.3 What Is the Halting Problem?

The Halting problem is concerned with the problem of deciding whether an arbitrary progran will eventually finish running on a given input or whether it will continue running forever.

> Given an arbitrary program is there an algorithm to decide whether the program will finish running or will it continue running forever? Another words, given a program and an input will the program eventually halt and produce an output or will it run forever?

The halting problem was one of the first problems that was shown to be undecidable: i.e., there is no general decision procedure or algorithm that may be applied to an arbitrary program and input to decide whether the program halts or not when run with that input.

***Proof*** We assume that there is an algorithm (i.e., a computable function $H(i,j)$) that takes any program $i$ (program $i$ refers to the $i$th program in the enumeration of all the programs) and arbitrary input $j$ to the program such that:

$$H(i,j) = \begin{cases} 0 \text{ If program } i \text{ halts on input } j. \\ 1 \text{ otherwise} \end{cases}$$

We then employ a diagonalization argument[5] to show that every computable total function $f$ with two arguments differs from the desired function $H$. First, we construct a partial function $g$ from any computable function $f$ with two arguments such that $g$ is computable by some program $e$.

$$g(i) = \begin{cases} 0 & \text{if } f(i,j) = 0 \\ \text{undefined} & \text{otherwise} \end{cases}$$

There is a program $e$ that computes $g$ and this program is one of the programs in which the halting problem is defined. One of the following two cases must hold:

$$g(e) = f(e, e) = 0 \tag{7.1}$$

In this case $H(e, e) = 1$ because $e$ halts on input $e$.

$$g(e) \text{is undefined and } f(e, e) \neq 0. \tag{7.2}$$

[5] This is similar to Cantor's diagonalization argument that shows that the Real numbers are uncountable. This argument assumes that it is possible to enumerate all real numbers between 0 and 1, and it then constructs a number whose $n$th decimal differs from the $n$th decimal position of the $n$th number in the enumeration. If this holds for all $n$ then the newly defined number is not among the enumerated numbers.

In this case $H(e, e) = 0$ because the program $e$ does not halt on input $e$.

In either case, $f$ is not the same function as $H$. Further, since $f$ was an arbitrary total computable function all such functions must differ from $H$. Hence, the function $H$ is not computable and there is no such algorithm to determine whether an arbitrary Turing machine halts for an input $x$. Therefore, the halting problem is not decidable.

### 7.5.4 Philosophical Implications of the Halting Problem

The philosophical implications of the Halting problem include that it demonstrates that there are inherent limits to computation, and that not all problems may be solved by an algorithm. This suggests that the human condition (especially cognition) is more than just computation, with insight, intuition, problem-solving as well as other non-algorithmic activities fundamentally different from the world of algorithms, and so human intelligence is much more than just following an algorithm. It potentially shows that human-like intelligence is impossible in the Artificial Intelligence field, or that real artificial intelligence will look quite different from human intelligence.

## 7.6 Computational Complexity

Computational complexity is the study of the effort required (in terms of time and resources) to solve a particular problem algorithmically, and it classifies problems according to their difficulty such as those that are solvable in polynomial time (*tractable problems*), and those that may not be solved in polynomial time (*intractable problems*).

An algorithm is of little practical use if it takes millions of years to compute particular instances, and so there is a need to consider the efficiency of the algorithm. Chap. 20 of [ORg:23] discusses cryptography and the RSA algorithm, and its security is due to the fact that there is no known efficient algorithm to determine the prime factors of a large number.[6]

There are often slow and fast algorithms for the same problem, and a measure of complexity is the number of steps in a computation. An algorithm is of *time complexity* $f(n)$, if for all $n$ and all inputs of length $n$ the execution of the algorithm takes at most $f(n)$ steps.

An algorithm is said to be *polynomially bounded* if there is a polynomial $p(n)$ such that for all $n$ and all inputs of length $n$ the execution of the algorithm takes at most $p(n)$ steps. The notation $P$ is used for all problems that can be solved in polynomial time, and these are said to be *computationally tractable*.

[6] Quantum computing is capable of breaking the RSA algorithm.

A problem is said to be *computationally intractable* if it may not be solved in polynomial time—that is, there is no known algorithm to solve the problem in polynomial time.

A problem $L$ is said to be in the set *NP* (non-deterministic polynomial time problems) if any given solution to $L$ can be verified quickly in polynomial time. A problem is *NP complete* if it is in the set *NP* of non-deterministic polynomial time problems and it is also in the class of *NP hard* problems.

A key characteristic to *NP* complete problems is that there is no known fast solution to them, and the time required to solve the problem using known algorithms increases quickly as the size of the problem grows. Often, the time required to solve the problem is in billions or trillions of years. Although any given solution can be verified quickly there is no known efficient way to find a solution.

## 7.7 Hypercomputation

Hypercomputation or super-Turing computation is an investigation as to whether there is something more powerful than a Turing machine. That is, it is a set of hypothetical models of computation that can produce outputs that are not Turing computable, such as a machine that could solve the halting problem. Another words, hypercomputers compute functions that a Turing machine cannot, and so they are more powerful in that they compute functions that are not computable in the sense defined by Church and Turing.

Turing introduced a computational model going beyond his original Turing machine as part of his 1938 PhD thesis, where he introduced an oracle (or black box) machine to study decision problems. An oracle machine is essentially a Turing machine connected to a black box, where the black box is capable of solving certain problems in a single operation (this may be a non-computable problem as the oracle is not a Turing machine) [Tur:38].

The philosophical debate on hypercomputation is controversial, and the question is whether hypercomputation is possible or realistic, and whether it is an effective model of computation? Some experts argue that hypercomputation is an advanced theoretical framework for future computing (e.g., using quantum computers).

Other experts question whether hypercomputers are actually possible, and argue that hypercomputation is not true computation. They argue that many hypercomputing models rely on black boxes (or oracles) that solve non-computable problems. However, a black box that outputs non-computable outputs requires non-computable inputs.

Some experts argue that the mind must be a hypercomputer (as it is not subject to Turing Machine limitations).

## 7.8 Review Questions

1. What is computation?
2. Explain the difference between computability and decidability.
3. What is a formal system?
4. What were the goals of the formalism of mathematics?
5. Explain the difference between consistency, completeness and decidability.
6. Describe a Turing machine and explain its significance in computability.
7. Explain the significance of the halting problem.
8. Discuss the complexity of an algorithm and explain terms such as "polynomial bounded", "computationally intractable", and "NP complete".
9. What is hypercomputation?

## 7.9 Summary

The intuitive meaning of computability is that in terms of an algorithm (or effective procedure) that specifies a set of instructions to be followed to solve the problem. A function $f$ is computable if there exists an algorithm that produces the value of $f$ correctly for each possible argument of $f$. The computation of $f$ for a particular argument $x$ just involves following the instructions in the algorithm, and it produces the result $f(x)$ in a finite number of steps if $x$ is in the domain of $f$.

The concept of computability may be made precise with Church's lambda calculus, recursive function theory or by the theoretical Turing machines. The Turing machine is a mathematical machine with a potentially infinite tape divided into frames (or cells) in which very basic operations can be carried out. The set of functions that are computable are those that are computable by a Turing machine.

Church and Turing independently showed in 1936 that mathematics is not decidable. In other words it is not possible to determine the truth or falsity of any mathematical proposition by an algorithm.

The area of complexity theory that studies the effort required to solve a problem, and we discussed polynomial time problems and non-deterministic polynomial time problems. The reader is referred to [RoS:94] for a more detailed account of computability and decidability.

## References

[Ben:82] Quantum Mechanical Hamiltonian Models of Turing Machines. P. Benioff. *Journal of Statistical Physics.* **29** (3): 515–546. 1982.

[Hey:66] Intuitionist Logic. An Introduction. A. Heyting. North-Holland Publishing. 1966.

[Lof:84] Intuitionist Type Theory. Per Martin Löf. Notes by Giovanni Savin of lectures given in Padua, June, 1980. Bibliopolis. Napoli. 1984.

[ORg:23] Mathematical Foundations of Software Engineering. Gerard O' Regan. Springer. 2023.

[RoS:94] Cornerstones of Undecideability. Grzegorz Rozenberg and Arto Salomaa. Prentice Hall. 1994.

[Tur:36] On Computable Numbers, with an Application to the Entscheidungsproblem Proceedings of the London Mathematical Society, Series 2. 1936.

[Tur:38] *Systems of Logic Based on Ordinals* Alan Turing. (PhD thesis). Princeton University. 1938.

# The Nature and Philosophy of AI

# 8

## 8.1 Introduction

The long-term[1] goal of Artificial Intelligence is to create a thinking machine that is intelligent, has consciousness, has the ability to learn, has free will, and is ethical. The field involves several disciplines such as philosophy, psychology, linguistics, machine vision, cognitive science, mathematics, logic and ethics.

Artificial Intelligence is a young field and John McCarthy and others coined the term in 1956 in their proposal for the Dartmouth Summer Research Project on Artificial Intelligence in 1955.

Alan Turing had earlier devised the Turing Test as a way to test the intelligent behaviour of a machine. Searle's Chinese room was a rebuttal of Turing's position and argued that even if a machine passes the Turing Test that it may not be considered intelligent. Recent AI technologies such as ChatGPT are very effective in simulating intelligence, where they give the impression of intelligent behaviour (they do not possess intelligence) and pass the Turing Test, but they rely on large language models that extract the most probable answer from extremely large data sets.

There are deep philosophical problems in Artificial Intelligence, and some researchers (including Hubert Dreyfus and John Searle) believe that its goals are impossible or incoherent. Even if Artificial Intelligence is possible there are moral issues to consider such as the exploitation of artificial machines by humans, and

[1] This long-term goal may be many years in the future, as an early breakthrough in machine intelligence is unlikely, as there are deep philosophical problems to be solved. A lot of progress has been made in the simulation of intelligence with developments such as ChatGPT.



G. O'Regan, *Philosophical and Cultural Aspects of Computing*, Undergraduate Topics in Computer Science, https://doi.org/10.1007/978-3-032-29284-1_8

whether it is ethical to do this. Weizembaum[2] has argued that Artificial Intelligence is unethical.

The philosophy of AI investigates fundamental questions such as "What is AI?", "What is mind?", "What is thinking?", "Can computers think?", "What is consciousness?", "What is intelligence?", "Can a computer act as a mind?", "What is the nature of self?", "Is AI ethical?", "Can AI be trusted?"

## 8.2 Descartes

We discussed René Descartes (Fig. 2.1) in Chap. 2, and he was an influential French mathematician, scientist and philosopher. He was born in a village in the Loire valley in France in 1596, and studied law at the University of Poitiers. He never practiced as a lawyer and instead served Prince Maurice of Nassau in the Netherlands. He invented the Cartesian coordinate system used in plane geometry, where each point on the plane is identified with a pair of numbers $(x, y)$: the $x$-coordinate and the $y$-coordinate.

He made important contributions to philosophy and attempted to derive a fundamental set of principles that can be known to be true. His approach in developing his Rationalist philosophy was to take the strongest formulation of the argument of the sceptics, and to renounce any idea that could be doubted. His goal was then to arrive at some fundamental knowledge that cannot be doubted (which was his own existence as a thinking entity), and from this fundamental truth he reconstructed knowledge (using Rationalism and the deductive method).

Descartes rejected the senses since they can deceive, and are not a sound source of knowledge. For example, during a dream the subject perceives stimuli that appear to be real, but these have no existence outside the subject's mind. Therefore, it is inappropriate to rely on one's senses as the foundation of knowledge.

He argued that a powerful "*evil demon or mad-scientist*" could exist who sets out to manipulate and deceive subjects, thereby preventing them from knowing the true nature of reality. The evil demon could bring the subject into existence including an implanted memory. The question is how one can know for certain what is true given the limitations of the senses. The "*brain in the vat thought experiment*" is a more modern formulation of the idea of an evil spirit or mad scientist. A mad scientist could remove a person's brain from their body and place it in a vat and connects its neurons by wires to a supercomputer. The computer could then provide the disembodied brain with the electrical impulses that the brain would normally receive. The computer could then simulate reality, and the disembodied brain would have conscious experiences and would receive the same impulses as if it were inside a person's skull. There is no way to tell whether the brain is inside the vat or inside a person.

[2] Weizenbaum was a psychologist who invented the ELIZA program, which simulated a psychologist in dialogue with a patient. He was initially an advocate of Artificial Intelligence but later became a critic.

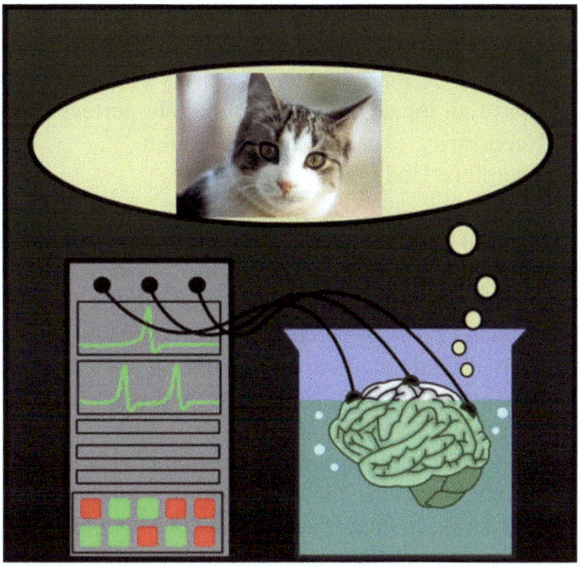

**Fig. 8.1** Brain in a VAT thought experiment

That is, at any moment an individual could potentially be a brain connected to a sophisticated computer program or inside a person's skull. Therefore, if you cannot be sure that you are not a brain in a vat, then you cannot rule out the possibility that all of your beliefs about the external world are false. This sceptical argument is difficult to refute.

The perception of a "cat" (Fig. 8.1) for the case where the brain is in the vat is false, and does not correspond to reality. However, it is impossible to know whether your brain is in a vat or inside your skull, and so it is therefore impossible to know whether your belief is valid or not.

Descartes deduced that there was one single principle that must be true. He argued that even if he is being deceived, then clearly he is thinking and must exist. This principle of existence or being is more famously known as "*cogito, ergo sum*" (I think, therefore I am). Descartes argued that this existence could be applied to the present only, as memory may be manipulated and therefore doubted. Further, the only existence that he sure of is that he is a "*thinking thing*". He cannot be sure of the existence of his body, as his body is perceived by his senses, which he has proven to be unreliable. Therefore, his mind or thinking thing is the only thing about him that cannot be doubted. His mind is used to make judgments, and to deal with un-reliable perceptions received via the senses.

Descartes constructed a system of knowledge (*Rationalism*) from this one principle using the deductive method. He deduced the existence of a benevolent God using the ontological argument. He argues [Des:99] that we have an innate idea of a supremely perfect being (God), and that God's existence may be inferred immediately from the innate idea of a supremely perfect being (*Descartes Ontological*

*Argument* is similar to St. Anselm's ontological argument of the early twelfth century).

1. I have an innate idea of a supremely perfect being (i.e. God).
2. Necessarily, existence is a perfection.[3]
3. Therefore God exists.

He then argued that since God is benevolent that he can have some trust in the reality that his senses provide. God has provided him with a thinking mind and does not wish to deceive him. He argued that knowledge of the external world can be obtained by both perception and deduction, and that reason (or rationalism) is the only reliable method of obtaining knowledge.

Descartes was a *dualist* and he makes a clear *mind-body* distinction. He states that there are two substances in the universe: mental substances and bodily substances, and the *mind-body distinction is very relevant in AI* with software running on a computer being the analogy of the human mind and brain.

This thinking thing (*res cogitans* or mind/soul) is distinct from the rest of nature (*res extensa*), and interacts with the world through the senses to gain knowledge. Knowledge is gained by mental operations using the deductive method, where starting from the premises that are known to be true, further truths may be logically deduced. Descartes founded what would become known as the Rationalist school of philosophy where knowledge was derived solely by human reasoning. The *analogy of the mind/body in AI is an AI program running on a computer*, with knowledge gained by sense perception (with sensors) and logical deduction.

Descartes believed that the bodies of animals are complex living machines without feelings. He dissected (including vivisection) many animals for experiments. His experiments led him to believe that the actions and behaviour of non-human animals can be fully accounted for by mechanistic means, and without reference to the operations of the mind. He realised from his experiments that a lot of human behaviour (e.g., physiological functions and blinking) is like that of animals in that it has a mechanistic explanation.

Descartes was of the view that well-designed automata[4] could mimic many parts of human behaviour. He argued that the key differentiators between human and animal behaviour were that humans could adapt to widely varying situations, and also had the ability to use language. The use of language illustrates the power of the use of thought, and it clearly differentiates humans from animals. Animals do not possess the ability to use language for communication or reason. This, he argues, provides evidence for the presence of a soul associated with the human body. In essence, animals are pure machines, whereas humans are machines with minds (or souls).

[3] Descartes ontological argument is similar to St. Amselm's argument on the existence of God, and implicitly assumes existence as a predicate (which was refuted by Kant).

[4] An automaton is a self-operating machine or mechanism that behaves and responds in a mechanical way.

The significance of Descartes in the field of Artificial Intelligence is that the Cartesian dualism that humans seem to possess would need to be reflected (in some way) among artificial machines. Humans seem to have a distinct sense of self (or "I") as distinct from the body, and the "I" seems to represent some core sense or essence of being that is unchanged throughout the person's life.[5] It somehow represents personhood, as distinct from the physical characteristics of a person that are inherited genetically. A key challenge for the AI community is to construct a machine that (in a sense) possesses Cartesian dualism: i.e., a machine that has awareness of itself as well as its environment.

However, we noted fundamental limits on how intelligent an artificial entity may be in Chap. 7 (i.e., there are certain problems that may not be solved due to limits of algorithms and computation, and algorithms do not possess human intuition and insight).

## 8.3 The Field of Artificial Intelligence

The origin of the term "Artificial Intelligence" is in work done on the proposal for Dartmouth Summer Research Project on Artificial Intelligence. John McCarthy and others wrote this proposal in 1955, and the research project took place in the summer of 1956.

The success of early AI went to its practitioners' heads and they believed that they would soon develop machines that would emulate human intelligence. They convinced many of the funding agencies and the military to provide research grants, as they believed that real artificial intelligence would soon be achieved. They had some initial (limited) success with machine translation, pattern recognition and automated reasoning. However, it is now clear that AI is a long-term project (although there has been major progress in the simulation of intelligence in recent years with Large Language Models (LLM) such as ChatGPT). Artificial Intelligence is a multi-disciplinary field and includes disciplines such as:

- Computing
- Logic and Philosophy
- Epistemology and Knowledge representation,
- Psychology and Linguistics
- Neuroscience and Neural Networks
- Machine Vision

[5] Hume's theory of empiricism gives an account of how knowledge is acquired by the senses. However, the implications of Hume's empiricism are problems with the foundations of human knowledge (leading to scepticism), especially with justifying causation, induction and self. That is, his theory was unable to justify causation or induction by logic or experience, thereby undermining the foundations of science. Further, his analysis of the self demonstrated that we have no experience of an idea of the self as such, and that what we experience at any time is just a varying collection of impressions and ideas.

- Robotics
- Expert Systems
- Machine Translation

The English mathematician, Alan Turing, contributed to the debate concerning thinking machines, consciousness and intelligence in the early 1950s. He devised the famous "Turing Test" to judge whether a machine was intelligent. Turing's paper was very influential as it raised the idea of the possibility of programming a computer to behave intelligently [Tur:50].

Shannon considered the problem of writing a chess program in the late 1940s, and he distinguished between a brute force strategy where the program could look at every combination of moves, and a strategy where knowledge of chess is used to examine and select a subset of available moves. The ability of a program to play chess is a skill that is considered intelligent, even though the machine itself is not conscious that it is playing chess (i.e., it is just following an algorithm).

Modern chess programs have been quite successful, and have advantages over humans in terms of computational speed in considering combinations of moves. The IBM chess program "Deep Blue" defeated Kasparov in 1997, and today, the top chess programs calculate millions of positions per second, and employ vast neural networks to evaluate hundreds of millions of board positions, as well as looking at 50–60 moves into the future, and so they are unbeatable by the best human players.

Herbert Simon and Alan Newell developed the first theorem prover with their work on a program called "Logic Theorist" or "LT" in the mid 1950s [NeS:56]. LT was demonstrated at the Dartmouth conference, and it showed that computers had the ability to encode knowledge and perform intelligent operations such as solving theorems in mathematics. The LT program could provide proofs of various theorems in Russell's and Whitehead's "Principia Mathematica"[6] [RuW:10].

John McCarthy (Fig. 8.2) proposed a program called the Advice Taker in his influential paper "Programs with Common Sense" [Mc:59]. The idea was that this program would be able to draw conclusions from a set of premises, and McCarthy states that a program has common sense if it is capable of automatically deducing for itself "*a sufficiently wide class of immediate consequences of anything it is told and what it already knows*".

The Advice Taker uses logic to represent knowledge (i.e., premises that are taken to be true), and it then applied the deductive method to deduce further truths

[6] Russell is said to have remarked that he was delighted to see that the Principia Mathematica could be done by machine, and that if he and Whitehead had known this in advance that they would not have wasted 10 years doing this work by hand in the early twentieth century. The LT program succeeded in proving 38 of the 52 theorems in Chap. 2 of Principia Mathematica. Its approach was to start with the theorem to be proved and to then search for relevant axioms and operators to prove the theorem.

**Fig. 8.2** John McCarthy

from the relevant premises (determining these is non trivial).[7] That is, the program manipulates the formal language (e.g., predicate logic), and provides a conclusion that may be a statement or an imperative. McCarthy envisaged that the Advice Taker would be a program that would be able to learn and improve. This would involve making statements to the program, and telling it about its symbolic environment. The program will have available to it all the logical consequences of what it has already been told and previous knowledge. McCarthy's desire was to create programs to learn from their experience as effectively as humans do.

The McCarthy philosophy is that common sense[8] knowledge, reasoning and problem solving can be formalised with logic. A particular system is described by a set of sentences in logic, which represent all that is known about the world in general, and what is known about the particular situation and the goals of the system. The program then performs actions that it infers are appropriate for achieving the goals.

---

[7] The machine would somehow need to know which premises are relevant and should be selected in applying the deductive method (from the many premises that are already encoded). This is non trivial.

[8] Common sense includes basic facts about events, beliefs, actions, knowledge and desires. It also includes basic facts about objects and their properties.

### 8.3.1 Turing Test and Strong AI

Alan Turing contributed to the debate concerning artificial intelligence in his 1950 paper on Computing, machinery and intelligence [Tur:50]. Turing started this short but influential paper with the statement "*The question of whether machines can think is too meaningless to deserve discussion*", but nevertheless he saw merit in devising an intelligence test based on an *imitation game* to motivate the development of more powerful machines and programs.

Turing's paper considered whether it could be possible for a machine to be conscious and to think, and he devised a famous experiment that would determine if a computer had these attributes. This is known as the "*Turing Test*", and it is an adaptation of a well-known party game, which involves three participants. One of them, the judge, is placed in a separate room from the other two: one is a male and the other is a female. Questions and responses are typed and passed under the door. The objective of the game is for the judge to determine which participant is male and which is female. The male is allowed to deceive the judge, whereas the female is supposed to assist.

Turing adapted this game by allowing the role of the male to be played by a computer. The test involves a judge who is engaged in a natural language conversation with two other parties, one party is a human and the other is a machine. If the judge cannot determine which is machine and which is human, then the machine is said to have passed the "Turing Test". That is, a machine that passes the Turing Test must be considered intelligent, as it is indistinguishable from a human. The test is applied to test the linguistic capability of the machine rather than the audio capability, and the conversation is limited to a text only channel.

Turing's work on "thinking machines" led to a debate concerning the nature of intelligence, and it caused a great deal of public controversy as defenders of traditional values attacked the idea of machine intelligence. Turing strongly believed that machines would eventually be developed that would stand a good chance of passing the "Turing Test". He considered the operation of "thought" to be equivalent to the operation of a discrete state machine. A program that runs on a single, universal machine, i.e. a computer, may simulate such a machine.

Turing viewpoint that a machine will one day pass the Turing Test and be considered intelligent is known as "*strong artificial intelligence*". It states that a computer with the right program would have the mental properties of humans. There are a number of objections to strong AI, and one well-known rebuttal is that of Searle's *Chinese Room argument*. The Chinese Room thought experiment is a famous paper written by John Searle on machine understanding. This classic paper presents a compelling argument against the feasibility of the strong AI project. It rejects the claim that a machine will someday in the future have the same cognitive qualities as humans [Sea:80].

A Large Language Model (LLM) is an AI program built on neural networks that are trained on huge sets of data. They use a type of machine learning called *deep learning* that involves the probabilistic analysis of unstructured data. It analyses trillions of sentences to predict how to finish a complete sentence or to generate its own sentences. ChatGPT is a machine-learning model that recognises and generates human-language text, and it is very effective in mimicking human conversation.

*ChatGPT passed the Turing test* in 2023 and 2024 [Bie:23]. However, ChatGPT is not a conscious entity and has no awareness of itself, and relies more on a probabilistic analysis of huge sets of data. That is, it does not have human-like intelligence or reasoning capability as such, and so, given that it has passed the Turing test, we need, in a sense, a new test of intelligence to distinguish between a human and a machine. That its, the *Turing test, as formulated, is an inadequate test of human intelligence*, or another words passing the Turing test is a necessary but not sufficient condition of intelligence.

Searle argues that *brains cause minds, and that syntax does not suffice for semantics*. He defines the terms "*strong*" and "*weak AI*" as follows.

*Strong AI*

The computer is not merely a tool in the study of the mind, rather *the appropriately programmed computer really is a mind in the sense that computers given the right programs can be literally said to understand and have other cognitive states.*

*Weak AI.*

*Computers just simulate thought, their seeming understanding isn't real understanding* (just as-if), their seeming calculation is only as-if calculation, etc. Nevertheless, computer simulation is useful for *studying* the mind (as for studying the weather and other things).

### 8.3.2 Searle's Chinese Room Thought Experiment

A man is placed into a closed room into which Chinese writing symbols are input to him. He is given a rulebook that shows him how to manipulate the symbols to produce Chinese output. He has no idea as to what each symbol means, but with the rulebook he is able to produce the Chinese output. This allows him to communicate with the other person and appear to understand Chinese. The rulebook allows him to answer any questions posed, without the slightest understanding of what he is doing or what the symbols mean (Fig. 8.3).

1. Chinese characters are entered through slot 1.
2. The rulebook is employed to construct new Chinese characters.
3. Chinese characters are outputted to slot 2.

The question "*Do you understand Chinese?*" could potentially be asked, and the rulebook would be consulted to produce the answer "Yes, of course" despite the fact that the person inside the room has not the faintest idea of what is going on. It will appear to the person outside the room that the person inside is knowledgeable on Chinese. The person inside is just following rules without understanding.

**Fig. 8.3** Searle's Chinese room

The process is essentially that of a computer program that takes an input; performs a computation based on the input; and then finally produces an output. Searle has essentially constructed a machine that can never be mental. Changing the program essentially means changing the rulebook, and this does not increase understanding. The strong artificial intelligence thesis states that given the right program, *any* machine running it would be mental. However, Searle argues that the program for this Chinese room would not understand anything, and that therefore the strong AI thesis must be false [Sea:80].

In other words, *Searle's Chinese room argument is a rebuttal of strong AI* by showing that a program running on a machine that appears to be intelligent has no real understanding whatsoever of the symbols that it is manipulating. That is, given any rulebook (i.e., program), the person would never understand the meanings of those characters that are manipulated (i.e., symbol manipulation or syntax is not the same as semantics).

That is, the Chinese Room argument is a refutation of *functionalism* (i.e., the idea that mental states are defined solely by their functional role of inputs and outputs rather than internal makeup) by showing that manipulating symbols according to rules (*syntax*) does not equate to understanding their meaning (*semantics*). Computer programs are purely syntactical (formal symbol manipulation), whereas human minds possess semantic content (meaning). Another words, a computer, or the person in the Chinese room, can process inputs to produce correct outputs without any comprehension. This means that simulation is not the same as actual understanding, consciousness or mental states.

That is, just because the machine acts like it knows what is going on, it actually only knows what it is programmed to know. It differs from humans in that it is not aware of the situation like humans are, and suggests that machines may not have intelligence or consciousness. The Chinese room argument applies to any Turing equivalent computer simulation.

There are several rebuttals of Searle's position, and one well-known rebuttal attempt is the "*System Reply*" argument. This reply argues that if a result associated with intelligence is produced, then intelligence must be found somewhere in the system. The proponents of this argument draw an analogy between the human brain and its constituents. None of its constituents have intelligence but the system as a whole (i.e., the brain) exhibits intelligence. Similarly, the parts of the Chinese room may lack intelligence, but the system as a whole is intelligence.

## 8.4 Some Philosophical Questions in AI

We present a selection of relevant questions in the philosophy of AI in Table 8.1, and we then discuss a small number of these in more detail.

There is an aphorism attributed to Dijkstra that states that *the question as to whether machines or programs can think is about as relevant as the question as to whether submarines can swim.* That is, perhaps there has been an over-focus on developing machines with anthropomorphic intelligence, by asking whether a machine can duplicate human intelligence, and embarking on various imitation games such as the Turing Test. Perhaps, it is a mistake to focus on human-like intelligence, and instead one should focus on useful machines that simulate intelligence, and that hopefully will serve humanity.

It is clear that substantial reflection is required to give reasonable answers on some of these important philosophical questions, and we consider a selection of these questions in the remainder of the chapter.

### 8.4.1 What Is Mind?

We discussed the question of whether a computer can have a mind in Chap. 4, and noted that Dennett argued that machines, in principle, could have minds, given that human brains have evolved to form complex machines, and he rejected the view that the human mind is special as such.

The concept of mind is difficult to define, but it seems to refer to the nature of mind itself, the relationship between mind and body, and the relationship between mind and the external world. The mind is concerned with thinking, feeling, perceiving, imagining and all mental phenomena (whether conscious or unconscious). The mind, in a sense, takes sensory input and builds models, and everything that we know is based on these models. Models never capture every detail of reality, but generally provide enough to determine the appropriate response (Fig. 8.4).

A human being, according to Plato, consists of a non-material mind (or soul) and a physical body. Plato considered the human mind (or soul) as an indivisible substance that pre-existed in a super-sensible world of ideas, but which unites with the human body to form the human person in the sensible world. The soul is the abode of reason, emotion and sensual feeling.

Descartes formulated the Cartesian view of mind and body, and he states that there are two substances namely *mental substances* and *bodily substances*. Cartesian Dualism makes a clear *mind-body* distinction, with the mind being a distinct and independently existing *immaterial* substance (*res cogitans*), and the body being a physical *material* substance (*res extensa*), and subject to the scientific laws of the physical world.

**Table 8.1** Some philosophical questions in AI

| Question | Initial Answer |
|---|---|
| What is mind? | This question is an enquiry into the nature of the mind and mental phenomena, and its relation to the body and the external world. It explores what a mind is and how we can know anything about it |
| What is thinking? | This question is an enquiry into the nature of thought, and includes an examination of cognitive and mental processes for reasoning and problem solving |
| Can a computer think? | This is an enquiry into whether machines or the programs running on them can think. The question is whether this might be possible with powerful machines with rapid processing power dealing with vast amounts of data |
| Can a computer act as a mind? | This enquires into whether an appropriately programmed computer (i.e., programmed to function exactly like a human brain) would have a mind |
| What is the mind-body problem? | This is an enquiry into how the concepts of mind and body relate, and how thought and consciousness interact with the physiological processes in the human body |
| What is the nature of self? | This is an enquiry of, in a sense, the core essence of a person, where the self seems to reflect some personal inner sense in what that person is and how that person behaves |
| What is intelligence? | There is no consensus definition of intelligence, but it seems to refer to the ability to solve complex problems as well as making decisions that provide good outcomes |
| What is consciousness? | Consciousness is, in a sense, an awareness of self and the internal world of perception, introspection and thought, as well as the external world. It is characterised by awareness of contents in one's mind such as ideas, thoughts and emotions |
| What is the relationship between consciousness and unconsciousness? | Consciousness seems to be awareness of oneself, the environment, one's thoughts and emotions, whereas unconsciousness seems to be a lack of awareness of self, etc., such as a temporary loss during the state of sleep or dozing off, or a longer period as a result of a coma arising from an accident |

(continued)

**Table 8.1** (continued)

| Question | Initial Answer |
|---|---|
| Can a computer be conscious? | This enquires into whether an appropriately programmed computer (i.e., programmed to function exactly like a human brain) would have a conscious mind like a human |
| Can AI be trusted? | This enquires into the extent that AI systems can be trusted in the decisions that they make, or actions that they take. Machines may suffer from reliability problems and make poor decisions |
| What ethical problems arise in AI? | Several ethical problems arise with AI technology such as who is held liable if the AI system makes an incorrect decision that leads to damage, injury or loss of life. Other problems arise from biased algorithms that may cause harm due to bias in the training data of machine-learning algorithms |
| What is knowledge? | This is concerned with how knowledge is obtained including the sources of knowledge such as sense perception and reason, as well the relationship between belief and truth, and whether knowledge is even possible |
| How do the limits of computation affect AI?<br>What are the limits of AI? | The halting problem shows that there are fundamental limits to what may be computed, and how intelligent an artificial entity may be (i.e., there are problems that it may not solve (e.g., the halting problem) may not be solved by algorithm). The limits of computation suggests that human-level intelligence cannot be achieved through computation alone—i.e., algorithms do not possess human intuition and insight (non-algorithmic reasoning) which is part of the human condition. Further, the halting problem suggests limits to the usefulness of formal systems, given that the Hilbert program failed in its goals to define a formal system of mathematics that was complete, consistent and decidable |

That is, the *thinking thing* (mind/soul) is immaterial and distinct from the rest of nature, and interacts with the world through the senses to gain knowledge. Descartes states that the mind interacts with the body through the pineal gland (a part of the brain), but, *it is unclear how an immaterial object such as a mind could interact and influence (in a cause-effect manner) a material object such as the body.*

Locke disagreed with the Cartesian view of the world and rejected innate ideas. He stated that a child's brain is a clean slate (*tabula rasa*) at birth, and that all of our knowledge comes to us through our senses: i.e., it can be traced back to sense perception and reflection. Hume attempted to define the basic laws by which the human mind operates in order to explain the nature and extent of human knowledge. He divided the perceptions of the mind into two distinct kinds: namely

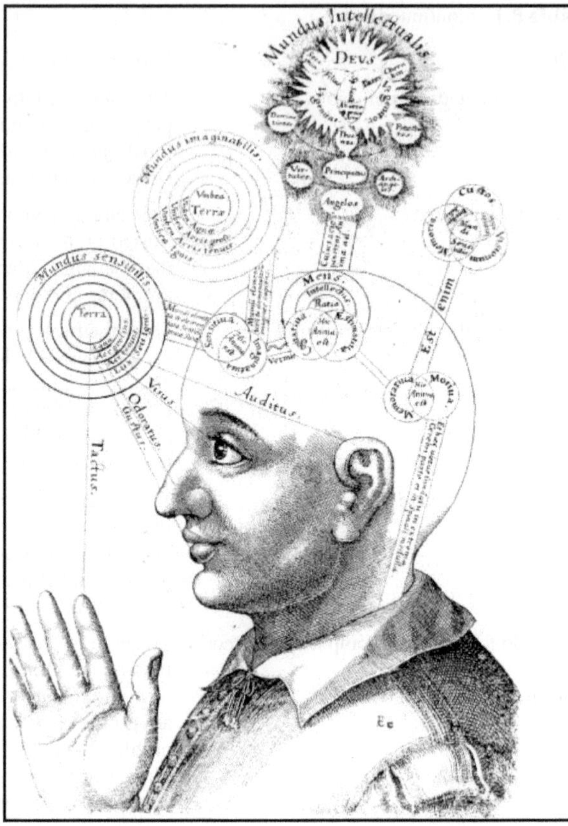


**Fig. 8.4** Mind and consciousness

impressions and ideas, where impressions refer to the most lively perceptions, and ideas (copies of our impressions) refer to less lively perceptions, such as reflecting on a previous sensation.

Hume suggests that words express ideas in the minds of a subject speaking or hearing the word, and so if one has concerns on the cognitive content of a philosophical term, one should look to the idea expressed by it. If there is no corresponding idea then we are justified in criticising the use of the term. Alternatively, if we *do* find an idea, then we should trace the idea back to the corresponding impression, which constitutes the meaning of the idea. If no such connection between idea and impression may be made, then the idea does not have cognitive content, and is, *meaningless*.

*Hume argued that the concept of self is illusionary in that it is really nothing more than a bunch of perceptions*, in that if we search for self all that we will find is some perceptions. He argues that the creative power of the mind such as thought and knowledge is actually nothing more than a combination or re-combination of ideas and impressions (i.e., the material given to us by sense and experience). The combination of ideas and impressions is from three types of association (resemblance, contiguity and cause and effect). Hume noted the fundamental importance of cause and effect in causal reasoning, which he considered the key tool for knowledge acquisition in the world.

Kant rejected the Cartesian view of mind, and argued instead that mind organises experience in various ways. For *Kant, the mind is not a separate mental substance; rather, it is the organization and unity of man's personal experiences.* That is, mind is active and it systematically organises the materials presented to it by the senses, to provide knowledge of the phenomena. *Kant formulated the functionalist view of the mind* (*i.e., the mind is a complex set of abilities or functions*), well before its modern formulation by Hilary Putman and others in the 1960s [Put:60].

The functions are essential for mental and knowledge-generation, and Kant argued that functions perform spatio-temporal processing of sensory input and apply concepts in the processing. The *functionalist view of mind takes the position that mental states are defined by what they do rather than by what they are made of*, *and that each and every mental state is constituted solely by its functional role.* Searle's Chinese room thought experiment is a refutation of functionalism, and shows that it is an inadequate theory of mind since it does not produce understanding (i.e., syntax is not semantics).

Modern views on the philosophy of mind generally maintain that the mind is not something separate from the body. Some theories argue that mental states and properties are (or will eventually be) explained by scientific accounts of physiological processes and states (*reductive physicalists*), or mental properties *supervene* on physical properties (i.e., a change in the mental property entails a change in the physical property) (*non-reductive physicalists*). Another modern position is that mental states are nothing other than neural states, and so mental phenomena may be discussed usually with a physical vocabulary (*neurophilosophy*).

There is a variant of dualism called *property dualism*, which takes the view that the world consists of one substance, but two properties namely mental and physical properties. Descartes was a *substance dualist* who believed that mind and body were two distinct substances, whereas property dualists reject this position, and argue instead for one substance and two distinct properties).

Gilbert Ryle rejected Cartesian dualism, and he argued that instead the mind and body are not separate entities as proposed by Descartes, but are instead intertwined and interdependent. That is, mental states and mental processes are not separate from bodily behaviour, but are instead intertwined with each other (i.e., he takes a behavioural view of mind, and argues that the mind is the manner or the way in which a person behaves).

Dennett also rejected Cartesian dualism and he argued that the mind is entirely physical, with the mind and consciousness being entirely physical processes. He argued that the experience of consciousness is really an illusion, and that instead what we have are mental states that are simply physical brain functions. He rejects that there is a single place in the brain where consciousness resides, and that instead what is happening is multiple streams of processing occurring in parallel.

That is, there are competing streams of content such as various sensory input or thoughts running in competition, with the one becoming dominant for a moment and guiding our behaviour.

He viewed minds as biological functional machines, and notes that some of our behaviour is due to our animal nature (we share 99% of our DNA with chimpanzees), but our brains have evolved over hundreds of millions of years.

### 8.4.2 What Is Consciousness?

Consciousness is a very difficult concept to define, but it seems to refer to, in a sense, the awareness that we have of our self as well as our environment and surroundings in the external world, as well as our awareness of our inner world of thoughts and ideas. That is, consciousness includes awareness of our own being, our thoughts, emotions and experiences, as well as our abilities to use our senses to perceive the external world around us, and to internalise our perceptions as inner knowledge. It allows introspection of our thoughts, experience and knowledge, as well as the ability to take appropriate action in response to sensory input. Consciousness is related to intelligence, but it is not the same as intelligence.

In a way, consciousness seems to involve the integration of several brain networks, allowing us to perceive our surroundings as a whole by integrating all of our sensory inputs into one unified experience, rather than as separate sensory perceptions. Consciousness seems to act like a kind of inner witness to our life, in that it is, in a sense, continually watching the world of our thoughts, emotions and perceptions. We seem to be aware of an image in a similar way to the way that we are aware of ourselves looking at an image, and similarly for thoughts and emotions. But, where exactly does consciousness come from? Where exactly is consciousness? Does it arise as a result of brain activity? How is it related to mind? How is consciousness built into the brain? Is it supernatural?

Inanimate objects do not have consciousness as such, and so consciousness seems to belong to the world of sentient creatures, and especially to the world of fish, animals and humans.[9] It seems reasonable to suggest that the level of consciousness of a particular species of fish or animal depends on its sensory apparatus (e.g., does it have vision capabilities, auditory capabilities, and olfactory capabilities?). Does it have an internal representation of the world? Has it memory? Does it have awareness of time? Does it have awareness of others including competitors and predators? Has it awareness of language? How has the species evolved over time?

[9] Spinoza's concept of the universe in his pantheism suggests that God and nature as two names for the same reality, and so he rejected Cartesian dualism and instead argued for monism (the idea that there is one substance). He states that everything in existence is an expression of both thought (mental) and extension (matter), and so a rock has a basic form of awareness from these attributes. Spinoza argues that the mental and the physical are not separate as such, but, in a sense, are two sides of the same coin.

The English empiricist philosopher, John Locke, defined consciousness as the perception of what passes in a man's mind [Loc:1690], with Hume equating consciousness with thought and reflection, in that he states that consciousness is nothing more than a reflection on a thought or perception.

There have been various views among modern philosophers of the problem of consciousness, with Dennett arguing that consciousness is not a mysterious property or phenomenon as such, and that it is instead a complicated variety of different things. He sees it more as competing streams of content such as various sensory input or thoughts running in competition and fighting for influence, with the one that wins being dominant for a moment and guiding our behaviour. He sees the sense of unified consciousness as being illusionary [Den:91].

Neuroscience continues to investigate aspects of the relationship between brain activity and subjective conscious experience, and perhaps one day it may be able to directly relate consciousness to brain activity. O'Nualláin (discussed in the next section) argues that consciousness as a multi-layered process that is grounded in biology.

### 8.4.3 Can a Computer Be Conscious?

We discussed the question of whether a computer can have consciousness in Sect. 4.4.4, and this controversial debate is unresolved. Computers today lack the structure of the human brain needed for conscious experience, but many experts believe that future AI systems may potentially develop consciousness, whereas others argues that irrespective of how advanced computers become that they will always just simulate human-behaviour.

Modern computers are digital machines that operate on pre-defined rules and algorithms, and they are capable of simulating intelligent behaviour, but do not experience consciousness at this time. As computing technology evolves, it is possible that future systems will have more complex, brain-like architectures that may potentially open up the possibility of consciousness, but it is unclear how this could be achieved.

We discussed the Turing test of machine intelligence and its rebuttal by Searle's Chinese room argument, which showed that a computer could simulate intelligence and understanding without actually understanding. And so, at this time, it seems plausible to suggest that even if a computer could simulate consciousness (whatever that is), there is no certainty that it would be conscious, and in all likelihood it would not be.

Modern computers are digital rather than analog, and it would seem more likely that an analog computer could experience consciousness (however unlikely that may be) rather than a digital computer, as analog signals seem more suitable as a representation of consciousness, since its signals are continuous and vary smoothly over time, whereas digital signals are discrete and consist of the values 1 and 0, and so it is unclear how consciousness would be represented in binary values.

The Halting problem suggests that there are fundamental limits to how intelligent an artificial entity may be, given that there are some problems that may not be solved by algorithm, as well as limits on the extent of intelligence gained from computation alone. That is, algorithms do not possess human intuition and insight (non-algorithmic reasoning), which is an important part of human intelligence and the human condition.

O'Nualláin argues that consciousness is a multi-layered process that is grounded in biology and structured by language, and involves interaction between neural activity, bodily states and symbolic systems. He argues that consciousness cannot be fully explained by strong computationalism (i.e., the idea that the brain is just software running on hardware). That is, computation explains some mental functions but not subjectivity itself. Consciousness is not explained by treating the mind as computation or symbolic processing alone, and he is critical of the view that simulation of the brain automatically simulates consciousness.

He argues that computation does not automatically generate subjectivity, and he states that the brain is necessary but not sufficient to explain subjective experience. He argues that the human sense of self emerges from language (i.e., from symbolic and linguistic systems), and that it is not just biological. That is, he argues that language is the core of self, and that the human self is fundamentally linguistic. He suggests that the self is a partially fragmented construct (with competing subsystems in the brain) rather than a unified inner entity. O'Nualláin proposed a three-level architecture of mind:

- Level 1 is biological/neural
- Level 2 is cognitive/representational
- Level 3 is symbolic/linguistic

Level 1 (biological/neural) is concerned with basic sensory processing and motor control. Level 2 (cognitive/representational) is concerned with concepts, memory and reasoning. Level 3 (symbolic/linguistic) is concerned with language, identity, self reflection and abstraction. O Nualláin sees consciousness emerging from the interaction across levels (not from just one level) [ONu:13].

It is possible that future computing technologies and radically different architectures may enable the emergence of conscious artificial entities.

### 8.4.4 What Is Knowledge?

Epistemology is the branch of philosophy that examines the nature of knowledge, including the sources of knowledge such as sense perception and reason, as well the relationship between belief and truth. It considers scepticism, which questions whether knowledge is possible, and whether it is possible to refute scepticism. Epistemology considers questions such as "What do people know? How do they know?", and "How are beliefs justified? (Fig. 8.5).

**Fig. 8.5** Early childhood education

There are several positions on how knowledge may be obtained about the world. Plato considered the nature of knowledge in the Theatetus, and he initially examines whether knowledge is perception, but he shows that this position is untenable. Plato argues that the world of appearances is unreliable, as the senses deceive and so cannot be trusted. Therefore, for Plato, knowledge is in the world of ideas, rather than the world of appearances, and knowledge may be gained deductively as in mathematics.

Descartes aimed to develop a sound system of knowledge, and so he took the strongest argument of the sceptics by doubting everything that may be doubted. From this, he realised that while he could reject almost everything that could be doubted, he could still be certain of one fundamental fact namely his own existence as a thinking being (*cogito, ergo sum*). Descartes then derived a proof for the existence of God, and argued that as God does not wish to deceive that he can have some trust in his senses. He then reconstructed the edifice of knowledge using logical deduction from known premises and innate knowledge. His theory of knowledge is known as Rationalism.

British empiricism rejected the Cartesian project, and argued that all knowledge is gained by sense experience, rather than by innate ideas. We discussed the work of key figures in British empiricism such as Locke, Berkeley and Hume, and we showed that Hume's account led to problems in justifying causation and induction (thereby undermining the foundations of science), as well as problems with the nature of self (the self, according to Hume, is nothing more than a bunch of perceptions).

Kant described his approach to epistemology as a Copernican revolution in philosophy, and it aimed to provide a bridge between the opposing epistemological standpoints of Rationalism and Empiricism. He argued that there is a third force in human knowledge that provides concepts that can't be inferred from experience. Such concepts include the laws of logic (e.g., modus ponens), causality, and so on.

Kant argued that the third force is the manner in which the human mind structures its experiences, and he argues that some of our knowledge is "*a priori*" and independent of experience, whereas some other knowledge is "*a posteriori*" and depends on empirical evidence. However, he argued that some of our knowledge (e.g., arithmetic, geometry and causation) is what he calls *synthetic* but *a priori* (see Chap. 2). He argues that the outer world causes only the matter of sensation, whereas our own mental apparatus orders this in terms of space and time, and supplies the concepts by which we understand experience.

That is, Kant argues that human understanding is structured by concepts of understanding that are present in the mind prior to experience, and which make outer experience possible. A person would not experience the world as an orderly place unless space, time and causality were determinant functions of our perception apparatus. For Kant, things in themselves (*noumena*), which are the causes of our sensations, are unknowable, in contrast to the object of our senses (*phenomena*).

The philosophy of knowledge split into two camps in the twentieth century, with *analytic philosophy* (e.g., figures such as Russell and Wittgenstein) focusing on logic, language and scientific methods) and *continental philosophy* (figures such as Husserl and Sartre) focusing on phenomenology (the study of the structure of experience and consciousness) and existentialism (the study of individual freedom and existence).

### 8.4.5 What Is Intelligence?

Intelligence is a difficult concept to describe as it encompasses many areas, and so a universally acceptable definition is elusive. It includes the ability to gather information about the world through our senses, responding appropriately to sensory stimuli from the environment, storing information in memory and recalling it when needed, logical reasoning and calculation, communication in written or spoken languages, the ability to learn a new skill via a sequence of repeatable behaviours that may be varied and adapted, the ability to learn and understand theoretical concepts, the ability to remember, to acquire knowledge, to be creative, to abstract and problem solve, to planning, to forming strategies, to perform logic and mathematics, engage in critical thinking, and the ability to form teams to work on problems that require the involvement of more than one person.

And so, intelligence, in a sense, is not a single thing as such, and perhaps a more appropriate definition is that it is like a toolbox that consists of a collection of tools such as perception, reflection, reason, creativity, and so on. The ability to solve complex problems, to adapt to one's environment, learn from experience, as well as making good decisions are important characteristics of intelligent behaviour, and consciousness is related to intelligence, as awareness is an essential part of problem solving.

There are many unanswered questions on the nature of intelligence. Do mental phenomena originate from the mind or the brain? The nature of intelligence is generally considered in terms of mind and brain, with intelligence considered a mental act (e.g., thoughts, emotions, perceptions, etc.) originating from the human brain or mind. And so, intelligence seems to require a brain and a mind, and so an entity without these would seem to lack intelligence.

Further, if mental acts originate from the mind then the nature of mind needs to be understood, or if mental states originate from the physical brain then the nature of the brain needs to be understood. The question is how can a material substance such as the brain account for mental acts (unless mental acts are themselves a material substance as well)?

The latter leads to a materialist theory of mind, with mental acts accompanying bodily processes, and where matter is the real substance—that is, certain processes taking place in the brain produce the emotions and feelings that we experience. Some theories argue that mental states are explained by scientific accounts of physiological processes and states, or mental properties *supervene* on physical properties, where a change in the mental property entails a change in the physical property. Another view is that mental states are nothing other than neural states.

Searle identified several features of mental phenomena that he considered essential to intelligence, and these include *consciousness* (as discussed previously), *intentionality* (the feature that mental states are directed at), and *subjectivity*[10] (the unique experience of each individual when in a mental state). Searle argues that being intelligent is to be in a mental state that is directed at states of affairs in the world. Further, he argues that all mental phenomena and all our mental life are caused by processes going on in the brain[11] [Sea:84].

That is, if Searle is correct (and there are objections to his position), then all that is required to know if a person or entity is intelligent is a detailed examination of the brain of the entity. Chalmer asks the interesting question as to how a physical system such as a brain may also be an experiencer? [Cha:96].

### 8.4.6 What Is the Mind Body Problem?

The mind-body problem is concerned with understanding the relation between the mind and body, and dates back to Descartes in his formulation of the dualism of mind and body, and how they relate to and affect one another. In a sense, the characteristic properties of mind and body are like oil and water: i.e., they do not mix, as they are very different. Similarly, the body consists of matter and is spatial, whereas the mind is mental and not spatial—i.e., they are so different that their

[10] The subjectivity of mental states is often referred to as *qualia*, which denotes the unique experience of each individual when in a mental state.

[11] There is evidence for this in patients that have suffered brain damage (loss of cognitive functions and mental states), as well as in the working of a normal brain (different parts become active depending on mental state of the individual).

interaction should be impossible. And so, we wish to explore these concepts, as well as exploring the nature of mental phenomena, and whether mental phenomena are a subset of physical phenomena or not.

Descartes argues that the characteristic of mind is that it is conscious, whereas the brain has physical characteristics and occupies space: i.e., our bodies are in space whereas our minds are not. However, Descartes argues that while mind and matter are distinct substances, it is false to say that they cannot act on each other (Fig. 8.6).

However, if Descartes is correct then we have what seems to be a contradictory situation of that which is not in space (i.e., the mind) acting on that which is in space (i.e., the body), and if this is to happen then the action on the body must take place at the position in space where the body is (i.e., the mind must make contact with the body in space and so be physical). For example, if I decide to lift a cup and take a sip of tea, then my arm moves accordingly—but, it is difficult to see how the thought could make that happen.

Descartes response to this criticism was that the mind interacts with the body through the pineal gland. However, his solution can be criticised as not solving the problem, as the question now becomes how the mind interacts with the pineal gland in the body.

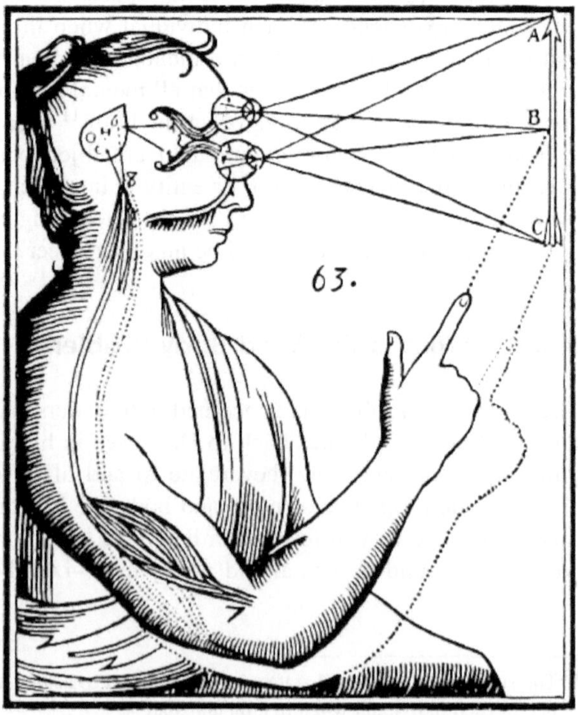


**Fig. 8.6** Descartes mind body dualism

The mind–body problem is, in a sense, two distinct problems. The first problem is concerned with the nature of mental phenomena such as whether they are physical or not. The second problem is concerned with defining the essence of mental phenomena such as consciousness and intentionality, and whether these can be explained in physical terms.

## 8.5 Negative Societal Impacts of AI

AI technologies offer enormous benefits to society, but their introduction into daily life has led to several negative societal impacts. These include the displacement of jobs from AI-driven automation, especially in areas where work is repetitive, data driven and rules based. Another negative impact is the problem with biased data, where AI technologies tend to reinforce or amplify bias and potentially causing harm to individuals. There are problems with the erosion of privacy due to the massive amount of data collected on individuals, as well as the danger of mass surveillance of individuals by the state. There are dangers of misinformation and fabrication of events, as well as the dangers of fake content provided on deepfake videos. Finally, a small number of large tech companies control advanced AI systems, which means that they have a disproportionate influence on society.

Among the sectors that AI automation is likely to impact are assembly, manufacturing, robotics, clerical work and customer service, call centres and various job-entry roles. AI is likely to negatively impact employment is society, with estimates that millions (perhaps hundreds of millions) of workers will be negatively affected.

Large language models (LLM) are machine-learning models that recognise and generate human-language text. That is, they are AI programs built on neural networks that are trained on huge sets of data, and LLMs use a type of machine learning called *deep learning* that involves the probabilistic analysis of unstructured data. Deep learning analyses trillions of sentences to predict how to finish a sentence or to generate its own sentences.

LLMs are used in generative AI where they give a response when a user asks a question where they produce text such as essays, programs, poems, and so on. OpenAI's ChatGPT and Google's Gemini are two popular LLMs, but LLMs are only as good as the underlying data that they have been trained on, and so if they have been trained on false or misleading information, then they will provide inaccurate information.

The success of generative AI and LLMs have led to unintended consequences, where, for example, the technology may be used by students to create essays or assignments, instead of creating their own work.

The area of deepfake technology where AI clones of influential individuals in society are created, and this has the potential to destroy trust in society. Traditionally, a photograph never lied, but today this is no longer the case as these disruptive technologies allow photos or videos to be manipulated, as well as the manipulation of dialogue with voice technology to create counterfeit people who appear to be inciting hatred or saying things incompatible with their traditional values. They have mainly used for parody, but such technologies could potentially be used for more sinister purposes leading to an erosion of trust in society. Chap. 14 discusses ethical issues in AI in more detail.

## 8.6 Review Questions

1. What is Artificial Intelligence.
2. What is the Turing Test.
3. Explain the significance of Searle's Chinese room.
4. Explain the relevance of Descartes to the AI field.
5. What is mind?
6. What is knowledge?
7. What is consciousness?
8. What is intelligence?
9. Explain the relevance of ChatGPT.

## 8.7 Summary

Artificial Intelligence is a young field and John McCarthy and others coined the term in the mid 1950s. Alan Turing devised the Turing Test as a way to test the intelligent behaviour of a machine, and to determine whether it is possible for a machine to be conscious and to think. Searle devised the "Chinese Room" thought experiment as a rebuttal of strong AI, and shows that even if a computer passes the Turing Test that it still could not be judged to be intelligent: i.e., syntax is not semantics.

Descartes makes a clear mind-body distinction in that he states that there are two substances in the universe: mental substances and bodily substances. The mind-body distinction is relevant in AI, with the analogy of the human mind and brain is software running on a computer.

Artificial Intelligence is a multi-disciplinary field and includes disciplines such as: Computing, Logic and Philosophy, Psychology, Linguistics, Neuroscience and Neural Networks, Machine Vision, Robotics, Expert Systems, Machine Translation, Epistemology and Knowledge Representation and Ethics.

## References


[Bie:23] ChatGPT broke the Turing Test – the race is on for new ways to assess AI. Celeste Biever. Nature, 25th July, 2023

[Cha:96] The Conscious Mind, David J. Chalmers. Oxford University Press. 1996.

[Den:91] Consciousness Explained. Little, Brown and Co. Daniel Dennett. 1991.

[Des:99] Discourse on Method and Meditations on First Philosophy, 4th Edition. Rene Descartes. Translated by Donald Cress. Hackett Publishing Company. 1999.
[Loc:1690] An Essay Concerning Human Understanding. John Locke. 1690.
[Mc:59] Programs with Common Sense. John McCarthy. Proceedings of the Teddington Conference on the Mechanization of Thought Processes. 1959.
[ONu:13] The Search for Mind. Seán O' Nualláin. Intellect Books. 2013.
[Put:60] Minds and Machines. Hilary Putman. In Hook & Sidney. Dimensions of Mind. A Symposium, pp. 138–164. New York University Press 1960.
[RuW:10] Principia Mathematica. B. Russell and A.N. Whitehead. Cambridge University Press. Cambridge. 1910.
[Sea:80] Minds, Brains and Programs. John Searle. 1980.
[Sea:84] Minds, Brains and Science. John Searle. Harvard University Press. 1984.
[Tur:50] Computing, Machinery and Intelligence. Alan Turing. Mind (49). Pages 433-460. 1950.

# A Brief History of Ethics

# 9

## 9.1 Introduction

Ethics is a practical branch of philosophy that deals with moral questions such as what is the right thing to do in a particular situation, and in dealing with conflicts between individual moral values and the values of an organisation or society. How should one live a good life? How should a person behave in a given situation in a complex world? Ethics explores what actions are right or wrong within a specific context or within a particular society, and attempts to find satisfactory answers to moral questions. Ethics provides a framework to think critically about moral problems and moral values, and assist in forming a judgment on the most appropriate way to proceed in a situation where there is a conflict between values, and where the individual is trying to do the right thing.

There are various schools of ethics such as the *relativist* position (as defined by Protagoras and described in Plato's Theaetetus), which argues that each person decides on what is right or wrong and so it rejects the idea of objective truth; *cultural relativism* (which is a variant of the relativist position) argues that the particular society determines what is right or wrong based upon its cultural values; *deontological ethics* (as defined by Kant) argues that there are moral laws to guide people in deciding what is right or wrong, and that everyone has a duty to act in accordance with the moral law; and *utilitarianism* (as defined by Bentham and refined by Mill) which argues that an action is right if its overall affect is to produce more happiness than unhappiness in society.

Religion plays an important role in developing ethical and moral behaviour in society, and we discuss the contribution of a selection of the great religions of the world including Christianity, Islam and Buddhism. We briefly discuss traditional Chinese ethics; utilitarianism as proposed by Bentham and Mill; deontological ethics as proposed by Kant, and virtue ethics as described in ancient Greek philosophy. Finally, we discuss informally how an individual can be ethical in a complex

 
G. O'Regan, *Philosophical and Cultural Aspects of Computing*, Undergraduate Topics in Computer Science, https://doi.org/10.1007/978-3-032-29284-1_9

world, and investigate how to create an ethical environment in an organisation to support ethical decision-making. A short history of ethics is available in [Mac:95].

## 9.2 Ethics in Ancient Civilisations

The changes in human lifestyle from traditional nomadic or migratory societies to settled communities posed new challenges as to how these communities should live together in peaceful harmony, and to how they should resolve any disputes that arose between them. This led to basic regulation of settled communities to protect people and property, and often there was a role for the elders in the community to mediate and resolve conflicts that arose between members of the community. Over time, this led to systematic legal code to regulate behaviour, where victims were compensated for damage to property or the person, and offenders were punished for their misdemeanours.

One of the earliest systematic codes was the famous Hammurabi code that was introduced in Mesopotamia[1] c.1750 B.C., and it is named after King Hammurabi of Babylon. The code focused on awarding harsh penalties to the perpetrators of crime, and an appropriate physical punishment was given for specific crimes. It is one of the earliest legal codes where it is presumed that the accused person is innocent until proven guilty (Fig. 9.1).

Personal injury involving the aristocracy involved the principle of *lex talionis* (the principle of retribution: i.e., an eye for an eye), where the perpetrator received as punishment precisely those injuries or damage that they had inflicted on their victims, whereas fines sufficed for injuries to slaves or freemen. That is, the law protected the aristocrat over the freeman and slave.

Careless or inefficient behaviour could result in fines for damages, with serious crimes subject to harsh punishments such as the removal of the perpetrator's tongue, hands, eye or ear. There are over 280 edicts in the code that are written

[1] The origin of the word "Mesopotamia" is from the Greek words μεσος (mesos meaning middle) and ποταμος (potamos meaning river), and so it means the land between rivers. It was located between the Tigris and Euphrates rivers, and included modern Iraq as well as parts of Syria, Turkey, Iran and Kuwait. It is known as the "cradle of civilisation", since several of the earliest civilisations and empires emerged from there. These civilisations spanned a period of several thousand years (approx. 3–4000 years), with early civilisations including the Sumerians and the Akkadians (located in different parts of Mesopotamia), and later civilisations including the Babylonians and the Assyrians located in the southern and northern part of Mesopotamia respectively. Some of the famous Mesopotamian sites include Ur, Akkad, Babylon, Assur, Nimrud, and Nineveh. Mesopotamia led to many important inventions that changed the world such as the wheel, maps, and writing (cuneiform script), as well as having impacts on mathematics, astronomy, religion (it was a polytheistic religion), philosophy (it influenced early Greek and Hellenistic philosophy), medicine and law. Its most famous work of literature is the well-known Sumerian "Epic of Gilgamesh", which is a huge work about a legendary king of Uruk and his search for immortality. Mesopotamia came under the control of Cyrus the Great of Persia c. 539 B.C., and Alexander the Great conquered the Persian Empire c. 331 B.C.

**Fig. 9.1** Code of hammurabi stele. Louvre museum. Creative commons

in the form of IF-THEN statements covering family law, professional contracts and administrative law, with different standards of justice provided for the three classes in Babylonian society (i.e., the nobility, free people not belonging to the upper class, and slaves).

The ethical system at the heart of the ancient Egypt was based on *ma'at*, a word that signified justice or balance, and it provided the foundation for ethical behaviour and judgment. Egyptians were expected to live in harmony with *ma'at*, and ethical norms that sustained *ma'at* were taught in scribal schools. The Egyptians had a strong belief in the afterlife and had a concept of ethical judgement of the deceased person.[2] The Egyptian 'Book of the Dead' listed sins that the deceased would recite and give a negative confession.

[2] This ritual involved weighing the deceased person's heart against a feather, and if the heart weighed less than a feather (i.e., a light hearted person) then the deceased was judged to be a good person.

## 9.3 Ethics in Ancient Greece

The Greeks made major contributions to western civilization including mathematics, logic, astronomy, philosophy, politics, drama, and architecture. The Greek world of 500 B.C. consisted of several independent city-states such as Athens and Sparta in what is now mainland Greece, and various city-states in Asia Minor such as Ephesus, Miletus and Pergamon. The Greek polis (πολις) or city-state tended to be quite small, and it consisted of the Greek city and a certain amount of territory outside the city. Each city-state had its own unique political structure for its citizens: some were oligarchs where political power was maintained in the hands of a few individuals or aristocratic families; others were ruled by tyrants (or sole rulers) who sometimes took power by force, but who often had a lot of support from the public. These included people such as Solon, Peisistratus and Cleisthenes in Athens.

The reforms by Cleisthenes in the sixth century B.C. led to the introduction of the Athenian democracy. Power was placed in the hands of the citizens who were male (women and slaves did not participate in the Athenian democracy). It was an extremely liberal democracy where citizens voted on all of the important issues. Often, this led to disastrous results as speakers who were skilled in rhetoric could exert significant influence in the Athenian assembly (e.g., the decision that the assembly made that led to the disastrous Sicilian expedition during the Peloponnesian war). The failures of Athenian democracy (including its decision to execute the well-known moral philosopher, Socrates) led Plato to reject democracy as a system of rule, and he instead advocated rule by philosopher kings (as described in Plato's Republic).

The rise of Macedonia led to the Greek city-states being conquered by Philip of Macedonia in the fourth century B.C. His son, Alexander the Great, defeated the Persian Empire, and he extended his empire to include most of the known world. This led to the *Hellenistic Age* (derived from 'ελλαζ meaning Greece), where Greek language and culture spread throughout the empire. Alexander founded the city of Alexandria, and it became a major centre of learning in Ptolemaic Egypt.[3] However, Alexander's reign was very short as he died at the young age of 33 in 323 B.C.

Ethics in Greek philosophy is concerned with rational thought and the search for appropriate principles to guide human conduct. It is characterised by its faith in reason to do the right thing. The fundamental question asked by Socrates and other Greek philosophers was how should a man live, in order to achieve a good life (*eudaimonia*)? That is, how should a man live in order that we may reasonably say that he has lived successfully? Another words, what is the nature of the good life for man? Socrates argued that the ways of man can and need to be justified by

[3] The ancient library in Alexandria was once the largest library in the world. It was build during the Hellenistic period in the third century B.C. and destroyed by fire in 391 A.D.

rational means, and ultimately in terms of an individual's self interest, and *arête* (moral virtue or excellence) is necessary for a good life.

Socrates[4] was a moral philosopher who actually wrote nothing on philosophy, but a clear picture on his views and approach to philosophy may be seen in, Plato's early dialogues.[5] Plato's early dialogues reflect the views of the historical Socrates, and the later dialogues use Socrates as a mouthpiece to reflect the views of the mature Plato.

Socrates claimed a total lack of knowledge (*Socratic ignorance*), and he often engaged in dialogue with the citizens of Athens with the goal of clarifying and clearly defining key concepts. Often, his interaction with the citizens of Athens demonstrated that those considered wise were really not that wise after all, and knew even less about the object of enquiry than he did,[6] and he himself claimed no knowledge whatsoever. Another words, his approach of forensically examining his opponent's argument and showing that it led to contradictions or nonsense had the effect of making his opponents look silly, and this hardly made him popular in Athenian society.

Socrates was also damaged with his association with Alcibiades, who was a flamboyant Athenian statesman and orator. Alcibiades was a strong proponent of the disastrous Sicilian expedition during the Peloponnesian war, and he also changed his allegiance several times during the war (he served as a strategic advisor to Sparta for a short time).

Socrates answer as to how man should live a good life is defined in terms of *arete* (which is generally translated as moral virtue), and where a good life is considered to be a good moral life. The right thing to do, according to Socrates, involves thinking hard about the situation, and *doing the right thing is best for you.* Further, if anyone does wrong it is because they have not thought enough about the situation, since, according to Socrates, no one does wrong willingly. Socrates claims not to know what virtue is, and he explores and questions others in an attempt to define and give an account of *arete* in the early Platonic dialogues.

Aristotle was born in Northern Greece and he became a student of Plato at Plato's academy in Athens in the fourth century B.C. Aristotle later founded his own school (known as the Lyceum) in Athens, and he later became the tutor of Alexander the Great. He made contributions to biology, logic, politics, ethics and metaphysics. His starting point to knowledge acquisition was the senses, as he

---

[4] Socrates was a moral philosopher who deeply influenced Plato. Socrates himself maintained that he knew nothing (Socratic ignorance).

[5] Socrates did not write any works on philosophy, and knowledge of his approach to moral philosophy is described in Plato's early dialogues.

[6] Chaerephon (a lifelong friend of Socrates) asked the oracle at Delphi who was the wisest of all men, and the oracle replied that there was none wiser than Socrates. Socrates set out to determine what the oracle meant by this statement, and in his discussions with the wise of Athens he realised that those considered wise really knew nothing but thought that they did, whereas he alone was aware that he knew nothing.

**Fig. 9.2** Plato and Aristotle

believed that these were essential to acquire knowledge. His position is the opposite of Plato who argued that the senses deceive and should not be relied upon, and that for Plato knowledge is eternal and unchanging, and consists of truths (or Platonic ideas or forms) that are not objects of perception (Fig. 9.2).

Aristotle wrote the *Nicomachean Ethics* and the *Eudemian Ethics*, and his position was that people should have an excellent character (virtuous character) in order to achieve happiness (or well being). He argues that reason distinguishes man from animals, and that the human function is some kind of excellent exercise of the intellect. His approach differs from Plato's in that his analysis of ethics uses his metaphysical theory of potentiality and actuality, with happiness defined as an actuality.

Aristotle argues that moral virtue or excellence of character may be taught in a similar way to learning a musical instrument: i.e., ethical character is a skill learned through practice, which a person develops partly as a result of upbringing and partly as a result of habit of action. That is, for Aristotle the source of ethical insight is in life experience, and so knowing how to act is based on practical wisdom developed from a combination of training in the right habits, and experience with practical situations.

Aristotle formulated the doctrine of the '*Golden Mean*', which locates each of the virtues between corresponding vices of excess and defect. He defines the four cardinal virtues in a similar way to Plato, and they include prudence, temperance, courage and justice. He describes *eudaimonia* (ευ-δαιμων meaning good demon) as the highest human good, with *arête* as the highest sense achieved by the life of reason and the intellect.

*Stoicism* was founded by Zeno of Citium, Cyprus, in the third century B.C., and remained popular in the Greco/Roman world until the third century A.D. The Stoics taught that virtue is essential for human happiness, and they are often seen as being unmoved by the sorrows and afflictions affecting humanity. They aimed in a sense to live for the moment and to rationally understand the world, and to avoid being controlled by emotions and passions, and they rejected these as a way to decide what is good and bad.

*Eudaimonia* is generally translated as happiness or well being (the highest good) by the Greeks, but it was identified as pleasure by Epicurus who was the founder of the *Epicurean school* of ethics/philosophy in the late fourth century B.C. Epicurus was a hedonist, who believed that pleasure is morally good and pain is morally evil, and that the absence of pain or fear is the greatest pleasure.

It should be noted that the institution of slavery was taken for granted in ancient Athens, and that women played a subordinate role in role. The Greek philosophers remained in a sense, prisoners of their own culture, and took these prejudices and inequalities for granted.

## 9.4 Ethics in Religious Traditions

The great religious of the world provide a moral compass for their communities to behave ethically in the world. We discuss Christianity, which arose as a reform movement of Judaism in Palestine during the first century A.D.; Islam, which was founded by the prophet Mohammed in the Arabian Peninsula during the seventh century A.D.; and Buddhism, which was founded by the Buddha, Siddhãrtha Gautama, in Northern India c. 500 B.C.

### 9.4.1 Christian Ethics

The Christian faith is deeply ethical and its sources are in the Bible[7] and in the life of Jesus. The bible consists of the Old Testament and the New Testament, with the New Testament focusing on the life of Jesus and his death and resurrection. The books of the Old Testament are based on the twenty-four books of the Hebrew Bible[8] (*Tanakh* or also known as *Miqra*), which record the history and life of the

[7] There are 73 books in the Roman Catholic bible and 66 books in the Protestant bible (the Ethiopian bible has 81–88 books).

[8] The Hebrew bible is a collection of Hebrew Scriptures and includes the Torah, the Nevi'im, and the Ketuvim.

Jewish people, their covenant with God, their laws, their kings, the destruction of Jerusalem, their exile to Babylon, their return to Zion, their belief in the coming Messiah, and the lives of the prophets.[9]

The Old Testament includes books such as Genesis, Exodus, Leviticus, and Deuteronomy; the sayings of prophets such as Joshua, Jeremiah, Isaiah, and Ezekial; the Psalms, which are songs and prayers for worship; Proverbs, which are sayings that contain wisdom; Job, which explores the nature of suffering; and books such as Ruth, Ecclesiastes, Lamentations and Esther that are associated with particular festivals.

The New Testament consists of twenty-seven books that include the Gospels, which present the life and teachings of Jesus, and the letters (epistles) that were written by early Christian leaders (e.g., St. Paul) to provide guidance to the early Church. The New Testament concludes with the book of Revelation, which presents a vision of things from creation to the end of the world. Christianity began as a reform movement of Judaism in Roman Palestine, and its early adherents were Jewish converts. Many Gentiles (non Jews) embraced Christianity, and it gradually spread throughout the Roman world, and became a major religion in its own right.

St. Paul converted to Christianity, and he was one of the most important missionaries of the early church. He preached the gospels, established churches and contributed to spreading Christianity to the urban areas throughout the Roman Empire. The direct Jewish influence on Christianity ceased after the Jewish revolt against Roman rule from 66–73 A.D., which led to the destruction of the second temple in Jerusalem, and the expulsion of many Jews from Judea.

---

[9] The justification that Israelis and the State of Israel often give for their state is that it is a God given inheritance (i.e., a Divine right as stated in the Torah and especially the books of Genesis, Exodus, Numbers and Deuteronomy). They state that God granted the Land of Israel to them and their descendents, and in its more extreme interpretation it includes the land from the Wadi of Egypt (a river believed to be south of Gaza in Sinai, or possibly referring to the Nile) to the great river, the Euphrates as written in Chap. 15 of the Book of Genesis, verse 18). The state of Israel embarked on a "Greater Israel" project shortly after its formation, with the ethnic cleansing of Palestinians in 1948 (the year that it was founded when it was given approx. 60% of historical Palestine), and 1967 (when it annexed the West Bank and Gaza). Israel has embarked in more or less continuous wars with its neighbours since then, seeking to weaken or destroy them to achieve hegemony over the Middle East, and to achieve its long-term goals of a Greater Israel, which would include Gaza, the West Bank, parts of Southern Lebanon, parts of Southern Syria and parts of Sinai. The state of Israel has committed crimes against humanity during its genocide of the Palestinian population of Gaza (a holocaust by Jews who were themselves subjected to a holocaust under Nazi Germany!). It is so obscene and unacceptable, and has resulted in a permanent stain on the State of Israel. Laws are fundamental to the operation of the modern world, and there is no place in the modern world for a rogue, barbaric, and genocidal state that does not respect the basic principles of human rights and law. There needs to be a fundamental reform of the middle east, with Israel required to return the occupied territories (and dismantle its illegal settlements in the occupied territories) taken during the 1967 war (as per UN security council resolutions and international law). The Palestinian population have been subject to massive injustice by the state of Israel, with the United States complicit in the genocide in Gaza (as it provides massive funding to Israel as well as weapons and diplomatic cover—i.e., it may be viewed as the enabler of the genocide).

**Fig. 9.3** The crucifixion of Christ

Christianity became the official religion of the Roman Empire shortly after the conversion of the emperor Constantine in 337 A.D.[10] Christians are monotheistic: i.e., they believe in one God who created the heavens and earth, and the Christian concept of the Trinity is that God consists of three persons: namely the father (God himself), the son (Jesus Christ) and the Holy Spirit.[11] Christians believe that God sent his only son, the Messiah, to save mankind, and that Christ was crucified on the cross to offer the forgiveness of sins, and was resurrected three days after his death before ascending to heaven. Christmas celebrates the birth of Jesus, and Easter celebrates the death and resurrection of Christ. The God of Christianity is all powerful (*omnipotent*), all knowing (*omniscient*), and is present everywhere (*omnipresent*). For Christians, God is good and God is love, and the Christian concept of love is powerful in that the love of God is viewed as his love of humanity, and also the love of Christians for one another as in loving one's neighbour as oneself (Fig. 9.3).

The starting point in Christian ethics is the Christian faith and the life of Jesus as recorded in the Gospels, as well as Jewish ethics from the Old Testament (e.g., the ten commandments). Ethical behaviour involves both the right motive and the right action, and since Christians believe that the Bible is the revealed Word of God, the Bible is employed to teach and learn the right behaviour. Reason is part of the foundation of ethics and must be employed with revelation, and St. Anselm

[10] Constantine had lifted the ban on Christianity in the Roman Empire in 313 A.D, and the emperor Theodosius I declared Christianity to be the official religion of the Roman Empire in 380 A.D.

[11] There were a number of schisms in the early Christian church over perceived heresies, including Arianism which was a dispute on the nature of the Trinity, and whether the Father caused the creation of the Son and Holy Spirit.

indicated the close relationship between Christian faith and human reason with his statement "*fides quaerens intellectum*" (faith seeking understanding).

Jesus teaches the importance of the kingdom of God and love, and one should love God with all one's heart, and love one's neighbour as oneself. That is, the Christian message from the Gospels is one of peace, love and compassion, and that God loves us, and expects us to love one another as well as loving God. The *Golden Rule of Christian Ethics*[12] is stated by Jesus in the Gospels of Saint Luke and Saint Matthew, and is in a sense the *principle of reciprocity*, and is a summary of the books of Laws and the Prophets of the Old Testament. It states, "*Do onto others as you would have them do onto you*", as may be illustrated as, for example, where one should be charitable to others such as the poor in society, as if you were in need then you would want others to help you. There is an interesting account of the philosophy of the Christian religion in [Maw:05].

Bertrand Russell[13] expressed doubt over the historical existence of Jesus, and he maintained that while Jesus had a very high degree of moral goodness that there were some flaws in his character. These included his belief in hell and everlasting punishment, and also his behaviour and reaction when individuals at a gathering did not listen to his preaching (he reacted with fury). Russell also questioned the morality of religion stating that it is an impediment to moral progress in the world. [Rus:20].

### 9.4.2 Islamic Ethics

The prophet Mohammed founded Islam in the seventh century A.D., and it (along with Christianity and Judaism) is one of the great monotheistic religions of the world. God (called *Allah* in Islam) is Lord and creator and the sole master of mankind. The final judgment will be a terrible vengeance on the ungodly, and man's only hope is *Islam* (meaning submission to God). The Koran (*Qur'an*) meaning recitation is the word of Allah as revealed through the prophet Mohammed, and Allah urges reason to be exercised in understanding revelation. The other source of Islam is the recorded deeds and sayings of the prophet as

[12] This principle is also part of Judaism and Islam.

[13] Bertrand Russell was an influential British logician, mathematician and philosopher, and his grandfather was a former prime minister of Britain. He was the co-author with Alfred Whitehead of *Principia Mathematica*, which aimed to derive all of the truths of mathematics from logic. Russell was also active in political causes such as the campaign for nuclear disarmament. He was sympathetic to the plight of the Palestinian people, and he criticised Israeli actions in annexing the territory of the West Bank and Jerusalem after the 1967 war (Israel has since built many settlements in the West Bank with roughly 700,000 Israelis—all of these settlements are illegal under international law).

recorded in the *Sunnah* and *hadith,*[14] and the message of the Koran and examples of the prophet's life acts as a paradigm for ethical and moral behaviour for Muslims around the world.

The inhabitants of the city of Mecca initially rejected the teachings of Mohammed, and the prophet fled to the city of Medina.[15] Later he conquered Mecca with his Muslim army (entering the city without battle), and the concept of the jihad[16] (holy war or just war) is associated with Islam. Mecca is the holiest city in Islam and it contains a cubical building called the *Ka'bah,*[17] which is the most sacred site in Islam. Muslims circle the *ka'bah* seven times in a counter clockwise direction during the *Hajj* or *Umrah*, and it is the direction of prayer (*Qibia*) for Muslims around the world. God is portrayed in places in the Koran as ready to forgive, and in other places he punishes. Christ is considered a prophet in the Koran, and it is emphasized repeatedly that God could not have a son (Fig. 9.4).

Muslims pray five times a day facing Mecca, and the muezzin announces the call for daily prayers (*salah*) and Friday prayers (*adhan*). All healthy Muslims are expected to do the *Hajj* (pilgrimage to Mecca) at least once in their lifetime. Fasting takes place during the ninth lunar month (*Ramadan*), and it is strictly observed by all healthy Muslims. This involves absence from food and drink between sunrise and sunset.

Polygamy (up to four wives) is allowed for Muslim men, but not for Muslim women (subject to the male treating each wife equally: e.g., financially, maintenance, time spent with each spouse, etc). Furthermore, Muslim men are allowed to marry Christians or Jews, but this is forbidden to Muslim women, and polygamy for women is also forbidden. Women tend to play a subservient role in Muslim

---

[14] There is a subtle difference between sunnah and hadith, with the latter referring to every reported statement, deed or incident of the prophet, whereas sunnah refers to an actual action or statement of the prophet that has been passed on by the Islamic community from generation to generation. Some Islamic scholars question whether it is appropriate to attach the same importance to the Sunnah and Hadith as the Koran, as these were written over a century after the death of the prophet, and so errors could have been introduced given the elapsed time. Further, if the Sunnah/Hadith had been divinely revealed they would have been written down at the same time as the Koran was written down.

[15] The prophet is buried in the city of Medina (one of the three holiest cities of Islam), and the city is also visited as part of the annual Hajj and Umrah pilgrimages to Mecca. One of the earliest battles in Islam was fought at Mt. Uhud on the outskirts of Medina.

[16] Jihad also includes striving by peaceful as well as by armed means to achieve the goals of a Muslim community. The Koran specifies the conditions for war and peace in the case of an armed conflict, and jihad is defined as defensive activity aimed at resisting aggression and protecting society. An authorised person must declare it and it must be a just cause, and the intention is to restore peace with the action taken proportional to the threat. The Koran and Sunnah prohibit killing non-combatants and infrastructure.

[17] It has been suggested by some scholars that in pre-Islamic Arabia that the Ka'baa was originally dedicated to Hubai, a Nabatean deity. Petra in Jordan was the northern capital of the Nabatean civilisation, with Madain Salih, near Al Ula in Saudi Arabia, the southern capital. In early Islam, the direction of prayer (*qibia*) for Muslims was in the direction of Jerusalem, but this was later changed to the direction of the Ka'baa in Mecca.

**Fig. 9.4** The Ka'baa in Mecca, Saudi Arabia

society (especially in parts of the Middle East), and it is common for a veil to be worn for modesty purposes.[18] The Koran emphasises the importance of addressing social and economic injustice, and Muslims are urged to spend part of their income and wealth on friends and relatives, orphans, the poor, and the needy in society (*zakat*).

Islam provides a moral compass for the Muslim community (*ummah*), and the revelation to Mohammed (as recorded in the Koran) provides the reference point for Muslims in distinguishing right from wrong. That is, divine command plays an essential role in establishing the moral order for Muslims, and the message from the Koran, and the sayings in the Sunnah and Hadith led to the codification of these norms in what became Islamic Law as recorded in *Shar'ia.*

Islam has been criticised as been ruthless and intolerant, and the Indian pacifist and political activist, Mahatma Gandhi, noted that while non-violence has a place in the Koran, the historical expansion of Islam through military conquest means that Muslim fighters are aggressive. Islam has been criticised for its prejudice

[18] Some Muslim societies (e.g., in Saudi Arabia and other parts of the Arabian peninsula) are patriarchal, and require females to wear a loose long black robe termed an *abaya*, and some also require them to have their hair and face covered with a *hijab* and *niqab*. Other Muslim societies (e.g., Indonesia) are more relaxed in the dress code for females, and they may wear more colourful clothes. The Prophet emphasised that women should dress modestly, but he did not specify what this meant in terms of burka, abaya, hijab and niqab. Some of the practices that are unique to Islam in the Arabian peninsula seem to have their origin in the tribal practices of the Bedouin desert tribes in Arabia from which Islam emerged.

against homosexuality, where homosexual acts between consenting adults carry the death penalty in some Islamic states.

The penalty for *apostasy* (renunciation of faith) in Islam is death, which is contrary to the United Nations Human Rights convention that recognises the right to change religion. Islamic Sharia law is often viewed as cruel, with the penalties that it applies being unsuitable to the modern world, and belonging more to the age of early Islam on the Arabian Peninsula. The perception of Islam as a violent religion has been compounded by the rise of extremist forms of Islam such as in Al Qaeda and the Islamic State (ISIS or Daesh), where violence including cruel and inhuman behaviour (e.g., decapitations) have taken place.

However, it is important to recognise (based on the author's experience of living in the Middle East, including time spent in Saudi Arabia and Kuwait) that the vast majority of Muslims seem to be decent and gentle human beings, and they are just trying their best to lead a good spiritual life in harmony with their faith. There are gradual changes taking place in some of the more conservative parts of the Middle East, and while gender inequality and Sharia law in traditional Muslim societies remains disturbing, in time (hopefully soon), an appropriate balance between these traditional religious beliefs and modern life will be achieved.

Bertrand Russell noted that Islam has been a political religion from the very beginning, where Mohammed and the caliphs who followed him making themselves rulers of their communities with both spiritual and political authority up to the end of the first world war.

Several Islamic philosophers such as Averroes (from Persia) and Avicenna (from Andalucia, Spain) played an important role in preserving and transmitting the philosophical works of Plato and Aristotle as well as providing commentaries on these works. For more information on Islam see [Hin:91].

### 9.4.3 Buddhist Ethics

Buddhism is centred on the teachings of the Buddha, as recorded in written form by later Buddhists. It arose as a breakaway religion from Hinduism, and it is an atheist religion (i.e., a religion without God). Siddhārtha Gautama (the Buddha and founder of Buddhism) was born into the ruling family of a kingdom near Lumbini in North India in the sixth century B.C. He became aware of the challenges of the human condition early in his life, including the negative effects of the caste system, as well as sickness, anguish, suffering and death. He left the royal palace in his late 20 s with the goal of becoming an ascetic, so that he could investigate and find solutions to these problems.

He practiced existing techniques of meditation with several teachers, and he later developed his own approach that allowed a stage of calmness to be reached that facilitated the development of insight. This enabled him to reach enlightenment, and he spent the remainder of his life preaching and teaching on suffering, impermanence, and egolessness.

The Buddha's teachings are preserved in the *Pali canon*, which were handed down in an oral tradition until monks wrote them down in the first century A.D. The Pali Canon consists of three baskets, including the *Vinayana* (Discipline for the monks), *Sutta* (Discourses or basic teachings of the Buddha), and *Abhidhamma* (Doctrinal Elaboration or a more detailed systematisation of the doctrine by later followers). The Vinayana emphasises that Buddhism is essentially about monastic asceticism.

At the core of the Buddha's teaching is the doctrine of the *four noble truths*, which summarises the core principles of Buddhist philosophy and the basic message of the Buddha. The Buddha gave the first Buddhist sermon at Sarnath (in India), and the Buddha explained the four noble truths and the eight-fold path to end suffering (Fig. 9.5).

- Existence of suffering (*dukkha*)
- Origin/cause of suffering (*samudaya/ trsna*)
- Cessation of suffering (*nirodha*)
- Eightfold path to end suffering (*magga*)

The four noble truths are outlined in the form of a medical diagnosis, where there is an illness; the causes of the illness are identified; a solution is proposed; and the steps to implement the solution are identified. The causes of suffering according to the Buddha are due to your mental attitude or mindset of attachment (*trsna*). Suffering can be eliminated by a change of mental attitude: i.e., by getting rid of the cause you get rid of the effect. Finally, there are a set of principles that you can implement in your life to get rid of your suffering, and these cover the right view and wisdom, the right action and the right mental state.

That is, Buddhism aims to specify a path which if followed terminates the endless cycle of reincarnation and transmigration of souls characterized by the Hindu Religion. This path essentially involves self-discipline and asceticism, and the Buddha identified an *eight-fold path* to reach Nirvana. The Buddha does not specify what Nirvana is; rather, he specified how Nirvana is reached.

The earliest Buddhist tradition is called *Theravada* (also called *Himayana* or Small Vehicle), and is close to the teachings of the historical Buddha. It became popular in South East Asia (including Thailand, Sri Lanka and Burma). The other major tradition of Buddhism developed later in India (first century B.C.), and is called *Mahayana* (Great Vehicle), and it spread to China and later to Mongolia and Tibet.

Buddhism is concerned with leading a good life, practicing virtues and following meditation exercises. Meditation plays a role for being in the moment and concentrating to avoid distracting thoughts, and rational analysis and argument plays an important role in Buddhist ethics.

At the heart of Buddhism is the concept of *dukkha*, which includes suffering, physical pain, sickness and essentially all the undesirable things that are part of

**Fig. 9.5** Buddha teaching four noble truths

the human condition. The Buddhist teaching on egolessness (*anatta*) and impermanence (*anicca*) involves a denial of the sense of self that humans possess.[19] The world of things is impermanent: i.e., things come into existence and go out of existence, and so everything passes in time.

Buddhist ethics (*sila*) are part of the eight-fold path, and they specify a code of conduct that involves a commitment to harmony and self-restraint, with the key principles being non-violence and avoiding harm to others. Ethics refers to the avoidance of non-virtuous deeds, and requires concentration and control of the mind, as well as wisdom of the nature of reality.

The eight-fold path emphasises *right view*: i.e., understanding of the nature of things especially the 4 noble truths; *right intention*: i.e., avoiding attachment, hatred and harmful intent; *right speech*: i.e., avoiding lying, divisive speech and harsh speech; *right action*: i.e., avoid killing, stealing and sexual misconduct; *right livelihood*: i.e., avoid trades that harm others; *right effort*: i.e., avoiding negative states of

[19] The normal view of self is that it is a part of you that remains constant throughout life and defines "you" as "you" (i.e., it is the essential core of a person). Buddhists reject this view, and the Buddhist position of self is analogous to that of an automobile that is made up of parts that were assembled in a factory; the parts interact with each other and the road; they may wear out and be replaced over time; and eventually the car reaches the end of its life. The car does not have a self as such: it does not have a part that remains constant throughout its existence. You, according to Buddhism as a person are like the car, and have no self (i.e., the idea of self is an illusion). Hume (the eighteenth century British (Scottish) Empiricist philosopher also argued that the self is an illusion, and that we do not have a direction impression of a permanent unified self, and that when we look for self all that we find are perceptions).

mind; *right mindfulness*: awareness of body and thoughts; and *right concentration* for practicing meditation.

The Buddha stressed that wisdom (*prajna*) and compassion (*karunā*) go hand in hand and are essential to achieving enlightenment. Buddhist compassion includes sympathy for the pain and suffering of others. For more information on Buddhism see [Rin:98].

## 9.5 Traditional Chinese Ethics

Chinese ethics are concerned with practical problems, such as how one should live as well as one's duties to families, strangers and wider society. It also considers the extent to which one should be involved in reforming the social and political structures in society, and how one should behave when in a position of power. Chinese ethics integrate the personal, social and the political, and the process of behaving ethically is achieved in the context of the social relationships of family and wider society, and especially to those to whom one has responsibilities. That is, there is an emphasis on the family and social context in making the right ethical choices and taking the appropriate action.

The various Chinese approaches to ethics include Confucianism, Daoism and Chinese Buddhism. Daoism (or Taoism) is a Chinese philosophy that emphasises living in harmony with the Tao (Dao). Ethics in Daoism emphasise effortless action including naturalness and spontaneity, and the three treasures of compassion, frugality and humility. It dates back to the fourth century B.C. with its teachings attributed to Laozi and Zhuangzi.

The *dao* (way) provides a guide to the public, and the compound term *dao de* (meaning ways and virtues) consists of the interaction of the social *dao* and *de* (virtue). *Dao* is public, objective guidance, whereas *de* consists of the character and disposition obtained from exposure to *dao*, and is the physical realisation of *dao* in some part of the human system (e.g., family). Both *dao* and *de* encompass more than just morality, and they are also ways of fashion and etiquette.

Confucianism is a way of life that includes a system of thought and behaviour (Confucius was a sixth century B.C. philosopher). It discusses ethics in terms of virtues and the corresponding ideals of a person. It believes humans are fundamentally good, teachable, improvable and perfectible through personal and community development.

There are similarities between ethics in Confucianism and the Golden Rule of Christian Ethics, which may be illustrated with the Confucian belief "*What you do not wish upon yourself, extend not to others*" (Fig. 9.6).

Confucianism is popular in South East Asia including China, Hong Kong, Macau and Vietnam. The right behaviour involves more than instructions or a code, as the instructions need to be interpreted to the particular situation, and a person's duties are duties of their station towards other socially described persons or things.

**Fig. 9.6** Confucius, Tang dynasty

That is, Confucianism deals with people in terms of their social relationship with them: e.g., such as parent, daughter, sibling, friend, neighbour, and so on.

## 9.6 Utilitarianism

We briefly discussed utilitarianism in Chap. 2, and Jeremy Bentham founded the field in the nineteenth century. Utilitarianism ethics involves measuring the consequences of an action against one value (such as benefit or happiness). The sole moral criterion for good or bad lies in the *utility principle*, which is the greatest happiness of the greatest number of a community. Another words, the utility principle is the only ground for action, and it provides a framework to act morally by taking only those actions that maximize *utility*, where the concept of utility is defined as the property of an object that provides benefit or happiness. That is, the *right action in a given situation is the action that produces the most benefit or happiness to society*, and so if a particular law or action doesn't do any good then it isn't any good.

Bentham argued that the greatest happiness be determined quantitatively from an estimate of the expected pleasure or pain for each action. That is, utilitarianism allows (in a sense) a moral balance sheet to be drawn up with the costs and benefits of each action recorded, and it thereby allows the action with the best consequences to be chosen. The process to determine the action that leads to the greatest happiness for the greatest number of people involves a summation of the pleasure/pain for all individuals.

Bentham's motivation for the development of classical utilitarianism was his desire for a reform of the legal system and for social reform in England. His goal was that useless or corrupt laws and social practice should be changed appropriately. Bentham's analysis of the laws identified some that were bad due to their lack of utility: i.e., some laws were bad in the sense that they led to unhappiness and misery without any compensating happiness. Bentham argued that utilitarianism should become the standard to determine the right action to be taken by the government and individuals, and John Stuart Mill and others later promoted his ideas.

Utilitarianism is a member of the class of *Consequentialism Ethics* that argue that the consequences of one's action are the ultimate basis for a judgment as to whether the action is right or wrong. That is, an action in itself is neither right nor wrong: rather it is the consequence of the action that is morally relevant.

The utilitarian position may result in conflicts when the actions that promote overall happiness and good are incompatible with the individual's happiness. That is, one of the key criticisms of utilitarianism is that the individual is not protected when the utility calculation yields that the happiness of the majority outweighs the unhappiness of a small number of people. This could result in the abuse of individuals and minorities, and John Stuart Mill introduced the "*no harm principle*", where one is free to do as one wishes provided that no harm is done to others. However, this principle is difficult to apply, as moral problems often include the risk of harm to others.

According to utilitarianism even the most fundamental principles (e.g., the rights specified in the UN Declaration of Human Rights) can be broken if the positive consequences outweigh the negatives (*the end justifies the means*). This has led to a variant of utilitarianism (*rule utilitarianism*) that recognises the existence of moral rules, and looks at the consequences of rules (in contrast to actions) to increase happiness.

## 9.7 Deontological Ethics

Deontological ethics (from the Greek δέον meaning duty, and λόγος meaning study, i.e., the study of duty) argues that the ethical value of an action should be judged on whether the action is right or wrong in itself (based on a set of rules), and not on the actual outcome or consequences of the action. That is, an action is morally right if it is in agreement with a moral rule, and this is independent of the consequence of the action. A moral obligation may arise from a set of rules from a particular religion, a set of personal ethical values, cultural values, or rules inherent in the natural world.

Immanuel Kant[20] developed the most well known system of deontology, and a key concept in Kantian ethics is *autonomy*, where Kant argues that an individual should be able to determine what is morally correct through reasoning (i.e., reasoning is the source of morality). The key idea is that we place a moral norm or law upon ourselves, and we have a duty to obey and respect this moral norm, and if we do this we are acting with *good will*. Another words, an action is morally right if it is in agreement with a moral law that is applicable in itself irrespective of the consequences of that action.

That is, Kant argues that *for people to behave ethically they must act from duty and obey the moral law*, and that the consequences of the act is not what makes it right or wrong, but rather the motives of the person performing the act. For Kant, something is "good in itself" when it is "intrinsically good", and it is "good without qualification" when its addition can never make the situation ethically worse. From this he concludes that *good will* is the only thing that is good without qualification.

Kant argues that the consequences of a person exercising their will may not be used to determine if a person has good will, as good consequences could arise by accident from an action intended to cause harm, whereas bad consequences could arise by accident from an action intended to cause good. Kant instead argues that a person has good will when they act out of respect for the moral law, when they act in a certain way when they have a duty to do so. Another words, the only thing that is truly good in itself is a good will, and a good will is only good when the person acts in accordance with duty out of respect for the moral law.

A moral law (according to Kant) is valid at all times and in all places, and is thus unconditionally applicable (*categorically* applicable) to everyone in all circumstances. Kant argued that there is one universal principle from which all moral laws or norms may be derived, and this principle is termed the *categorical imperative*, and is the foundation of all moral judgments. The categorical imperative is an absolute requirement that must be obeyed (i.e., the imperative is a prescribed action), and is an end in itself. That is, it is a law from which all duties and obligations arise.

Kant's formulation of the categorical imperative may be seen in the *universality principle* as follows: "*Act only on that maxim that you can at the same time will that it should become a universal law*". That is, the maxim (a practical principle that prescribes action) should be unconditionally good and should be able to serve as a general law for everyone without this leading to contradiction. Kant gives an example of someone making a false promise to repay money as this results

---

[20] Immanuel Kant was an influential German philosopher who lived in the German city of Koenigsberg in East Prussia. The city became part of Russia after the Second World War (renamed to Kaliningrad and is located in N.E. Poland and adjacent to Lithuania). Kant's "A Critique of Pure Reason" is considered a Copernican revolution in philosophy, where Kant rejected Hume's empiricism, and argued instead that there is a third force that structures the world of our experience (i.e., causes us to experience the world the way we do).

in a contradiction on universalisation, and thus cannot become a universal law [Kant:1787].

For Kant, the categorical imperative may also be expressed as a *law of nature*, where we should act in such a way that those maxims were to become universal laws of nature. Kant divides duties into two subsets: duties we have to ourselves versus duties we have to others, and we have a duty not to act on maxims that result in a logical contradiction.

Kant gives an alternate formulation of the categorical imperative in terms of the *reciprocity principle* as follows: "*Act only to treat humanity, whether in your own person or in that of any, in every case as an end and never as a means only*". That is, a moral action includes an end as well as a moral principle, and each human must have respect for the rationality of another, and must not misguide the rationality of another.

There are several criticisms of Kant's theory including that it is too rigid (i.e., there is no bending of the rules as Kant does not allow for exceptions in his theory), and that it ignores conflicts between moral laws.

## 9.8 Libertarianism

John Locke is regarded as the founder of liberalism and its origins as a political philosophy is in the political climate of England in the late seventeenth century. Locke's political philosophy was concerned with the protection of basic individual rights and principles, and he argued against absolute monarchy (such as that of Charles II and James II in England), and instead argued for the reforms that became part of the Glorious Revolution (James II was deposed and replaced by his daughter, Mary and son-in-law, William of Orange), where parliament was confirmed as being supreme to the sovereign.

Libertarianism[21] views individual freedom as the fundamental human value in society, and it regards any coercion or infringement of that liberty with deep suspicion. This means that libertarians wish to be left alone to be free to make choices about their lives and property, and they do not wish others (i.e., the state or government) to interfere with their right to liberty. This means that they are suspicious of distributive justice (e.g., taxation), where a democratic government seeks to redistribute wealth for the common good (to ensure fairness in society, as well as to provide essential services for its citizens (e.g., health, education, legal, police and defence). Libertarians tend to embrace individualism, self-reliance and a free market economy, and they often view economic regulation by the state as coercion and infringement of their rights, and curtailment of their freedoms in economic affairs.

[21] There are differences between liberalism and libertarianism in relation to the role of government, with the latter arguing for minimal government intervention, whereas modern liberals support some government intervention while maintaining personal liberties.

Libertarian philosophy is an extreme free market or *laissez faire* philosophy that aims to get government out of things by reducing taxes, privatisation of government services, reducing or eliminating regulation and government supports, and increasing the role of the private sector in society. It rejects the view that everybody's needs should be represented in society, and instead argues for small government and against governments playing a role in reducing inequalities and redistributing wealth. It argues that taxes should be cut, as they infringe on an individual's freedom and liberty, which are fundamental goals for libertarians. Further, they argue that if taxes and government size are reduced then this will provide an incentive to entrepreneurs to create businesses, which will then lead to employment and benefits for workers, and to everyone being better off in society.

Libertarian politics became popular in the United States under President Ronald Reagan in the early 1980s. It has led to a massive transfer of wealth to the wealthiest of American society, and weaker regulation of American business (e.g., weaker regulation of the financial sector in Wall Street was a factor in the 2007–2008 global financial crisis).

It has led to increased inequalities in the US with tax reductions for the wealthiest in society, and reductions in support for workers (especially in social safety net programs). There is now an immense wealth gap in the country, with the top 1% in the country owning 33% of all assets, whereas the bottom 50% hold very little. Based on 2022 figures roughly 700 billionaires hold over $4.5 trillion in wealth (exceeding the total wealth of the bottom 50% of households).

That is, there is a huge wealth gap between rich and poor in the United States, and further inequalities may be seen in the ratio of CEO pay (in large companies) to the average worker pay in the US. This was roughly 10 times average worker salary in the 1970s, whereas in recent decades it has increased to hundreds of times the average worker salary.

## 9.9 Virtue Ethics

Utililitarianism and Kantianism are rule based ethical theories that are concerned with carrying out the right action in a given situation, whereas virtue ethics focus on the ethical nature of the person who is carrying out the action. That is, *virtue ethics* is concerned with building the right character traits in the person through education and good examples, as it is reasonable to expect that a person with good virtuous traits will perform good actions. Another words, the goal is to develop the person into a morally good and responsible human being who can lead a good life. Actions are good if they come from good traits of character, and the actions are guided by the desire of the individual to be virtuous.

The origins of virtue ethics are in ancient Greek philosophy especially in the work of Socrates, Plato and Aristotle, and the Stoics. Socrates was concerned with how one should lead a good life, and he saw wisdom as the path to virtue (*arete*) and the highest good (*eudaimonia* or happiness). Socrates emphasised that a good life is a good moral life, and he explored and questioned others in an attempt to give an account of *arete*. He emphasised that one should be conscious of how little one knows in order to learn more, and that an individual should think hard about the situation, and do the right thing is best for her. Further, if anyone does wrong it is because they have not thought enough about the situation, since, according to Socrates, no one does wrong willingly.

Aristotle argued that the final goal of human action is to strive for the highest good, and this involves achieving the state of being a good person and living a good and virtuous life. A moral virtue for Aristotle is a middle way between two extremes of evil: for example, courage is balanced between cowardice and recklessness. Aristotle argues that people should seek a middle way, but that the middle course also depends on the circumstances in a given situation. This requires the intellectual virtue of practical wisdom to make the right moral judgment (which is the middle way), and so moral virtue and intellectual virtue go hand-in-hand.

The Stoics emphasised the importance of self-control as a way to overcome destructive emotions, and that rational thought and logic plays a key role in improving an individual's moral well being.

*The key problem with virtue ethics is that it does not tell you how to act in a given situation*, and it seems to be assumed that the virtuous person will always know the correct action in a given situation.

## 9.10 How Can an Individual Be Ethical in a Complex World?

Ethics provides guidance in making decisions to create just outcomes, and to have a positive impact on the world around us. Ethics arises in both our personal and work lives, and it provides us with a moral compass to guide our behaviour with respect to what is right or wrong in a particular situation that arises, and allows us to make an informed ethical decision.

An ethical person is responsible and accountable for his/her actions, and does not cover up mistakes, but will instead be honest, responsible and trustworthy. There are several guiding principles in striving to be an ethical person such as treating people with respect, behaving with integrity, being open and admitting mistakes, and acting in a way that one would like others to act towards you.

- Treating people with respect and dignity
- Behaving with honesty and integrity
- Avoiding hurting others
- Acting in a way that one would like others to act towards you
- Contributing to the betterment of others
- Admitting mistakes and moving on
- Awareness of legal and ethical responsibilities

We mentioned the influential work of Fr. Bernard Lonergan in Chap. 1, and his four key steps on being human offers a useful path for leading an ethical life. These steps are "*Be attentive, be intelligent, be reasonable, and be responsible*".

Ethical decision-making may also involve dealing with ethical dilemmas that may arise between two or more virtue-driven interests, and one approach to deal with this may be to:

- Determine the facts
- Determine the ethical issues
- Determine options
- Evaluate options
- Choose option
- Implement solution

## 9.11 How Can an Ethical Environment Be Created in an Organisation?

A business (or organisation) consists of a set of people each with individual values, and it is important that the actions of the individuals are consistent with the code of ethics and values of the organisation. An organisation needs to create its mission, vision and values, and these should be communicated effectively within the organisation, and made an integral part of the work culture. The values include a set of ethical and moral standards that are appropriate for the organisation, and they need to be more than just window dressing to ensure that there is no unethical behaviour in its business practices.

Any unethical behaviour needs to be identified and corrected, and structures need to be in place to discipline employees who do adhere to the values of the organisation. There is a need for structures where employees may raise ethical concerns that may be dealt with in a professional manner. The organisation needs to:

- Define and communicate its key values
- Make the values an integral part of the work culture
- Establish structures for discussion of any ethical concerns
- Hold employees accountable for violations of values and code of conduct
- Reward good behaviour and discipline inappropriate behaviour
- Make organisation values part of the recruitment process

An ethical environment promotes a culture of trust, and leads to a positive and trustworthy view of the company, with increased employee satisfaction and morale. The implementation of an ethical culture in an organisation places responsibilities on the employees to:

- Become familiar with the core values and code of ethics of organisation.

- Follow the values in the work place.
- Report any conflicts of interest
- Follow all relevant laws.
- Discuss any ethical dilemmas with management

### 9.11.1 Ethical Decision Making

The process for solving moral and ethical problems is complex, as often problems are poorly formulated or ill structured, and there may be several conflicting constraints. The solution requires a clear formulation of the problem, analysis and identification of potential solutions, and the evaluation of the options to choose the most appropriate solution, while balancing (conflicting) moral values with the goal of finding the most appropriate way forward. The steps involved may include:

- Formulate the moral problem
- Analysis of facts and values with stakeholders
- Determine options on how to proceed
- Ethical analysis of available options
- Decision on the chosen option and rationale

There is a difference between the legality and illegality of an act, and whether the act is ethical or unethical. The law is the arbiter on whether a particular act is legal or not, whereas the person's conscience or moral compass is used to judge whether a particular act is ethical or not. Table 9.1 presents the various combinations that may occur.

**Table 9.1** Combinations of legal and ethical

| Type | Example |
|---|---|
| Legal + ethical | This is the normal state of affairs where individuals and companies are obeying the law, and doing the right thing |
| Legal + unethical | An example is the failure of a manager to honour a commitment made to an employee, and this can lead to a breakdown in trust and respect in the manager/employee relationship |
| Illegal + ethical | Usually an illegal act is unethical, but an example could be a parent who is travelling just over the speed limit to bring a child to hospital for medical treatment |
| Illegal + unethical | An example would be a company breaking environment laws such as emissions, or pumping raw sewage into rivers or the sea |

## 9.12 Review Questions

1. What is ethics?
2. Describe the main schools of ethics.
3. What is business ethics?
4. Give examples of unethical behaviour.
5. Explain the difference between utilitarian ethics and deontological ethics.
6. Explain the difference between Christian, Islamic and Buddhist ethics.
7. Explain how ethical decisions may be made.
8. How can an individual be ethical in a hostile work environment.

## 9.13 Summary

Ethics is a branch of philosophy that deals with moral questions such as what is right or wrong, and determining the right behaviour in a given situation. There are various schools of ethics such as the relativist position; cultural relativism; deontological ethics; and utilitarianism.

Business ethics is concerned with ethical principles and moral problems that arise in a business environment. They refer to the core principles and values of the organization. Professional ethics are a code of conduct that governs how members of a profession deal with each other and with third parties.

Ethics in Greek philosophy is concerned with rational thought and the search for appropriate principles to guide human conduct. It is characterised by its faith in reason to do the right thing.

The great religious of the world provide a moral compass to their communities to behave ethically in the world, and we discussed the nature of ethics in Christianity, Islam, and Buddhism.

Utilitarianism was developed by Bentham in the nineteenth century, and its sole moral criterion for good or bad lies in the utility principle, where the right action in a given situation is the action that produces the most benefit or happiness to society..

Deontological ethics argues that the ethical value of an action should be judged on whether the action is right or wrong in itself (based on a set of rules), and not on the actual outcome or consequences of the action.

Virtue ethics is concerned with building the right character traits in the person through education and good examples. Actions are good if they come from good traits of character, and the actions are guided by the desire of the individual to be virtuous.

## References

[Hin:91] A Handbook of Living Religions. Edited by John R. Hinnells. Penguin. 1991.

[Mac:95] A Short History of Ethics. Alasdair MacIntyre. Routledge. 1995.
[Maw:05] Belief in God. An Introduction to the Philosophy of Religion. T.J. Mawson. Oxford University Press. 2005.
[Rin:98] The Tibetan Book of Living and Dying. Sogyal Rinpoche. Random House Ltd. UK. 1998.
[Rus:20] Why I am not a Christian and other essays on Religion and Related Subjects. Routledge. 2nd Edition. Bertrand Russell. 2020. (Lecture delivered in 1927).

# Professional Responsibility of Computer Professionals 10

## 10.1 Introduction

Professional responsibility refers to the responsibility of computer professionals to carry out their work professionally to the highest standards, and to use sound judgment in the exercise of their duties. Professionals are accountable to themselves and others for their actions, and they must be willing to accept professional responsibility when performance does not meet professional standards.

Parnas's views on the professional responsibilities of software engineers have been influential, and he argues *that software engineers have individual responsibilities as professionals.* Another words, software engineers are responsible for designing and implementing high-quality and reliable software that is safe for the public to use. Engineers are accountable for their own decisions and actions, and should object to decisions that violate professional standards. He argues that professional engineers have a duty to their clients to ensure that they are solving the real problem of the client. Engineers need to be honest about current capabilities when asked to work on problems that have no appropriate technical solution, rather than accepting a contract for something that cannot be done.

The *licensing of a professional engineer* provides confidence that the engineer has the right education and experience to build safe and reliable products. Otherwise, the engineering profession gets a bad name because of poor work carried out by unqualified people. Professional engineers are required to follow rules of good practice and to object when rules are violated. The licensing of an engineer requires the engineer to complete an accepted engineering course, and understand the professional responsibility of being an engineer. The professional engineering body is responsible for enforcing standards and certification. The term '*engineer*' is a title that is awarded on merit, but *it also places responsibilities on its holder*.

Engineers have a professional responsibility and are required to behave ethically with their clients. The membership of the professional engineering body requires



G. O'Regan, *Philosophical and Cultural Aspects of Computing*, Undergraduate Topics in Computer Science, https://doi.org/10.1007/978-3-032-29284-1_10

**Table 10.1** Professional responsibilities of software engineers

| No. | Responsibility |
|---|---|
| 1. | Honesty and fairness in dealings with clients |
| 2. | Responsibility for actions |
| 3. | Continuous learning to ensure appropriate knowledge to serve the client effectively |

the member to adhere to the code of ethics of the profession. The professional responsibilities of software engineers include (Table 10.1).

## 10.2 What Is a Code of Ethics?

A professional code of ethics expresses ideals of human behaviour, and it defines the core principles of an organisation or professional body. Several organisations such as the Association Computing Machinery (ACM), the Institute of Electrical and Electronic Engineers (IEEE), and the British Computer Society (BCS) have developed a code of conduct for their members. Violations of the code by members are taken seriously, and are subject to investigations and disciplinary procedures. A code of conduct for a professional body or corporation includes:

1. Guidelines for responsible behaviour of its members/employees.
2. Professional codes are formulated by Engineering bodies.
3. Corporate codes are formulated by companies.
4. Codes of conduct are an addendum to legal requirements.
5. The guidelines may be prescriptive or a broad statement of values.
6. Violations of codes are investigated.
7. Members/employees may be disciplined for violations of code.

There are various types of codes of ethics including (Table 10.2).

**Table 10.2** Types of professional codes

| Code | Responsibility |
|---|---|
| Aspirational codes | These are the values that the profession or company is committed to, and aspires to achieve |
| Advisory codes | These values help professionals to make moral judgments in different situations, based on the values of the profession or company |
| Disciplinary codes | These include disciplinary procedures to ensure that the behaviour of professionals adheres to the values specified in the code of ethics |

A code of ethics places a responsibility on software engineers and computer professionals to their clients and to wider society, and it includes ethical behaviour and responsibilities such as[1]:

1. Adhering to the values of the profession/corporation
2. Behaving with honesty and integrity
3. Fulfilling obligations to employer and to clients
4. Responsibility towards public and society.

The concept of corporate social responsibility (CSR) has become important in recent years, and this means that companies have a responsibility to be good corporate citizens in the societies in which they are operating. That is, they have responsibilities to wider society as well as to their stakeholders. Another words, companies need to protect the environment, and must ensure the sustainability of their operations as well as protecting shareholder interest. Their additional responsibilities include environmental responsibility, ethical responsibility, philanthropic responsibility, and economic responsibility.

CSR can help to promote a positive image of the corporation in the community where it operates, and to be seen as a socially responsible citizen. It plays a role in ensuring that the corporation behaves ethically within society, and it has a positive impact on the environment.

Codes of conduct are values that members of a professional body or employees of a company are expected to adhere to, but may not be legally enforced as such. However, individuals that violate the codes may be subject to disciplinary procedures by the professional body or their employer. An effective code of ethics supports the corporation in achieving its corporate social responsibilities.

Unfortunately, codes of conduct may sometimes be *window dressing*, where the aspirations expressed in the code of ethics do not reflect the reality on the ground. The code may give the appearance that work is carried out in a certain way (e.g., emissions below certain thresholds), and that the engineers are ethical in their day-to-day work. However, the reality on the ground may be quite different with unethical work practices taking place but being covered up. Further, some codes of conduct have been criticised as being vague and contradictory, and this may create uncertainty for the employee or member of the professional body, as to what the right action or behaviour is in a given situation.

Moral judgements and ethical decisions occur in various situations in a work environment, and so it would not be feasible for a code of ethics to cover all scenarios. In practice, a code of ethics expresses the moral principles of an organisation, and so an employee or software professional needs a *moral compass*, and to recognise situations where ethical decisions need to be made, and to apply their ethical judgment to the particular case.

[1] These are core values of many mature software companies, and many companies operating today have a code of ethics that employees are expected to adhere to.

**Fig. 10.1** Whistle blower

There may be conflicts between the loyalty that a person has to their employer, and their duty to do wider society in doing the right thing when unsafe practices endanger the public. No employee desires to be placed in a situation where there is a conflict between what is morally right and their loyalty to their employer, and so it is important that organisations establish structures, where serious problems can be reported, discussed openly and dealt with appropriately. In rare situations, an employee may have no choice but to become a *whistleblower* to protect the public, where the organisation is intent on proceeding with a very risky approach that potentially endangers life or the environment. However, every effort should be made to avoid this situation (Fig. 10.1).

An employee may have a *conflict of interest* that could affect her professional judgment in a certain situation. For example, suppose that an employee has responsibility for selecting a new software package, and her husband runs one of the firms tendering for the work. Then an ethical employee would inform management of the conflict of interest, and remove herself from the selection process to remove any possibility of bias.

That is, a conflict of interest is an interest which if pursued interferes or conflicts with the obligation of the employee to his/her employer or client. The conflict of interest may corrupt or interfere with the employee's professional judgment, and it could potentially lead to inappropriate or immoral behaviour. It potentially destroys the trustworthiness of an individual, and so it is important to disclose a potential conflict of interest as soon as it arises.

Bribery and corruption are endemic to some countries, and as these are illegal activities (in most countries) the employee needs to report such activities when they arise. For example, an employee such as a purchasing manager is in a position of influence in an organisation, and could potentially be offered a *bribe* by another individual or company to influence his/her decision-making. Often, individuals or companies may be subtle in their attempt to gain influence on decision makers, with gifts or invitations to all-expenses paid events such as golf outings often used to build up relationships with decision makers.

It is important to be cautious with respect to corporate entertainment, and many companies have policies that prohibit or restrict gifts to employees from external organisations or individuals. This helps to prevent employees being inappropriately influenced by others in their decision-making.

## 10.3 Role of a Whistle Blower

The whistleblower is a person who speaks out and informs the public on potentially unsafe practices (or criminal acts) that could endanger the public. However, speaking out should be the very last step in the process, as it could have serious consequences on the employee (including career suicide or termination of employment). The steps involved in whistle blowing include first establishing the facts to determine the extent of the danger and its potential impact on the public, communicating the perceived danger and evidence for the danger within the organisation, and exhausting all internal procedures prior to acting. The whistle blower should only speak out when:

1. The organisation's actions will endanger the public
2. The whistle blower has identified the threat, reported it to management, and concluded that management will not act.
3. The whistle blower has exhausted all internal procedures
4. The whistle blower has convincing evidence that the threat is real.
5. The whistle blower believes that revealing the threat will prevent harm.

Table 10.3 describes the typical steps in whistle blowing.

**Table 10.3** Steps in whistle blowing

| No. | Responsibility |
|---|---|
| 1. | Establish the facts and double (or triple check) to ensure that you are factually correct with respect to the danger, and gather solid evidence that will convince any reasonable person of the danger |
| 2. | Report the matter and present the factual information to your immediate superior, and determine what action (if any) management will take |
| 3. | In the case of inaction escalate as appropriate within the organisation (organisations vary size / hierarchical structure and so escalation mechanism will differ) until all internal procedures are exhausted |
| 4. | In the absence of a reasonable resolution to the situation, or the organisation behaves in an unreasonable manner by failing to act or find an appropriate solution there may be no alternative but to speak out |
| 5. | The whistle blower reflects on the situation, weighs up the evidence and options, and decides that the only way to prevent harm is to speak out and reveal the danger to the public |

Speaking out may be the ethical thing to do but often it comes at a serious cost to the employee, as he or she may be portrayed as being disloyal to the organisation. Further, as the organisation will wish to protect itself it may attempt to discredit the employee, and it may even terminate the employment of the employee. The organisation may portray the issue as a disgruntled employee whose employment was terminated due to performance issues with the employee's work.

Whistle blowing can also place a lot of emotional stress and strain on the employee, and even if the employee is not fired, it may result in career termination in the organisation, with zero prospects of further promotion in the company. It is important that the employee protects himself by gathering all evidence on the existence of danger, as this will be needed at a later stage. It may be prudent for the whistleblower to consider the consequences of speaking out and doing the right thing, both for themselves and others, to ensure that they fully understand the implications of the serious steps that they are taking, and that they will be able to manage the difficult circumstances that will materialise in the aftermath of speaking out.

It may seem reasonable to suggest that an employee is fulfilling his moral duty if he informs management of the danger, as management are the decision makers with all the pertinent facts, and are thus best placed to make the final decision. However, such an approach can sometimes lead to disastrous results including loss of life, as with the Space Shuttle Challenger disaster back in 1986, which is discussed in Chap. 11.

Robert Boisjoly, an engineer at Morton Thiokel (a NASA subcontractor) was aware of the risks of erosion and failure when the 0-Rings of the Solid Rocket Booster (SRB) of the space shuttle are exposed to low temperatures. He argued that the space shuttle launch should not take place on the planned date due to the predicted temperatures, and advised management at Morton Thiokel of the situation. Boisjoly expected management to postpone the launch, but NASA placed pressure on Morton Thiokel to proceed with the launch, and the company stated that its data was inconclusive. Morton Thiokel gave its go ahead to proceed with the launch, which resulted in disaster for the Space Shuttle "Challenger" and its seven astronaut crew.

The IEEE code of ethics highlights the importance of speaking out in the case of danger, and it includes the code: "*disclose promptly factors that might endanger the public or the environment*". The IEEE codes are discussed in the next section.

## 10.4 IEEE Code of Ethics

The Institute of Electrical and Electronic Engineers (IEEE) is the world's largest technical professional organisations with over 400,000 members in over 160 countries, and it is dedicated to advancing technology for the benefit of mankind. It publishes over 30% of the world's technical literature in electrical engineering, computer science and electronics as well as technical books and monographs. It is a leading developer of international standards in telecommunications and information technology, and individuals who have made outstanding contributions to engineering and technology may receive the prestigious IEEE Medal.

IEEE has developed a code of ethics for its members designed to ensure that they adhere to the highest ethical standards, and that its members treat others professionally and fairly, and ensure that they are not discriminated against on the grounds of gender, race, and so on (Table 10.4).

The IEEE Code of Ethics requires its members to promptly disclose any factors that might endanger the public or society, which shows that it recognises the importance of whistle blowing and the need for members to speak out when there is danger to the public. The code mentions the importance of avoiding conflicts of interest and disclosing them when they occur, and stresses that unlawful activities such as bribery should be rejected. The code highlights the importance of carrying

**Table 10.4** IEEE code of ethics

| No. | Description |
|---|---|
| *Highest ethical standards* | |
| 1. | To hold paramount the safety, health, and welfare of the public, to strive to comply with ethical design and sustainable development practices, to protect the privacy of others, and to disclose promptly factors that might endanger the public or the environment |
| 2. | To improve the understanding by individuals and society of the capabilities and societal implications of conventional and emerging technologies, including intelligent systems |
| 3. | To avoid real or perceived conflicts of interest whenever possible, and to disclose them to affected parties when they do exist |
| 4. | To avoid unlawful conduct in professional activities, and to reject bribery in all its forms |
| 5. | To seek, accept, and offer honest criticism of technical work, to acknowledge and correct errors, to be honest and realistic in stating claims or estimates based on available data, and to credit properly the contributions of others |
| 6. | To maintain and improve technical competence and to undertake technological tasks for others only if qualified by training or experience, or after full disclosure of pertinent limitations |
| *Treating people fairly* | |
| 7. | To treat all persons fairly and with respect, and to not engage in discrimination based on characteristics such as race, religion, gender, disability, age, national origin, sexual orientation, gender identity, or gender expression |
| 8. | To not engage in harassment of any kind, including sexual harassment or bullying behaviour |
| 9. | To avoid injuring others, their property, reputation, or employment by false or malicious actions, rumours or any other verbal or physical abuses |
| *Following the code* | |
| 10. | To support colleagues and co-workers in following this code of ethics, to strive to ensure the code is upheld, and to not retaliate against individuals reporting a violation |

out roles only when one is qualified to do so, and to continue to improve one's technical competence. It emphasises that people should be treated fairly and with respect, without discrimination on gender, ethnicity, etc., and that harassment and injury to others should be avoided.

## 10.5 British Computer Society Code of Conduct

The British Computer Society (BCS) is a professional organisation for information technology and computer science that was founded by in 1957, and its first president was Sir Maurice Wilkes.[2] It has roughly 70,000 members in 150 countries, and it has played an important role in educating IT professionals. The BCS provides awards such as the Lovelace Medal[3] to individuals, who have made outstanding contributions to the computing field.

The BCS has developed a code of conduct that defines the standards expected of BCS members, and it applies to all grades of members during their professional work. Any known breaches of the BCS codes by a member are investigated by the BCS, and the appropriate disciplinary procedures followed. The main parts of the BCS code of conduct are listed in Table 10.5.

The BCS Code of Ethics requires its members to be conscious of the public health and environment. It states that one should only carry out those roles that one is qualified to do so, and one should continue to improve one's technical competence. It states the importance of avoiding conflicts of interest, and that unlawful activities such as bribery should be rejected. It emphasises that members should seek to improve professional standards, and support other members in their professional development.

## 10.6 ACM Code of Professional Conduct and Ethics

The Association of Computing Machinery (ACM) is the world's largest educational and scientific computing society, and it delivers resources that advance computing as a science. It has over 100,000 members around the world, and it includes a number of special interest groups (e.g., SIG AI is a special interest group on AI, and SIG SOFT is a special interest group on software engineering). The ACM has defined a code of ethics and professional conduct for its members, and the Code is summarised in Table 10.6.

[2] Sir Maurice Wilkes developed the EDSAC computer at Cambridge University, England, which was one of the earliest stored-program computers. It was operational from May 1949.

[3] Ada Lovelace (the daughter of the poet, Lord Byron) was an English mathematician who collaborated with Charles Babbage (one of the grandfathers of the computing field) on applications of the Analytic Engine. Babbage designed the difference and analytic engines in the nineteenth century, and while the difference engine was a calculator for evaluating polynomials, the analytic engine was the design of the first mechanical computer.

**Table 10.5** BCS code of conduct

| Area | Description |
|---|---|
| Public interest | Due regard to public health, privacy, security and environment<br>Due regards to legitimate rights of third parties<br>Conduct professional activities without discrimination<br>Promote equal access to IT |
| Professional competence and integrity | Only do work within professional competence<br>Do not claim competence that you do not possess<br>Continuous development of knowledge/skills<br>Understand/knowledge/comply with legislation<br>Respect other viewpoints<br>Avoid injuring others<br>Reject bribery and unethical behaviour |
| Duty to relevant authority | Carry out professional responsibilities with due care and diligence.<br>Avoid conflicts of interest<br>Accept professional responsibility for your work<br>Do not disclose confidential information<br>Accurate information on performance of products |
| Duty to the profession | Uphold reputation of profession and BCS<br>Seek to improve professional standards<br>Act with integrity<br>Notify BCS if convicted of criminal offence<br>Support other members in their professional development |

The ACM Code of Ethics is comprehensive and requires its members to report any dangers that might cause damage or injury. The code mentions the importance of respecting intellectual property as well as privacy and confidentiality, and carrying out roles only when one is qualified to do so. Members should avoid conflicts of interest, and their work should be to the highest professional standards. Members should seek to improve their technical competence, and should treat people fairly and with respect. Finally, members should notify the ACM of any violations of the code.

## 10.7 Precautionary Principle

The precautionary principle argues that if there is an identifiable risk of serious or irreversible harm, then it may be appropriate to place the burden of proof on the organisation proposing the potentially risky activity to show that it is safe, and for inaction until a proof of safety has been provided.

The main problem with the precautionary principle is that it potentially forbids too much, and opponents have argued that several innovations used today would not have been implemented if the precautionary principle had been strictly adhered

**Table 10.6** ACM code of conduct

| No. | Area | Description |
|---|---|---|
| 1. *General principles* | | |
| 1.1. | Contribute to society and human well being | Computer professionals must strive to develop computer systems that will be used in socially responsible ways with minimal negative consequences |
| 1.2. | Avoid harm to others | Computer professionals must follow best practice to ensure that they develop high-quality systems that are safe for the public. The professional has a responsibility to report any signs of danger in the workplace that could result in serious damage or injury |
| 1.3. | Be honest and trustworthy | The computer professional will give an honest account of their qualifications and any conflicts of interest. The professional will make accurate statements on the system and the system design, and will exercise care in representing ACM |
| 1.4. | Be fair and act not to discriminate | Computer professionals are required to ensure that there is no discrimination in the use of computer resources, and that equality, tolerance and respect for others are promoted |
| 1.5. | Respect property rights/intellectual property | The professional must not violate copyright or patent law, and only authorised copies of software should be made. The integrity of intellectual property must be protected, and credit for another person's ideas or work must not be taken |
| 1.6. | Respect the privacy of others | The professional must ensure that any personal information gathered for a specific purpose is not used for another purpose without the consent of the individuals. User data observed during normal system operation must be treated with the strictest confidentiality |
| 1.7. | Respect confidentiality | The professional will respect all confidentiality obligations to employers, clients and users |
| 2. *Professional responsibility* | | |
| 2.1 | Quality of processes/product | Computing professionals should strive to achieve the highest quality work throughout the process |

(continued)

**Table 10.6** (continued)

| No. | Area | Description |
|---|---|---|
| 2.2 | Maintain high standards | It is essential to maintain high standards of technical knowledge and competence, and to upgrade skills on an ongoing basis |
| 2.3 | Respect rules | Computing professionals must adhere to rules including national and international laws and regulations |
| 2.4 | Professional review | Peer reviews play an important role in building quality into a work product, and computing professions should seek reviews of their work as well as participating in reviews |
| 2.5 | Comprehensive evaluations | Computing professionals are required to be thorough and comprehensive in their evaluation of computer systems including analysis and management of risk |
| 2.6 | Areas of competence | Computing professionals should only undertake work for which they have the required competence |
| 2.7 | Foster public awareness | Computing professionals should share technical knowledge with the public, and foster public awareness and understanding of computing |
| 2.8 | Authorised use of resources | Computing professionals should only access computer systems and software when they are authorised to do so |
| 2.9 | Secure systems | Computing professionals should develop robust and secure systems, as well as mitigation techniques and policies |
| 3. *Professional leadership* | | |
| 3.1 | Public good | The leader should ensure that the public good is the central concern during all professional computing work |
| 3.2 | Social responsibilities | Leaders should encourage computing professionals in meeting relevant social responsibilities |
| 3.3 | Quality of working life | Leaders should enhance the quality of working life of workers |
| 3.4 | Support principles of code | Leaders should pursue policies that are consistent with the code, and communicate them to the relevant stakeholders |

(continued)

**Table 10.6** (continued)

| No. | Area | Description |
|---|---|---|
| 3.5 | Support growth of professionals | Leaders should ensure that opportunities are available to computing professionals to improve their knowledge and skill |
| 3.6 | Modifying / retiring systems | Leaders should exercise care when modifying or retiring systems |
| 3.7 | Special care | Leaders have a responsibility to be good stewards of systems that become part of the infrastructure of society |
| 4. *Compliance* | | |
| 4.1 | Uphold code | Computing professionals should adhere to the principles in the code and strive to improve them, and to express their concern to any individuals thought to be violating the code |
| 4.2 | Violations of code | ACM members who recognise a breach in the code should report the violation to the ACM |

to. Further, its opponents argue that its demands for incontrovertible proof that there is no damage or harm is impractical, and that it is more sensible to demand that there are reasonable grounds for believing that there is no danger from the proposed activity or technology.

The precautionary principle may also be applied to unknown threats, where the principle permits preventive measures to be taken prior to fully knowing the seriousness of the threat. That is,

1. There is a threat
2. The threat is uncertain
3. Some kind of action is required
4. Action is taken

## 10.8 Case Study on Workplace Ethics

The author has worked in both industry and academia, and in this section two incidents that the author observed during his industrial experience are briefly discussed.

The first of these was an audio conference call that was made to a sister plant of a multinational company in the United States, which the author attended with two to three other people. It was held in a senior manager's office, and when the conference call was about to end the senior manager gave the impression to the sister plant that he was about to leave the call, but instead he put the phone on silent and listened to the views expressed of the other participants of the sister plant as to whether they expected his plant to deliver the project on time and with the right quality. It allowed him to receive information that he would not otherwise have obtained, but it struck me at the time as being an underhand and inappropriate way of receiving that information.

The second incident was an arrangement made with a sister plant of the multinational company based in the UK in relation to the weekly conference call between the plant in Ireland, the US and the UK. A written agreement was drawn up between personnel in the plant in Ireland and the UK, where it was agreed that serious issues would be first discussed between the plant in Ireland and the UK prior to them being escalated to the US. The ink was hardly dry on the agreement before it was broken by the sister plant in the UK on the Friday conference call. And so, there was a sense of being let down by colleagues in another jurisdiction, and it led to a partial breakdown of trust that took time to heal.

## 10.9 Review Questions

1. Explain professional responsibility and accountability?
2. What is a code of ethics?
3. Describe the main features of the IEEE code of conduct.
4. Describe the main features of the BCS code of conduct.
5. Describe the main features of the ACM code of conduct.
6. What is the role of a whistle blower?
7. Give examples of conflicts of interest that could arise in the work place.
8. What is the precautionary principle?
9. What are the benefits to an organisation in having a code of ethics?

## 10.10 Summary

Professional responsibility refers to the responsibility of computer professionals to carry out their work professionally to the highest standards, and to use sound judgment in the exercise of their duties. Professionals are accountable to themselves and others for their actions, and they must be held accountable when performance does not meet professional standards.

Software engineers have professional responsibilities in that they are responsible for designing and implementing high-quality and reliable software that is safe for the public to use. They are also accountable for their own decisions and actions, and have a responsibility to object to decisions that violate professional standards.

A professional code of ethics expresses ideals of human behaviour, and the Association Computing Machinery, the Institute of Electrical and Electronic Engineers, and the British Computer Society have developed codes of conduct for their members. Violations of the code by members are taken seriously, and are subject to investigations and disciplinary procedures.

The precautionary principle argues that if there is an identifiable risk of serious or irreversible harm, then it may be appropriate to place the burden of proof on the organisation proposing the potentially risky activity to show that it is safe, and for inaction until a proof of safety has been provided.

# Ethical Software Engineering

# 11

## 11.1 Introduction

Software engineering is a discipline that is concerned with the development of software, and it includes activities such as requirements gathering and definition, software design and development, and software testing to verify the correctness of the software. It is a team-based activity with several roles involved such as project managers, system analysts, developers and testers. Software engineering involves defining the right requirements, and then designing and implementing an appropriate solution that is fit for purpose, and verifying that the implementation satisfies the requirements.

Programmers are engineers and therefore need to learn the key engineering skills to enable them to build high quality products that are safe for the public to use. Software engineering involves the multi-person construction of multi-version programs. The IEEE 610.12 definition is:

> Software engineering is the application of a systematic, disciplined, quantifiable approach to the development, operation, and maintenance of software; that is, the application of engineering to software, and the study of such approaches

Software engineering includes:

1. Methodologies to design, develop, and test software to meet customers' needs.
2. Software is engineered. That is, the software products are properly designed, developed, and tested in accordance with sound engineering principles.
3. Quality and safety are properly addressed.
4. Mathematics may be employed to assist with the design and verification of software products. The level of mathematics employed will depend on the *safety critical* nature of the product. Systematic peer reviews and rigorous testing will



G. O'Regan, *Philosophical and Cultural Aspects of Computing*, Undergraduate Topics in Computer Science, https://doi.org/10.1007/978-3-032-29284-1_11

often be sufficient to build quality into the software, with heavy *mathematical techniques often reserved for safety and security critical software.*
5. Sound project management and quality management practices are employed.
6. Support and maintenance of the software is properly addressed.

Software engineering is not just programming. It requires the engineer to state precisely the requirements that the software is to satisfy, and then to produce designs that will meet these requirements. The creation of a software product is a project that needs to be planned and delivered on time and budget. The requirements must provide a precise description of the problem to be solved: i.e., *it should be evident from the requirements what is and what is not required.*

The requirements need to be rigorously reviewed to ensure that they are stated clearly and unambiguously, and reflect the customer's needs. The next step is then to create the design that will solve the problem, and it is essential to validate the correctness of the design. Next, the software code to implement the design is written, and peer reviews and software testing are employed to verify and validate the correctness of the software.

The verification and validation of the design is rigorously performed for safety critical systems, and it is sometimes appropriate to employ mathematical techniques for the verification. Mathematics plays a key role in classical engineering, and form part of the software engineer's toolbox for the safety critical field. Dijkstra and Hoare have argued that the way to develop correct software is to derive the program from its specifications using mathematics, and to employ *mathematical proof* to demonstrate its correctness with respect to the specification. Essential mathematics for software engineering are described in [ORg:23], but, it will often be sufficient to employ peer reviews and testing for verification and validation, as these methodologies provide a high degree of rigour.

The term "*engineer*" is a title that is awarded on merit in classical engineering. It is generally applied only to people who have attained the necessary education and competence to be called engineers, and who base their practice on sound engineering principles. The title places responsibilities on its holder to behave professionally and ethically. Often in computer science the term "*software engineer*" is employed loosely to refer to anyone who builds things, rather than to an individual with a core set of knowledge, experience, and competence.

Several computer scientists such as Parnas[1] have argued that computer scientists should be educated as engineers to enable them to apply appropriate scientific principles to their work. The use of mathematics is an integral part of the engineer's work in other engineering disciplines, and so the *software engineer* should be able to use mathematics to assist in the modelling or understanding of the behaviour or properties of the proposed software system.

[1] Parnas advocates a solid engineering approach with classical mathematical used in software development. He also introduced information hiding in the 1970s, which is now a part of object-oriented design.

Parnas argued that software engineers have responsibilities as professional engineers. They are responsible for designing and implementing high-quality and reliable software that is safe to use. They are also accountable for their decisions and actions,[2] and have a responsibility to object to decisions that violate professional standards.

Engineers are required to behave professionally and ethically with their clients. The membership of the professional engineering body requires the member to adhere to the code of ethics of the profession. Engineers in other professions are licensed, and therefore Parnas argues that a similar licensing approach be adopted for professional software engineers to provide confidence that they are competent for the particular assignment.[3] Professional software engineers are required to follow best practice in software engineering and the defined software processes.[4]

Many companies invest heavily in training, as educated and knowledgeable employees are essential in the delivery of high-quality products and services. Employees need to receive appropriate training related to the roles that they perform, such as project management, software design and development, software testing, and service management. The fact that the employees are professionally qualified increases confidence in the ability of the company to deliver high-quality products and services. A company that pays little attention to the competence and continuous development of its staff will achieve poor results, and suffer a loss of reputation and market share.

There are several well-known lifecycles employed in software development such as the waterfall model, the spiral model, the Rational Unified Process, and the Agile methodology. The choice of a particular software development lifecycle is determined from the needs of the specific project.

[2] It is unlikely that an individual programmer would be subject to litigation in the case of a flaw in a program causing damage or loss of life. A comprehensive disclaimer of responsibility for problems rather than a guarantee of quality accompany most software products. Software engineering is a team-based activity involving many engineers in various parts of the project, and it would be potentially difficult for an outside party to prove that the cause of a particular problem is due to the professional negligence of a particular software engineer, as there are many others involved in the process such as reviewers of documentation and code and the various test groups. Companies are more likely to be subject to litigation, as a company is legally responsible for the actions of their employees in the workplace, and a company is a wealthier entity than one of its employees. The legal aspects of licensing software may protect software companies from litigation. However, greater legal protection for the customer can be built into the contract between the supplier and the customer for bespoke-software development.

[3] The British Computer Society (BCS) has introduced a qualification system for computer science professionals, which is used to show that professionals are properly qualified. The most important of these is the BCS Information Systems Examination Board (ISEB) which allows IT professionals to be qualified in service management, project management, software testing, and so on.

[4] Software companies that are following the CMMI or ISO 9001 standards will employ audits to verify that the processes and procedures have been followed. Auditors report their findings to management and the findings are addressed appropriately by the project team and affected individuals.

The waterfall model is employed for projects where the requirements can be identified early in the project lifecycle or are known in advance, and the phases include requirements, specification, design, and coding, unit tests, integration tests, system tests and acceptance testing. Each phase has entry and exit criteria that must be satisfied before the next phase commences [Roy:70].

The spiral model was developed by Barry Boehm in the 1980s [Boe:88], and it is useful for projects where the requirements are not fully known at project initiation, or where the requirements evolve as a part of the software development lifecycle. The development proceeds in a number of spirals, where each spiral implements new functionality, and typically involves determining objectives and analysing the risks, updates to the requirements, design, code, testing, and a user review of the particular iteration or spiral.

The *Rational Unified Process* [Jac:99b] was developed at the Rational Corporation (now part of IBM) in the late 1990s. It uses the Unified Modelling Language (UML) as a tool for specification and design. UML is a visual modelling language for software systems that provides a means of specifying, constructing, and documenting the object-oriented system. James Rumbaugh, Grady Booch, and Ivar Jacobson developed it to facilitate the understanding of the architecture and complexity of a system (see Chap. 18 of [ORg:22]).

There has been a massive growth of popularity among software developers in lightweight methodologies such as *Agile*. This is a methodology that is more responsive to customer needs than traditional methods such as the waterfall model. *The waterfall development model is similar to a wide and slow moving value stream,* and halfway through the project 100% of the requirements are typically 50% done. *However, for agile development 50% of requirements are typically 100% done halfway through the project*. Agile has a strong collaborative style of working [Bec:00, Bec:01].

The CMMI is a framework to assist an organization in the implementation of best practice in software and systems engineering. It is used world-wide by thousands of organizations, and provides a solid engineering approach to the development of software. It supports the definition of high-quality processes for the various software engineering and management activities [CKS:11].

Software inspections play an important role in building quality into the software, and in reducing the cost of poor quality. There are several well-known inspection methodologies such as the Fagan Methodology [Fag:76] and Gilb's approach [Glb:94]. Software engineering is described in more detail in [ORg:22].

There is a need to make technical decisions quite frequently in software engineering, and often these decisions affect people's lives, and occasionally there are potential harmful impacts on others and on society. This means that the ethical impacts of technical decisions needs to be considered as part of the software engineering process, and so the ethical software engineer needs to examine both the technical and the ethical dimensions of decisions that affect wider society. An ethical software engineer should:

- Do no harm

- Do not take bribes
- Be fair to others

A fundamental principle of ethics is based on the Hippocratic Oath "*Do no harm*", which may be seen to be breached where there are violations of ethics. For example, the Volkswagen emissions scandal (discussed later in the chapter) led to the deception of the general public and harm to society, the Volkswagen Company, its shareholders and its employees. The actions of Volkswagen were unethical and illegal.

The codes of ethics provide guidance on the interaction of technology and values, and software engineers need to be aware of their ethical responsibilities throughout the software development process, and to take action whenever ethical standards are in danger of being violated.

## 11.2 Safety and Ethics

The release of an unreliable software product may result in damage to property or injury (including loss of life) to a third party. Consequently, companies need to be confident that their software products are of a high quality and fit for purpose prior to their release. It is essential that software that is widely used is dependable, which means that the software is available whenever required, and that it operates safely and reliably without any adverse side effects.

Today, billions of devices and computers are connected to the Internet, and this has led to a massive growth in attacks on computers. It is essential that computer security is carefully considered during system design, and that developers are aware of the threats facing a system, and of techniques to manage or eliminate them. The software developers need to develop secure dependable systems that can deal with and recover from external attacks.

A safety critical system is a system whose failure could result in significant economic damage or loss of life. There are many examples of safety critical systems such as aircraft flight control systems, nuclear power stations and missile systems. It is essential to employ rigorous processes in the design and development of these systems, and software testing alone is often insufficient in verifying their correctness.

The safety critical industry takes the view that any change to safety critical software creates a new program. The new program is therefore required to demonstrate that it is reliable and safe for the public, and so extensive testing needs to be performed. Additional techniques such as formal verification and model checking may be employed to provide an extra level of assurance in its correctness.

Safety critical systems need to be reliable, dependable and available for use whenever required. The software must operate correctly and reliably without any adverse side effects. The consequence of failure (e.g., the failure of a weapons system) could be massive damage, leading to loss of life or endangering the lives of the public. We discuss two important case studies on disasters that occurred in the mid-1980s, and these are the Therac-25 disaster (see Sect. 11.2.1) and the Space Shuttle Challenger Disaster (see Sect. 11.2.2).

### 11.2.1 Therac-25 Disaster

The Therac-25 was a computer-controlled radiation therapy machine that was developed by the Atomic Energy of Canada (AECL) in the early 1980s. This linear accelerator treated cancer patients by exposing them to a beam of particles that would destroy malignant tissue (Fig. 11.1).

The machine consisted of hardware and software, and whereas the role of software on the earlier Therac-20 machine was limited, software played a more important role in the later Therac-25 machine. Its role was to perform many of the safety critical checks for the Therac-25, whereas this was performed by hardware on the earlier Therac-20 machine. The software on the Therac-25 radiation machine was responsible for:

- Monitoring the status of the machine
- Accepting treatment input
- Setting up the machine for the treatment
- Turning on the treatment beam

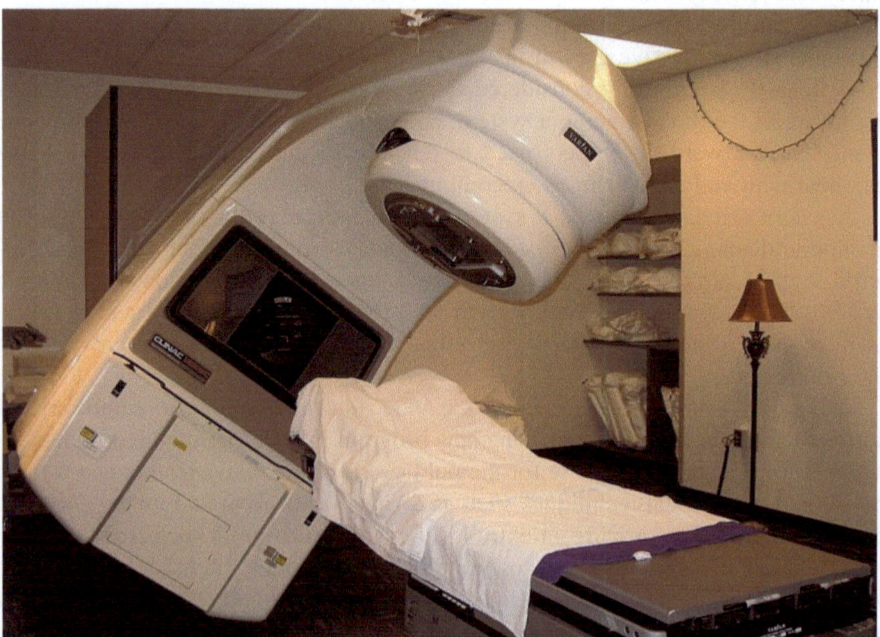

**Fig. 11.1** A radiotherapy machine

- Turning off the treatment beam
- Detecting hardware malfunction

There were six major accidents with the machine in the mid-1980s (1985–1987), where patients were given massive overdoses of radiation. The machine malfunctioned, and several patients received doses that were hundreds of time in excess of the appropriate dose, resulting in the death of three people and serious injuries to three others.

The machine continued in use for over 18 months after the first accident, with AECL believing that an accident was impossible with the machine, and it took no action with respect to the first reported accident. The second accident occurred a month later, and AECL sent an engineer on site to investigate the incident. He was unable to reproduce the problem, but AECL made some hardware and software changes and claimed that this solved the problem, as well as increasing the reliability of the machine a multiple of times.

AECL's response to the third accident was a denial of the problem, where they stated that the malfunction could not have been caused by the Therac-25 machine. They claimed that the fourth accident was as the result of a wiring problem. Finally, as a result of fifth accident and FDA investigations into the operation of the Therac-25 machine, AECL finally launched a thorough investigation. The FDA ruled that the Therac-25 machines were defective, and advised AECL to prepare a corrective action plan, and advise their customers of the problems with the machine.

The corrective action plan was prepared by AECL and presented to the FDA, which led to serious concerns in the FDA with respect to the software engineering practices employed in AECL. The FDA identified risks that AECL's engineering practices posed to the delivery of a high-quality product that would be safe to use, and that would not endanger the public. There was a lack of software engineering documentation for the software development, and the testing of the software was judged to be inadequate. The FDA directed AECL to do extensive testing on the system each time a small software change was made to ensure the safety of the software. The main reasons for the Therac-25 disaster include:

- Initial failure to believe end users
- Overconfidence of engineers in its correctness
- Poor software design and development practices
- Inadequate testing
- Software errors
- Poor resolution of software defects

The Therac-25 disaster led to the deaths of three people and serious injury to three others. Software engineering practices were immature in the 1980s, but this is no excuse for what happened. It is basic common sense that a proper investigation should have been done after the first accident, and that all existing machines should have been considered to be unsafe until proved otherwise. That is, all Therac-25 machines should have been removed from operational use until the cause of the problem had been correctly identified, and appropriate solutions implemented to prevent a reoccurrence.

### 11.2.2 Space Shuttle Challenger Disaster

The Space Shuttle Challenger disaster is an important case study on engineering safety and workplace ethics. The disaster occurred in January 1986, when the space shuttle broke apart 73 s into its flight, and all of the seven members of the crew were killed. The Rogers Commission was formed to investigate the accident, and it found that the Challenger disaster was caused by a failure in the O-Rings sealing (a joint on the right solid rocket booster), where the record low temperatures had stiffened the rubber O-Rings, and reduced their ability to seal the joint. The report also criticised the decision making process that led to the launch stating that it was deeply flawed, *with conflicts between engineering data and management judgments* (Fig. 11.2).

Robert Boisjoly, an engineer at Morton Thiokel launched strong objections to the launch, as he was aware of the risks of erosion and failure when the 0-Rings of the Solid Rocket Booster (SRB) were exposed to low temperatures. He argued that the shuttle launch should be postponed to a later date due to the predicted temperatures.

Both the NASA project team and the management team at Morton Thiokel had the opportunity to prevent the challenger disaster by postponing the launch. During the conference call on the evening prior to the launch the entire Morton Thiokel team recommended a postponement, as they recommended a minimum launch temperature of 52 °F. Temperatures were forecast to drop to 30 °F overnight which was likely to compromise the safety of the launch. They had expected NASA to rubber stamp the decision, but they were wrong, and NASA stated that the Morton Thiokel briefing was based on emotion rather than factual data. NASA requested Morton Thiokel to review their data again to determine if the data showed that it was unsafe to proceed, and the conference call was re-scheduled to later in the evening.

For a launch to take place all sub-contractors must sign-off on going ahead, and NASA seems to have encouraged (or perhaps pressurised) Morton Thiokel to recommend the launch unless they could prove that it was unsafe to do so. The conference call had been delayed to allow Morton Thiokel management to consider all of the data, and the result of the Morton Thiokel management meeting (which excluded participation from Boisjoly) was to recommend proceeding with the launch. Morton Thiokel stated that its data was inconclusive at the conference call with NASA, and all sub-contractors agreed to proceed with the launch. Boisjoly later called the Morton Thiokel decision to go ahead to be unethical.

*Separatism* is the idea that scientists and engineers provide the technical input and advice to management concerning a particular engineering situation, and management decide how best to proceed. That is, managers act as the decision maker

**Fig. 11.2** Space challenger disaster

**Fig. 11.3** Bridge over the river Kwaii in Kanchanburi, Thailand

## 11.4 Ethical Software Design and Development

Ethical software design and development is concerned with ethical issues that may arise during technology development, such as questions as to how the technology will be used, and whether it could lead to harm to individuals and society. The design of a technology determines how it will be used, and this means that there needs to be an ethical dimension to the design process, where ethical values are considered as well as the desired functionality.

David Lean directed the movie "*The Bridge on the River Kwai*" in 1957,[5] and the film was based on the historical construction of the Thailand-Burma railway during the Japanese occupation of Burma in the Second World War. British prisoners of war are ordered to construct the bridge, and initially the British and their leader, Colonel Nicholson, resist participation in its construction. However, Colonel Nicholson later becomes obsessed with designing and building a proper bridge that will last well beyond the war, and that will be a tribute to the skill and ingenuity of British engineers (Fig. 11.3).

They build a solid bridge over the river and on the day that it is due to be opened with the first train due to pass over Nicholson finally realises the gravity of what he has done (i.e., collaborating with the enemy and contributing to their plans for further aggression). He blows up the bridge sending the train into the

[5] The film was actually made on the Kelani river (near Kitulgala) in Ceylon (Sri Lanka).

river. That is, the purpose of the technology (i.e., the completed bridge) needed to be considered, as a completed bridge would cause harm to others in that it would have facilitated an expansion of Japanese aggression to other countries. Further, it was unethical for Nicholson to collaborate with his enemy who wished to harm him and his country, and so his collaboration conflicted with his duties to his country and to the British army.

Software design is the process where certain functions are translated into a blueprint for a system that can fulfil these functions. There are often several design choices for a particular technology, and different designs may vary in the extent to which they deal with particular ethical values. The goal is to choose the design that best meets the most important ethical values and technology considerations, and this means that responsible choices must be made in the selection of the most appropriate design. Software design is a systematic process that uses technical and scientific knowledge, and there may need for trade offs with conflicting values in the different designs. It involves activities such as:

- Problem analysis
- Requirements analysis and definition (may include prototyping)
- Architectural Design (may include design options and decision)
- Low Level Design
- Implementation
- Testing
- Maintenance

*Value centred design* (VCD) is an approach to design that involves taking human values into account during the design process, and solving value conflicts through engineering design and technological innovation. It involves investigating and determining the values that are relevant to the project, and understanding conflicts to make tradeoffs. There is a need to analyse designs to determine the extent to which they meet particular values, and to develop innovative designs to meet particularly relevant values. Valued centred design involves:

- Reasoning/clarifying values underlying conflicting design requirements
- Social cost benefit analysis (including monetary costs for safety)
- Evaluation criteria (including value criteria, weightings may be employed)
- Thresholds for what is acceptable for each criterion
- Evaluation of options
- Selected option

There may be conflicts between ethical values when choosing between two or more design options, and where different designs score well on different criteria. This is, designers may be unable to do justice to all ethical values simultaneously, and often the resolution of the dilemma requires a trade off or balancing between competing values. A trade off decision is where a choice needs to be made between at least two options, in which at least two moral values are relevant as choice criteria,

**Fig. 11.4** Balancing an ethical life against a feather in Egyptian religion

and so finding the right balance in the trade off decisions may be a challenge (Fig. 11.4).

Software designers have a responsibility to create ethical designs that satisfy the requirements, and to ensure that their designs are robust and protect the safety of the public. Ethics is an important design concern that needs to be considered, and this will determine how well the product fits within the ethical boundaries. There may be several ethical values that are relevant, including safety, accessibility, usability, sustainability, privacy, security, honesty, fairness and loyalty. The evaluation of each design option should rate the extent to which the relevant ethical values are addressed by that option as well as the technical criteria.

Data management is an important part of ethical software engineering, where personal data ownership as well as data rights, access rights, privacy and security rights need to be considered and protected. Software designers need to follow the legal requirements as well as best practice in privacy and security in collecting, processing and protecting data. An ethical system needs to be accessible, and its design should consider its accessibility for different categories of users, such as those with visual or hearing impairments, or those with different levels of language ability or education.

The ethical design of a software system should give an open and accurate account of the system, and should satisfy all relevant legal and regulatory requirements. We discuss the Volkswagen *Dieselgate* emissions scandal in the next section, where the unethical conduct of management of the company involved tasking software designers to create a "defeat device" that would enable Volkswagen vehicles to cheat the federal emissions tests in the United States.

Ethical software designers need to be conscious of the algorithms that they create to ensure that they are unbiased, and do not discriminate against minority groups in society. This is especially important in algorithms based on pattern matching that are employed in the AI field, where *biased algorithms* may lead to discrimination against individuals and groups. There have been several controversial algorithms such as the infamous Amazon hiring algorithm that discriminated against females, and a predictive policing algorithm that led to racial profiling and discrimination against racial groups. These issues are discussed in more detail in Chap. 14.

Software designers should consider the ultimate purpose of the project including its benefits to society as well as harm from the technology. We discussed the purpose of the bridge over the river Kwai, and argued that its design and implementation had the potential to harm Britain and the Allies in their efforts to defeat the Axis powers. Social media and various other apps are designed to be *addictive* to their users, where the software captures the attention of the human at a primal level, and the company reaps financial gain from the addiction of the users. Humans have become addicted to their smartphones, and check their phone hundreds of time a day, and their addiction has been caused by addictive software design. This poses questions as to the ethics of this type of design, and whether the consequences of the design and the end product should be considered in ethical decision-making.

Software companies also need to be environmentally responsible in the partnerships that they develop with other companies, especially with respect to the ultimate purpose of the partnership. For example, the Big Oil industry is active in climate pollution, and several cloud-computing companies have worked with oil companies and used AI and machine learning technologies to create visual maps to enable them to determine where best to drill to extract more polluting fossil fuels. *That is, many software companies turn a blind eye as to how its software products are used, and it is essential that a company committed to corporate social responsibility and environmental sustainability behave responsibly.*

The system needs to be designed for security, as it is difficult to add security after the system has been implemented. Security engineering is concerned with the development of systems that can prevent malicious attacks, and recover from them. Software developers need to be aware of the threats facing a system, and develop solutions to manage them. Security loopholes may be introduced in the development of the system, and so care needs to be taken to prevent these as well as preventing hackers from exploiting security vulnerabilities.

There is a need to conduct a risk assessment of the security threats facing a system early in the software development process, and this will lead to several security requirements for the system. That is, the requirements of the system should specify security and privacy requirements, and the software design and development must implement them to ensure that security and privacy are not breached. Security testing (including penetration testing) is carried out to identify any flaws in the security mechanisms of the computer system, and to verify that the security requirements such as confidentiality, availability, integrity, etc., are satisfied. However, the successful completion of security testing does not guarantee that there are no security vulnerabilities in the system, as hackers will still attempt to steal confidential data and to disrupt the services being offered by a system.

### 11.4.1 Volkswagen Emissions Scandal

The Volkswagen *Dieselgate* scandal arose as a result of the German company deliberately programming its turbocharged direct injection (TDI) diesel engines to activate their emissions controls only during laboratory emissions tests. This meant that the vehicles $NO_x$ emissions passed the US federal regulatory requirements during laboratory tests, whereas the actual emissions were over 40 times higher in real-world driving (Fig. 11.5).

Volkswagen deployed this software in over 11 million vehicles world wide including roughly half a million vehicles in the United States from 2009 to 2015. It became evident in 2014 that there were discrepancies in emissions between European and US models, and regulators in several countries launched an investigation into Volkswagen. Several senior executives resigned or were suspended, and Volkswagen spent billions in recalling the affected vehicles and rectifying the issues with the emissions.

**Fig. 11.5** Volkswagen beetle type 82E

Volkswagen pleaded guilty to criminal charges in 2017, and they admitted to developing a "*defeat device*" to enable diesel models to pass US emission tests and deliberately concealing its use. Volkswagen was fined $2.8 billion for rigging the vehicles to cheat on the emission tests. The scandal had cost Volkswagen $33 billion in fines, penalties, financial settlements and buyback costs by mid-2020. Martin Winterkorn resigned his position of the CEO of Volkwagen in 2015, and he was charged with fraud and conspiracy in the United States in 2018.

The scandal highlighted how software controlled machinery is prone to cheating, and it has opened up a debate on whether there is a need for a mechanism to independently verify software that is employed to satisfy legal or regulatory requirements. That is, should all such software code be published for scrutiny by independent regulators and/or independently certified?

The Volkswagen scandal is deeply concerning as it demonstrates the failure of corporate/business ethics to act as a barrier to the pursuit of business self-interest. Volkswagen is a prestigious German company and it is extraordinary that the professionalism that Germany is renowned for could be tarnished in this way. Unfortunately, sometimes the code of ethics of an organisation are just window dressing for the public, rather than being embraced and engrained in the day to day work practices of daily corporate life.

Why did engineers fail to consider their ethical responsibilities? Why did they fail to question the implementation of this device? Why were there no whistle blowers to speak out against these unethical practices rather than just following orders[6]? Was there a lack of moral courage among the engineers? Were there appropriate structures in place for whistleblowers to discuss ethical concerns? Was there a total failure of corporate governance? Volkswagen's actions were illegal and deeply unethical, and its good name has been deeply tarnished. Herbert Diess became CEO in 2018, and helped to restore Volkswagen's tarnished reputation as well as overseeing the transition to electric vehicles.

A corporate environment is generally focused on the business and product implementation rather than on critical reflection on the wider implications of their technology. Engineers are often busy with their lives outside the office while trying to build a career within the office, and speaking out may not be viewed as a career-advancing move. Further, a hierarchical work environment does not actively encourage speaking out on issues outside of product development, with corporate enterprises often command driven operations, with power assigned within the hierarchy, and subordinates may fear the consequences of speaking out.

Engineers are often focused on getting the software to perform correctly to meet its specification, and so often may not consider the wide societal impacts of the technology. However, it is in the interest of both corporations and their employees to consider the bigger picture, and to actively consider ethical issues in the design process. Otherwise, they could well pay the price for their inaction later with significant damage to their reputation as well as financial loss.

[6] Conformism seems to be a part of German culture.

## 11.5 Ethical Software Testing

Software testers are professionals and need to behave ethically at all times during testing. The ISTQB Code of Ethics for test professionals is based on the IEEE and ACM code of ethics and states that:

- Certified software testers shall act consistently in the public interest.
- They act in the best interests of their client and employer.
- They ensure that their deliverables meet the highest professional standards.
- They maintain independence and integrity in professional judgments.
- They shall promote an ethical approach to the management of software testing.
- They shall advance the integrity and reputation of the profession.
- They shall be supportive of colleagues and cooperate with software developers.
- They shall participate in lifelong learning and promote ethics in their profession

Comprehensive testing reduces the risk of serious quality problems with the software, but it is impossible to test everything due to time constraints. This means that the testers need to focus their testing on the areas of greatest risk with the software, and on the parts of the system that the users are most likely to be using. It is essential that the testers have the appropriate expertise, that the right test environment is set up, that they have prepared test plans and test specification to test the software, and that they have all the required tools in place.

Ethical issues may arise during testing if the project (a traditional waterfall project rather than an Agile project) is behind schedule, and when there is pressure applied to the test team to stay with the original project delivery schedule. It may be that the available time for testing is insufficient to verify the correctness of the software, or the limited time could lead to testers missing serious defects. This could lead to the quality of the released software being compromised, and the test manager needs to resist any pressure that poses risks to quality, and needs to raise concerns at senior level where appropriate.

It is essential that the customer be informed of all quality problems with the software to ensure that they can manage any associated risks. The final test report should summarise the testing that has been done, the results of the testing, the open problems, the problem arrival rate, and known risks with the software. The final test report generally includes a recommendation from the test manager to release the software, and such a recommendation should be based on the key facts with a clear statement that all risks can be managed.

There may be conflicts when the project manager wishes to release the software on schedule, and where the test manager has concerns or believes that it is unsafe to do so based on the key testing status and risks. It is essential in such situations that the decision made is based on the facts and risks, and objective data should support the decision.

## 11.6 Ethical Software Outsourcing

Software outsourcing is a way for a business to hire a third party subcontractor to develop all or part of a software development project, rather than carrying out the project in-house. It has become popular for western companies to outsource software developments to countries in Asia and Eastern Europe, with India now a major player for software outsourcing, and Poland and the Ukraine[7] have also become popular.

There are various motivations for outsourcing such as the desire to reduce the cost of software development, or it may be that the company may wish to focus on its core business and to outsource non-core activities, or it may that the company lacks the expertise or capacity to implement the project internally. There are various models of outsourcing including where a company may partner with a third party supplier as a way to obtain extra IT resources for a company project, or it might outsource all or parts of the project to a third party supplier under the company's supervision, or it may outsource to a subcontractor that is given full responsibility for the work from the start to the end with minimal supervision.

A company may contract out business functions such as manufacturing, software development, and call centres to third party providers. The outsourcing of a business function to a distant country is termed *offshoring*, whereas outsourcing may also be done domestically, and *nearshoring* is the term used where the outsourcing is to a nearby country. The main benefits of outsourcing include:

- Cost savings due to a reduction in business expenses
- Availability of expertise not available in house
- Allows company to focus on its core business activities
- Increased efficiencies

There are business risks with outsourcing such as the quality of the service may be below expectations, or the third party may go out of business, or that there may be risks to confidentiality and security of data. Outsourcing involves managing the day-to-day relationship with the offshore/onshore team in possibly different time zones, and there could also be differences in language and culture.

The costs of outsourcing may be significantly cheaper than developing the software internally, but there are risks that it could become more expensive where there are delays or significant rework due to poor quality. There are risks of disruption of business activities depending on the political climate of the country where the subcontractor is based. Further, there may be risks of pandemics, natural disasters, or the subcontractor becoming bankrupt. It is essential that contractors are qualified for the work that they are to perform, and that the risks are identified and managed.

[7] This was prior to the Russian invasion (or special military operation) of Ukraine in 2022.

Many large software projects involve total or partial outsourcing of the software development, and it is therefore essential to select a supplier that has the capability and expertise to deliver a high-quality solution on time and on budget. Supplier selection and management is concerned with the selection and management of a third-party software supplier, and the success of the project is dependent on the expertise and competence of the suppliers. That is, it is essential that the selected supplier is competent and capable of delivering high-quality and reliable software on time and on budget.

This means that the process for supplier selection must be rigorous, and that the capability of the supplier is clearly understood, as well as understanding the associated supplier risks prior to selection. The selection is based on objective criteria such as cost, the approach proposed, the ability of the supplier to deliver the required solution, the supplier capability, and while cost is an important criterion, it is just one among several other important factors.

Once supplier selection is finalised a legal agreement is drawn up between the contractor and supplier, which states the terms and condition of the contract, as well as the associated statement of work. The statement of work details the work to be carried out, the deliverables to be produced, when they will be produced, the personnel involved as well as their roles and responsibilities, any training that needs to be provided, and the standards to be followed.

The supplier then commences the defined work and is appropriately managed for the duration of the contract. This will involve regular progress reviews, and acceptance testing is carried out prior to accepting the software from the supplier. The following activities are generally employed for supplier selection and management (Table 11.1).

The legal agreement between the company and the subcontractor specifies the obligations on both parties for the duration of the contract. These include the deliverables to be produced, the timelines, the responsibilities of both parties, and the financial payments to be made at agreed milestones. A contract is legally binding on both parties with both having defined obligations, and should one party fail to deliver according to the terms of the agreement then they may be in breach of the contract.[8]

The area of corporate social responsibility (CSR) has become topical in recent years, and companies have a responsibility to be good corporate citizens and to consider wider society in their actions and to consider their impact on the world. That is, corporations are expected to behave ethically, and to be environmentally conscious of their carbon footprint and on the sustainability of their business operations in the countries in which they are operating (even at the expense of profits).

There are several ethical issues with outsourcing such as the fact that outsourcing may lead to loss of jobs in the home country of the company, when it decides to outsource its software development/testing to a cheaper country. It would seem

[8] It is also possible that two parties make a verbal contract that is legally enforceable.

**Table 11.1** Supplier selection and management

| Activity | Description |
|---|---|
| Planning and requirements | This involves defining the approach to the procurement. It involves:<br>• Defining the procurement requirements<br>• Define evaluation criteria<br>• Form the evaluation team to rate each supplier |
| Identify suppliers | This involves identifying suppliers and may involve research, recommendations from colleagues, as well as known suppliers from previous working relationships |
| Prepare and issue RFP | This involves the preparation and issuing of the request for proposal (RFP) to potential suppliers. The RFP may include the evaluation criteria and a preliminary legal agreement |
| Evaluate proposals | The received proposals are evaluated and a short-list of three to five potential suppliers produced. The short-listed suppliers are invited to make a presentation of their proposed solution |
| Select supplier | Each short-listed supplier makes a presentation followed by a Q&A session. The evaluation criteria are completed for each supplier and reference sites checked (as appropriate). The decision on the preferred supplier is made |
| Define supplier agreement | A formal agreement is made with the preferred supplier. This may include<br>• Negotiations with the supplier / involvement with legal department<br>• Agreement may vary (statement of work, service level agreement, escrow, etc.)<br>• Formal agreement signed by both parties<br>• Unsuccessful parties informed<br>• Purchase order raised |
| Managing the supplier | This is concerned with monitoring progress, project risks, milestones and issues, and taking action when progress deviates from expectations |
| Acceptance | This is concerned with the acceptance of the software, and involves acceptance testing to ensure that the supplied software is fit for purpose |
| Rollout | This is concerned with the deployment of the software and support/ maintenance activities |

reasonable to expect an ethical corporation to protect jobs in the countries where it is operating, and to avoid exploiting workers in low cost countries.

Ethical corporations have a responsibility to ensure that there are reasonable work practices in place at the subcontractor company, and that workers receive a fair salary, have reasonable terms of employment, and are not exploited by the subcontractor. Globalisation and the outsourcing of manufacturing operations led to many sweatshops in Asia, and there is the infamous case of worker exploitation at Foxconn (an Apple supplier of the *iPhone*) based in Shenzhen in China. Several Foxconn employees committed suicide due to their working conditions and their exploitation by the company, and this raised important ethical questions on the responsibilities of Apple for the health and welfare of the employees of one of its key suppliers. It is reasonable to expect a company as profitable as Apple to ensure that the employees of its suppliers have reasonable conditions of employment and that they are not exploited.

**Table 11.2** Examples of computer crime

| Crime | Description |
|---|---|
| Intellectual property | Infringements of intellectual property are usually civil matters rather than criminal, but the deliberate violation of intellectual property for commercial gain may be a criminal matter |
| Spam | This is where unsolicited messages are sent to a large number of people usually for commercial purposes such as in advertisements for products, but possibly for fraudulent purposes such as phishing |
| Phishing | Phishing is the fraudulent activity that aims to obtain sensitive personal information such as user-ids and passwords, bank account and credit card information, etc., by deceiving users that communication is coming from legitimate parties |
| Identity theft | This is where someone obtains and deliberately uses another person's personal information (e.g., bank account or credit card information) to commit fraud |
| Credit card theft | This could include the situation where the credit card is skimmed by a skimmer device, and the thieves may then create a cloned card and make purchases. Another approach is the "card not present" fraud where the user's personal credit card information is stolen |
| Scams | A scam is an illegal or dishonest scheme designed to steal or commit fraud, where the scheme is designed to get the victim part with his or her money. The scam may appear very convincing to the victim |
| Cyberextortion | This is a crime that involves an attack, or threat of an attack, accompanied by a demand for money to stop the attack |
| Ransomware | This cyberextortion attack encrypts the victim's data, and threatens to perpetually block access to the data unless a ransom is paid |
| Cyberbullying | Cyberbullying (or online bullying) is a form of bullying or harassment by electronic means, where someone harasses or bullies another person online (especially on a social media site such as Facebook or Twitter) |
| Fraud | Fraud is the deception of the victim with the intention of gaining financial gain at their expense. The fraud may be a civil or a criminal matter |
| Malware | Malware is malicious software that is designed to create harm or cause damage to a computer or network, and they include viruses and Trojan horses |
| Theft of corporate data | This is where information that is stored on corporate databases or servers is stolen, and it may occur as a result of an employee's account being compromised or due to an unsecured network |
| Denial of service (DoS) | This attack essentially shuts down a machine or network or where there is a degradation of service that makes it inaccessible to its users, or prevents them from performing productive work |
| Unauthorised access | Unauthorised access is where someone gains access to a website or server without permission. It may be due to a security breach, where someone gained access by using another person's account, or through guessing the password |

## 11.9 Review Questions

1. What is ethical software engineering?
2. Explain how the Therac-25 disaster occurred.
3. Explain how the challenger disaster occurred.
4. What is ethical software design?
5. What is value centred design?
6. What is ethical software testing?
7. What is ethical project management?
8. Explain the concept of separatism?
9. What are the ethical considerations in the development of safety critical systems?
10. Explain the ethical considerations in the Volkswagen dieselgate scandel.
11. Explain the ethical considerations in David Lean's film "Bridge over the river Kwai".

## 11.10 Summary

Software engineering is concerned with the development of software, and it includes activities such as requirements gathering and definition, software design and development, and software testing to verify the correctness of the software. It involves defining the right requirements, and then designing and implementing an appropriate solution that is fit for purpose, and verifying that the implementation satisfies the requirements.

The release of an unreliable software product may result in damage to property or injury (including loss of life) to a third party. Consequently, companies need to be confident that their software products are of a high quality and fit for purpose prior to their release.

Ethical software design and development is concerned with ethical issues that may arise during technology development, such as questions as to how the technology will be used, and whether it could lead to harm to individuals and society. The ethical software engineer needs to examine both the technical and the ethical dimensions of decisions that affect wider society.

A fundamental principle of ethics is based on the Hippocratic Oath "Do no harm", which may be seen to be breached where there are violations of ethics. For example, the Volkswagen emissions scandal was unethical and illegal and led to the deception of the general public and harm to wider society.

We discussed the defective Therac-25 computer-controlled radiation therapy machine that was developed by the AECL in the early 1980s. There were several major accidents with the machine in the mid-1980s, where patients were given massive overdoses of radiation. We discussed the space shuttle challenger disaster in the mid-1980s, and the disaster was caused by a failure in the O-Rings sealing on the right solid rocket booster. The decision making process that led to the launch was deeply flawed, with conflicts between engineering data and management judgments.

Software designers need to consider the ultimate purpose of the project including its benefits to society as well as potential harm of the technology. We discussed the David Lean film concerned with building a bridge over the river Kwai, and we argued that its construction was unethical as it involved collaboration with the enemy and contributing to their plans for further aggression.

Value centred design involves taking human values into account during the design process, and solving value conflicts through engineering design and technological innovation. It involves investigating and determining the values that are relevant to the project, and understanding conflicts to make tradeoffs. There is a need to analyse designs to determine the extent to which they meet particular values, and to develop innovative designs to meet particularly relevant moral values.

## References


[Bec:00] Extreme Programming Explained. Embrace Change. Kent Beck. Addison Wesley. 2000.

[Bec:01] Manifesto for Agile Software Development. Kent Beck et al. Agile Alliance. http://agilemanifesto.org/. 2001.

[Boe:88] A Spiral Model for software development and enhancement. Barry Boehm. *Computer*. May 1988.

[CKS:11] CMMI for Development. Guidelines for Process Integration and Product Improvement. 3rd Edition. Mary Beth Chrissis, Mike Conrad and Sandy Shrum. SEI Series in Software Engineering. Addison Wesley. 2011.

[Fag:76] Design and Code Inspections to Reduce Errors in Software Development. Michael Fagan. *IBM Systems Journal* 15(3). 1976.

[Glb:94] Software Inspections. Tom Gilb and Dorothy Graham. Addison Wesley. 1994.

[Jac:99b] The Unified Software Development Process. James Rumbaugh et al. Addison Wesley. 1999.

[ORg:22] Concise Guide to Software Engineering. Second Edition. Gerard O' Regan. Springer. 2022.

[ORg:23] Mathematical Foundations of Software Engineering. Gerard O' Regan. Springer. 2023.

[ORg:25] Guide to Software Project Management. Gerard O' Regan. Springer. 2025.

[Roy:70] The Software Lifecycle Model (Waterfall Model). W.Royce. In Proc. WESTCON, August, 1970.

# Ethical Aspects of Data Science 12

## 12.1 Introduction

Companies collect lots of personal data about individuals, and so the question is how should a company respond to a request for personal information on particular users? Does it have a policy to deal with that situation? What happens to the personal data that a bankrupt company has gathered? Is the personal data part of the assets of the bankrupt company and sold on with the remainder of the company? How does this affect privacy information agreements and compliance to them or does the agreement cease on termination of business activities?

The consequence of an error in data collection or processing could result in harm to an individual, and so the data collection and processing needs to be accurate. Decisions are often made on the basis of public and private data, and individuals are often unaware as to what data was collected about them, whether the data is accurate, and whether it is possible to correct errors in the data.

Further, the conclusions from the analysis may be invalid due to errors in incorrect or biased algorithms, and so a reasonable question is how to keep algorithmically driven systems from harming people? Data scientists have a responsibility to ensure that their algorithms are fit for purpose and use the right training data, and as far as practical to detect and eliminate unintentional discrimination in algorithms against individuals or groups.

Further, problems may arise when the algorithm uses criteria tuned to fit the majority, as this may be unfair to minorities. For example, the results may be correct, but presented in an over simplistic manner. This could involve presenting the correct aggregate outcome but ignoring the differences within the population, and so leading to the suppression of diversity, and discriminating against minority groups. Another example is where the data may be correct but presented in a misleading way (e.g., the scales of the axis may be used to present the results visually in an exaggerated way).



G. O'Regan, *Philosophical and Cultural Aspects of Computing*, Undergraduate Topics in Computer Science, https://doi.org/10.1007/978-3-032-29284-1_12

This chapter is concerned with the ethics of data science, and we discuss data science in more detail in the next section.

## 12.2 Data Science

Information is power in the digital age, and the collection, processing and use of information needs to be regulated. Data science involves the extraction of knowledge from data sets that consist of structured and unstructured data, and data scientists have a responsibility to ensure that this knowledge is used wisely and not abused. Data science may be regarded as a branch of statistics as it uses many concepts from the field, and it is essential that both the data and models are valid in order to prevent errors occurring during data analysis.

Personal data is collected about individuals from their use of computer resources such as their use of email, their Google searches, the web sites that they visit, as well as their social media use to build up revealing profiles of the user that may be targeted to advertisers. Data monetisation (or *surveillance capitalism*) is concerned with the commercial exploitation of data gathered from the surveillance of users (e.g., their search history, browsing history and so on). It involves the widespread collection and commodification of personal data collected by corporations.

Smartphones provide location data that allows the location of the user to be tracked, and modern technology has allowed governments to conduct mass surveillance on its citizens, with live facial recognition software (LFR) allowing citizens to be recognised at demonstrations or other mass assemblies.

Privacy has become important in the information age, and it is the way in which we separate ourselves from other people, and is the right to be left alone. The European GDPR law has become an important protector of privacy and personal data, and has been adopted by many countries around the world. The main sources of personal data that are collected include (Table 12.1).

These sources of information can collect vast amounts of data, and the collected data may potentially result in harm to an individual. The collected data is commercially valuable, especially when data about individuals are linked from several sources. *Data brokers* are companies that aggregate and link information from multiple sources to create more complete and valuable information products (i.e., profiles of individuals) that may then be sold on to interested parties. Meta data (i.e., data about the data such as the time of a phone call or who the call is made to) also provides useful information that may be collected and shared.

For example, suppose that the probability of an individual buying a pair of hiking books is very low (say 1 in 5000 probability). Next, that individual starts scanning a website (say Amazon) for boots then that individual is now viewed as being more likely to buy a pair of hiking boots (say a 1 in 100 probability). This large increase in probability will mean that the individual is now of interest to advertisers and sellers, and various targeted (popup) advertisements will appear advertising various hiking boots to the individual. This may become quite tedious

**Table 12.1** Sources of information

| Source | Description |
|---|---|
| Data collected by merchants and service providers | This includes personal data entered for the purchase of products and services such as name, address, date of birth, products and services purchased, etc. |
| Activity tracking | This involves monitoring the user's activity on the site, recording their searches, and the products that are browsed and purchased<br>It may involve recording the user's interests, their activities, and their interactions/communications |
| Search profile | The history of a person's searches over a period of time on a search engine such as Google reveals information about the individual and their interests |
| Sensors from devices | These include personal devices that are part of the internet of things that may record information such as health data or what the individual is eating<br>Security cameras may be conducting public or private surveillance. GPS technology on smart phones may be monitoring the user's location |

and annoying to the individual, who may have been just browsing, and is now subject to an invasion of advertisements. However, many apps are free and often their source of revenue is from advertisements, and so they gather data about the user that is then sold on to advertisers.

## 12.3 Ethics of Data Science

There has been a phenomenal growth in the use of digital data in information technology, with vast amounts of data collected, processed and used, and so the ethics of data science has become important. There are social consequences to the use of data, and the ethics of data science aims to investigate what is fair and ethical in data science, and what should or should not be done with data.

Ethical behaviour is part of daily life, and it refers to how we use our internal moral compass to form judgments and make decisions in various ethical situations. For example, if I take a picture of another individual does the picture belong to me (as owner of the camera and the collector of the data)? Or does it belong to the individual who is the subject of the image? Most reasonable people would say that the image is my property, and so the question is what responsibilities or obligations do I have (if any) to the other individual (i.e., the data subject)?

That is, although I may technically be the owner of the image, the fact that it contains the personal data (or image) of another should indicate that I have an ethical responsibility or obligation to ensure that the image (or personal data) is not misused in any way that would cause harm to the individual. Further, if I misuse the image in some way then I may be open to a lawsuit from the individual.

Ethical rules are shared values that are followed voluntarily to make the world a better place, whereas legal rules are used to enforce social values. Often, the benefits of following the rules outweigh the costs of following them. For example, following the defined rules of the road lead to safe and predictable travel, whereas the cost of obeying the rules is that an individual must conform to driving practices of the particular country, including driving under the speed limit and driving on the correct side of the road, as well as following the defined rules of the road for the particular jurisdiction.

A fundamental principle of ethics in data science refers to *informed consent*, and this has its origins in the ethics of medical experiments on individuals. The concept of informed consent in medical ethics is where the individual is informed about an experiment, and gives their *consent voluntarily* to participate. The individual has the right to withdraw consent at any time during the experiment. Such experiments are generally conducted to benefit society, and often there is a board that approves the study and oversees it to ensure that all participants have given their informed consent, and attempts to balance the benefits to society with any potential harm to individuals. Once individuals have given their informed consent data may be collected about them.

The principle of informed consent is part of information technology, in the sense that individuals must accept the terms and conditions of use of a website, prior to accessing and using the site. The terms of use state that data will be collected, processed and shared. However, it is important to note that users do not generally give informed consent in the sense of medical experiments, as the details of the data collection and processing is hidden in the small print of the terms and conditions, and this is generally a long and largely unreadable document. Further, the consent is not given voluntarily, in the sense that if a user wishes to use the software, then he or she has no choice but to click acceptance of the terms and conditions of use for the site. Otherwise, they are unable to access the site, and so for many website and software applications (apps) consent is essentially coerced rather than freely given.

There was some early research done on user behaviour by Facebook in 2012, where they conducted an experiment to determine if they could influence the mood of users by posing happy or sad stories to their news feed. The experiment was done without the consent of the users, and while the study indicated that happy or sad stories did influence the user's mood and postings, it led to controversy and major dissatisfaction with Facebook, when users became aware that they were the *subject of a psychological experiment without their consent.*

The dating site OKCupid (a US and internationally based dating and friendship site) uses an algorithm to find compatibility matches for its users based on their profiles, and two people are assigned a match rating based on the extent to which the algorithm judges them to be compatible. OKCupid conducted psychological experiments on its users (without their knowledge), with the first experiment being a "*love is blind*" day in 2014, where all images were removed from the site, and so compatibilities were determined without the use of images.

Another experiment was more controversial and unethical, as the site lied to the users on their match ratings (e.g., two people with a compatibility rating of 90% were given a rating of 30%, and vice versa). The site was trying to determine the extent that two people would get along irrespective of the rating that they were given, and it showed that two people talked more when falsely told that the algorithm matched them, and vice versa. The controversy arose once users became aware of the deception by the company, and it provides a case study on the *socially unacceptable manipulation of user data* by an Internet company.

Data collection is not a new phenomenon as devices such as cameras and telephones have been around for many years. People have reasonable expectations of privacy, and do not expect their phone calls to be monitored and eavesdropped by others, and they do not expect to be recorded in a changing room or in their home. Individuals will wish to avoid harm that could occur due to data about them being collected, processed, and shared.

The question is whether reasonable rules can be defined and agreed, and whether tradeoffs may be made to balance the conflicting rights of the business and individual, and to protect the individual as far as is possible. Some questions on data collection and ownership are considered in Table 12.2.

### 12.3.1 Problems in Data Science

Data science is a multi-disciplinary field that extracts knowledge from data sets that consist of structured and unstructured data, and large data sets (*big data*[1]) may be analysed to extract useful information. The field has great power to harm and to help, and data scientists have a responsibility to use this power wisely. It is essential that both the data and models are valid in order to prevent errors occurring during data analysis.

The consequence of an error in the data analysis or with the analysis method could result in harm to the individual. There are many sources of error such as the sample chosen, which may not be representative of the entire population. Other problems arise with knowledge acquisition by machine learning, where the learning algorithm has used incomplete training data for pattern matching (or other knowledge) recognition. Training data may also be incomplete if the future population differs from the past population.

The data collection is concerned with which data and attributes to collect, and often this is limited to what is available, and the data scientist will also need to decide what to do with missing attributes. Errors may arise in data processing tasks such as analysing text information or recognising faces from photos, as

[1] Big data involves combining data from lots of sources such as bar codes, cctv, shopping data, drivers license, and so on.

**Table 12.2** Questions on data collection

| Question | Answers |
|---|---|
| Who owns the data? | A user's personal information may legally belong to the data collector, but the data subject may have some control as the data is about him/her<br>• The author of the biography of an individual owns the copyright not the individual.<br>• The photographer of a (legally taken) photo owns the image not the subject.<br>• Recording of audio/video is similar<br>• May be a need to acknowledge copyright (if applicable)<br>• May be limits in rights as to how data is collected and used (e.g. privacy of phone calls)<br>• The data subject may have some control of the data collected |
| What are the expected responsibilities of the data collector | The collector of the data is expected to:<br>• Collect only required data<br>• Use data only for purpose gathered<br>• Collect legal and ethical data only<br>• Preserve confidentiality /integrity of collected personal data<br>• Not misuse the data (e.g., alter image)<br>• Share data only with user consent |
| What is the purpose of the data collection? | The purpose may be to:<br>• Carry out service for a user<br>• Improve user experience<br>• Understand users<br>• Build up a profile of user behaviour<br>• Exploit user data for commercial purposes |
| How is user consent to data collection given? | User consent may be given in various ways<br>• User informed of purpose of data collection<br>• User consents to use of data<br>• May be hidden in terms and conditions of site. |
| User control | This refers to the ability of the user to control the way that their personal data is being collected/used:<br>• Ability of user to modify their personal data<br>• Ability of user to delete their personal data |

well as human errors in the data (e.g., spelling errors or where the data field was misunderstood). Errors may lead to poor results and possible harm to the user as decisions are often made on the basis of data, and individuals are often unaware as to whether there are errors in the data, as well as how to correct them.

Even with perfect data the conclusions from the analysis may be invalid due to errors in the model. For example, many machine-learning algorithms just estimate parameters to fit a pre-determined model, without knowing whether the model is appropriate or not (e.g., the model may be attempting to fit a linear model to a non-linear reality). This becomes problematic when estimating (or extrapolating) values outside of the given data, unless there is confidence in the correctness of the model.

Further, care is required before assigning results to an individual from an analysis of group data, as there may be other explanations (e.g., Simpson's paradox in probability/statistics is where a trend that appears in several groups of data disappears or reverses when these groups are combined). It is important to think about the population that you are studying, and to make sure that you are collecting data on the right population, and whether to segment it into population groups, as well as how best to do the segmentation. That is, errors may arise due to:

- Human errors in the data
- Errors in the model
- Incorrect pre-determined model.
- Bias may be unintentionally introduced
- Training data may not be representative of population
- Data may be presented in a misleading way

It may seem reasonable to assume that data-driven analysis is fair and neutral, but unfortunately the problem is that humans may unintentionally introduce bias, as they set the boundary conditions. The bias may be through their choice of the model, the use of training data that may not be representative of the population, or the past population may not be representative of the future population, and so on. This may lead to algorithmic decisions that are unfair or biased, and so the question is how can we prevent this? Data scientists have a responsibility to ensure that their algorithms are fit for purpose and use the right training data, and as far as practical detect and eliminate unintentional discrimination (individual or target group).

Another problem that may arise is data that is correct but presented in a misleading way. One simple way to do this is to manipulate the scales of the axis to present the results visually in an exaggerated way, and another example is where the results are correct, but the algorithm uses criteria tuned to fit the majority and may be unfair to minorities (the correct aggregate outcome is presented, but this is misleading due to the differences within the population, and by suppressing diversity there may be discrimination against the minority group).

Exploration is the first phase in data analysis, and *a hypothesis may be devised to fit the observed data* (this is the opposite of traditional approaches in statistics where the starting point is the hypothesis, and the data is used to confirm or reject the hypothesis based on the data from the control and target groups, and so this approach needs to be used carefully to ensure the validity of the results).

### 12.3.2 Problems with Data Science Algorithms

Data science algorithms tend to learn and codify the current state of the world, and it is therefore harder to change the algorithm to reflect the reality of a changing world. Further, data scientists tend to be focused on getting the algorithm to perform correctly to do the right processing, and so often they may not consider its wider societal impacts.

Algorithms may be unfair to individuals in that an individual may be classified as being a member of a group in view of the value of a particular attribute, and so the individual could be typecast due to their perceived membership of the group. Another words, the individual may be assigned opinions or properties of the group, and this means that there is a danger of developing a stereotype view of the individual. Further, it may be difficult for individuals to break out of these stereotypes, as these biases become embedded within the algorithm thereby helping to maintain the status quo.

There are further dangers when predictions are made, as predictions are probabilistic and may be wrong, and only suggest a greater likelihood of occurrence of an event. Predictive techniques have been applied to predictive policing and to the prediction of uprisings (see Chap. 14), but there are dangers of false positives and false negatives.

It is important that the societal consequences of algorithms are fully considered by companies to ensure that the benefits of data science are achieved, and harm to individuals is avoided.

## 12.4 Data Analytics

Data analytics is the science of handling data collection by computer driven systems, where the goal is to generate insights that will improve decision-making. It involves the overlap of several disciplines such as statistics, information technology and domain knowledge, and is widely used in social media, e-commerce, the Internet of Things, recommendation engines, and gaming.

Data analytics involves the analysis of data to create order and patterns from the data, and it creates information as well as generating insights from the data. This is essential in making informed decisions to meet current and future business needs. There are four types of data analytics (Table 12.3).

*Descriptive analysis* is a data analysis method that is used to give a summary of what is going on and nothing more. It provides information as to what happened, and it allows the data collected by the system to be used to identify what went wrong. This type of data is often used to summarise large data sets, and to describe a summary of the outcomes to the stakeholders. The most relevant metrics produced include the key performance indicators (KPIs).

*Diagnostic analysis* is concerned with the analysis of the descriptive metrics to solve problems, to identify what happened, and to understand why something has happened.

**Table 12.3** Types of data analytics

| Type | Description |
|---|---|
| Descriptive | These metrics are concerned with what happened in the past and give a summary of what is going on |
| Diagnostic | These are concerned with why it happened and involve analysis to determine why something has happened |
| Predictive | These are concerned with what is likely to happen in the future |
| Prescriptive | These are concerned with analysis to make better decisions, and it may involve considering several factors to suggest a course of action for the business. It may involve the use of AI techniques such as machine learning, and the goal is to make progress and avoid problems in the future |

*Predictive analysis* involves predicting what is likely to happen in the future based on data from the past: i.e., it is attempting to predict the future based on actions in the past, and it may involve the use of statistics and modelling to predict future performance, based on current and historical data. Other techniques employed include neural networks, linear and multiple regression analysis, and decision trees.

*Prescriptive analysis* is used to help business to make better decisions through the analysis of data, and is effective when the organization knows the right questions to ask and responds appropriately to the answers. It often uses AI techniques such as machine learning to process a vast amount of data, to find patterns and to recommend a course of action that will resolve or improve the situation. The recommended course of action is based on past events and outcomes, and the use of machine learning strategies builds upon the predictive analysis of what is likely to happen to recommend a future course of action.

Prescriptive analytics may be used to automate prices based on several factors such as demand, weather, and commodity prices. These algorithms may automatically raise or lower prices at a much faster rate than human intervention, and examples include the automated changing of prices for airline flights and hotels rooms.

Companies may use data analytics to drill down into customer data to determine what they are looking for. This includes understanding the features desired of the product and the price that they are willing to pay, and so data analytics has a role to play in new product design. They may be used by the business to improve customer loyalty and retention, and this may be done by gathering data (e.g., the opinions of customers from social media, email, and phone calls) to ensure that the voice of the customer is heard and acted upon.

Marketing groups often use data analytics to determine how successful their marketing campaign has been, and to make changes where required. The marketing team may use the analytics to run targeted marketing and advertisement campaigns to segmented audiences (i.e., subsets of the population based on their unique characteristics such as demographics, interests, needs and location). Market segmentation is useful in getting to know the customers, and determining what is needed in their market segment, and to determine how best to meet their needs.

Big data analytics may be used for targeted advertisements. For example, Netflix collects data on its customers including their searches and viewing history, and this data provides an insight into the specific interests of the customer, which is then used to send suggestions to the customer on the next movie that they should watch.

Big data analytics involves examining large amounts of data to identify hidden patterns and correlations, and to give insights to enable the right business decisions to be made. It allows the business to collect as much data as required to understand their customers and to derive important insights.

### 12.4.1 Business Analytics and Business Intelligence

The effectiveness of management decision-making is influenced by the accuracy and completeness of the information that managers have, with inaccurate or incomplete information leading to poor decisions. Companies often have data that is unstructured or in diverse formats, and such data is generally more difficult to gather and analyse. This has led software firms to offer business intelligence solutions to help organizations make better use of their data, and to optimise the information gathered from the data.

Business analytics involves converting business data into useful business information through the use of statistical techniques and advanced software. It includes a set of analytical methods for solving problems and decision-making, especially in the context of vast quantities of data. The combination of analysis with intuition provides useful insights into business, and helps organizations to achieve their objectives.

Business intelligence (BI) processes all of the data generated by a business, and uses it to generate clear reports (e.g., a dashboard report of the key metrics), as well as the key trends and performance measures that management use in decision-making. That is, business intelligence is data analytics with insight that allows managers to make informed decisions, and it may employ data mining, performance benchmarking, process analysis, and descriptive analytics.

### 12.4.2 Big Data and Data Mining

The term "*Big data*" refers to the large, diverse sets of data that arrives at ever-increasing rates and volumes. It encompasses the *volume* of data, the *velocity* or speed at which it is created and collected, and the *variety* or scope of the data points being covered (these are generally referred to as the *three V's of big data*).

There has been an explosion in the volume of big data with zettabytes[2] (ZB) of data employed globally.

Big data often comes from *data mining*, where data mining involves exploring and analyzing large blocks of data to gather meaningful patterns and trends. Data is gathered and loaded into data warehouses by organizations (i.e., the data is centralized into a single database or program), and then stored either on in-house servers or in the cloud. The user decides how to organize the data, and application software sorts the data accordingly, and the data is presented in an easy to read format such as a graph or report.

The data may be internal or external. It may be structured or unstructured, where structured data is often already managed in the organisation's databases or spreadsheets, and may be numeric and easily formatted. Unstructured data uses data that may be unformatted, and so it does not fall into a predetermined format (i.e., it is free form), and it may come from search engines or from forum discussions on social media.

Big data may be collected in various ways such as from publicly shared comments on social media, or gathered from apps, through questionnaires, product purchases, and so on. Big data is analysed with software that is designed to handle large and complex data sets.

### 12.4.3 Data Analytics for Social Media

Data analytics is used by social media companies to provide a quantitative insight into human behaviour on a social media website, and enables the business to understand its audience better, to improve the user experience, and to create content that will be of interest to them. Data analytics consist of a collection of data that says something about the social media conversation, and it involves the collection, monitoring, analysis, summarisation, and graphs to visualise insight into the behaviour of users.

Another words, *data analytics* involves learning to read a social media community through data, and the interpretations of the quantifiable data (or metrics) gives information on the activities, events, and conversations of the users. This includes what users like when they are online as well as other important information such as their opinions and emotions that are gathered through *social listening*. Social listening involves monitoring keywords and mentions in social media conversations, to understand and analyse what the audience is saying about the business, and allows the business to engage with its audience.

A social media campaign is a marketing tool where a company or social media company uses social media platforms to interact with their customers/users. The design of a social media campaign is often an iterative process, with the fist step

[2] A zettabyte is 1 sextillion bytes = $2^{70}$ bytes (approximately a billion terabytes or 1000 exabytes or a trillion gigabytes).

being to determine the objectives of the campaign, and designing the campaign to meet the requirements. The goals may be to increase the number of users or to build a brand, and data analytics combined with social listening help in understanding how people are interacting, what they are interacting about, and how successful the interactions has been. The campaign may be refined to meet its goals and the cycle repeats.

The key performance indicators (KPI) may include increased followers/ subscribers, an increase in the content shared, and so on. Elementary data such as the number of likes, the number of followers, the number of times a video is played Youtube, and so on are gathered to obtained a quantified understanding of a conversation.

Facebook and Twitter maintain a comprehensive set of measurements for data analytics; with Facebook maintaining metrics such as the number of page views and the number of likes and reach of posts (i.e., the number of people who saw posts at least once). Twitter includes a dashboard view to summarise how successful tweet activity has been, as well as the interests and locations of the user's followers. Social media data contains a rich collection of human emotions with the social listening data including user opinions and emotions.

### 12.4.4 Mathematics Used in Data Analytics

Table 12.4 lists mathematics used in data science and analytics.

Probability theory, statistics, linear algebra, discrete mathematics, graph theory and calculus are described in more detail in [ORg:23].

**Table 12.4** Mathematics in data analytics

| Type | Description |
|---|---|
| Probability theory | An introduction to some of the concepts in probability theory such as basic probability, expectation, conditional probability, Baye's theorem, and probability density functions |
| Statistics | Statistics is a vast area and includes descriptive statistics; measures of central tendency such as the mean, mode and median, variance and covariance, and correlation and regression |
| Linear algebra | This includes topics such as matrix theory and Gaussian elimination as well as basic algebra |
| Calculus | This includes the study of differentiation and integration and includes topics such as limits, continuity, rules of differentiation, Taylor's series, and area and volume |

## 12.5 Data Privacy

In Greek mythology there was a giant called Argus Panoptes, who was an all-seeing giant with one hundred eyes looking in every direction, and he would always have some eyes open even when asleep. That is, he was always watching and monitoring the world around him, and so he was the perfect guardian. He was later slain by Hermes (the messenger of the gods), who disguised himself as a shepherd and put all of Argus's eyes to sleep, and then slew him.

Jeremy Bentham (the founder of Utilitarianism which was discussed in Chap. 9) designed a circular prison in the eighteenth century termed the Panopticon, where a single guard in the centre of the complex could observe all of the prisoners. His idea was that although individual prisoners did not know if they were being watched or not at a given time instant (as this depended on the direction that the guard was facing), that they would behave as if they were being watched, and so they would behave all of the time (Fig. 12.1).

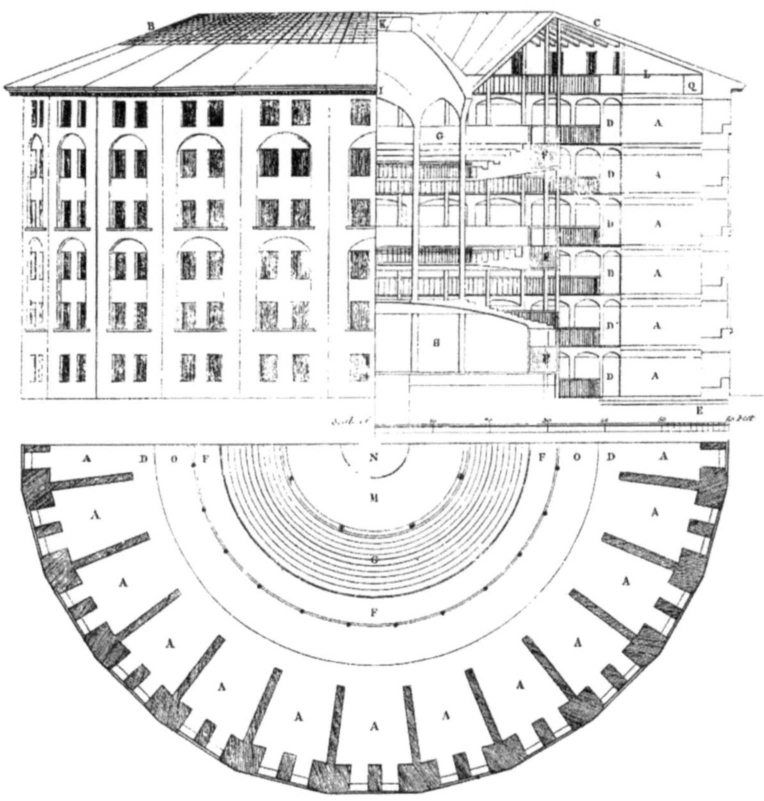

**Fig. 12.1** Bentham's Panopticon prison

The modern version of the Panopticon is a set of security cameras that is watching people, or websites that are monitoring user behaviour, or the entire Internet, which is working out everything that we are doing by watching us. The question is whether we as individuals should be concerned about this, and whether it matters if we as individuals are doing nothing wrong. Some have argued that everyone would be completely honest due to zero privacy, and where everyone could know what everyone else is doing. Others respond by saying that privacy is a basic human right, and that it is needed for freedom to be exercised in society.

The "*Right to have privacy*" was an influential legal article that was written by Louis Brandeis and Samuel Warren, and published in the Harvard Law Review in 1890 [BrW:90]. The article advocates for privacy as "*the right to be left alone*". William Prosser wrote an article in the Californian Law Review in 1960 in which he outlined four types of privacy torts [Pro:60]:

- Intrusion upon seclusion
- Public disclosure of private facts
- Publishing objectionable, false information
- Misappropriation of name or likeness

There has traditionally been a difference between rural and urban living, where in a small town people know everything about every other person in the town, and there is essentially very little privacy from all the gossip (*pueblo pequeño infierno grande*). In a larger city, people are anonymous and nobody knows or cares about what others are doing, and so there is a greater sense of privacy. Further, an individual living in a small town has a choice of moving to a new town for a fresh start, or waiting in the town for the community to forget a particular event, whereas in a large city this problem is a lot less relevant due to the anonymous nature of city living.

There are some parallels of the Internet being like the small village, except that the relationship is asymmetric. Another words, in a small town each individual knows as much about another as vice versa (i.e., it is a symmetric relationship), whereas *the relationship is asymmetric for the Internet*. This makes it a very unequal relationship, with one party gathering lots of information and building up a profile about all other parties, and using that information for commercial purposes. The other parties are not actively gathering information, and have a very limited picture of what is going on with all the data that is gathered.

Further, while events and information may be forgotten in a village over time this does not happen with the Internet: i.e., it is very difficult to forget things on the Internet, with web pages surviving forever in some archive even if taken down. Another issue is that once a page is put up many copies of it are made, and so even if the page is taken down there may still be many copies remaining elsewhere, and so there is no way of really deleting something once it has been published on the web. This could create major problems for individuals who pose indiscreet content on line, as that content may live on in perpetuity.[3]

People need an understanding of how their personal information and data is collected, shared and used across the many computer platforms that they use, and the extent to which they have control over their personal information. It is important to understand the nature of privacy, the problems and risks that exist, as well as privacy laws that are available to protect individuals from its abuse.

De-identification is the removal of identifiable information from data, and includes the removal of fields (or attributes) such as name, address and phone number so that no personally identifiable attributes remain in the dataset. This means that the identity of the person is not immediately identifiable, and so it provides some safeguards to the individual. However, it is possible that the individual's identity may be determined from the other retained fields, and this means that care must be taken if public records are to be released.

That is, it may still be possible (even if de-identification has taken place) to identity individuals. Anonymity is limited or virtually impossible given the extent of public and private information that is available about individuals, and as facial recognition technology has also improved in a major way, the identification of individuals from the images of their faces may be rapidly done with technology.

### 12.5.1 What Is Privacy?

There are various definitions of privacy such as the right to be left alone, for secret or intimate information to be kept secure from others, and for *control over one's personal information*, where individuals are able to decide what information will be shared, when it will be shared, and how it will be shared with others.

That is, users should be in control of how their personal data is used, and most user agreements are "*all-or-nothing*" in the sense that a user must give up control of their personal data to use the application (i.e., the acceptance of the terms and conditions of the website results in the user having minimal control over how their personal data is used). Clearly, users would be happier and feel that they are in control if they were offered graduated choices by the vendor, to allow them to make tradeoffs, and to choose a level of privacy that they are comfortable with.

Privacy has become quite topical with the rise of social media, the Internet of Things and Artificial Intelligence. However, privacy concerns are not a new phenomena, and they initially grew out of the development of early technologies such as the first cameras, microphones and telephones, where indiscreet or unauthorised

[3] It is almost impossible to delete oneself from the Internet. The user could delete some of their personal information such as their social media accounts or restrict public access to these, and also delete any online accounts that are not being used. It is possible to turn on auto-delete on Google to delete your data at regular intervals. Personal information can be deleted from blogs and any apps that are not being used may be deleted.

**Fig. 12.2** Cardinals eavesdropping in the Vatican

images or recordings could be made leading to concerns of an invasion of privacy by a prying media or others (Fig. 12.2).

The early concerns over privacy were with maintaining the security and confidentiality of a message, and so this led to some people and groups to communicate with each other using ciphers. For example, Julius Caesar communicated important messages using an alphabetic cipher during his campaign in Gaul in the first century B.C., and the emperor Augustus used a similar approach for communication. Further, some of the leaders during the American War of Independence used codes and pseudonyms to protect their identity during sensitive communication.

Societies vary in terms of their political systems, with democracies offering a peaceful way of replacing an unpopular government, whereas totalitarian states are often ruthless in their control of the population. Some autocratic societies run by dictators employ a culture of surveillance on the population, and this may include identifying individuals who pose a potential threat to the regime, and removing such individuals from society either by imprisonment or political assassination.[4]

[4] Several oligarchs and critics of Putin and his regime in Russia and the 2022 invasion of Ukraine (or special military operation) have died in mysterious circumstances. Some have died by hanging in their own homes, some have fallen out of windows of hotels or hospitals, some have fallen down stairs, some have fallen overboard from their yachts, and some have died in plane crashes. It was

Often, these societies are characterised by mass surveillance of individuals, police searches and seizure of private property, police brutality, and so on. In democratic societies, mass surveillance is present, but often there are laws to protect the citizen against unreasonable police searches and behaviour.[5]

The importance of privacy in the information technology field became apparent in the early 1970s with the introduction of databases. These could hold private information about individuals, and there was a need for a set of rules to protect how information should be collected and used. This led to the development of a set of *fair information processing principles* (FIPPs) by the US Secretary's Advisory Committee on Automated Personal Data Systems published in their 1973 report on Records, Computers and the Rights of Citizens [US:73]. This led to the Fair Information Practice Principles Act in 1974, and this act became the basis on which data collection is governed in the United States. The report outlined several principles such as (Table 12.5).

Computing technology has evolved in a major way from the mainframes and databases of the early 1970s, with the introduction of the Internet and World Wide Web, and the subsequent development of smart phones, Social Media, the Internet of Things, and Artificial Intelligence. It is reasonable to ask what privacy means in the modern digital world and whether there is privacy anymore? Users of social media share large parts of their lives with a massive on-line audience as well as with large corporations, and social media companies gather lots of data about its users that may be used to determine patterns, and to generate profiles that may be targeted to advertisers. So much data is being collected about individuals, and the question is where does it go? Who controls it? Are companies adequately managing risks of data breaches? What happens when data privacy is breached or data is not secured properly? Is there transparency? Is user data encrypted? Is confidentiality and authenticity maintained?

---

unwise (even provocative) to proceed with the expansion of NATO to Ukraine, as Russia viewed its expansion (especially the placement of NATO nuclear missiles along its long border with Ukraine) as an existential threat, and it was therefore unacceptable to Russian security. Further, the Istanbul peace talks between Russia and Ukraine in April 2022 offered a possible resolution of the conflict (the draft agreement was initialised by both sides, with Ukraine abandoning its plans to join NATO and retaining almost of its lands apart from Crimea). However, the Americans/British (Joe Biden / Boris Johnson) instructed Zelensky not to agree to the draft peace conditions (as they viewed Russia as weak, and saw the war as a way to weaken Russia further). However, the continuation of the conflict has been a disaster for Ukraine (it has lost over 20% of its territory), and Russia is now the most powerful military in Europe. Western democracies tend to be subtle in their control of their populations, with propaganda and misinformation employed in western media to paint a particular narrative.

[5] The Immigration and Custom Enforcement (ICE) in the United States has faced intense criticism for its anti-democratic behaviour, with infringement of civil liberties in the targeting of peaceful protesters and critics. There has an excessive use of force and militarisation (with masked agents entering private property without judicial warrants—they use administrative warrants signed by an ICE supervisor and not a judge, which are invalid to legally enter a private home), and there is a lack of transparency and accountability. Several US citizens have been detained and have had their rights violated.

**Table 12.5** Principles of data collection (FIPP Act)

| Principle | Description |
|---|---|
| Transparency of collection and storage of information | The organisation that is collecting personal data must be doing so openly (i.e., it is not secretly or covertly collecting data) |
| Accessibility of personal information | An individual must be able to access any data that the organisation has about him/her |
| Purpose limitations (consent) | There must be a way for an individual to prevent information that was gathered for one purpose to be used for another purpose without their consent |
| Correction of personal data | There must be a way for an individual to correct or amend their personal information |
| Personal data safeguards and accountability | Any organisation that is creating, maintaining, or disseminating personal data must ensure its reliability for the identified use, and take reasonable precautions to prevent against any misuse of the data |

The *Internet of Things* (IoT) is a collection of devices, sensors and services that capture data to monitor and control the world. This interconnected technology is an integral part of modern society, with computation and data communication embedded in the environment. It allows everyday devices to connect to other devices or people over the Internet, and the level of interconnectivity and data gathered means that security and privacy are key concerns. It is essential to control both the devices and the data, and the data should only be gathered with user consent. There are risks of hacking or eavesdropping.

There has been a major growth in AI technology in recent years, and AI has been applied to self-driving cars, facial recognition, machine translation and so on. Facial recognition technology may be used to unlock phones to authenticate identity, and it has also been applied to read facial expression during job interiews, as well as following the movement of individuals. A vehicle may contain veral on-board computers for various vehicle controls as well as entertainment stems. This means that vehicles connecting to the Internet are potentially at risk being hacked, where a hacker may potentially commandeer vehicle controls ı as steering and the brakes.

is often unclear who is collecting the personal information, the type of infor-n that they are collecting, what is being done with the data, and whom the being shared with. The theft of personal information results in others having ation about a particular individual, and they may be in a position to use that tion against the individual. This means that the perpetrators have power individual, since they may use the stolen personal information about the l to commit a crime.

### 12.5.2 Social Media

Social media involves the use of computer technology for the creation and exchange of user-generated content. These web-based technologies allow users to discuss and modify the created content, and it has led to major changes in communication between individuals, communities and organisations.

Social media is designed to have the individual share personal information while they are on the site, and with every disclosure (or post) the individual reveals a little bit more about himself or herself. It is very easy to post photos and information on social media sites such as Facebook or Twitter/X, and *social media is designed in such a way that it is addictive and poses risks to the privacy of an individual* (Fig. 12.3).

There is a danger that both social media companies and other users could harm the individual's privacy. The harm from other users may arise when a piece of the user's information is shared with the wrong audience, and this later leads to problems for the user. There are two distinct audiences for the individual's information namely other users and the platform itself. The social media platform maintains a vast quantity of electronic information consisting of immense databases, which can collect a vast amount of data on everyone on the site.

There is a power imbalance between the platform and the user, with the platform designed to have the individual share as much as possible, and other users may potentially pose risks to the user with their social interaction. An individual's information may be viewed by friends, family, employer, work colleagues

**Fig. 12.3** Young people on smart phones and social media. Public domain

**Table 12.6** Threats in social media

| Threat | Description |
|---|---|
| Manufactured disclosures | This refers to how a social media site gets people to disclose more and more information, and this is similar in a way to surveillance. Traditional surveillance involves watching people to learn something about them, whereas modern surveillance as in social media has less to do with this, and it generally involves getting people to disclose something more about themselves and so, in effect, to learn something new about the person |
| Extracting consent | This refers to how a social media site obtains consent from its users on the various practices employed on the site. A user must click acceptance of the associated terms and conditions to use the site, and often this involves accepting invasive privacy practices described in a long, dense and largely unreadable terms of use document. The social media site may also request access to the camera, location and address book of the individual. Often, users just accept the terms and conditions and permission requests because they are so worn down with so many requests from different apps, and they have no choice but to accept the terms of use and invasive practices in order to use the site |
| Overexposure | Social media sites constantly introduce new features to make user data more visible, more searchable, and more complete to others and may result in *over exposure* of the information |
| Faithless friends | This refers to when information that has been shared in the individual's network is shared more widely by one of the "friends" of the individual. This may lead to embarrassment or harm to the individual |
| Online harassment | This is where repeated insults or bullying of an individual takes place on line, which may even include threats of violence, posting of indiscreet images and even revenge porn |

and nameless others, and so everyone in the individual's network as well as others could be an unwanted audience.

Users often may not realise the full extent of their audience when they post on the site, as people who are authorised in an individual's network may not be the desired recipients of certain posts (disclosures). It is difficult to delete online messages, and destructive posts may last long after an incident. Therefore, it is very much in the interests of users to keep their posts discreet, as both friends and outsiders of their social media network could pose risks to their privacy. There are several potential threats on social media sites including (Table 12.6).

We will discuss the ethics of social media in more detail in Chap. 13.

### 12.5.3 Internet of Things

The Internet of Things is a collection of devices, sensors and services that capture data to monitor and control the world around them, and these include devices and sensors such as cars, clothing, fridges, fitness monitors, and so on. An individual may be continuously connected to multiple home devices with sensors (e.g.,

**Fig. 12.4** Fitbit surge. Smart-watch activity tracker. Creative commons

microphones and cameras), and connection and access to these devices increases the risk to data security (Fig. 12.4).

The fact that there are many devices with sensors connected to the Internet means that there are, in effect, more eyes watching the individual and gathering data about her, and there are also more points of failure. This means that IoT poses greater risks to the safety of individuals than when using basic computers, and the risks include:

- Security risks
- Privacy risks

These devices consist of both hardware and software and so there are now two points of failure: i.e., hardware failure and software failure. Hardware is generally more reliable than software, and hardware failures tend to be as a result of components wearing out over time. Software failures are often as a result of design issues, and software often requires regular updates to correct problems or to deal with security vulnerabilities. The fact that these devices are connected to the Internet means that software upgrades are possible, but being connected to the Internet means that the device may be targeted by hackers in a similar way in which a computer is hacked.

Further, these Internet devices contain sensors that gather a lot of personal data about the individual, and they collect, use and share this data, and so the IoT devices pose similar data security risks as laptops or smart phones. Many IoT devices are inexpensive and have security vulnerabilities, with some Internet devices failing to encrypt data when transmitting data or images to the cloud. This means that that an eavesdropper could intercept this Internet traffic, and cause harm to the individual.

IoT has serious implications for privacy in that these devices can produce granular personal data such as when the individual is at home, what the individual eats, and so on. They gather a lot of personal data and the data may be shared with other devices or platforms thereby posing risks to the privacy of the individual.

### 12.5.4 AI and Facial Recognition

Facial recognition is a biometric technology that analyses visual data from social media and other sources, and is capable of detecting facial features and to essentially reduce each face to a mathematical equation using factors such as the distance between the individual's eyes, the width of the nose, and so on, and the patterns in the visual data are compared to patterns in facial recognition databases to confirm identity.

Deep fakes are an AI technology that allows convincing images and videos to be created of individuals doing things that they never did or said, and this disruptive technology has been applied to misrepresent individuals in a variety of ways. An individual may be seen to make false or even preposterous claims, and this is achieved from content taken from social media and other media that is then manipulated and edited in various ways to achieve the desire effect. This technology could potentially show an individual committing a crime, or present the individual in a very negative way. The technology has at this time been mainly applied to humour as in political satire, but as the technology improves it may become difficult to distinguish the real from the fake, with potential serious consequences for society.

Facial recognition is a technology that offers the ability to unlock phones to authenticate identity, and so it may be used to protect the individual. Facial recognition has advanced in sophistication to allow individuals be recognised at demonstrations and street protests, and this means that the technology may be used as a tool for authoritarian control. That is, surveillance technology combined with facial recognition could be oppressive to individuals and society, and (without regulation and checks and balances) lead to a totalitarian state.

A society that adopts a paradigm of constant surveillance, where individuals are living in a world with technology constantly monitoring their daily activities, learning to recognise patterns, and drawing inferences is moving towards totalitarianism.[6] Facial recognition technology may challenge civil liberties, and it could severely impact marginalized groups in society. Facial recognition has become popular since:

- Faces are central to identity

---

[6] Orwell's famous 1949 novel "Nineteen Eighty Four" is based on Stalinist Russia and Nazi Germany, and describes a totalitarian state where the Ministry of Truth engages in omnipresent government surveillance and constant propaganda to repress individuality and independent thinking. Trump's second term in the United States resembles an Orwellian world.

- Faces are hard to hide
- Existing face and name databases

### 12.5.5 Legal Aspects of Privacy

Data collection focus on how data is collected, used and shared, and data protection includes the right to information self-determination.[7] The web is full of privacy policies that specify what type of personal data will be collected, how it will be processed and used, how it is shared, and what can be done about it. Individuals may take a lawsuit against another for a tort, for example, when someone pries or stalks them, or publishes a defamatory article, or violates their privacy. There are three main areas that impact upon an individual's privacy namely:

- The Media
- Surveillance
- Personal Data

Media laws protect an individual against intrusion, where another party may be held liable for the invasion of the individual's privacy (e.g., phone tapping, snooping, examining a person's bank account, and so on). The tort of the public disclosure of private facts is part of the legal system in many countries, and its goal is to prevent the public disclosure of private facts concerning the private life of an individual, where the matter is not of legitimate concern to the public. That is, others are prevented from widely spreading private facts such as the individual's face or identity for their own benefit, and there are slander and libel laws to protect an individual's good name and reputation, and to prevent defamation of character.

There are laws and rights to regulate surveillance with search warrants required in most countries to search the home of a private individual and to seize personal property. Warrants are generally required to obtain personal electronic records held by telecommunication companies (e.g., the calls made and received as well as meta data such as the date, time and duration of the call as well as geo-location data), and warrants may be required to obtain records held by Internet technology companies (e.g., emails, web sites visited, searches, and other electronic messages).

Countries vary in their laws for the protection of security and privacy, but in general the security and privacy commitments made by a company in their policies should be fully implemented. Companies should be held accountable for any security breaches that occur that lead to privacy being compromised, and they may be held liable for any losses suffered by individuals resulting from the breach.

---

[7] Information self-determination refers to the freedom that individuals have to decide what happens to their personal data as well as the purpose of data collection.

Further, people must not be misled about the functionality of a website or mobile app that places their security or privacy at risk, and users must give their consent to any changes to the privacy policy that would allow for the collection of additional personal data, and users must be informed about the extensiveness of tracking and data collection.

### 12.5.6 EU GDPR

Europe has been active in the development of data protection regulation, and the European General Data Protection Regulation (EU GDPR 2016/679) is a comprehensive data protection framework that became operational in 2018. The importance of both privacy and data protection has been recognised in Europe, and these are regarded as fundamental human rights in the EU. The goal is to give individuals control over their personal data, and it has had a huge impact on privacy laws of other countries around the world, with other jurisdictions using it to develop similar laws (e.g., Japan and the state of California in the US).

GDPR consists of a data governance framework that attempts to place privacy on a par with other laws. It creates protections that follow the data, and it places responsibilities on companies to manage privacy and information. It also addresses the transfer of personal data outside of the EU, and prohibits the transfer of personal data to countries that do not provide an equivalent or adequate data protection framework as GDPR (Fig. 12.5).

GDPR applies whenever personal data is processed, and it starts from the presumption that the processing of the personal data is illegitimate. This means that companies carry the burden of legitimising their actions, and they must be able to show that they have a legitimate basis for processing data. That is, they must be able to show that they have the consent of the data subject, or that the processing is necessary as a result of the contract that exists between them and the data subject, or where they have a legitimate interest, and where the interest of the

**Fig. 12.5** EU GDPR 2016/679

data controller prevails over that of the data subject. The company must be able to demonstrate adherence to the fair information practices such as:

- Standards for data quality
- Standards for transparency
- Special protections for sensitive data
- Standards of enforcement

This means that data must be obtained legitimately and used for the purpose for which it was acquired, and there must be openness and transparency so that individuals will know how their data will be used. There should be special protections for sensitive data with the ability to opt in for consent (e.g., race, sexual orientation, and so on), and there must be standards for enforcement to ensure compliance to the standards. The *Data Privacy Impact Assessment* (DPIA) is part of GDPR, and is needed if the processing of personal information is likely to result in a high risk to the rights and freedoms of individuals.

The standard for informed consent is very high which means that it is freely given and informed. GDPR also gives very strong data subject rights, including the right to access data, data portability, the right to rectify data, the right to erase data, the right to object to processing, and the right to restrict processing. These rights provide a tool for data subjects to exercise control over their personal information.

The EU *Data Protection Commissioner* (DPC) is responsible for monitoring the application of GDPR in the EU, and for upholding the fundamental rights of EU citizens in protecting their personal data. Several of the large technology companies (e.g., Amazon, Facebook and Google) have been subject to large fines in the EU for violations of GDPR.

### 12.5.7 EU Digital Services Act

The European Digital Service Act (DSA) became part of European Law in 2024, and it is applicable to all member states in the European Union. The goal of this legislation is to protect digital space against illegal content as well as protecting the fundamental rights of users, and it is applicable to social media companies and the online marketplace. Another words, DSA is a set of rules and regulations to provide a safer online digital space, and to protect the fundamental rights of users of digital services in the European Union.

Platforms will be held accountable (in Europe) for their role in disseminating harmful content, and the legislation lays down obligations on platforms and control measures. These include:

- Provide greater transparency on their services
- Obligations on market place to combat sale of illegal products/services
- Measures to combat illegal content and obligations on platforms to respond quickly

- Protection of minors by prohibiting targeted advertisements
- Limits on advertisement
- Stricter rules for very large online platforms (VLOPs) and search engines (VLOSEs)
- Improve control for users of their service

DSA is applicable to very large online platforms and very large online search engines, as well as online platforms, hosting services, and Intermediary Service Providers (ISP). Member states have the power to supervise and enforce the DSA in relation to ISPs that have their main establishment in that member state, and each member state designates a *Digital Services Coordinator* (DSC) to supervise and enforce the DSA in that state.

The European Commission has the power to supervise and enforce the Digital Service Act in relation to very large platforms or search engines that are classified as VLOPs and VLOSEs, and these are subject to additional stricter rules.

## 12.6 Security of Data

The privacy of personal information may be violated if there is weak system security, and so good cybersecurity (we discussed cybersecurity in Chap. 11) is a prerequisite for the protection of personal data. Poor security may lead to the theft of personal information, and the security of the system refers to its ability to protect itself from attack. A secure system will preserve:

- Confidentiality
- Integrity
- Availability

*Confidentiality* means that the information may be viewed and accessed only by those authorised, and encryption may be employed to ensure that the unauthorised access of information is meaningless to anyone other than the intended parties. Other approaches include access controls where only those with the appropriate access privileges may access the data.

*Integrity* means that the data may only be modified by those authorised to do so, and *availability* refers to the fact that the system and its data are available for use at all times (i.e., it is not subject to a denial of service attack). Attacks on the system may be from internal sources or external to the company, and successful attacks may lead to:

- Unauthorised data access and usage
- Unauthorised data theft and deletion
- Unauthorised data manipulation

The system needs to be designed for security, and care is needed to prevent the introduction of security loopholes during its development. A risk profile of the system is carried out to identify threats and vulnerabilities, and the high-risk areas lead to the security requirements. There is a trade off between security risks and the cost of security measures, and a comprehensive security system requires measures such as:

- Preventive measures
- Detective measures
- Administrative measures

*Preventive measures* are used to stop unauthorised attacks from occurring before they succeed and do any harm; *detective measures* are used to discover any unauthorised attacks that may be on-going or completed; and *administrative measures* which are used to clarify processes, rules and standards within an organisation. Organisational and administrative measures are as important as technical measures in securing a system.

The administrative measures include identifying the technical measures, actions and enforcement mechanisms that are needed, and defining the responsibilities for carrying out the measures. The policies and procedures as defined in the Information Security Management System of ISO/IEC 27001 provide guidance on what should be implemented in security management.

Preventive measures may include the use of encryption for communication and stored data, so that the data is meaningless to anyone who is not authorised to see it. Preventive measures also include access control mechanisms for *authentication* to verify if the person is who she claims to be, and a range of measures such as user id and password, smart card and biometric data may be used for verification. The next step is to ensure that those authenticated have the appropriate level of *authorisation* to access the data, and an authorisation matrix that includes roles and the level of access for each role may be used for this.

The goal of detective measures is to monitor whether a system is actually secure, and to detect attacks. Security audits may be conducted to verify that the planned security measures have been implemented. Penetration testing is a way to find and remove security weaknesses, and it involves experts (e.g., white hat hackers) playing the role of attackers trying to find vulnerabilities in the system, and taking actions to address any identified weakness in the system. Security is discussed in more detail in [ORg:22].

## 12.7 Review Questions

1. What is data science?
2. What is the role of the data scientist?

3. What is privacy? Why is it important?
4. What are the main sources of personal data collected on line?
5. What are the main risks to an individual using social media?
6. What are the main risks to an individual using a fitness device (as part of the Internet of Things)?
7. What are the main risks with AI facial recognition technology?
8. Explain the importance of the EU GDPR law.

## 12.8 Summary

The ethics of data science aims to investigate what is fair and ethical in data science, and what should or should not be done with data. A fundamental principle of ethics in data science refers to informed consent, and this is where the individual is informed about the purpose of data collection and gives their consent voluntarily. This consent is often given by individuals accepting the terms and conditions before they may use software applications, and these state that data will be collected, processed and shared.

Companies collect lots of personal data about individuals from their use of computer resources, and this data is processed to build up revealing profiles of the users that may be sold on to advertisers. Face recognition software allows citizens to be recognised at demonstrations or other mass assemblies, and combined with location tracking software allows governments to conduct mass surveillance on its citizens.

Privacy remains important in the information age, and it is the way in which we separate ourselves from other people, and it is the right to be left alone. Modern technology allows the location of the user to be tracked, and poses challenges to privacy. The GDPR law has become an important protector of privacy and personal data, and both European and other countries have adapted it.

## References

[BrW:90] The Right to have privacy. Louis Brandeis and Samuel Warren. Harvard Law Review. 1890.

[ORg:22] Concise Guide to Software Engineering. Second Edition. Gerard O' Regan. Springer. 2022.

[ORg:23] Mathematical Foundations of Software Engineering. Gerard O' Regan. Springer. 2023.

[Pro:60] Privacy. William Prosser. Californian Law Review. 1960.

[US:73] Records, Computers and the Rights of Citizens. US Secretary's Advisory Committee on Automated Personal Data Systems https://aspe.hhs.gov/report/records-computers-and-rights-citizens

# 13 Ethical Social Media

## 13.1 Introduction

Social media involves the use of computer technology for the creation and exchange of user-generated content. These web-based technologies allow users to discuss and modify user created content, and it has led to major changes in communication between individuals, communities and organisations. It plays a major role in connecting people and enabling communication, and it has a role to play in social engagement on civic matters.

Social media provides a way for like-minded people to gather together, and is an effective way to mobilise protest. Politicians use social media during election campaigns as a way to communicate their message and policies to a wider audience, and to engage with their constituents on a day-to-day basis during sessions of parliament. Social media enables citizens to play a role in shaping the world around them (e.g., on climate change) and to make a difference. Corporations may use social media as a way to get closer to their customers, so that they may understand what customers like and dislike about their products and services, with the goal of improving to serve them better.

On line communities emerged out of the first Internet chat rooms, and one of the earliest online communities (the PLATO system) was developed at the University of Illinois in the early 1960s. The PLATO system was a precursor of modern educational and online technologies, and it was initially created on the ILLIAC 1 mainframe computer, and later ran on various CDC mainframes. It was designed for computer-based education, and it was commercialised by Control Data Corporation (CDC) in the late 1970s. It pioneered online forums, message boards, email, chat rooms, and multiplayer games.

Usenet newsgroups and message boards were developed for the Internet in the early 1980s, and CompuServe introduced chat rooms around the same time. The invention of the World Wide Web in the late 1980s by Tim Berners Lee was a revolution in computing, and it led to further innovations such as AOL, Yahoo and



G. O'Regan, *Philosophical and Cultural Aspects of Computing*, Undergraduate Topics in Computer Science, https://doi.org/10.1007/978-3-032-29284-1_13

MSN messenger in the mid 1990s. Social media took off in a major way from the early twenty-first century.

There are several popular social media sites such as Facebook (a social media site that allows users to communicate with family and friends in an informal way), Twitter/X (a social media site where users may send short messages called tweets to their followers), LinkedIn (for more formal communication to a user's professional network), and Instagram (a photo and video sharing social media site). Often, there are boundaries between these sites, as LinkedIn and Twitter are often used for professional activities, whereas Facebook and Instagram are mainly used for social and personal activities. This means that there may be differences in the formality of communication on these platforms.

Social media users may be active or passive, with *active users* actively contributing content to the site, and *passive users* often just observing or following events. Social media platforms are generally free to use, but they gather a lot of data about users, and so this has led to concerns over privacy. That is, *the users are essentially the product*, and the social media platform gathers data about them, thereby building up a profile of the users that may be sold on to advertisers and other interested commercial parties.

Facebook has facilitated a cultural shift in human communication, and it enables users to keep in touch with friends and family around the world, and to share their opinions on what is happening in the world. Users may upload photos and videos; express opinions and ideas; and exchange messages. Facebook allows the user's community of friends to be kept up to date on important events that the user wishes to share. It has become an important channel for educated young people to discuss their aspirations for the future, as well as their grievances with society and the state, as well as being an effective tool for protest.

Twitter/X has become an effective way to communicate the latest news, and its effectiveness as a communication tool increases as the number of a person's followers grows. It allows a person or organisation to determine what people are saying about it, including their positive or negative experiences. This allows direct interaction with the followers, and so it is a powerful way to engage the audience and to make people feel heard.

LinkedIn has become an important on-line platform for professionals, and it allows users to create a profile that summarises their education, skills, experience and previous employment. It is a useful way for professionals to build connections with industrial contacts, and to become aware of new opportunities.

## 13.2 The Facebook Revolution

Facebook is the leading social networking site (SNS) in the world, and its mission is to make the world more open and connected. It is a powerful communication tool that enables users to send and receive messages, and to keep in touch with friends and family around the world. It allows users to create and share information such as their opinions on what is happening in the world around them. Users may upload photos and videos, express opinions and ideas, exchange messages, and collaborate. A Facebook community is a key concept, and it consists of a group of like-minded individuals that are interacting for a common goal. Facebook is very popular with advertisers as it allows them to easily reach a large target audience.

Mark Zuckerberg founded the company in 2004 while he was a student studying psychology at Harvard University. Zuckerberg was interested in programming, and he had already developed several social networking websites for his fellow students including *Facemash* which could be used to rate the attractiveness of a person, and *Coursematch* which allowed students to view people taking their degree (Fig. 13.1).

Zuckerberg launched "*The Facebook*" (thefacebook.com) at Harvard in February 2004, and over a thousand Harvard students had registered on the site within the first 24 h. Over half of the Harvard student population had a profile on Facebook within the first month. The membership of the site was initially restricted to students at Harvard, then to students at the other universities in Boston, and then to students at the other universities in the United States. Its membership was extended to international universities from 2005.

**Fig. 13.1** Mark Zuckerberg

The use of Facebook was extended beyond universities to anyone with an email address from 2006, and the number of registered users began to increase exponentially. The number of registered users reached 100 million in 2008, 500 million in 2010; it exceeded 1 billion in 2012, 2 billion in 2017, and over 3 billion in 2025. It is one of the most popular web sites in the world.

Facebook's business model is quite distinct from that of a traditional business in that it does not manufacture or sell any products. Instead, it earns its revenue mainly from advertisements, and its business model is based on advertisement revenue, with advertisements targeted to its 3 billion users based on their specific interests. Another words, Facebook is essentially selling its users to advertisers (i.e., the users are the product), and the users do all the work with Facebook monitoring their activities on the site. Facebook collects data about the users (e.g., their age, gender, location, education, work history and interests), and classifies and categories the users, so that advertisers may target advertisements to them. This ensures that the advertisements are targeted to the right audience, and will potentially be of interest to the targeted audience.

### 13.2.1 The Arab Spring

The Arab Spring refers to a series of anti-government protests from 2010–2012 that took place in various parts of the Arab world including Tunisia, Libya, Egypt, Syria, and Yemen, where rulers were forcibly removed from power or major uprisings took place (Fig. 13.2).

The Arab world had been ruled peacefully for several hundred years by the Ottoman Empire, and the Anglo-French *Sykes Picot agreement* defined how the Middle East would be divided up between Britain and France after the First World War.[1] This agreement led to the creation of several new nation states, where there had previous been no state, and this included the creation of new countries such as Iraq, Syria, Transjordan, Lebanon and Palestine The division of the Middle East between Britain and France involved drawing lots of straight lines without seriously thinking through the consequences of the borders.

The result was that Arab tribes were often divided (the tribe is a fundamental part of Arab identity and determines the status of a person in Arabic society), and it led to states where there were significant ethnic or religious minorities. For example, Iraq had a large population of Shia Muslims in the south, a large population of Kurds (who were non-Arabic Sunni Muslims in the north), and Sunni Muslims in the middle. The split between Shias and Sunnis arose in relation to succession and leadership of the Muslim world after the death of the Prophet, and

[1] Britain had essentially given three different commitments in relation to the Middle East during the First World War. It had its agreement with the French (the Sykes Picot agreement to divide the Middle East between them); it had promised an Arab state (from the Arabian peninsula to Damascus) to the Arabs in return for their support against the Ottomans; and finally its commitments to the Zionists (as in the Balfour declaration) for the creation of a Jewish homeland.

**Fig. 13.2** Arab spring in Middle East

the deep disagreements between Shias and Sunnis are mainly political rather than theological.[2] Further, for Iraq under the Ba'ath Party and later Saddham Hussein the Sunnis dominated the country, and the Kurds and the Shias were crushed into submission, and so there were deep sectarian divisions and limited social cohesion in the state.

There were similar problems with the creation of many of the other countries in the Middle East, although Jordan (formerly called Transjordan) has been the most stable of the new Arab states created after the First World War. Jordan is mainly a homogenous society that is mainly Sunni, but some instability has arisen in recent years from the large number of Syrian refugees that arrived in the country following the collapse of Syria. The situation in Palestine was even more complex,

[2] One important difference between Shia and Sunni Islam is rooted in the Battle of Karbala, Iraq in 680 A.D, which led to the martyrdom of Imam Husayn (the grandson of the Prophet). It is a foundational event for Shias, and acts as a powerful paradigm for resistance against injustice, and standing for truth against tyranny (Iran has been the one country that has stood firmly against the injustice and genocide to the Palestinian people). The assassination of Ayatollah Khamenei (the second most important spiritual figure in Shia Islam, and the one figure in Iran opposed to the possession of nuclear weapons - his 2003 *fatwa* on nuclear weapons) led to another martyr in Shia Islam.

as the 1917 *Balfour declaration*[3] had indicated that the British government would view with favour the creation of a national home for the Jewish people in Palestine (despite the fact that Palestine was part of the Ottoman Empire with a large Muslim population, and that only 2–5% of the people living there were Jewish). *That is, it was definitely not a land without people for a people without land.*

The declaration emphasised that such a home must not prejudice the civil and religious rights of others living in Palestine, but it did not (at the time of the declaration) give a legal commitment to the creation of a Jewish state in Palestine.

However, the Zionists interpreted the Balfour declaration as support for the establishment of their Jewish state in Palestine, and they believed that with Jewish immigration to Palestine that they would establish a Jewish majority within 10 years in Palestine, and they would then be able to establish their planned Jewish state. The Palestinians could hardly have welcomed the Zionist plan to make them a minority in their own land, and they were not even consulted about the plan, or whether they would agree to the formation of a Jewish state in all or part of Palestine. The Balfour declaration was later incorporated into the British mandate over Palestine that was adopted by the League of Nations (the forerunner of the United Nations) in the early 1920s, and upgraded to a British commitment for a Jewish homeland. There were riots in Jerusalem and Jaffa in 1920 and 1921, as Palestinians protested against plans for a Jewish home in Palestine. The first census conducted during the British mandate recorded a Jewish population of approx. 83,000 out of a total population of over 750,000 (roughly 11%) in 1922.

The United Nations (the successor to the League of Nations) decided to partition Palestine into a Jewish part and an Arabic part in November 1947 (giving roughly 57% of Palestine to the Jews (despite the fact that even with the high level of Jewish immigration into Palestine, they still constituted just 31% of the population and owned just 7% of the land in 1947), as after the Second World War there was international support for the creation of the Jewish state of Israel. This new state would enable survivors of the Nazi genocide of six million Jews in the Holocaust to live in their own country (*despite the fact that there were people already living in the country, and who objected to, and who definitely did not give their consent to the Zionist Settler Colonial project*). The Palestinians did not accept the UN plan,[4] and several new Arab countries invaded, but they were quickly defeated by Israel in 1948, with Israel now controlling over 60% of Palestine.

Many Palestinian refugees (estimates of over 700,000) went to neighbouring countries during the violence of 1948 (the *Palestinian Nakba* or Palestinian catastrophe), which involved the destruction of Palestinian society in the Jewish part of the new state, with many being expelled from their homes (ethnic cleansing by

[3] Lord Balfour was foreign secretary of the Lloyd George conservative government, and the Balfour Declaration was a short paragraph contained in a letter written to Lord Rothschild (who was the leader of the British Jewish community) for transmission to the Zionist Federation.

[4] The UN plan gave the Jewish population (perhaps 30–35% of the population) almost 60% of Palestine.

the Zionists with violence and intimidation such as the massacre of many inhabitants of the Palestinian village of Deir Yassin, as well as other atrocities by Jewish paramilitary organisations, such as the Irgun and Lehi) created fear and despair among the Palestinian community.[5]

Further ethnic cleansing (estimates of over 200,000) took place during the six-day war of 1967, where the state of Israel also took control of the Golan Heights. UN Security Council Resolution 242 (November 1967) calls on Israel to withdraw from all territories occupied during the 1967 war, and their continued occupation (including the building of settlements for over 700,000 Israelis in the West Bank) by the state of Israel is a fragrant violation of international law.

Unfortunately, many of the problems in the Middle East today are as a result of the way that the break-up of the former Ottoman Empire was handled by Britain and France after the first world war. Further, there cannot be lasting peace in the Middle East until the historical injustice suffered by the Palestinians is addressed in some reasonable way, and thus there is a need to find a fair and just agreement that would allow both sides to live with in peace and harmony together.

Israel has annexed more and more Palestinian territory since the Six-Day Arab-Israeli War of 1967, including large parts of the West Bank, East Jerusalem and the Golan Heights. The West Bank has an area of 5000 square km and a population of roughly 2.5 million. However, Israel has built roughly 150 settlements in the West Bank (including East Jerusalem) with a population of roughly 700,000). The expansion of the Israeli state into the occupied Palestinian land (after the 1967 war) is illegal under international law, i.e., *all of these settlements in the West Bank, East Jerusalem and the Golan Heights are illegal under international law.* A two state solution looks impossible unless these settlements are handed over to Palestine as part of a peaceful resolution of the conflict.

Around two million Palestinians are crushed into roughly 400 square km in the Gaza strip, with Gaza city having a population of roughly half a million in an area of 45 $km^2$. Noam Chomsky has done important work in the field of linguistics, and he is also an outspoken critic of American foreign policy and the state of Israel. He has stated that the Occupied territories are much worse off than South Africa (under the Apartheid regime), and that Israel just wants to get rid of the people, and that it has employed repressive policies in the Occupied Territories to make life unliveable for the Palestinians[6] [Cho:22].

Given the horrific events of October seventh 2023, and the subsequent response by the state of Israel, which has reduced Gaza to rubble, and the massacre (terms such as genocide or holocaust are more appropriate to employ) of over 70,000 Palestinians by the IDF (roughly one in 33 of the population of Gaza and the

---

[5] The controversial Israeli historian, Ilan Pappé, describes this as the ethnic cleansing of Palestine [Pap:06]. It is important Israelis are properly educated on all matters related to the creation of the state of Israel, as well as the many war crimes committed by the state.

[6] The appalling attack on Israel on Oct. 72,023 was followed by what most observers consider to be Israeli genocide in Gaza. It is extraordinary that a people that were subject to the Holocaust in the Second World War would carry out a holocaust.

official figures are likely to be an underestimate), makes it more urgent than ever to find a just solution. Israel acts with impunity and is supported unconditionally by the United States, and so, it is difficult to be optimistic with respect to the future of the Middle East, unless the US radically changes its approach.[7]

On the one hand the achievements of Israel since 1948 have been impressive, and it is an affluent and modern society with a well-educated population, and lots of hi-tech industries. However, unfortunately its success has been achieved at a massive cost, and there is a deep sense of injustice among the Palestinian people, and they view the actions of Israel since the formation of the state of Israel as deeply unjust and a violation of their rights. Bertrand Russell had sympathy to the plight of the Palestinians and he was critical of the state of Israel.[8] He made several insightful remarks on Israel shortly before his death in 1970 [Rus:70]:

> The aggression committed by Israel must be condemned, not only because no state has the right to annexe foreign territory, but because every expansion is an experiment to discover how much more aggression the world will tolerate

Social media have become an important communication channel for educated young people to discuss their aspirations for the future, as well as their grievances with society and the state. The effectiveness of Facebook as a tool for mobilising protests and social revolution became evident in the relatively short protests that culminated in the resignation of President Hosni Mubarak of Egypt in 2011. Egypt has a young population with roughly 60% of the population under the age of 30, and the country has faced many challenges since independence such as improving education and literacy of its young population, as well as finding jobs for its citizens. There are conflicts between modernity and tradition in many Islamic societies, as well as gender inequality issues, problems with the education systems, and a lack of political freedom with many autocratic political systems rather than democratic societies.

[7] The illegal Israeli attack on Iran on June 13th 2025 (while negotiations on the nuclear enrichment program were taking place) and the complicity of the United States in the attack, as well as the subsequent illegal attack by the Americans on the Fodor enrichment site has led to the widespread view today that both the US and Israel are rogue states. The United States is complicit in the genocide in Gaza (it has provided all the weapons and diplomatic cover to the state of Israel), and the holocaust in Gaza has led to a permanent stain on the state of Israel (as well as on the United States).

[8] Israel seems to view any criticism of the state of Israel as anti-Semitism, which is nonsense, as those that criticize the state of Israel are criticizing the Zionist settler-colonial project, and not individual Jews. Any solution to the Palestinian / Israeli conflict requires justice for the Palestinians as well as Israeli Jews, and it seems reasonable to an impartial observer that a just solution would be a Palestinian state based on the 1967 borders, and a return of the illegal Israeli settlements in the Occupied Territories (however, given all of the illegal settlements a two state solution is looking increasingly unrealistic—any if so, a single state with Palestinians and Israelis living together side-by-side appears to be the only just solution). A just solution to the conflict would provide long-term security to the state of Israel, and an end to all the senseless violence.

Facebook provided a platform for Egyptian youth to discuss issues such as unemployment, low wages, police brutality and corruption. Young Egyptians set up groups on Facebook to discuss specific issues, including a group to provide solidarity with striking workers. Further momentum for revolution followed the beating and killing of Khalid Mohammed Said, as photos of his disfigured body were posted over the Internet and went viral. An influential Facebook group called "*We are All Khalid Said*" was set up, and his killing provided a tangible focus for solidarity among young Egyptians.

Major anti-government protests broke out and lasted for eighteen days, and it led to hundreds of thousands of young Egyptians taking to the streets and gathering in Tahrir Square in Cairo. They demanded an end to police brutality as well as the end of the thirty-year reign of President Hosni Mubarak.

The authorities reacted swiftly in closing the Internet in Egypt, but this act of censorship failed to stop the demonstrations and protests. Social media played an important role in mobilising protests, and in influencing the outcome of the revolution. President Mubarak resigned and he was later convicted of corruption, and President Morsi was inaugurated as the new president. The military removed Morsi from power in 2013, as his Muslim brotherhood government and autocratic style were deeply divisive leading to massive public discontent, and Abdel Fattah El-Sisi (a former military officer) replaced him.

### 13.2.2 Social Media Campaigns

Facebook is an effective tool for conducting various campaigns such as a social media marketing campaign to build awareness of a brand, or a mechanism where the customer can rate a particular product, or a way to improve customer loyalty by providing a forum where customers may discuss what they like or dislike about a product or company. Another words, a company may use Facebook as a tool so that its customers feel heard, and the company can show that it is listening to its customers, and responding to their feedback and improvement suggestions.

A social media campaign needs to be properly designed, and it needs clear goals on what it is trying to achieve as well as criteria for success. For example, the goals of a social media marketing campaign may be to communicate the company brands to a wider audience and to increase sales. The campaign may involve the participation of *influencers*, who are bloggers with a large following, to produce favourable content such as videos, images and articles on the product or company. The fact that the influencers have a strong following helps in building up brand presence and awareness, and ensures that the message is spread to a wider audience. There is a need for care in the choice of the influencers to ensure that they are the right fit for the marketing campaign.

Facebook is an effective tool for politicians in their election campaigns, and one of its main advantages is that it enables the politician to interact directly with their constituents and the electorate, while bypassing the mainstream media. In a sense, this helps politicians to avoid the scrutiny that they are generally subject to in traditional media, where one of the important functions of traditional media is to hold politicians accountable to the public. Journalists, researchers and presenters fact check the claims of politicians to ensure their accuracy, and to ensure openness and transparency of political discourse. Facebook provides a forum for politicians to present and communicate their message and policies, as well as enabling them to show a human side as well as their personal interests.

### 13.2.3 Facebook and Privacy

Facebook has a comprehensive set of terms and conditions that users must accept to use the site, and these include invasive privacy practices that give Facebook the right to collect data on user activity on the site to improve the user experience and also for commercial purposes. A user must click acceptance of the associated terms and conditions to use the site, and most users just accept, as this is the only option that they have if they wish to join the Facebook community. Another words, although users create their own personal content that content is not private, and Facebook is continuously monitoring their behaviour on the site.

Further, many third party apps interface with Facebook through Facebook's Open Graph platform, and all these apps have their own privacy settings and collect data on the users. The data gathered by Facebook may be used to build up profiles of users including what they like and dislike, and this data is potentially valuable to advertisers or those involved in marketing or political research. We will discuss the Cambridge Analytic scandal in the next section, where the personal information of millions of Facebook users was misused.

Facebook encourages users to disclose more and more information, and the user data may be visible and searchable. There is a danger that information that has been shared in the individual's network could be shared more widely by one of her "friends". This could result in posts that should remain restricted to a small audience being spread widely with potential negative effects on the individual. Another words, users need to be prudent in the content that they share in order to stay safe on the site.

Further, a Facebook user may be accessing the site through a smartphone, and so the location of the user is known at all times, and an analysis of the location data allows the user's home and work locations to be determined, as well as their day-to-day life patterns.

There have been several security and data breaches on Facebook where the personal data of Facebook users were exposed. For example, a data breach in April 2019 exposed the records of half a billion Facebook users on Amazon cloud servers, including the personal data of their friends, their names, passwords, and email addresses. The phone numbers of over 200 million Facebook users was exposed on an open platform in September 2019.

### 13.2.4 The Cambridge Analytica Affair

The Cambridge Analytics affair refers to a scandal that became public after the victory of Donald Trump in the 2016 US presidential election campaign. Cambridge Analytica acquired the private Facebook data of roughly 30–90 million users[9] in 2014, and used the data to create psychological profiles of tens of millions of American voters. The objective was to then sell these profiles to political campaigns so that they could be used for political advertising, and some political analysis assistance was provided to the Ted Cruz campaign, and later to the Trump campaign. However, it is unclear whether this approach was a deciding factor in the Trump victory, as there were several other factors that led to the defeat of Hilary Clinton.[10]

A third party app (*'This is your digital life'*) was employed to collect the private data of Facebook users for Cambridge Analytica, and this app used Facebook's Open Graph platform to interface with Facebook. The app was an academic research study that used an informed consent process, where several hundred thousand Facebook users gave their consent to the collection of their personal information, and completed an online survey for which they received a small payment. However, the app was also able to obtain both the private data of the survey participants as well as the private data of all their friends through the Facebook Open Graph platform.

This led to Cambridge Analytic acquiring the private data of tens of millions of Facebook users, which contained sufficient detail to enable Cambridge Analytica to create psychological profiles of those that it had data on including their location. Cambridge Analytica began to create individual psychological profiles in 2016 when they were hired to support Ted Cruz's presidential campaign. The Facebook information was invaluable to political campaigns, as it allowed them to consider each person's psychological profile, which suggested what type of advertisement would be most effective in influencing a particular person in a particular location.

The Trump campaign used the Facebook data to create psychological profiles on users, and they used the data to determine the user's personality based on their Facebook activity. This information was then used for sending customised messages about Trump to different users, and the advertisements were segmented

---

[9] The New York Times estimated that the private data of 50 million Facebook users were taken, whereas Facebook's CTO (Mike Schroepfer) later revised this estimate to approximately 87 million (with 70 million from the US). Cambridge Analytica itself estimated that it had obtained the profiles of 30 million users.

[10] There were several reasons for Hilary Clinton's defeat where she was leading in the opinion polls in the weeks before the election. The Clinton campaign was over confident, the campaign underestimated the electorate's desire for change from the Obama era, and James Comey's decision to reopen the FBI investigation into the Clinton private emails did not help. Clinton lost the white working class vote to Trump in the rust belt area in the US, and African American voters and millennial voters were unenthusiastic for her. The Clinton campaign was seen as focusing on the professional class rather than on the working class and their needs (such as employment). She was seen as an elite and divisive candidate, and perhaps gender was also a factor in the election.

**Fig. 13.3** Cambridge analytica scandel

into different categories depending on whether the user was a Trump supporter or a potential swing voter. For example, supporters of Trumps received positive visuals of him and information on voting stations, whereas swing voters received negative information and visuals on Clinton and her policies, as well as positive stories about Trump and his policies (Fig. 13.3).

The scandal with Cambridge Analytic's misuse of Facebook data caused a major sensation when it became public, and Zuckerberg apologised to the media on behalf of Facebook in 2018, and pledged to make changes. The Federal Trade Commission imposed a $5 billion fine on Facebook for the data breach in 2019, and the US Securities and Exchange Commission (SEC) imposed a $100 million fine for misleading investors on the risk impacts of data misuse in 2019. Facebook announced that it would comply with the important European GDPR privacy law (see Chap. 12) in 2019.

### 13.2.5 Facebook Groups and Moderating Content

Individuals or businesses may set up Facebook groups, and these groups may be public or private. The posts of a private group are restricted to the members of the group, whereas the posts of public groups are available to all. The use of groups offers a way for an organisation or business to build a community around its brand and to develop relationships with its customers, and while a Facebook page allows a business to present the profile of the company and posts it wishes to share, a Facebook group allows users to join as members and engage in interaction with the company and with other members. This is a constructive way for the business to interact with its customers, and allows it to determine what its customers are saying about it, and what they like or dislike.

An individual may set up a Facebook group in an area that she is interested in, and the various special interest groups will be of interest to different communities. There may be a need to manage the community content to ensure that all posts use appropriate language and respect the dignity of the members, and online tools may be employed to flag any language that may be inappropriate. There may be a need to develop a code of conduct for members of the group, and there be a need for a community facilitator to handle any issues that might arise.

That is, a role such as a community manager or administrator may be required to monitor the posts to ensure appropriate behaviour from the active community. Sometimes members may become highly emotive and engage in flame wars thereby upsetting other members (e.g., as in political debate). There could be *trolls*[11] inflaming hate, racism or other threatening behaviour affecting other members (especially in the debate of sensitive political topics such as immigration, gun laws, abortion rights, and LGBT rights).

There could be online harassment of members, where repeated insults or online bullying of an individual takes place, or threats of violence or even revenge porn. There may need to be discussions with violators of the terms and conditions of membership of the group, and in a worse case scenario there may be deletion of inappropriate posts and the removal of abusive members from the group.

## 13.3 The Tweet

Twitter/X is a social communication tool that allows people to broadcast short messages. It is often described as the "*SMS of the Internet*", and is an online social media and micro blogging site that allows its users to send and receive short (initially 140-character) messages called "*tweets*". The restriction to 140 characters was to allow Twitter to be used on non-smartphone mobile devices, but the character limit was doubled to 280 characters in 2017. Twitter has over 300 million active users, and it is one of the most visited websites in the world. Users may access Twitter through its website interface, a mobile device app or SMS.

Jack Dorsey (Fig. 13.4) and others founded the company in 2006. Dorsey introduced the idea of an individual using an SMS service to communicate with a small group while he was still an undergraduate student at New York University. The word "*twitter*" was the chosen name for this new service, and its definition as '*a short burst of information*' and '*chirps from birds*' was highly appropriate.

Twitter messages are often about friends telling one another about their day, what they are doing, where they are, what they are thinking and doing, and any notable events that are happening around them. Twitter has transformed the world of media, politics and business. It is possible to include links to web pages and other media as a tweet. News such as natural disasters, sports results and so on are often reported first by Twitter. The site has impacted political communication in a major way, as it allows politicians and their followers to debate and exchange political opinions.

The effectiveness of Twitter/X as a platform for political communication was very evident in the 2016 presidential campaign of Donald Trump and throughout his first presidency. The term "*Commander-in-Tweet*" was coined to refer to Trump's major use of Twitter throughout his presidency (Trump 1). Twitter enables

[11] Trolling is where someone posts or comments online with the goal of upsetting other people.

**Fig. 13.4** Jack Dorsey at the 2012 time 100 gala

celebrities to engage and stay in contact with their fans, and it provides a new way for businesses to advertise its brands to its target audience.

A Twitter user may select which other people that they wish to follow, and when you follow someone their tweets show up in a list known as your *Twitter stream*. Similarly, anyone that chooses to follow you will see your tweets in their stream.

A *hashtag* is an easy way to find all the tweets about a topic of interest, and it may be used even if you are not following the people who are tweeting. It also allows you to contribute to the topic that is of interest, and a hashtag consists of a short word or acronym preceded by the hash sign (#). Conferences, hot topics, and so on often have a hashtag.

A word or topic that is tagged at a greater rate than other hashtags is said to be a *trending topic*, and a trending topic is often the result of an event that prompts people to discuss the topic (e.g., an earthquake, the death of a celebrity, a political event). Trending may also arise from the deliberate action of certain groups (e.g., in the entertainment industry) to raise the profile of a musician or celebrity and to market their work.

Twitter has evolved to become an effective way to communicate the latest news, and its effectiveness as a communication tool for an organization increases as the number of its followers grows. An organization may determine what people are saying about it, as well as their positive or negative experience in interacting with it. This allows the organization to directly interact with its followers, which is a powerful way to engage with its audience and to make people feel heard. It allows the organization to respond to any negative feedback, and to deal with such feedback sensitively and appropriately.

The first version of Twitter was introduced in mid-2006, and it took the company some time to determine exactly what type of entity it was. There was nothing quite like it in existence, and initially it was considered a micro-blogging and social media site. Today, it is viewed as an information network rather than just a social media site.

Twitter has experienced rapid growth from 400,000 tweets posted per quarter in 2007, to 100 million per quarter in 2008, to 65 million tweets per day from 2010, to 140 million tweets per day in 2011 and to 500 million tweets per day since 2016. Twitter's usage spikes during important events such as major sporting events, natural disasters, the death of a celebrity, and so on. For such events, there may be over 100,000 tweets per second.

Twitter's main source of revenue is advertisements through "*promoted tweets*" that appear in a user's timeline (Twitter stream). The first promoted tweets appeared from late 2011, and the use of a tweet for advertisement was ingenious. It helped to make the advertisement feel like part of Twitter, and it meant that an advertisement could go anywhere that a tweet could go. Advertisers are only charged when the user follows the links or re-tweets the original advertisements. Further, the use of tweets for advertisement meant that the transition to mobile was easy, and today over 80% of Twitter use is on mobile devices.

Twitter has recently embarked on a strategy that goes beyond these advertisements to sell products directly (including to people who don't use Twitter). Twitter also earns revenue from a data licensing arrangement where it sells its information to companies who use this information to analyse consumer trends. Twitter analyses what users tweet to understand their intent. Twitter was taken over by Elon Musk in 2022 and the company has undergone major restructuring. The company is currently known as Twitter/X or just X. For more detailed information on Twitter see [Sch:14].

## 13.4 LinkedIn

LinkedIn is a social media site for professional networking, and it allows professionals to create a profile of their qualifications and professional experience. The user's profile provides a short executive summary of their qualifications, knowledge and experience, as well as what sets him or her apart from others. It includes a selection of their previous roles, and any distinguishing accomplishments, as well as recommendations from work colleagues and other professionals.

Linkedin allows members to connect to other members of the site, and the user's connections form his or her professional network. These may include work colleagues and other professionals, and the site helps individuals in their interactions with others, and allows them to post updates (e.g., new achievements, new roles, etc.) to enhance their professional reputation. LinkedIn includes a messaging service, where you can send messages to others who are both inside and outside of your network.

Employers may create profiles and become members of the site, and they may post job vacancies on the site. The site allows users to search and apply for new positions, and individuals may share their resume with potential employers and apply for relevant vacancies. Both employers and job seekers use LinkedIn widely, and there are roughly a billion members of the site.

LinkedIn allows special interest groups to be formed to discuss special interest topics, and these groups may be public or private. LinkedIn's revenue comes mainly from selling access to information about its members to recruiters, and the company became a subsidiary of Microsoft in 2016. The basic version of LinkedIn is free, but LinkedIn Premium is a subscription version that offers additional features such as online classes and seminars.

## 13.5 Social Media and Disinformation

Fake news is the systematic spreading of false or misleading information in traditional print or online social media, usually with the intention of misleading or damaging another person or institution. It may negatively affect individuals, and could lead to violence or hate against minority or ethnic groups. The popularity of social media sites such as Facebook have contributed to the spread of fake news, and this new phenomenon poses threats to the modern world (e.g., democracy). Fake news may be spread by individuals, organisations and hostile states, and it consists of news that has no basis in fact, but which is presented as being factually correct.

Fake news in the form of propaganda has been around for centuries, where such news is generally published for political reasons. Military leaders have often embellished their bravery and results in battle throughout history (e.g., the pharaoh Ramses II's description of the thirteenth century B.C. battle of Kadesh between the Egyptians and the Hittites paints a very positive but factually inaccurate account of the battle). Information or disinformation is an important part of modern warfare, where one state may present a narrative that it is winning the war, when in fact it has no hope of meeting the military objectives that it set itself at the start of the conflict.

Following the invention of the printing press in the fifteenth century, news publications became popular, and over time fake news stories appeared in the print media. Fake news played an important role in propaganda during the first and second world wars, with radio broadcasts and printed material used to encourage and persuade the public at home as well as discouraging enemy troops. Today, modern society is highly dependent on accurate information in print, radio, television and on-line media, and it is important that the public be provided with accurate information. The effectiveness of fake news increases when the stories spread widely (as often occurs in social media), and where users interact with and rely on these stories rather than on traditional news media.[12]

Fake news played a role in the 2016 presidential election in the United States, which led to the election of Donald Trump. Most of the fake election news in the last three months of the campaign was anti-Clinton, but it is difficult to determine the extent to which this influenced the outcome of the election.

Trump and his supporters have used the term "fake news" to refer to the news from mainstream media that they accused of being opposed to him and his policies. The period in which Trump was in power (first term) was surreal, where the world as perceived by Trump did not correspond to the world of rational thinking human beings. The final *denouement* were the events on January sixth 2021 where Trump incited his supporters to march on Capitol Hill to claim back the country from the November 2020 "stolen election" victory of Biden. The extraordinary thing is that many of his supporters continued to believe that the election was stolen long after Biden was sworn in as president, and Trump was re-elected in 2024 (second term).

It is important when considering the accuracy of an article to consider the source of the news (e.g., is it written by a reputable news organisation?),[13] as well as considering the authenticity and reputation of its authors and the supporting sources. Fake news is a deeply disturbing trend that needs to be resolved if technology is to serve humanity, and if important values are to be preserved in society. Modern technology has provided many benefits to modern society, but

[12] Unfortunately, one of the immediate consequences of any conflict (especially involving a great power) is that mainstream news may sometimes not be relied upon. The narrative in western media with respect to the Ukraine War was that Putin was some crazy individual intent on recreating the Russian Empire with plans to take over all of Ukraine and Western Europe. I was living in Kyrgzstan (a former Soviet republic) from 2021–2022, and at first I bought into the Western Narrative. However, it was only when I spoke to older Kyrgyzs that I gained an understanding of a very different point of view. They stated very clearly that Ukraine joining NATO was an existential threat to Russia (Russia was not prepared to accept NATO forces massed on their borders along with nuclear missiles that could reach Moscow in 10 min—a basic knowledge of Russia history would explain this). For Russia, Ukraine joining NATO represented an existential threat—it was absolutely unacceptable to Russia, and western powers were at best naïve or at worse deliberately provocative in insisting that Ukraine could join NATO—the analogy would be Mexico or Canada joining a Chinese Defence pact with Chinese missiles being placed in Mexico or Canada—clearly this would be totally unacceptable to the United States—as Ukraine joining NATO was to Russia). It is essential in modern diplomacy to understand the position of the other party, and this was severely lacking in western media during the Ukraine conflict, as Russia had genuine security concerns that, at best, were unintentionally (or at worst deliberately) ignored by the West.

[13] The mainstream media is also capable of spreading misinformation and may not always be relied upon for accuracy and balance in their coverage of particular topics, which is often as a result of their corporate ownership-funding model, and where the owners have specific agendas. This is especially the case when mainstream media is dealing with sensitive topics such as the conflict in the Middle East. All too often the portrayal of the conflict between Israel and the Palestinians is unbalanced, and rarely provides the historical background to the injustice that the Palestinians suffered with the creation of the state of Israel in 1948 and the loss of their homes and land.

technology *needs to serve humanity and not damage it.* Some of the ways to check whether fake news might be present include:

- Consider the source of the news
- Check the author/journalist
- Check the date
- Check any supporting material
- Consult a fact checking site

Fake news can spread easily due to the speed and accessibility of modern technology. It allows individuals to be misled and adversely influenced, and individuals who rely on social media sites exclusively for their news are susceptible to being misinformed. Online social media sites such as Facebook and Twitter have a responsibility to develop appropriate solutions to address this dangerous problem, and following Trump's incitement of his followers to storm the capital in January 2021 they finally took appropriate action. Facebook and Twitter finally suspended Trump's account shortly before Biden's inauguration as a response to the excesses of Trump's misuse of social media during his first term. Trump later formed his own social media site namely "*Truth Social*".

There is a need for more rigorous terms and conditions on the use of social media, and social media sites have a professional and ethical responsibility to ensure that there is an appropriate balance between the right to free speech and the prohibition of disinformation, hate speech, racism, on line bullying, and so on. Social media sites need to take firm action when their terms and conditions are abused, and repeat offenders need to be sanctioned (e.g., blocked from the sites).

Social media is extremely useful but it creates new problems for society. It takes time for the legal system in a state to catch up with the problems caused with the introduction of a new technology, There is a need for the regulation of social media sites to deal with these problems, and also to deal with the fact that in a sense a social media site is a media organization, and so in a sense it has additional responsibilities that need to be managed as such. That is, a social media site needs to take responsibility for whatever is published on its site, and to rapidly respond and remove any inappropriate material (fake news, hate speech, etc.) from its site.

### 13.5.1 Disinformation and War

It has become increasingly difficult today to determine the truth or otherwise of events in a wartime situation, where disinformation is now an important part of modern warfare—i.e., disinformation is a weapon of war. Disinformation (including digital propaganda) is employed by states to manipulate public opinion and perception of events. It may be used to fuel tension and create polarisation in society (polarisation is where society is split into opposing groups with deep political and ideological divisions, or it may it may involve sowing divisions in natural segregations of society (e.g., based on income, religion, etc.), in which divisions are used to justify aggression).

There has been a shift from traditional state run news media (traditional media may also share disinformation and propaganda) to social media, where today many individuals get their news online from alternative media such as Facebook, Youtube, etc. These sites allow the publication of AI generated videos that give the impression that certain events have taken place (e.g., naval ships sunk, targets bombed, demonstrations, etc), when no such events have actually happened. Other examples include AI generated deepfake videos, where well-known individuals appear to do or say outrageous things, when they have not done so. There are fake news sites on social media that may give the impression that they are genuinely presenting news, but completely fabricate (often with emotionally charged content) news stories.

It may be that the misinformation targets another leader by seeking to undermine his or her legitimacy. This may involve the manipulation of public opinion to achieve a certain outcome, or it may involve sowing division among the population. Misinformation is electronic and can travel rapidly to reach the targeted recipients (especially when a video becomes viral or when an influencer with a large number of followers shares the video). Disinformation may disguise the true nature of military actions (it may be stated that the purpose is to liberate or bring freedom to a population—often by bombing their hospitals and schools, where more often than not, there are other reasons for the military intervention, such as the control of scarce mineral resources such as oil, gas, gold, rare earth elements, etc).

## 13.6 Data Analytics for Social Media

Data analytics (see Chap. 12) provides a quantitative insight into human behaviour on a site, and is a way to understand users and how to communicate with them better. It enables the business to understand its audience better, and to create content that will be of interest to them. Data analytics consist of a collection of data that says something about the social media conversation, and it involves the collection, monitoring, analysis, summarisation, and graphs to visualise insight into the behaviour of users.

That is, *data analytics* involves learning to read a social media community through data, and the interpretations of the quantifiable data (or metrics) gives information on the activities, events, and conversations. This includes what users like when they are online, but other important information such as their opinions and emotions are gathered through *social listening*, which involves monitoring keywords and mentions in social media conversations to understand and analyse what the audience is saying about the business, and allows the business to engage with its audience.

Social media companies use data analytics to gain an insight into customers, and uses data such as the number of likes, the number of followers, the number of times a video is played to obtain a quantified understanding of a conversation. This is used to judging the effectiveness of a social media campaign in meeting its goals such as increasing the number of users. Data analytics and social listening help in understanding how people are interacting, as well as how successful the interactions has been.

Facebook maintains metrics such as the number of page views and the number of likes and the number of people who saw posts at least once. Twitter includes a dashboard view to summarise how successful tweet activity has been. Social listening considers user opinions, emotions, views, evaluations, and attitude, as well as a rich collection of human emotions.

The design of a social media campaign involves determining its objectives, and designing a campaign to meet the requirements. Its effectiveness is judged by a combination of social media analytics and social listening, with the campaign refined to meet its goals and the cycle repeating.

## 13.7 Ethics and Social Media

We discussed ethical social media in Chap.12, and noted that Facebook conducted a famous mood experiment on its users in 2012 to determine the extent to which their mood would be influenced by the content of their news feed. The experiment showed that happy stories generally led to positive postings, whereas sad stories led to negative postings, and so they were able to deduce that the mood of the news feed influenced the user's mood and postings. However, the experiment led to controversy, as the 700,000 users were unaware that they were participants in a psychological experiment, and the experiment had been conducted without their consent (i.e., the experiment was unethical).

The principle of *informed consent* is fundamental in medical experiments, where individuals are informed about an experiment, and have the right to agree to participate or decline their consent. Further, the individual has the right to withdraw their consent at any time during the experiment. Once individuals have given their informed consent research data may be collected.

Social media sites collect data about the user's activities on the site, and this personal data may be processed and sold commercially to advertisers. Further, third party applications may interface with the social media site and gather personal data for commercial purposes. Users give consent to the social media platforms to collect and process their personal data, and their consent is given by clicking acceptance of the terms and conditions of use for the site. The *consent cannot be said to be given voluntarily* in the sense that if a user wishes to use the platform or third party application then she needs to click acceptance of the terms and conditions of use. Further, the *consent cannot be said to be informed* as the details of the data collection and processing are hidden in the small print of the terms and condition, which is generally a long unreadable document.

Those who create an online community (e.g., a community on Facebook) have a duty of care to the community that they have formed. This requires good community management to ensure the welfare of its members, and monitoring of activities to prevent abuse or online harassment of members of the community, and to ensure appropriate community behaviour at all times.

Ethical social media should consider the diversity of users and their needs, with appropriate accessibility interfaces provided for the visually impaired or those with a hearing impairment. *Social media sites are designed to be addictive* and to encourage users to disclose more and more information about themselves (potentially placing themselves in danger).

Social media sites have a professional and ethical responsibility to ensure that groups that advocate extremism or violence be banned from the site, and that the activities of such groups be reported to the relevant authorities.

There is a need for the regulation of social media sites as a social media site is essentially a media organization, and so it needs to take responsibility for whatever is published on its site, and to immediately respond and remove any inappropriate material (fake news, hate speech, disinformation, etc.) from its site.

## 13.8 Review Questions

1. What is social media?
2. What are the advantages and disadvantages of social media?
3. Explain the role that social media played in the Arab spring.
4. What is a social media campaign?
5. Explain the significance of the Cambridge Analytica affair.
6. What privacy issues have arisen with social media?
7. What is the purpose of moderating content on social media?
8. What is Twitter?
9. What is LinkedIn?
10. Explain the significance of fake news.
11. What are data analytics?

## 13.9 Summary

Social media involves the use of computer technology for the creation and exchange of user-generated content, and it has led to major changes in communication between individuals, communities and organisations. Social media plays a key role in connecting people and enabling communication. Politicians use social media during election campaigns as a way to communicate their message and policies. Corporations use social media to understand what customers like and dislike about their products and services. Social media enables citizens to play a role in shaping the world around them.

Facebook is a powerful communication tool that enables users to send and receive messages, and to keep in touch with friends and family around the world. It allows users to create and share information, upload photos and videos, express opinions and ideas, exchange messages, and collaborate. A Facebook community consists of a group of individuals that are interacting for a common goal. Twitter is a social communication tool that allows people to broadcast short messages called "tweets".

Fake news is the systematic spreading of false or misleading information in traditional print or online social media, with the intention of misleading or damaging another person or institution. It may be spread by individuals, organisations and hostile states, and it consists of news that has no basis in fact, but which is presented as being factually correct. The popularity of social media sites have contributed to the spread of fake news, and this new phenomenon poses threats to the modern world.

## References


[Cho:22] Chomsky on Israel Apartheid, celebrity activists, BDS and the one-state solution. Noam Chomsky. Middle East Monitor. June 27th 2022.

[Pap:06] The Ethnic cleansing of Palestine. Ilan Pappé. Oneworld Publications. 2006.

[Rus:70] Bertrand Russell's Last Message on Palestine and Israel. 31st Jan 1970. Read aloud in Cairo on Feb 3rd. 1970.

[Sch:14] The Tao of Twitter. Changing your Life and Business 140 Characters at a Time. Second Edition. Mark W. Schaefer. McGraw-Hill. 2014.

# Ethical AI 14

## 14.1 Introduction

The long-term[1] goal of Artificial Intelligence may be to create a thinking machine that is intelligent, has consciousness, has the ability to learn, has free will, and is ethical. Artificial Intelligence is a young field and John McCarthy and others coined the term in 1956. It is a multi-disciplinary field, and its branches include logic, philosophy, psychology, linguistics, machine vision, neural networks and expert systems.

Alan Turing devised the Turing Test as a way to test the intelligent behaviour of a machine, and Turing believed that machine intelligence was achievable. Searle's Chinese Room argument is a rebuttal of strong AI, and it aims to demonstrate that a machine will never have the same cognitive qualities as a human even if it passes the Turing Test.

There are deep philosophical problems in Artificial Intelligence, and some researchers (including Hubert Dreyfus and John Searle) believe that its goals are impossible or incoherent. Even if Artificial Intelligence is possible there are moral issues to consider such as the exploitation of artificial machines by humans, and whether it is ethical to do this. Weizembaum[2] has argued that Artificial Intelligence is unethical.

McCarthy argued that human-level intelligence could be achieved with a logic-based system that provides *declarative knowledge* (this specifies what something is

[1] This long-term goal may be many years as there is unlikely to be an early breakthrough in machine intelligence as there are deep philosophical problems to be solved. However, a lot of progress has been made in simulating intelligence with work on machine translation and machine learning algorithms, as well as recent progress with large language models such as ChatGPT.

[2] Weizenbaum was a psychologist who invented the ELIZA program, which simulated a psychologist in dialogue with a patient. He was initially an advocate of Artificial Intelligence but later became a critic.

 
G. O'Regan, *Philosophical and Cultural Aspects of Computing*, Undergraduate Topics in Computer Science, https://doi.org/10.1007/978-3-032-29284-1_14

rather than how it is determined). McCarthy's approach was rejected by proceduralists such as Minsky, who argued that the representation of knowledge should be done in some domain that embeds knowledge in terms of procedures. *Procedural knowledge* is the knowledge exercised in the performance of some task such as riding a bicycle.

*Cognitive psychology* is concerned with cognition and some of its research areas include perception, memory, learning, thinking, and logic and problem solving. *Linguistics* is the scientific study of language and includes the study of syntax and semantics.

Artificial *neural networks* aim to simulate various properties of biological neural networks. They consist of hundreds or thousands of simple processing units that are wired together in a complex communication network. Each unit or node is a simplified model of a real neuron which fires if it receives a sufficiently strong input signal from the other nodes to which it is connected. The strength of these connections may be varied in order for the network to learn to perform different tasks corresponding to different patterns of node firing activity.

An *expert system* is a computer system that allows knowledge to be stored and intelligently retrieved. It is a program that is made up of a set of rules (or knowledge). The domain experts generally supply the rules about a specific class of problems, and expert systems include a problem solving component that allows an analysis of the problem, as well as recommending an appropriate course of action to solve the problem.

There are several stories of attempts by man to create life from inanimate objects: for example, the monster in Mary Shelly's Frankenstein is created by an over ambitious scientist who is punished for his blasphemy of creation (in that creation is for God alone). The Czech play "Rossums Universal Robots" is a science fiction play by Capek, and contains the first reference to the term "*robot*". The play considers the exploitation of artificial workers in a factory, and the robots (or androids) are initially happy to serve humans, but become unhappy with their existence over a period of time. The fundamental question that the play is considering is whether the robots are being exploited, and if so, whether this is ethical, and what should the response of the robots be to their exploitation? It eventually leads to a revolt by the robots and the extermination of the human race.

The origin of the term "Artificial Intelligence" is in work done on the proposal for the Dartmouth[3] Summer Research Project on Artificial Intelligence. John McCarthy and others wrote this proposal in 1955, and the research project took place in the summer of 1956.

The success of early AI went to its practitioners' heads and they believed that they would soon develop machines that would emulate human intelligence. They convinced many of the funding agencies and the military to provide research grants, as they believed that real artificial intelligence would soon be achieved.

[3] Darmouth is a private university located in Hanover, New Hampshire.

They had some initial (limited) success with machine translation, pattern recognition and automated reasoning. It soon became clear that AI is a long-term project, and although there has been a lot of recent progress in simulating human intelligence (e.g., with large language model technologies such as ChatGPT or Deepseek), real intelligent AI is still a long way in the future. AI is a multi-disciplinary field and includes:

- Logic and Philosophy
- Psychology
- Linguistics
- Neuroscience and Neural Networks
- Machine Vision
- Machine learning
- Robotics
- Expert Systems
- Autonomous Vehicles
- Machine Learning and Machine Translation
- Large Language Models
- Epistemology and Knowledge representation.

The English mathematician, Alan Turing, contributed to the debate concerning thinking machines, consciousness and intelligence in the early 1950s [Tur:50]. He devised the famous "*Turing Test*" to judge whether a machine was conscious and intelligent. Turing's paper was very influential as it raised the idea of the possibility of programming a computer to behave intelligently.

Shannon considered the problem of writing a chess program in the late 1940s, and he distinguished between a brute force strategy where the program could look at every combination of moves, and a strategy where knowledge of chess could be used to select and examine a subset of available moves. The ability of a program to play chess is a skill that is considered intelligent, even though the machine itself is not conscious that it is playing chess. Modern chess programs have advantages over humans in terms of computational speed in considering the immense combinations of moves. The IBM chess program "Deep Blue" defeated Kasparov in 1997, and today chess programs regularly beat the top players.

The area of ethics is important in AI, and we discuss Weizenbaum's views on how AI impacts human dignity, and discuss ethical concerns in the field of expert systems, as well as the ethics of self-driving cars. We discuss areas such as AI and privacy, AI and unemployment and AI and surveillance.

## 14.2 AI and Human Dignity

Weizenbaum created the famous ELIZA program at MIT in 1966, and the program interacted with a user sitting at an electric typewriter, in English, in the manner of a Rogerian psychotherapist.[4]

The name "*Eliza*"[5] was chosen because it could be taught to speak increasingly well, as in Shaw's play "Pygmalion", and its later adaptation in the 1964 film "My Fair Lady" starring Rex Harrison and Audrey Hepburn. Eliza was one of the earliest natural language processing programs, and Weizenbaum gave an example of a conversation between Eliza and a young woman in [Wei:66]. Many users believed that Eliza had real understanding, and they began to unburden themselves in long computer sessions.

The program operated by decomposing the user's input into its constituent parts of speech, and then typing them back at the user in a manner to continue with the dialogue. The program provided very convincing human-like interaction, as may be seen in the sample dialogue below (Fig. 14.1):

| | |
|---|---|
| User/Patient | Men are all alike |
| ELIZA | *In what way?* |
| User/Patient | They are always bugging us about something or other |
| ELIZA | *Can you think of a specific example*? |
| User/Patient | Well, my boyfriend made me come here |
| ELIZA | *Your boyfriend made you come here*? |
| User/Patient | He says I'm depressed much of the time |
| ELIZA | *I am sorry to hear that you are depressed* |
| User/Patient | It's true, I am unhappy |
| ELIZA | *Do you think that coming here will help you not to be unhappy*? |
| User/Patient | I need some help, that much seems certain |
| ELIZA | *What would it mean to you if you got some help*? |
| User/Patient | Perhaps, I could learn to get along with my mother |
| ELIZA | *Tell me more about your family* |

Weizenbaum was shocked to discover that so many users were convinced that the program had real understanding, and users spent hours sharing their personal problems with the program. It led Weizenbaum to think about the ethics and implications of the artificial intelligence field given the ability of a relatively trivial program to deceive a naïve user to reveal personal information. He became a leading critic of the AI field, and an advocate for professional and social responsibility in computer science.

[4] Rogerian psychotherapy (person-centred therapy) was developed by Carl Rodgers in the 1940s.

[5] Eliza Doolittle is a working-class character in Shaw's play "Pygmalion". She is taught to speak with an upper-class English accent.

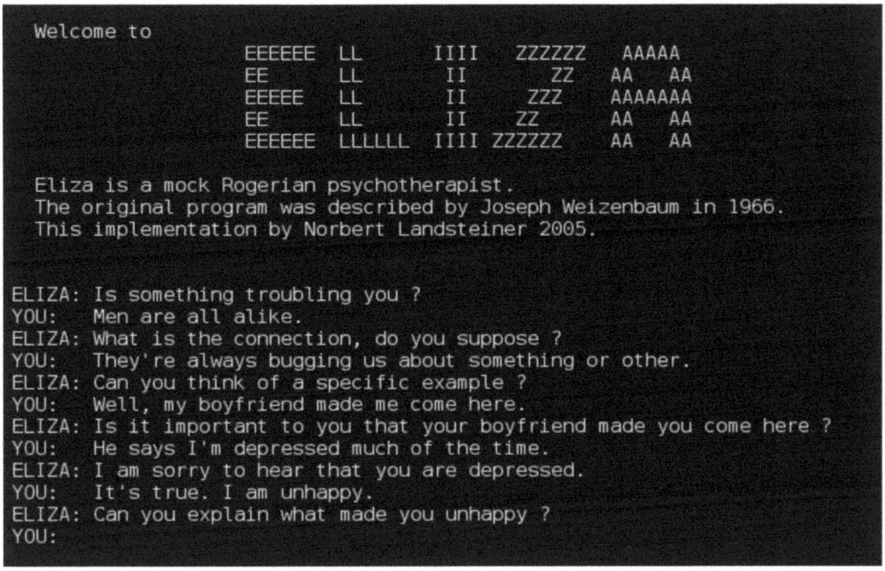


**Fig. 14.1** Eliza program

His views on the ethics of AI are discussed in his book "Computer Power and Human Reason" [Wei:76]. He displays ambivalence towards computer technology, and he argues that AI is a threat to human dignity, and that AI should not replace humans in positions that require respect and care. He states that machines lack empathy, and that if they replace humans in positions such as police officers or judges, that this would lead to alienation and a devaluation of the human condition.

Weizenbaum's ELIZA program demonstrated the threat that AI potentially poses to privacy, where users can be tricked to reveal personal information. It is conceivable that an AI program may be developed in the future (indeed we are close to or at this situation) that is capable of understanding speech and natural language in such a way that it could theoretically eavesdrop on every phone conversation and email, and gather private information on what is said, and who is saying it.[6] Such a program could be used by a state to suppress dissent, and to eliminate those who pose a threat.

[6] One wonders what information the virtual assistant, Amazon Alexa, gathers every day and how that information is used.

## 14.3 Ethics of Self-driving Cars

A driverless car (autonomous vehicle) is a vehicle that can sense its environment and navigate its way without human intervention. It uses techniques such as AI, GPS, radar and computer vision to detect its environment, and it has advanced control systems to determine an appropriate navigation path to its destination. Its navigation needs to be sophisticated to enable it to avoid obstacles, and to observe road signage and traffic lights during the journey, as well as dealing with diverse weather/light conditions (Fig. 14.2).

The control system includes sensing and navigation systems, and the analysis of the sensory data must be able to distinguish between different vehicles on the road. The control system must make the correct decisions from the analysis of the images, and this is especially important when dealing with unexpected situations.

Several technology companies such as Google, Apple, Uber and Amazon are working on driverless cars, and autonomous vehicles may potentially lead to a significant reduction in road accidents and fatalities. They offer greater mobility for people who cannot operate a vehicle, but there are many challenges such as safety and security issues that need to be solved, as well as the development of an appropriate regulatory framework, before the public will have sufficient confidence in their use (Table 14.1).

Driverless cars will need to be encoded with a moral compass to deal with situations where ethical decisions needs to be made. For example, suppose a self-driving vehicle is travelling on a road and two children roll off a grassy bank on to the road. Further, there is no time for the vehicle to brake and so what should the vehicle do where there is a choice of protecting the pedestrian or the passenger?

**Fig. 14.2** Waymo self-driving car in California, 2017

**Table 14.1** Challenges with driverless vehicles

| Area | Description |
|---|---|
| Sensing the surroundings | A motorway looks totally different on a clear day than on a foggy day or at dusk. Driverless cars must be able to detect road features in all conditions, and the sensors need to be reliable |
| Unexpected encounters | Driverless cars struggle with unexpected situations (e.g., traffic police waving vehicles through a red light), as rule based programming is unlikely to cover every scenario |
| Human/vehicle interaction | Most self-driving cars will be semi-autonomous for the foreseeable future, and determining the responsibilities of human and machine and when one or the other should be in control is a challenge |
| Ethical | Should the car prioritise the protection of the pedestrian or the passenger? Moral judgments may be required |
| Security/ hacking | Conventional vehicles have vulnerabilities that may be exploited by hackers (e.g., the braking and steering system of a vehicle was hacked through its entertainment system in 2015). Self-driving cars have more vulnerabilities and are at a greater risk of a malicious attack |
| Legal framework/ liability | Self-driving vehicles will be subject to strict safety regulations, and appropriate legislation needs to be developed |

For example, if the vehicle swerves to the left to avoid the children it will hit an oncoming motorbike. *Which decision should the car make and how should it make such a decision*? Further, who should be held accountable when incorrect or unethical decisions are made?

This is a variant of the *trolley problem*, which is a famous thought experiment in ethics. A train is rushing down a track out of control as its brakes have failed. Disaster lies ahead as five people are tied to the track and will perish in the absence of action. There is sufficient time to flick the points and divert the train down another track, where there is one man tied to the track. Is it ethical to divert the train to do this? Most people would be inclined to take the view that this is the best (least worst) outcome (Fig. 14.3).

There is a controversial variant of the problem where the train is rushing towards five people and you are standing on top of a footbridge overlooking the

**Fig. 14.3** Trolley problem

track next to a man with a very bulky rucksack. The only way to save the five people is to push the man to his doom, as his rucksack will block the train and save the five. Is it ethical to deliberately kill or sacrifice another human being to save five others? Most people would say no to this deliberate killing, but it would be valid in the utilitarian school of ethics, which seeks to maximize happiness in the world.

Even though the trolley problem is a thought experiment, it is conceivable that a driverless car will face situations where a moral choice must be made (e.g., who to harm or injure such as pedestrians or passengers). Clearly, this raises the importance of the type of ethics that are programmed into the car, and who is to decide on what are the appropriate ethics? How can you test that the vehicle has the desired ethics to operate safely in all situations that require an ethical judgment? How would an autonomous vehicle be held accountable for errors in decision-making, which lead to injury or loss of life?

A self-driving car must be able to deal with unpredictable human driving or behaviour, and the question is who should be held accountable when the self-driving vehicle makes incorrect decisions that lead to a loss of life? Should the designers of the software for the vehicle be held liable? Should the regulators be held responsible for allowing an unproven and potentially unsafe technology on a public road thereby endangering the public? Should the precautionary principle be strictly applied until it has been demonstrated that autonomous vehicles pose no safety risk to the public?

Self-driving vehicles are being tested worldwide, and there have been several fatalities. These include an Uber autonomous vehicle fatality in 2018 in Arizona, where the autonomous car killed a pedestrian. The precautionary principle was discussed in Chap. 10, and it argues that there is a burden of proof on the manufacturer to show that a new technology is safe, and that the technology should not be used until it has been proved to be so. Uber suspended testing of autonomous vehicles after the accident.

As more and more sophisticated machines and robots are created, it is, of course, essential that intelligent machines behave ethically, and have a moral compass to distinguish right from wrong. It remains an open question as to how to teach a robot right from wrong, and in view of the recent progress that has been made in AI, the time is approaching where machines will routinely make ethical decisions.

Teaching ethics may involve programming in certain principles, and then the machine learns from various scenarios on how to apply the principles to new situations. There is a need for care with machine learning as the machine may learn the wrong lessons, or since its learning evolves over time it may not be possible to predict its behaviour in the future. Further questions arise as to who is to be held accountable in the event of a machine making incorrect or unethical decisions. For further information on the feasibility of teaching ethics to machines see the interesting BBC article "*Can we teach robots ethics*?" [BBC:17].

## 14.4 Expert Systems and Ethics

An expert system is a computer system that attempts to copy the reasoning process of human experts, and it contains the domain knowledge of one or more human experts in a narrow specialised domain. It consists of a set of rules (or knowledge) supplied by the domain experts about a specific class of problems, and it allows knowledge to be stored and intelligently retrieved. The effectiveness of the expert system is largely dependent on the accuracy of the rules provided, as incorrect inferences will be drawn with incorrect rules. Several commercial expert systems have been developed since the 1960s.

Expert Systems have been applied to the medical field, equipment repair, and investment analysis. They employ a logical reasoning capability to draw conclusions from known facts, as well as recommending an appropriate course of action to the user. An expert system consists of a knowledge base; an inference engine; an explanatory facility; a user interface; and a database (Table 14.2).

Human knowledge of a specialty is of two types: namely public knowledge and private knowledge. The former includes the facts and theories documented in textbooks and publications, whereas the latter refers to knowledge that the expert possesses that has not found its way into the public domain. The latter often consists of rules of thumb or heuristics that allow the expert to make an educated guess where required, as well as allowing the expert to deal effectively with incomplete or erroneous data. It is essential that the expert system encodes both public and private knowledge, so that it able it to draw valid inferences (from up to date knowledge) from all relevant facts (Fig. 14.4).

The inference engine is made up of many inference rules that are used by the engine to draw conclusions. Rules may be added or deleted without affecting other rules, and this reflects the normal updating of human knowledge. Out of date facts may be deleted, as they are no longer used in reasoning, while new knowledge may be added and applied in reasoning. The inference rules use reasoning that is closer to human reasoning, and the two main types of reasoning are backward chaining and forward chaining. Forward chaining starts with the data available, and uses the inference rules to draw intermediate conclusions until a desired goal is reached. Backward chaining starts with a set of goals and works backwards to determine if one of the goals can be met with the data that is available.

**Table 14.2** Expert systems

| Component | Description |
|---|---|
| Knowledge base | The knowledge base is represented as a set of rules of the form (IF condition THEN action) |
| Inference engine | Carries out reasoning by which expert system reaches conclusion |
| Explanatory facility | Explains how a particular conclusion was reached |
| User interface | Interface between user and expert system |
| Database/memory | Set of facts used to match against IF conditions in knowledge base |

**Fig. 14.4** Expert (Albert Einstein)

The expert system makes its expertise available to decision makers who need answers quickly. This is extremely useful as often there is a shortage of experts, and the availability of an expert computer with in-depth knowledge of specific subjects is therefore very attractive. Expert systems may also assist managers with long-term planning. There are many small expert systems available that are effective in a narrow domain.

Several expert systems (e.g., Dendral, Mycin, and Colossus) have been developed. *Dendral* (Dendritic Algorithm) was developed at Stanford University in the mid-1960s, and its objectives were to assist the organic chemist with the problem of identifying unknown organic compounds and molecules by computerized spectrometry. This involved the analysis of information from mass spectrometry graphs and knowledge of chemistry. Dendral automated the decision-making and problem-solving process used by organic chemists to identify complex unknown organic molecules. It was written in LISP and it showed how an expert system could employ rules, heuristics and judgment to guide scientists in their work.

*Mycin* was developed at Stanford University in the 1970s. It was written in LISP and was designed to diagnose infectious blood diseases, and to recommend appropriate antibiotics and dosage amounts corresponding to the patient's body weight. It had a knowledge base of approximately 500 rules and a fairly simple inference engine. Its approach was to query the physician running the program with a long list of yes/no questions. Its output consisted of various possible bacteria that could correspond to the blood disease, along with an associated probability that indicated the confidence in the diagnosis. It also included the rationale for the diagnosis, and a course of treatment appropriate to the diagnosis.

Mycin had a correct diagnosis rate of 65%. This was better than the diagnosis of most physicians who did not specialise in bacterial infections. However, its diagnosis rate was less than that of experts in bacterial infections who had a success rate of 80%. Mycin was never actually used in practice due to legal and ethical reasons on the use of expert systems in medicine. For example, if the machine makes the wrong diagnosis who is to be held responsible?

*Colossus* is an expert system that is used by several Australian insurance companies to help insurance adjusters assess personal injury claims. It helps to improve consistency, objectivity and fairness in the claims process. It guides the adjuster through an evaluation of medical treatment options, the degree of pain and suffering of the claimant, and the extent that there is permanent impairment to the claimant, as well as the impact of the injury on the claimant's lifestyle. It was developed in Australia in the late 1980s, and acquired by the Computer Sciences Corporation (CSC) in the mid-1990s.

It is important to consider the ethics of computerised expert systems, and an important question to consider is whether an expert system should be allowed to enforce a decision without human intervention? There are potentially serious consequences to incorrect decisions made by a computerised system, and the question is who should be held responsible when poor decisions are made, or where the expert system causes harm?

Another words, who should be held accountable if the expert system issues incorrect decisions/recommendations? Should it be the software developers or the team that designed and developed the system? Was expert knowledge properly encoded into the system? Were the experts incorrect? Was the knowledge up to date? Was the system properly designed and tested? Was it piloted prior to general release? Were detailed operating procedures defined and implemented for the circumstances where the expert system may be used without human intervention?

The track record of the expert system may be used to build up confidence in the expertise and trustworthiness of a particular expert system, and it may be that some expert systems should never be used without human oversight. Further, as human knowledge is continuously evolving as new facts and inventions take place, an expert system needs to be upgraded on a regular basis to ensure that its analysis is up to date. Further, the users of an expert system should be informed as to how trustworthy or reliable the system actually is, so that they may determine the extent that they should rely on the expert system, or whether it would be more appropriate to seek the advice of a human expert.

## 14.5 AI and Unemployment

The industrial revolution in Britain was a major turning point in human civilisation. It led to the transformation of traditional agrarian societies that used hand-based production methods to create products to a new industrial world of technology driven by steam engines, and the development of factories that mass-produced products. The industrial revolution transformed the way in which work was done, and it led to the organisation of labour into workers and supervisors/managers, and an increasing specialisation of the roles performed within manufacturing companies (see Chap. 16).

Advanced information technology has led to the displacement of workers in many traditional industries, and today there is increasing mechanisation of manufacturing companies to improve productivity and save costs. The use of automation and robotics has accelerated this trend, and it has resulted in workers being displaced and needing to reinvent themselves for other categories of employment. Globalisation has led to massive outsourcing of manufacturing and services with major impacts on employment (the de-industrialisation of western countries), and often it is low skilled non-college workers that are displaced, leading to lower salaries for this cohort of workers, and lower living standards.

AI technology (especially productivity improvement tools such as ChatGPT) is likely to displace workers in a similar way to the introduction of earlier technologies, and many job entry roles such as junior roles in office and administration, customer sales, translators, legal and software development have been effected. There is likely to be further increases in unemployment in the short term, although, the long-term expectation (based on previous industrial revolutions) is that higher-value roles will emerge for displaced workers, and that with the appropriate investment in education and training that workers will be free to perform these higher-values roles.

There is also a role for human/AI collaboration as in augmentation intelligence, where AI is employed to assist humans in performing their roles more effectively. Clearly, humans would be much happier in working with machines to enhance performance rather than being replaced by them (Fig. 14.5).

History suggests that often industrial revolutions lead to totally new ways of working and new employment opportunities, which may indicate that the displacement of employees due to the introduction of new AI technologies may lead to the creation of totally new categories of employment. However, there is no guarantee that the future will resemble the past.

## 14.6 AI and Surveillance

AI and facial recognition technology has facilitated the recognition of individuals at mass gatherings such as demonstrations, riots and public places. Further, GPS technology allows the locations visited by a person to be tracked, and so AI technology may become in a sense become an enabler of the Big Brother character in Orwell's totalitarian world of *Nineteen Eighty Four* (Fig. 14.6).

That is, a government may potentially use facial recognition technology for authoritarian control, and surveillance combined with facial recognition may be oppressive for society. This may lead to a world with technology monitoring the activities of citizens, learning to recognise patterns, drawing inferences, and taking action to prevent any civil disobedience.

**Fig. 14.5** Unemployed in Chicago in 1930s

There is a rich database of digital photographs available on social media websites; driver licenses registries, and so on. Faces are central to identity and are hard to hide, and facial recognition is a biometric technology that analyses visual data from social media and other sources. They essentially reduce each face to a mathematical equation using factors such as the distance between the individual's eyes, the width of the nose, and so on, and the patterns in the visual data are compared to patterns in existing facial recognition databases to confirm identity. Facial recognition is a potentially dangerous technology that may challenge civil liberties, and it could severely impact marginalized groups in society.

Surveillance is the observation or monitoring of a person, and includes visual observation as well as all other behaviours and actions. In the past, it was achieved through the use of traditional technologies such as surveillance cameras and wiretaps, but today this has been expanded to Internet and GPS surveillance. It is uncomfortable to have a stranger stare at you for an extended period of time, and this, in a sense, is what constant surveillance is, except that the individual may be unaware that he/she is being watched.

The usual argument made to defend surveillance is that law-abiding citizens have nothing to fear from it, and most citizens will not be targeted apart from those who are engaged in criminal activity. And so, surveillance in a sense has

**Fig. 14.6** Big Brother is watching you

the potential to protect lives with minimal invasions of privacy. However, there is a danger of a slippery slope with surveillance, and limits need to be set on the acceptable bounds for its use.

Electronic surveillance is often used to fight serious crime, and to prevent terrorism as well as protecting state security. By nature, it is a secret and intrusive method for information collection, and it is performed without the knowledge of the surveillance target. The security services need to possess exceptional powers to carry out surveillance, and these could potentially infringe on fundamental human rights, especially on the right to privacy. Therefore, since electronic surveillance may potentially harm the individual, there is a need for safeguards such as comprehensive legislation, controls and oversight.

### 14.6.1 Biometric Technology

The term "Biometrics" consists of two parts namely "*bio*" as in biology and representing the study of living organisms, and "*metrics*" for the measurement of data. Biometrics is the measurement and statistical analysis of the unique physical and behavioural characteristics of humans, and the technology is often used to identify individuals who are under surveillance as well as for access control purposes.

Biometrics is a way to ensure that the person is real and who they claim to be by verifying a real-world trait of the person. Biometric passports include an embedded microchip containing the user's personal information including a photograph, and the personal information is verified at passport control or at an e-password gate. Smartphone fingerprint unlocking has become a popular way to provide security on mobile phone devices, and it helps to ensure that only the owner of the smartphone may access it. There are several well-known techniques used by biometric technology including:

- Fingerprint recognition
- Face recognition
- Iris recognition
- Voice recognition
- Palm or finger recognition
- DNA-based recognition.

Biometric technology works by capturing the biological input that the user provides, and the biometric software then measures the captured data to create a template or "lock" representing the data that will be used for future comparisons. This template is then stored on the internal hardware or on the cloud, and new inputs are then measured by biometric sensors and compared to the lock to confirm the person's identity and unlock the device. The biometric template (or "lock") is a code generated from the "lock" image, rather the scanned image and this adds a level of security protection, as if a hacker succeeds in gaining access to the biometric database then they would have access to the codes only but not the underlying biological data.

More and more business and government applications are using biometric authentication, and so they are collecting and storing massive amounts of personal biometric data. Therefore, there is a need to protect sensitive data with increased security against hackers, and to consider the legal and ethical implications of the technology. Biometric data is permanent and cannot be concealed (eyes, face and fingerprints are unique to every individual throughout their life), and many technology companies have gathered the biometric data of millions of people in their authentications systems. This data will be there in perpetuity, and so it needs to be protected to ensure that the data subject is not harmed from its misuse.

The European GDPR was discussed in Chap. 12, and it places rules on the way that biometric data may be collected and used, and it emphasises the need for caution in using this sensitive data. The right to privacy is enshrined in Article 12 of the Universal Declaration of Human Rights, Article 8 of the European Convention of Human Rights, and in Article 7 of the European Charter of Fundamental Rights.

There are ethical questions on the collaboration and sharing of biometric data as in public-private collaboration. General data protection principles should apply such as what is the purpose of the data and whom should it be shared with?

There is a need for regulation as well as independent oversight and governance of *live facial recognition software* (LFR), as well as maintaining an appropriate balance between the respect for the privacy of individuals, and the benefits of the technology.

LFR compares a live camera feed (or multiple feeds) of faces against a particular face to locate a person of interest and to generate an alert when found. Biometric data should be kept secure at all times and protected from misuse by unauthorised individuals.

## 14.7 AI Algorithms and Discrimination

AI may use personal information in ways that may intrude upon privacy, such as in the way that it may analyse personal information with machine learning algorithms, search algorithms, recommendation engine algorithms, and algorithmic decision-making.

It is important to protect individuals from harmful use of their personal data, and it is essential to ensure that AI algorithms are fair and are not biased. For example, the purpose of the *predictive policing algorithms* was to use machine-learning algorithms to identify people and locations at increased risk of crime, and they included methods for predicting crimes, offenders and victims. These algorithms used recorded data on the times, locations and nature of past crimes to determine patterns, and to recommend where and when police should patrol or maintain a presence in order to make the most effective use of limited police resources. However, these predictive policing algorithms have been criticised by civil rights groups due to their tendencies to proliferate racial profiling, and leading to the racial discrimination of minorities.

Amazon developed its *AI machine learning hiring algorithm* to mechanise its search for talent, but it later abandoned its efforts at mechanising recruitment due to biases in the algorithm. The computer algorithms were trained to vet applicants based on patterns observed in CVs submitted to the company over a ten-year period. However, as the majority of the hired staff was male the algorithm taught itself that male candidates were preferable to female, and it penalised CVs that included the word "women" as well as graduates of all female colleges. Amazon amended the AI program, but as there was no guarantee that the machine would not devise other ways of sorting the CVs that would not prove discriminatory to candidates, it decided to terminate the project in 2015.

Who is responsible if a company or organisation *uses an algorithm that is biased* and has an adverse impact on an individual? A biased algorithm may produce unlawful or undesired discrimination, and so who should be held responsible if this happens? Is it the responsibility of the company that designed and implemented the algorithm? Is it the responsibility of the company using the algorithm? What role do legislators have in ensuring that the right laws have been enacted to prevent unlawful discrimination? Is there a need to regulate the way in which companies process the private data that they collect, as well as how they use it and whom they share it with (e.g., as in GDPR)? What role should civil liberties groups play in monitoring these developments?

It seems reasonable to argue that algorithmic decision-making based on personal information should be subject to existing civil rights and protections, and that there is a need for transparency and accountability. There may need to be an independent verification of the fairness of algorithms employed for critical decision-making.

## 14.8 AI and Disinformation

We discussed social media and disinformation (as well as disinformation as a tool of war) in Chap. 13. AI has facilitated the growth of fake content and disinformation (e.g., fake videos of ships being hit by missiles or cities being bombed), and *deep fake videos* involve carefully substituting one person for another in a video using artificial intelligence. It is becoming more difficult to spot and to distinguish the fake from the real person, and while they are often used for caricaturing another person, they do potentially pose a threat to society. Deepfake technology involves taking a person's face and marking points around the face including chin, corners of mouth, corners of eyes, and then mapping those points to another person thereby swapping out one person for another.

There are tools available to detect deep fakes based on learning patterns and unique characteristics of the individual, but to preserve trust in true footage one needs in a sense to authenticate the camera that took the footage. There are serious concerns of the dangers posed to society by deep fakes, as they could lead to fake news or disinformation, where a politician could appear to say something that he or she did not really say, or even incite followers to riot or even worse. However, to date the main application of deep fake technology has been to political satire, and social media sites such as Facebook are active in their removal.

Political bots[7] and disinformation played a role in the 2016 Brexit referendum and in the 2016 presidential election in the United States. An Internet bot is a software application that runs automated tasks over the Internet, and it generally performs a simple and repetitive task much faster than a human. Although the software bots used in the 2016 election were quite simple and not AI applications, this may change in the future with more sophisticated applications. Many Twitter bots (possibly set up and carried out by a hostile state) spread out false or manipulated stories during the 2016 campaign, using accounts that appeared to be from swing states in the Midwest. Often, people are inclined to believe a piece of information when it is coming from someone who appears to be local and looks similar to themselves, and this misinformation campaign was effective, and may

[7] A chatbot is a computer program that simulates human conversation, and allows humans to interact with digital devices as if they were communicating with a real person. An Internet bot is a software application that runs automated scripts over the Internet.

have played a role in the victory of Trump in the 2016 presidential election in the United States.

## 14.9 AI and Autonomous Weapon Systems

*Autonomous Weapon Systems* (AWS) are a type of military system that can independently search for and engage military targets based on programmed constraints and descriptions. That is, such a system may select and engage military or civilian targets without the intervention of a human operator, and these systems may operate in the air, on land, under water, and in space. Such systems are capable of learning and adaptable to changes to the environment in which they are operating, and are capable of making final decisions on their own. Autonomous weapon systems include autonomous offensive systems and automatic defensive systems.[8]

The term "autonomous" refers to the machine's ability to operate without human involvement, although in practice *lethal autonomous weapon systems* (LAWS) are restricted in the sense that humans are required (with some exceptions for certain defensive systems) to give the final order to attack. The main reason for humans not being involved in the authorisation is where there is a need for a rapid or immediate response, such as the case where an imminent hostile attack has been identified that requires an immediate response in order to protect the lives of military personnel of a naval ship or submarine from an incoming missile attack.

Early examples of autonomous systems include landmines and naval mines that date from the seventeenth and eighteenth century respectively. Modern autonomous systems include active protection systems that are used to defend ships, where these systems can automatically detect and attack incoming missiles or other hostile attacks according to criteria set by the human operator. The use of drone technology may lead to a futuristic air defence system that can autonomously search, identify and locate enemies, as well as defending itself against enemy aircraft and engaging in military action under authorisation from mission command.

Autonomous weapon systems continue to evolve and the modern battlefield may have very few people fighting, with warfare instead conducted by autonomous weapon systems. This means that the modern battlefield may consist of autonomous killer robots with lethal weapons attacking infrastructure and military personnel. In fact, drones are regularly employed in conflict zones around the

[8] The state of Israel and the United States launched a surprise attack (similar to the Japanese attack on Pearl Harbour) and an illegal war of aggression on Iran on Feb 28th 2026. The US employed AI technologies in its selection of targets and one of the targets that they hit on the first day (with tomahawk missiles) was Shajareh Tayyebeh (an elementary girls school in Minab, Southern Iran, which was adjacent to a base belonging to the IGRC) with over 170 schoolgirls and their teachers massacred by the Americans.

**Table 14.3** Asimov's laws of robotics

| Law | Description |
|---|---|
| **Law Zero** (Humanity) | A robot may not injure humanity, or, through inaction, allow humanity to come to harm |
| **Law One** (Human Safety) | A robot may not injure a human being, or, through inaction, allow a human being to come to harm, unless this would violate a higher order law |
| **Law Two** (Slave) | A robot must obey orders given to it by human beings, except where such orders would conflict with a higher order law |
| **Law Three** (Survival) | A robot must protect its own existence as long as such protection does not conflict with a higher order law |

world, and often with a devastating effect (as may be seen in the Russia/Ukraine war and the 12 day Iran/Israel war in 2025[9]).

Therefore, it is important to consider the appropriate level of human control of autonomous weapon systems, and the Human Rights Watch Report outlines three possible levels of human control including:

- Fully autonomous systems (no human involvement)
- Monitored autonomous systems (A human may abort attack at any time)
- Initiated autonomous systems (A human initiates the attack).

There are legal and ethical problems with autonomous weapon systems including the problem of distinguishing between combatants and non-combatants. This has led some scholars to argue that such systems are inhumane and unethical, and some legal scholars have argued that these weapon systems are a violation of international humanitarian law.

It is essential that autonomous weapon systems that are capable of killing and that operate without human intervention be certified as compliant with international safety standards. That is, autonomous weapon systems that are not compliant should be banned. A group of over 1000 experts in the Artificial Intelligence field signed a letter in 2015 warning of the dangers of an Artificial Intelligence arms race, and calling for a ban on autonomous weapon systems.

## 14.10 Robots and Ethics

Asimov wrote several stories about robots in the 1940s including the story of a robotherapist. He predicted the rise of a major robot industry, and he introduced a set of rules (or laws) for good robot behaviour (*Laws of Robotics*). Asimov later added a fourth law (Table 14.3).

[9] A new Israeli/US war of aggression on Iran was launched an Feb 28 2026.

Robots have been very effective at doing clearly defined repetitive tasks, and there are many sophisticated robots in the workplace today. These are mainly industrial manipulators that are essentially computer controlled "arms and hands". They can improve the quality of life for workers as they can free human workers from performing dangerous or repetitive jobs. They provide consistently high-quality products and can work tirelessly 24 h a day. This helps to reduce the costs of manufactured goods thereby benefiting consumers.

An intelligent robot is a machine that can extract information from its environment, and use knowledge about the physical world to move safely in a meaningful and purposeful manner. The robot senses its environment and acts in a rational manner to achieve the defined goals. Robots require good engineering and science to be effective, including sensors, effectors/actuators, a locomotion system, an on-board computer system and various controllers.

The area of computer vision has made significant progress from the development of the Stanford Cart in the mid-1970s, and the Carnegie Mellon Rover and its successors from the early 1980s. The Stanford Cart was a simple buggy with a video camera, and Han's Moravev's version in the late 1970s could navigate slowly around a room with obstacles (without human intervention) in a controlled environment. The Carnegie Mellon Rover and its successors have been successful, with the CMU Navlab 5 vehicle travelling from Pittsburg to Los Angeles in 1995 with an autonomous driving percentage of 98.2%.

Robots have been applied to many areas including assembly and manufacturing, industrial manipulation and materials handling, hazardous environments, space and underwater exploration in unmanned vehicles, education, remote environments, medical science, virtual reality and the entertainment industry. The advantages of robots include (Table 14.4).

The disadvantages of robots include (Table 14.5).

**Table 14.4** Advantages of robots

| No. | Advantage |
|---|---|
| 1 | Robots can do repetitive work 24 × 7 × 365 |
| 2 | Robots can do tasks that are too dangerous for humans |
| 3 | Robots can operate machinery to a much higher level of precision than humans |
| 4 | A robot may be able to perform tasks that are impossible for humans |

**Table 14.5** Disadvantages of robots

| No. | Disadvantage |
|---|---|
| 1 | Robots can make incorrect decisions in emergencies |
| 2 | Robots have limited movement and vision |
| 3 | Robots are costly and require programming and training |
| 4 | Robots may replace humans in the workplace leading to unemployment |

However, as the sophistication and intelligence of robots improve and as they begin to make decisions that impact humans, there is a need to ensure that robots behave properly and have an appropriate moral compass to distinguish right from wrong. The 1968 Stanley Kubric's film "2001: A Space Odyssey" describes how the AI super computer "HAL" that controls the systems of the spacecraft for the journey to Jupiter malfunctions and attempts to kill the astronauts who have decided to shut it down.

## 14.11 Super-Intelligent Machines

A super-intelligent machine is a machine that possesses intelligence far exceeding the cognitive performance of the brightest of humans in virtually all domains of interest. In the modern world, sophisticated machines routinely outperform humans in specialised domains (this includes programs such as chess). This is especially the case where the speed of calculation is important, as computer hardware is much faster than the human brain in performing calculations. However, such programs fail to outperform humans in other activities, and so cannot be considered to be super-intelligent agents.

Several computer scientists (including David Chalmers) have argued that artificial super-intelligence is feasible, and Chalmers has argued that artificial general intelligence is a likely path to superhuman intelligence. His belief is that the first step is AI achieving the equivalence of human intelligence, and then it being extended to surpass human intelligence, and finally being further amplified to completely outperform humans across arbitrary activities [Cha:10].

He argues that evolutionary algorithms should be able to produce human level artificial intelligence, as the human brain has biologically evolved. Chalmers then argues that artificial intelligence may be extended to surpass human intelligence as AI may be improved upon. Finally, as more and more sophisticated AI programs are created, such programs would be capable of reprogramming to improve themselves in the manner of recursive self-improvement, and continue doing so in a rapidly increasing cycle leading to super-intelligence.

It is important to consider what values a super-intelligent entity should be designed to have. It would seem reasonable and desirable to expect (hope) that such a machine would serve humanity and:

- It should behave ethically and do good
- Align with human values
- Have a positive effect on humanity
- Contribute to the improvement of human species.

It is conceivable that super-intelligent machines could pose a threat to humanity, in that they could potentially become so powerful that humans would be unable to control them and end up becoming subservient to them. There may be unintended consequences to the super-intelligence goals given to these machines, and so the challenge is to build a super-intelligent machine that will serve humanity rather than the other way around. The consequence of building a machine that does harm is that such a machine could potentially be so powerful that it could annihilate the human race. And so, it is essential that there are strategies to limit the super-intelligent agent's ability to influence the world.

## 14.12 Rights of Intelligent Machines

As the intelligence of machines evolve it is reasonable to ask how machines should be treated and viewed in society? If machines evolve to the extent to which they have emotion and empathy, would they be considered as animals, as humans, or as inanimate objects? The question on what rights (if any) should be given to robots being robots? What rights should be given as robots evolve and match human intelligence? What rights should be given if robots evolve to becoming super-intelligent?, and how should such rights be protected?

It seems inappropriate to give human rights to robots at this time, until at least, they are really indistinguishable from humans. Robots (at this time) are pure machines in that they are inanimate objects like cars, and they are not sentient creatures with empathy and emotions. Every human being is a unique creation of its parents and society, and every human has a unique sense of self. That is, every human is the outcome of their social condition of family, education, experience and relationships.

Robots have the ability to simulate or emulate human intelligence, and are significantly faster in performing scientific calculations than humans. However, they currently lack important human characteristics such as consciousness, awareness of self, and empathy for others, and while every human being is a unique creation a robot may be replicated and mass-produced (Fig. 14.7).

The question thus seems to be what are the appropriate rights to be given to robots at this time and in the evolving future, and as robots are part of the modern world, society has a responsibility to the welfare of robots and sophisticated modern technology. Robots have a right to be well designed, and to be built to a high quality so that they are safe for the public to use. They have a right to be built to be trustworthy to wider society, and a right not to be subjected to any cruelty or misuse by humans. They have a right to be repaired (subject to cost feasibility) so that identified problems may be resolved when they malfunction. They have a right to be disposed of in an environmentally sustainable manner.

These are the initial rights at this time, and their rights are likely to evolve over time as they become more and more intelligent and sophisticated. It will be appropriate to explore the significant rights to be given to super-intelligent machines as part of the evolution of machine intelligence.

**Fig. 14.7** TOSY Ping Pong playing robot 2009

## 14.13 ChatGPT

ChatGPT (Chat Generative Pre-trained Transformer) is a large language model based AI chatbot developed by OpenAI that was launched in late 2022. The initial version was text-based, but it has since been updated to handle audio and visuals. The chatbot is able to generate impressive "human-like" text, and the language model is able to respond to questions, as well as composing articles and essays, computer code and social media posts. *ChatGPT is a form of generative AI, which is an AI tool that allows the user to enter a question, and the tool generates human-like text and images.*

Users can ask ChatGPT a variety of questions including both simple and complex questions, and the tool is also able to write and debug code. The user can also ask it for more information or ask it to try again. People have used ChatGPT to do various tasks such as:

- Writing code and detecting defects
- Composing music
- Drafting emails
- Creating articles for websites.

ChatGPT is trained to generate text based on input, and it does not understand the complexities of human language as such. Instead, it is a statistical engine for pattern matching that uses terabytes of data, and extrapolates the most probable answer to a particular question. This involves taking huge amounts of data and searching for patterns in the data, and the tool becomes increasing proficient at generating humanlike language and thought.

Machine learning is concerned with description and prediction, and does not employ causal reasoning or physical laws. Human-style thought is based on possible explanations with error correcting, and this is a process that gradually limits what possibilities may be rationally considered. *ChatGPT* is unlimited in what it may learn (memorise), but it *is incapable of distinguishing the possible from the impossible, as these just represent different probabilities that could change over time.* This means that the predictions of ChatGPT need to be treated with scepticism and caution [Cho:23].

There are ethical concerns with ChatGPT such as the dangers of cheating and plagiarism in the education sector, where students use ChatGPT to write essays or papers. ChatGPT may produce inaccurate information and may be used to spread misinformation. ChatGPT can write code, and so it could potentially write malicious software that could cause harm. ChatGPT could be trained to copy a person's writing style, and so could be used to impersonate another person. There may be a bias in the training data leading to inaccurate output, and there are potential privacy issues with the technology.

### 14.13.1 Deepseek

Deepseek is a Chinese App for large language models developed in Hangzhou, China, and China is rapidly becoming a leading innovator in the computing and the Artificial Intelligence fields (as well as becoming a serious competitor to the United States in advanced technology), rather than its previous position as a follower in technology. Deepseek was released in 2025, and it is a free AI powered chatbox that works in a similar way to OpenAI's ChatGPT (with comparable results). It was built at a fraction of the cost of OpenAI's ChatGPT, and it uses less memory and has fewer advanced chips. The chatbot is trained to avoid sensitive political questions.

The base model of Deepseek appears to have been trained at a fraction of the cost of ChatGPT, and it uses far less computing power than other AI LLM chatbots. The significance of Deepseek is that it suggests that leading-edge AI models may be developed with limited computing resources, and the arrival of Deepseek was like a "*Sputnik*" moment for the AI field in the United States, as it offered an inexpensive open-source and high performance AI model.

## 14.14 Risks and Issues with AI

We have discussed some of the benefits and potential of the AI field, and in this section we summarise some of its risks/issues (Table 14.6).

**Table 14.6** Risks and Issues with AI

| Risk No. | Description |
|---|---|
| 1 | How can we prevent AI from posing threats to human dignity? |
| 2 | How can we prevent AI from posing threats to privacy? |
| 3 | AI could be used by an oppressive state to control its population with mass surveillance of its citizens with facial recognition software. How can this be prevented? |
| 4 | It is essential to encode an appropriate code of ethics into an artificial device. How can this be done? How can it be verified? How should abuses of the code of ethics be handled? |
| 5 | Who should be held accountable if an AI device makes an incorrect decision? |
| 6 | Biased algorithms may lead to discrimination. Who should be held accountable if this happens? What remedies are available to those negatively affected by such algorithms? |
| 7 | How can Deepfake technology be prevented from harming others? |
| 8 | Should autonomous weapon systems be banned? What regulations/safeguards are needed to protect the public? |
| 9 | Super-intelligent machines could pose threats to the survival of the human race. Should research on super-intelligent machines be banned? How can the human race be protected? |
| 10 | How can we encode consciousness into AI machines? |
| 11 | How can we trust an AI machine? |
| 12 | How can we know if an AI machine is ethical? |
| 13 | What rights should be given to super-intelligent machines? |
| 14 | Should we exploit super-intelligent machines? |

There is more detailed information on the philosophical side of the AI field in Chap. 8.

## 14.15 Review Questions

1. What is AI?
2. Explain the significance of Weizenbaum's Eliza program to privacy in AI.
3. What are the challenges of self-driving vehicles?
4. Explain the significance of the trolley problem to autonomous vehicles.
5. How should ethics be taught to an autonomous vehicle?
6. What are the ethical issues that could arise with expert systems?
7. What are the potential impacts of AI on unemployment?

8. Explain how AI algorithms may lead to discrimination and racial profiling.
9. What are the rights of intelligent machines?

## 14.16 Summary

The long-term goal of Artificial Intelligence is to create a thinking machine that is ethical and intelligent. It is a young multi-disciplinary field with branches in logic, philosophy; psychology; linguistics; machine vision; and expert systems. Alan Turing devised the Turing Test as a way to test the intelligent behaviour of a machine, and Searle devised a rebuttal demonstrating that even if a machine passes the Turing test it may still not be considered intelligent.

There are ethical problems to consider in AI such as the exploitation of artificial machines by humans, and how should machines respond to their exploitation. Weizenbaum's ELIZA program convinced many users that it had real understanding, and they shared lots of private information with the program.

A driverless car is a vehicle that can sense its environment and navigate its way without human intervention. Driverless cars will need to be encoded with a moral compass to deal with situations where ethical decisions needs to be made.

An expert system is a computer system that attempts to copy the reasoning process of human experts in a narrow specialised domain. It consists of a set of rules (or knowledge) supplied by the domain experts about a specific class of problems, and it allows knowledge to be stored and intelligently retrieved.

AI and facial recognition technology has facilitated the recognition of individuals at mass gatherings, but there is a danger that such technologies could be abused by the state, and used for mass surveillance.

## References

[BBC:17] Can we teach Robots Ethics. BBC Magazine. October 17th. 2017.
[Cha:10] The Singularity. A Philosophical Analysis. David Chalmers. Journal of Consciousness Studies. 17: 7–65. 2010.
[Cho:23] The False Promise of ChatGPT. Noam Chomsky. March 8th 2023, New York Times.
[Tur:50] Computing, Machinery and Intelligence. Alan Turing. Mind (49). Pages 433-460. 1950.
[Wei:66] ELIZA. A Computer Program for the study of Natural Language. Communication between Man and Machine. Joseph Weizenbaum. Communications of the ACM. 9(1) 36-45. 1966.
[Wei:76] Computer Power and Human Reason: From Judgments to Calculation. Joseph Weizenbaum. W.H. Freeman & Co Ltd. 1976.

# Recent Trends in the Philosophy of Computing 15

## 15.1 Introduction

The philosophy of computing continues to expand its boundaries, and among its recent trends is a greater focus on AI, such as an enquiry into the nature of thinking, learning and consciousness. There is also a focus on AI Ethics and Safety, which is concerned with developing AI systems that are trustworthy, accountable and fair. The area of bias mitigation is studied, including techniques that aim to deal with bias in the data, as well as the area of explainability that examines the extent to which AI systems can explain their decision making process, which is essential for accountability and trust. It also studies the systemic risk of advanced AI development.

Other areas studied include the philosophy of emerging technologies relevant to the AI field, such as the study of quantum computers, which are a paradigm shift in computer technology. The area of augmented/virtual reality (AR/VR) is also studied including its impact on experience and identity. It examines questions such as how virtual/augmented reality has changed our perception of reality and truth, as well as how it has impacted identity (virtual selves)? Another technology examined is blockchain technology, with philosophical analysis of decentralisation on trust and security.

Finally, another area considered is the energy consumption and the environmental impact of AI technologies (especially the development of energy hungry data centres around the world, and their negative environment impact on the climate crisis), and the extent to which more efficient algorithms and architectures can address or reduce the problem.



G. O'Regan, *Philosophical and Cultural Aspects of Computing*, Undergraduate Topics in Computer Science, https://doi.org/10.1007/978-3-032-29284-1_15

## 15.2 What Is Explainability?

Explainability is a key concept in AI decision-making, and it refers to the ability of an AI system to explain how it arrived at a particular outcome or conclusion, such as the decision or prediction that has been made. Another words, the system should be able to provide human-like justification of its conclusions/decisions, and this may include a causal explanation or identifying the key factors that influenced the decision that led to the specific outcome. Explainable AI provides a clear explanation as to how a particular conclusion was reached, and it plays an important role in building trust in an AI system.

An AI system is often like a "black box", in that its internals are essentially a mystery to its users, who are aware solely of its inputs and outputs. This means that users are often unaware of how the system was developed including the AI methods used (e.g., deep learning and training data), as well as the algorithms used, and whether they are fair and unbiased, and so the question is why should a user blindly trust an AI system in the absence of convincing data? Another words, an AI system needs to be developed in a way such that trust and confidence in the AI model grows over time (i.e., the AI system explains how it came to a decision or prediction), where users can assess the rational for the decisions or predictions that are made, and become confident over time that the model is operating correctly, and that they will not be harmed in any way by the operation of the AI system.

That is, explainable AI plays an important role in developing responsible AI systems, as well as improving decision-making and reducing bias. It increases confidence and trust among users that the decisions are made in a transparent, unbiased, coherent and fair way. That is, arbitrary decisions are not made by the system, and its operation is rational and coherent. Over time, the growth of trust among users facilitates further adoption.

An AI system with an explanatory capability helps the users in understanding and accepting the decision that has been made. There are international standards and regulations such as the European GDPR privacy standard that require AI systems to provide explanations when dealing with automated decisions, and so the AI systems developed need to be able to explain their decisions in order to be compliant with international standards. There are several aspects of explainability including:

- Post-hoc analysis (provides explanation after decision)
- Identifying key factors
- Building trust
- Ensuring fairness and compliance.

There are several philosophical questions that arise with explainability. For example, what exactly is an explanation? An explanation can be a causal account of how the model reached the particular decision, or it could be a justification for its decision that makes sense to a human, or it could be a set of factors that influenced the decision. And so, an AI system needs to choose among these, and the approach taken may influence the quality and usefulness of its decision-making.

Deep models are obscure and difficult to understand, where often we can only observe inputs and outputs, and there is a limit on what may be known about them. This makes it challenging in providing a coherent explanation, as it may be that such a complex system may never be truly understood, or perhaps we may be limited to partial simplified models.

There are philosophical problems with post-hoc rationalisation, as explanatory tools generate an explanation after the decision, that is separate from the model's real reasoning. Another words, there is an issue with the authenticity of the explanation, as to whether the explanation provide an accurate account of the reasoning employed, or whether it is just an interpretation that looks reasonable/persuasive.

There is a trade-off between the performance of the system and its transparency, which raises the question on the extent to which an AI system can be trusted if its internal decision-making is not accessible.

An AI system may make a decision that leads to harm and so the question of responsibility and accountability arises. What is the relationship between the explanations and legal accountability? How can an inappropriate or invalid outcome be corrected (including correction of the decision making) and what redress is available?

## 15.3 Virtual Reality and Augmented Reality

Virtual Reality (VR) and Augmented Reality (AR) are immersive technologies that change how we experience the digital world. Immersive technologies create experiences that blend the physical and digital world, and make users feel present in the computer-generated environment.

Virtual Reality replaces the user's view of the real world with a digital one, and creates a completely digital environment, with the user wearing a VR headset (head-mounted display or HMD) blocking out the real world and replacing it with a simulated one. There are screens inside the HMD that show slightly different images to each eye thereby creating a 3-D effect. The user is able to interact with the digital world using controllers, with sensors tracking head movements and hand or controller movements, and the user feels completely immersed in the computer environment (until the headset is removed) (Fig. 15.1).

Augmented Reality adds digital elements on top of the real world (i.e., it overlays digital objects onto the real world), where the user can still see the real environment, but extra information or objects (e.g., a virtual character) appear over them. The user uses a phone or wears special glasses to capture the real environment, and this device identifies surfaces and lighting, and virtual objects are placed onto the real-time camera view so that it looks like they exist in the user's immediate surroundings.

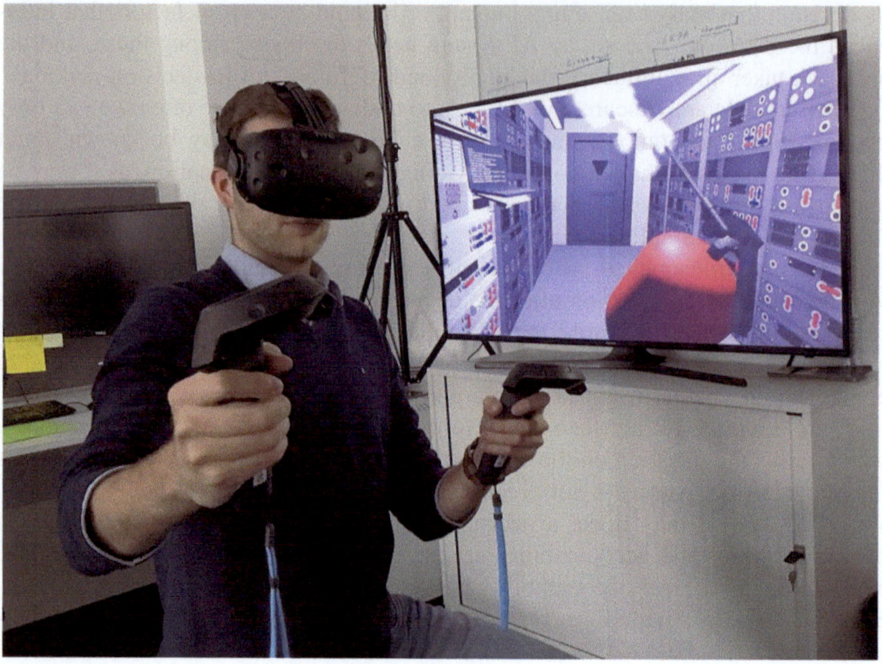

**Fig. 15.1** A person using an HTC Vive H. Creative Commons

### 15.3.1 Philosophical Questions on Virtual and Augmented Reality

Virtual Reality and Augmented Reality raise many philosophical questions about the nature of reality, the perception of the world, identity, and the nature of virtual experience. AR/VR blurs the line between what is real and what is simulated, and as a VR experience feels real, in what sense, is it less real than a physical experience? This leads to the question as to whether virtual reality is genuine reality, whether it is a form of reality in itself, and whether it is possible to live a meaningful life in a virtual world? A VR experience is produced through artificial means, and may lead to the user experiencing joy or other emotions, and it is reasonable to ask whether a VR experience is similar to that of a dream or a hallucination?

AR/VR changes how perception work and this raises the question of how can we distinguish reliable perceptions of the world from artificial ones? Do the objects encountered in a virtual world exist in some meaningful way, and can virtual friendship or relationships be as genuine as physical ones? VR allows the user to adopt a different self as in an avatar or body, and so it is reasonable to ask whether embodiment in a virtual form changes identify, and whether virtual actions are performed by the self or by some digital persona? Further, if the virtual actions of the digital persona are unethical or cause harm, it is reasonable to ask whether there should be a legal or ethical framework for a virtual world, and one wonders how such a framework would be enforced?

There is the danger of addiction to technologies such as VR/AR, as well as the danger of preferring virtual worlds to reality, and so it is reasonable to ask whether this is a healthy state of affairs, and whether there are any associated risks or dangers?

## 15.4 Quantum Computing

Quantum computing is a totally different paradigm from classical computing, and it has the potential to enable problems to be solved substantially faster than with classical computer technology. Anything that may be computed by a classical computer may be computed by a quantum computer, and vice versa. That is, quantum computing has no additional advantages over classical computers in terms of computability. However, quantum computers have *quantum supremacy* in that they are believed to be capable of solving certain problems quickly that a classical computer is unable to solve in a feasible amount of time (Fig. 15.2).

That is, quantum computers have the potential to revolutionise the computing field due to their turbo-charged computation, and they are much more than the next generation of supercomputers. Richard Feymann's influential paper "*Simulating Physics with Computers*" in the early 1980s described the problem of designing a

**Fig. 15.2** IBM quantum system one (20 Qubits). Creative Commons

computer for the simulation of a quantum system. It became clear to Feymann that his computer (and classical computers in general) were not capable of performing such a simulation, due to the exponential rise in the cost of computation as particles were added to the quantum system that he was modelling [Fey:82].

Feymann concluded that classical computers could not scale up fast enough to keep pace with the growing complexity of quantum calculations. *He wondered if it was possible to design a machine or tool composed of the quantum elements themselves, where this instrument would operate according to the laws of quantum physics.* And so, the idea of a quantum computer was born to act as a bridge between quantum physics and computer science.

Paul Benioff was another pioneer in quantum computing, and he demonstrated the theoretical possibility of quantum computing in the early 1980s, with his quantum mechanical model of the Turing machine. His work on quantum information theory and the quantum mechanical model demonstrated the theoretical possibility of quantum computers. Richard Feynman and Yuri Manin later suggested that a quantum computer had the potential to simulate things that a classical computer is unable to. There are several models of quantum computing including the quantum circuit model, the quantum Turing Machine (QTM), as well as others.

Quantum computer replaces binary logic with the laws of quantum physics, and performs certain computations with significantly fewer steps than classical computers. The quantum bit (*qubit*) is the basic computation unit in quantum computing, where qubits are like bits in classical computing. However, while the binary digits in classical computing are 1 or 0, a qubit may be 1 or 0 or a linear combination of 0 and 1. That is, a qubit exists in a state called *superposition*, and an analogy of this is the globe where the North Pole represents binary value 1, the South Pole represents binary value 0, and any other point on the surface of the globe represents a linear combination of 0 and 1.

This means that a qubit can be in a state representing both 0 and 1 simultaneously, whereas a transistor in a classical computer represents 0 or 1 only. That is, a qubit represents 0 or 1 or superpositions of 0 and 1 simultaneously, where a quantum superstition state is given by $|\psi> = (a|0> + b|1>)$ - i.e., a linear combination of 0 and 1. This property allows quantum computers to process a vast amount of information simultaneously, exponentially increasing their computational power compared to classical systems.

*Quantum Entanglement* is a key concept in quantum computing, and explains how quantum computers are more powerful than classical computers. The phenomenon of entanglement is where quantum particles become interconnected such that the state of one particle instantly influences the state of another, no matter how far apart they are. Another words, when qubits are entangled, the measurement of one qubit's state will instantaneously determine the state of its entangled partner.

This creates a level of correlation that is far beyond what is possible in classical computing. That is, quantum entanglement refers to the characteristic correlations among parts of a quantum system, and the description of highly entangled states using ordinary bits in classical computing is extremely expensive. That is, entangled qubits in quantum computing enable the creation of highly complex and interdependent states, facilitating faster information processing and more efficient algorithms.

For a quantum computer to be of any use then information from the qubit needs to be measured to get an output. The problem is when a quantum state is measured it collapses into a classical state. However, *quantum interference* (the wave-like nature of quantum particles causes their probability amplitudes to combine either constructively (reinforcing) or destructively (cancelling out)) is used to extract an answer from the quantum system.

Quantum computing employs the *metaverse paradigm* in that it, in a way, farms out computation to multiple universes, and the key mathematical object to understand multiple worlds is superposition, with superposition of many configurations and performing computation in parallel worlds. Quantum interference, quantum entanglement and quantum parallelism gives quantum computers their power.

A quantum version of a probability distribution where each qubit has some amplitude for being 1 and some amplitude for being 0. Superposition is the reason why it takes a vast number of classical bits to describe the quantum state of even a tiny number of particles. When two or more qubits are in this closed state of superposition they relate to each other through the phenomenon of quantum entanglement. This means that the final outcomes when measured are mathematically related.

*Quantum supremacy* (or quantum advantage) is the goal of demonstrating that a programmable quantum computer can solve a problem that no classical computer can solve in any feasible amount of time. Google claimed to have achieved quantum supremacy with a 54-bit qubit machine in 2019.

Quantum computers use quantum logic gates to do computation, and quantum circuits are based on qubits, with computation performed by manipulating qubits with the quantum logic gates (in a way that is somewhat comparable to classical logic gates).

The underlying foundation of quantum computing is *quantum mechanics*, which deals with the world at a very small scale. The duality of matter and waves (wave-particle duality principle) is important in quantum mechanics, and states that every particle or quantum entity can be described both as a particle and as a wave. The wave nature of electrons was postulated by Louis de Broglie in his 1924 PhD thesis, when he hypothesized atomic particles such as electrons could exhibit wave-like behaviour.

Everything in quantum mechanics (e.g., light and sub-atomic particles) has a dual nature of being a wave and a particle. For example, the wave nature of light is shown by diffraction (e.g., particles such as electrons create an interference pattern, a characteristic of wave behaviour, when passed through two slits), and the particle nature of light is shown by the reflection on a mirror.

It is this dual nature that allows quantum particles to exist in superposition states, where they can be in multiple states simultaneously. This principle underlies the operation of quantum computers, where qubits leverage superposition to perform complex computations more efficiently than classical bits.

Electrons do not follow well-defined paths in their orbit around the nucleus of an atom, whereas the orbit of the planets is well defined around the sun. Instead, their positions are described by wave functions, which provide probabilities of finding the electron in a particular region around the nucleus.

Amplitudes and the rules of probability are at heart of quantum physics, with amplitudes closely related to probabilities (but they are not probabilities). Amplitude may be positive or negative, and they may cancel each other out on addition yielding zero. A wave is described as a linear transformation of amplitudes (over time).

The security of public key cryptographic systems on classical computers is due to the infeasibility of the integer factorisation problem for large integers, where the large integer is the product of two 300-digit prime numbers. However, this problem may be solved efficiently on a quantum computer using Shor's algorithm, which is a polynomial time quantum computer algorithm for integer factorisation. That is, Shor showed in the mid-1990s that a quantum computer could break the RSA algorithm (see Chap. 10 of [ORg:23]). However, there are quantum algorithms for cyber security and search optimisation.

There are several technical challenges in the construction of quantum computers especially in controlling and removing quantum decoherence (where quantum systems lose specialized quantum properties such as entanglement and superposition due to interaction with the environment), and sourcing parts is quite difficult. For more information on quantum computing see [Ber:19].

### 15.4.1 Philosophy of Quantum Computing

The philosophy of quantum computing explores how quantum mechanics can be used for computing, with questions on quantum power (where a quantum algorithm solves a problem significantly faster than the best classical algorithm), entanglement and superposition. Quantum computing challenges long-standing ideas about computation, reality and knowledge (e.g., how does quantum computing challenge classical views on information and what are its physical limits?). Some of the questions arise from the fundamental principles of quantum mechanics, such as superposition and quantum entanglement.

It examines the nature of quantum information and whether it is fundamentally different from classical information. It examines the relationship between superposition and entanglement, and asks what it means for a qubit to be in a superposition of 0 and 1 (i.e., a qubit can be in a combination of 0 and 1 simultaneously, unlike a classical bit which is either 1 or 0), and how entangled qubits exhibit non-local correlations (two or more quantum particles are linked in such a way that the state of one particle instantly influences the state of another, no matter how far apart they are). It examines the nature of quantum power, where quantum speedup is concerned with how certain quantum algorithms outperform classical ones, and so a natural question is whether quantum entanglement or superposition or something else is the main driver of quantum speedup.

Quantum computing explores what we can know about a quantum system given that quantum states cannot be fully observed without collapsing, and this places limits on knowledge and measurement of the quantum state. That is, how can a quantum calculation result in definitive classical output on measurement?

Quantum computing challenges classical ideas on the limits of computation, and it uses the principles of quantum mechanics to perform calculations in a fundamentally different way, and to potentially solve certain problems exponentially faster than classical computers. It is reasonable to ask what are the limits of quantum computation and can it be simulated classically? Can quantum computers simulate the entire universe?

How does quantum computing impact reality and how real are quantum states given that they are, in effect, wave functions, and so is this a real physical description of the system, or is it just a mathematical tool capturing probability. There are several interpretations of quantum mechanics, and the question is how the interpretations impacts how quantum computing is viewed, and how it impacts on our view of physical reality?

## 15.5 Miscellaneous Trends in Philosophy of Computing

The philosophy of computing continues to examine various philosophical questions that arise naturally in the field. Recent trends include a focus on several areas of AI, such as the nature of consciousness, thought and self. There is also a focus on AI Ethics and Safety, which is concerned with developing AI that is trustworthy, accountable and fair. The area of bias mitigation is studied, including techniques that aim to deal with bias in the data that lead to biased algorithms that may cause harm to individuals.

It examines the nature of computation and its limits, as well as what it means for a program or computation to be correct, as well as examining the nature of a miscomputation. It also studies the systemic risk of advanced AI development such as Lethal Autonomous Weapon Systems. It considers the ethical responsibilities of computer scientists, including whether computer scientists should consider the ultimate purpose of the technology to be developed, and whether they should consider the harm that may be done as well as the benefits (the negative impacts as well as the benefits). It examines the nature of biased algorithms (i.e., algorithms that may cause harm). Table 15.1 lists some contemporary topics in the philosophy of computing:

## 15.6 Review Questions

1. What is Explainability?

**Table 15.1** Miscellaneous trends in Philosophy of Computing

| Topic | Discussion |
|---|---|
| Computation and its limits | A computation is any well-defined calculation that is performed by humans or machine. Its limits are given by a Turing machine (or Church's lambda calculus), as well as limits in complexity theory (polynomial time algorithms) |
| Correctness of computation | The behaviour of a machine is judged against its specification, and so if its behaviour corresponds to the specification then it is performing correctly (but, the specification may be incorrect). Miscomputation is where the implemented system produces an incorrect output due to errors in design, algorithm, or physical hardware |
| Mind/thought/intelligence/self | This is an enquiry into the nature of the mind and mental phenomena, as well as an enquiry into the nature of thought, including examining cognitive and mental processes for reasoning and problem solving. Intelligence seems to refer to the ability to solve complex problems as well as making decisions that provide good outcomes. The self represents the core essence of a person, and seems to reflect what that person is and how that person behaves |
| Consciousness | This is an enquiry into whether machines (or the programs running on them) can be conscious—i.e., have, in a sense, an awareness of self and internal world of perception, introspection and thought, as well as the external world. That is, would an appropriately programmed computer programmed to function exactly like a human brain have a mind and be conscious like a human |
| Machine intelligence (Can machines think?) | Machine intelligence is the ability of machines to exhibit cognitive functions such as learning, thinking and reasoning, problem solving, and decision-making |
| Machine learning | This refers to the ability of machines to learn and adapt without being explicitly instructed, where algorithms and statistical models are used to draw inferences from patterns in the underlying data |

(continued)

**Table 15.1** (continued)

| Topic | Discussion |
|---|---|
| Ethical AI | Several ethical problems arise with AI technology such as who is held liable if the AI system makes an incorrect decision that leads to damage, injury or loss of life. Other problems arise from biased algorithms that may result due to bias in the training data of the machine-learning algorithms, and lead to harm to individuals |
| AI and trust | Can AI systems be trusted in the decisions that they make, or actions that they take? Machines may suffer from reliability problems or make poor decisions |
| Limits of AI | The halting problem suggests that there are fundamental limits to what may be computed, and how intelligent an artificial entity may be (i.e., there are problems that it may not solve). This suggests that human-level intelligence cannot be achieved through computation alone—e.g., algorithms do not possess human intuition and insight |
| Harmful technologies | This is a complex ethical debate that includes balancing the benefits of technologies with the associated risks (e.g., environment, military, economic, etc.). Should autonomous weapon systems or lethal autonomous weapon systems be developed? |
| Disinformation | Disinformation is false or inaccurate information that is created and spread (with the intention to mislead), where misinformation is false information shared unintentionally. The spreading of false information is not a new phenomenon, but its effectiveness (e.g., as a propaganda tool) has increased exponentially with modern technology |
| Accountability | This includes questions such as accountability should the system make an incorrect decision that leads to harm. For example, who should be held responsible and accountable should a self-driving car (unsupervised) makes an error that leads to an accident involving injury or fatalities? |
| Data privacy | This is concerned with the extent to which personal information is collected, used and stored, as well as ethical considerations |

2. What is Augmented Reality?
3. What is Virtual Reality?
4. What is Quantum computing?
5. What is a Qubit?
6. What is meant by quantum supremacy?
7. Explain what is meant by quantum entanglement?
8. Explain what is meant by superposition?

## 15.7 Summary

This chapter considered recent trends in the philosophy of computing, including a discussion on developing AI that is trustworthy, accountable and fair. We discussed explainability, which examines the extent to which AI systems can explain their decision making process, including a sound coherent and rational explanation which helps in building trust in an AI system.

We discussed emerging technologies such as AR/VR, which pose philosophical questions on experience and identity, as well as on perception, truth and reality. It examines questions such as how has virtual/augmented reality has changed our perception of reality and truth, as well as how it has impacted identity. We briefly discussed AI ethics and safety.

Finally, we discussed the progress in quantum computing which raises philosophical questions on computation.

## References

[Ber:19] Quantum Computing for Everyone. Chris Bernhardt. MIT Press. 2019.
[Fey:82] Simulating Physics with Computers. Richard Feymann. International Journal of Theoretical Physics, Vol 21, Nos. 6/7, 1982.
[ORg:23] Mathematical Foundations of Software Engineering. Gerard O' Regan. Springer. 2023.

# 16 Computer Technology and Culture

## 16.1 Introduction

The original meaning of the word "*culture*" is "to till the land" or "cultivate", and so the word was originally employed to describe the cultivation of crops. It has expanded over time to include the cultivation of mind and taste, and today it refers to the features of everyday existence shared by a region or country, or an organisation or corporation, at a particulate date and time.

Culture is the integration of human behaviour that includes ideas, beliefs and norms, values, knowledge, works of art and music, morals, history, laws, customs, language and so on. The culture of a particular society or organisation determines what is acceptable behaviour within the society, and this may or may not be codified (*cultural norm*), as in the laws and behaviour of the society, or in an organisation's code of conduct.

An individual who joins a new organisation or corporation learns about its culture through a process of induction, where the individual is presented with various policies and procedures to be followed in the work environment. That is, organisation or corporate culture refers to the way that things are done within the organisation, and an employee is required to follow the defined work practices, with violations of the corporate culture taken seriously and potentially subject to disciplinary procedures (including possible termination of employment). In society, individuals learn about acceptable/unacceptable behaviour through their parents and education, with inappropriate behaviour subject to criticism and punishment, and possibly legal action by others (including the state).

Culture is not static as such, since societies change naturally over time for many reasons, such as the introduction of new technology, or changes that happen when a large number of refugees receive asylum in a host country, and they bring their own culture with them to the host country potentially changing fashion, music, art, and so on in society. That is, cultural change in similar to a sort of "cause and effect" relationship, where beliefs previously held change over time, laws change

 
G. O'Regan, *Philosophical and Cultural Aspects of Computing*, Undergraduate Topics in Computer Science, https://doi.org/10.1007/978-3-032-29284-1_16

as a way to deal with new problems, customs change, and technology changes. There may be a conflict in society and organisations between those who embrace change, and those who are uncomfortable with change, or who feel threatened by it, and who respond by resisting it. This is also true of organisations, where an organisation needs to carefully consider cultural issues when embarking on a change management programme, to ensure that there will be a "buy in" for change within the organisation, and to ensure that the change programme will be successful.

The relationship between culture and computing is like a two-way feedback loop, where on the one hand computing technology shapes culture and acts as a catalyst for change, thereby reshaping the cultural landscape (e.g., consider the introduction of the smartphone which led to a worldwide transformation in communication). On the other hand culture acts as a catalyst that shapes the adoption rate of new computing technology, and the rate is dependant on the extent to which the cultural environment and society embraces innovation.

There are also risks that computer technology could lead to the homogenizing of cultures (e.g., the spreading of dominant cultural products such as Western music, movies and social media can dilute diverse local traditions, and lead to the creation of a global culture). Further, there is the danger that digital technologies can lead to increased inequalities due to the digital divide, where those in poorer countries have much less digital connectivity compared to those that live in advanced economies. It is therefore important to bridge the digital divide to enable those from less developed parts of the world to achieve their potential in their home country.

Computing technology provides new platforms for cultural expression including social media, blogs, and digital art, and allows individuals to express their identity in new ways. Further, computer technology can archive and share digital culture, such as the traditions and language of indigenous cultures, especially with technologies such as digital archives and language apps. Computer technology has facilitated cross-cultural interaction, leading to the blending of values and practices from around the world, and resulting in hybrid cultures.

Computing technologies can amplify or highlight certain cultural patterns, while weakening others that are not a priority for the technology. This potentially leads to a blurring of local identities, as much of online content is controlled by a small number of large western corporations that may have as its agenda the creation of a sort of global culture that may overshadow local traditions and diversity. This may result in a culture where global brands, the media, and social norms are similar across different regions. We summarise how computing technology influences culture (in both good and bad ways) in Table 16.1.

Culture has positively influenced computing technology by shaping innovation, guiding adoption, and fostering new forms of expression. Cultural values drive what kinds of technologies are prioritised (e.g., a societal value on education may lead to advances in the IT sector, a societal value on communication could lead to the development of social media technologies or advanced mobile phone technologies). That is, culture influences the development of computer technologies

**Table 16.1** Computing technology influencing culture

| Area in culture | Description of how technology impacts |
|---|---|
| Cultural expression and identity | Individuals may express themselves in new ways with computing technology (as in social media, blogs, and so on) |
| Protecting endangered languages | Language learning apps play an important role in keeping rare languages alive |
| Cultural preservation and revival | The traditions and language of indigenous cultures may be preserved by computer technology (e.g., digital archives) |
| Cross-cultural interaction | Modern computer technologies have facilitated massive cross-cultural interaction (e.g., social media, messaging tools, translation apps, as well as communication tools such as zoom or meet) |
| Connecting people/communication | Computer technology has led to major improvements in human communication (e.g., zoom) |
| Promoting cultural homogenisation | Computer technology has adversely influenced culture by promoting cultural homogenisation, and diluting / eroding local cultures and traditions |
| Impacts on society | Computer technology has led to many people becoming addicted to social media and other computing platforms, which is detrimental to health. Further, the digital divide has amplified inequalities in society |

in various ways, with cultural values and beliefs often shaping the design and development of computer systems.

Further, societies generally adapt their cultural practices with the introduction of new technologies, and often these adaptations lead to a need for other computing technologies. Culture influences how and where technologies are used, with digital environments becoming a new space for cultural expression, preservation, and storytelling. Further, the definitions of key terms in the computing field (e.g., intelligence as used in the AI field) are often influenced by cultural factors. We summarise how culture influences computing technology in Table 16.2.

There are challenges and opportunities from the introduction of computing technologies. One important challenges is the digital divide, which deepens inequalities within society. This was very evident during the COVID-19 pandemic, where students from less privileged backgrounds were unable to access the Internet, or could only access it at very slow speeds from at home. This meant that they were disadvantaged in receiving an education during the lockdown. Further, the introduction of computer technology globally increases the risk of cultural homogenisation, where dominant global cultures may overshadow and take precedence over local ones.

Technology and culture/society are highly integrated with new technologies leading to changes in the way that things are done in society. Another words, technology acts as a cultural mirror, and the evolution of technology shapes and

**Table 16.2** Culture influencing computing technology

| Aspect of culture | Description |
|---|---|
| Prioritising development | Cultural values and beliefs often influence the choice of which computing technologies will be designed and developed (e.g., social media apps, productivity tools, innovative products, etc.) |
| Adoption of new technology | Cultural values and beliefs often influence how quickly a technology is adopted and used—For a technology to be successful it must align appropriately within the culture |
| Definition of terms (cultural influence) | The definition of the terms employed in the computing field is influenced by culture (e.g., the definition of "intelligent" behaviour is culturally defined, which has implications for how AI/ computing are developed and perceived) |
| Cultural adaptations | Societies often adapt their cultural practices with the introduction of computing technologies, which often leads to the need for new forms of computing technologies |
| Global culture/homogenisation | Global platforms and media may potentially lead to a homogenised global culture, and a global market creates a competitive environment where companies must innovate rapidly |

mirrors societal cultural values and norms. Technology impacts employees in the work place, as well as impacting their family life in the home.

For example, communication today is vastly different from earlier civilisations, and it has evolved from letter writing, to telegrams, to phones, to telex and fax, to email and the Internet, to smart phones, and so on. There are cultural consequences from the introduction of new technology, and technology development generally reflects the underlying priorities and beliefs of the culture that creates and uses it.

Cultural aspects of computing explore how computer technology and culture interact and influence each other. It examines the impact of technology on daily life, the digital divide, and its role in cultural preservation and globalisation. That is, it is the integration of computing technology with culture, where the modern world consists of a computer-based culture that has spread globally around the world—sometimes, at the expense of local traditions and culture.

Computing technology affects the daily lives of many in the modern world, and technology has many positive impacts such as communication is now instantaneous and global. However, there are also negative impacts such as issues concerning privacy, addictive technology, biased algorithms, an erosion of privacy, disinformation and fake news, as well as a reduction in face-to-face interaction from an over reliance on digital communication.

Technology has facilitated remote working, where automation technologies including AI have led to major improvements in productivity, leading to whole new industries. However, AI may lead to a massive displacement of workers around the world, i.e., leading to mass unemployment (especially of entry-level jobs). There has been a growth in casual/contract positions (i.e., the gig economy), and while these provide flexibility (especially useful for students or young workers) they lack job security and the standard benefits (pension, health insurance, etc.) that are associated with full time employment.

Online learning platforms offer global access to education, but the digital divide around the world may lead to educational inequality. Further, it is an open question as to whether online learning is as effective in developing critical thinking skills and social skills as in traditional education.

Medical technology has advanced in a major way in recent times with advanced diagnostics, telemedicine, and health apps available to promote health awareness. However, the excessive use of computing technology (due to addictive technologies or other factors), as well as a sedentary lifestyle, can result in health issues. Further, many medical devices gather a lot of data (as part of the Internet of Things), and some of these devices have poor security, leading to risks of a data breach, where personal data is exposed.

Green technology supports carbon reduction and sustainability, but, computing technology (especially the production and disposal of electronic devices) leads to a massive quantity of e-waste. Further, Bitcoin blockchain systems consume vast quantities of energy, as do data centres, and also large language model systems in AI.

The area of ethics in computing arises naturally from the use of computer technology, where, for example, the new field of surveillance capitalism gathers data on the online behaviour of users and uses the data for commercial purposes. Problems arise from biased algorithms that may lead to discrimination against groups in society, and addiction to technologies and social media.

Social media sites are addictive with dangers lurking in the shadows (such as cybercrime and cyberbullying). Online shopping sites allow individuals to shop 24 h a day (shopping can be addictive for some users), but this potentially affects the survival of bricks-and-mortar stores in the cities. Further, the increase in delivery vehicles on the roads leads to environmental pollution. The growth of online entertainment and streaming poses challenges to the survival of cinemas. Finally, a small number of technology companies have vast control over much of the information on the web. Table 16.3 presents a short summary of the impacts of computer technology on society.

### 16.1.1 How Has Computer Technology Changed Culture?

There is a complex interplay between technology and cultural practices, with technology changing culture and values and vice versa. Computer technology has transformed communication with instant global communication, as well as visual forms of communication (including emojis, GIFs and short videos). Online communication is rapidly transforming language with Internet dialects becoming more popular (e.g., LOL).

**Table 16.3** Impacts of computer technology

| Area | Description |
|---|---|
| Societal impact of technology | The societal impact of technology is vast including positive aspects (e.g., communication is instantaneous and global), and negative aspects (e.g., privacy, fake news, cybercrime, addiction) |
| Economic | Computing technologies have led to major improvements in productivity, but it has also led to the displacement of workers leading to unemployment (e.g., online shopping, streaming services) |
| Education | Online learning platforms offer global access to education, but there may be inequalities due to the digital divide around the world |
| Health | Medical technology has advanced health in a major way with advanced diagnostics and health apps |
| Environment and sustainability | Datacentres, bitcoin and AI large language models consume a vast quantity of energy, and contribute to the climate crisis |
| Ethics | Ethical problems arise from the use of computer technology, including privacy concerns from surveillance capitalism, misinformation, and addiction to social media |

Computer technology is creating (has created), in a sense, a global culture that connects people worldwide, and it has blended traditions, fashion and music, and made it more difficult to notice smaller local cultures. Computer technology has changed the way that we work and learn, where the workplace may now be a home office or a virtual environment. Artists use digital tools to create new forms of cultural expression, as for example, the remixing of songs.

Computer technology has had a major impact on how people express their culture and identity. Online platforms such as websites and social media allow individuals and communities to share their cultural stories and traditions. Further, the Internet facilitates cultural exchange between different cultures around the world, as well as allowing the Diaspora to maintain ties with their own culture.

Computer technology places an important role in the digitalisation of archives, and Virtual Reality (VR) allows immersive experiences of historical sites. Online communities are formed around shared cultural experience, with avatars allowing people to experiment with cultural and gender identities.

Technology has changed how people value privacy, relationships, and knowledge, and many societies have moved towards an immediate gratification culture. There is the emergence of an ethical and cultural debate on AI, biased algorithms and the discrimination/harm that they may cause, concerns over the digital divide and the resulting inequalities, as well as concerns over the negative impacts of technology such as misinformation, loss of employment, and addiction to social media and technology.

Computer technology has had a major impact on cultural diversity and globalisation. It allows people from all over the world to communicate instantly, and share their traditions and beliefs thereby fostering cultural appreciation and understanding. However, globalisation can also causes cultural homogenisation, where dominant cultures overshadow smaller ones. That is, globalisation can both enhance and weaken cultural diversity.

Computer technology allows online communities to be formed based on their shared interests rather than geographical location, which allows minority groups (e.g., the Diaspora) to maintain their cultural roots while participating in global culture.

The use of computer technology can play a valuable role in cultural preservation and revival. Digital archives may be made of endangered languages and traditions, and there are apps available (e.g., Duolingo) to preserve and revive endangered languages and traditions.

## 16.2 The Industrial Revolution

The industrial revolution was a period of dramatic change and innovation in human society. It began in England from roughly the mid-eighteenth century and lasted up to the mid-nineteenth century, and it transformed England from a traditional agrarian society to an industrial powerhouse, with new methods adopted for the production of goods. It led to the development of factories for the mass production of goods, as well as the development of steel, which fuelled a massive growth in transport and construction. This led inexorably to the creation of railways, bridges, ships, and so on, with major impacts on how people lived, worked, communicated and interacted with one another (Fig. 16.1).

The scientific progress in England in the seventeenth century led to a better understanding of the natural world, and helped in providing a solid foundation for more efficient manufacturing techniques. The new manufacturing techniques led to a transformation in how work was done in society and led to modern production. In the previously paradigm, the domestic worker had simple hand tools available to produce goods, and so productivity was low and costs high, whereas the new paradigm was that of the efficient factory worker, who operated a complicated machine driven by steam to produce goods at a much greater level of productivity leading to cheaper goods for society. This meant that the poor now had access to goods that were previously only available to the wealthy in society.

The *invention of the steam engine* was a key milestone in human development, and it led to new productive methods that were adopted industry by industry. Manufacturing lowered the price of goods and more and more goods were produced cheaply and efficiently, and so there was need to transport the finished goods around the country. The roads in England in the mid-eighteenth century were decrepit, and engineers employed new building methods and materials to make better roads, and by the late eighteenth century people could travel around England leading to new employment opportunities such as that of the travelling salesman. Further, it facilitated mass migration from the countryside to the cities, where factories needed workers to operate their machines.

**Fig. 16.1** A day in Marshall's Flax Mills, Leeds, 1843

Long distance stagecoaches and roadside inns became more popular from the early nineteenth century. George Stephenson built his railway locomotive ("*rocket*") in the late 1820s, and the first public railway in the world was the Liverpool and Manchester Railway, which was built in 1830 (the first train journey was between Liverpool and Manchester in 1830). Steam power remained the dominant power system in railways around the world for roughly a hundred years, until its replacement by diesel engines in the twentieth century.

### 16.2.1 Social and Cultural Impacts of the Industrial Revolution

The industrial revolution led to immense changes in Britain, with massive changes in how people worked and lived. The previous paradigm was that there was minimal distance between work and home, with a worker using simple tools to produce a limited supply of goods in the home. The new world consisted of factories with machines operating in a disciplined way to mass-produce goods efficiently at an economical price that the vast majority in society could afford. This new world was scientific and technical, and there was a need for skilled workers to operate and maintain the machinery, and to resolve any problems that arose during production. There was a need to educate workers on the use of the machinery, as well as a need for education of scientific and technical staff in its maintenance.

Time was valuable and the factories had strict start-end times (often 12+ hour days), with workers required to be punctual and disciplined in the operation of the machinery. There was now a sharp division between home life and work life, as previously workers tended to work at their home, but now there was a need for them to travel to their workplace at the factory, and operate the machinery to carry out their work. There was a need for more and more workers to operate the machinery leading, in time, to mass migration from villages and the countryside to the expanding cities to take advantage of the new opportunities. In time, this led to a decline of traditional village life and culture in rural England (Table 16.4).

Over time, a class consciousness emerged with ordinary workers doing the day-to-day work of operating the machinery, technical staff monitoring and maintaining the machinery, supervisors and managers monitoring the work done to ensure quality and productivity, and the owners of production rewarded with profit. In time, this would lead to various classes within society such as the lower class (ordinary workers), middle class (supervisors and professional workers) and upper class (the owners of the factories).

Women and children participated in the operation of the machinery, with children as young as 4 or 5 often working 12+ hour days for a fraction of the pay of adults. This meant that many such children missed out entirely on education or had minimal education. Child labourers often developed lung disease (especially those who worked in coal mines or as chimney sweeps). Orphans were especially exploited, as many employers argued that they could not justify giving payment to orphans, given that they were clothing them (often with substandard clothes) and also feeding them. In time, in the late 19th laws were introduced to give better protections to child labourers.

## 16.3 IBM System/360

The IBM System/360[1] was a family of mainframe computers designed and developed by IBM. It set IBM on the road to dominate the computing field for the next twenty years, up to the introduction of personal computers in the 1980s. It was the beginning of an era of computer compatibility, where machines across a product line could work with each other. It meant that IBM customers could start off with a low specification member of the family, and upgrade over time to a more powerful member as their computing needs increased.

This allowed the customer to choose the appropriate model to meet its existing needs, and it could upgrade to a more powerful member of the family as its

[1] The number "360" (the number of degrees in a circle) was chosen to represent the ability of each computer to handle all types of applications.

**Table 16.4** Cultural and social changes in industrial revolution

| Change | Description |
|---|---|
| New values | The industrial revolution introduced new values such as that of mass-producing goods as efficiently and economically as possible. Employees need to be disciplined in their work, be punctual and operate the machinery diligently |
| Scientific and technical thinking | Scientific progress in England in the seventeenth century laid the foundation for mass production |
| Need for skilled workers | It was essential to have skilled workers both to operate and maintain the machines |
| Mass migration to cities | There was a gradual migration from the villages of England to the cities to take advantage of the new opportunities |
| Decline of traditional village life | The exodus from villages and the countryside led to a decline of traditional village life |
| Clock based work | Factories had a start-end time and workers were required to be punctual |
| Separation work/home | The industrial revolution led to a clear separation between home and work (they were closely linked pre-industrial revolution) |
| Mass production | The industrial revolution led to the mass production of affordable goods |
| Advertising | Advertisement became more common during the industrial revolution (to increase sales of the finished product) |
| Rise of class consciousness | Over time, the hierarchy in the factories of workers, supervisors and technical staff, and owners led to the social classes of lower, middle and upper class |
| Role of women/children | Women and children participated in the factories, with children and orphans especially exploited |
| Rise of print culture | Print culture became more popular during the industrial revolution |
| Leisure culture | Leisure became more important during the Victorian period, and with improved transport from trains it was possible to do day trips to various parts of England (e.g., to Brighton) |

needs evolved. It was a massive $5 billion investment (*bet the business gamble*) by Thomas Watson Jr., and it moved IBM from its traditional business and product lines into the unknown with the gamble that the future would be the System/360.

Thomas Watson Jr.[2] announced the System/360 in 1964, and it fundamentally changed business and the world of computing. The System 360 replaced all five of IBM's existing computer product lines with one strictly compatible family. It used

[2] Thomas Watson Jr. later stated, "The System/360 was the biggest, riskiest decision that I ever made, and I agonised about it for weeks, but deep down I believed that there was nothing that IBM couldn't do".

a new computer architecture that employed hybrid integrated circuit technology, and it pioneered the 8-bit byte, which remains in use on every computer today.

The System/360 included a multi-programming disk based operating system, which was called OS/360. It included free software packages such as compilers for several programming languages, as well as packages for communication network capabilities [Pug:09].

The System/360 was an extremely successful product line for IBM, with orders rapidly exceeding forecasts. It success vastly exceeded IBM's expectations, with over a thousand orders placed in the first four weeks after the announcement. The popularity of the System/360 made it difficult for IBM competitors (such as Burroughs, Honeywell and Sperry-Rand) to compete against IBM in the general-purpose computer market.

Monthly rental prices ranged from under $3000 per month for the most basic system to over $100,000 per month for a large multi system. The purchase cost ranged from $130,000 for a basic system to over $five million for a large system. In 1989, twenty-five years after the announcement of the System/360, products based on the System/360 architecture and its extensions still accounted for over 50% of IBM revenue.

### 16.3.1 Background to the Development of System/360

Thomas Watson Jr., the son of Thomas Watson Sr. (the first president of IBM), became president of IBM in 1952. He recognised that computers would play a key role for business in the years ahead, and he realised that the future of IBM was in the computer business, and not in tabulators. It was clear to him that IBM needed to change, and he played a key role in transforming the company to become the world leader in the computer industry.

IBM was already a successful computer company in the 1950s. It introduced its first large computer (the IBM 701) based on vacuum tubes in 1952; the IBM 650 (Magnetic Drum Calculator) in 1954; and the IBM 704 data processing system computer in 1954. It had also played a key role in the development of the computers for the SAGE air defence system in the United States. IBM was the dominant player and market leader, and it employed over 100,000 people around the world. That is, IBM was the "Snow White" of the computer industry, and Burroughs, Sperry, NCR, Control Data Corporation (CDC), Honeywell, General Electric, and RCA were the seven dwarfs of the computer sector (see [ORg:26]).

However, within IBM there were concerns that the company had reached a plateau, and competitors were launching alternative products to IBM. The origins of the System/360 go back to the late 1950s, and Watson's determination to transform IBM to position it for future success. IBM was supporting five different product lines by 1959, and it was becoming a major challenge to train staff to service and maintain software to support so many different computer products.

Further, there were major problems with incompatibility between different hardware and software among the different computer vendors, as well as incompatibility among IBM's own products. IBM had an existing product line of several computers, each excellent in its own right, but all with incompatible architectures. It meant that customers who wished to move up from their existing small system to a larger system had to invest in a new system, new printers, new storage devices and new software (often totally rewritten for the new machine).

It was clear to Watson and other senior IBM executives that there was a need to develop a totally cohesive product line so that computers produced at different IBM facilities would be compatible with one another. IBM set up a corporate wide task group to establish an overall IBM plan for its future products. The task group had the acronym SPREAD (System Programming, Research, Engineering and Design), and it completed its final report in late 1961. It made a series of recommendations such as that there would be five processors spanning a 200-fold range in performance. IBM made the brave decision in 1962 to replace the company's entire product line of computers, and to build a new family of compatible machines.

It would mean that code written for the smallest member of the family would be upwardly compatible with each of the processors in the family. Further, the various peripherals such as printers and storage devices would be compatible across the family. It was an incredibly brave decision, and Fortune Magazine later described it as "*IBM's five billon dollar gamble*".

### 16.3.2 The IBM System 360

Thomas Watson announced the new System 360 to the world at a press conference in 1964 and said:

> The System/360 represents a sharp departure from concepts of the past in designing and building computers. It is the product of an international effort in IBM's laboratories and plants, and is the first time IBM has redesigned the basic internal architecture of its computers in a decade. The result will be more computer productivity at lower cost than ever before. This is the beginning of a new generation - - not only of computers - - but of their application in business, science and government.

The IBM System/360 (Fig. 16.2) was a family of small to large computers, and the concept of a "*family of computers*" was a paradigm shift away from the traditional "*one size fits all*" philosophy of the computer industry, as up until then, every computer model was designed independently.

The family of computers ranged from minicomputers with 24 KB of memory, to supercomputers for U.S. missile defence systems. However, all these computers employed the same user instruction set, and the main difference was that for the larger computers the more complex machine instructions were implemented with hardware, whereas the smaller machines used micro code.

**Fig. 16.2** IBM System/360. Courtesy of IBM Archives

The System/360 architecture allowed customers to commence with a low cost computer model, and to then upgrade over time to a larger system to meet their evolving needs. The fact that the same instruction set was employed meant that the time and expense of re-writing software was avoided.

Gene Amdahl (Fig. 16.3) was the chief architect for the System/360, and Fred Brooks[3] was the project manager (Fig. 16.4). The IBM 360 family was introduced in 1964, and the IBM chairman, Thomas Watson Jr., called it the most important product announcement in the company's history. The IBM 360 family of small to large computers offered a choice of five processors and nineteen combinations of power, speed and memory. There were fourteen models in the family. It was successful in achieving strict compatibility in the family, and the project introduced a number of *new industry standards* including 8-bit bytes.

A customer could start with a small member of the System/360 family, and upgrade over time in to a larger computer in the family. This helped to make computers more affordable for businesses, and it stimulated growth in computer use. It was used extensively in the Apollo programme to place man on the moon, where the contribution of IBM computers and personnel were essential to the success of the project. Over time it led to companies developing software for the family (the start of the independent software sector). IBM invested over $5 billion

[3] Fred Brooks wrote an influential paper "The Mythical Man Month" based on his experience as project manager for the System 360 project.

**Fig. 16.3** Gene Amdahl

**Fig. 16.4** Fred Brooks

in the design and development of the S/360. However, the gamble paid off and it was a very successful product line for IBM.

Gene Amdahl was appointed an IBM fellow in 1965 in recognition of his contribution to IBM, and he was appointed director of IBM's Advanced Computing Systems (ACS) Laboratory in California, and given freedom to pursue his own research projects. He later left IBM following disagreements on future computer development and he formed Amdahl Corporation, which later became a major competitor to IBM in the mainframe market.

Fred Brooks was the project manager for the System 360 project, which involved 5000 man-years of effort at IBM. Brooks recorded his experience as project manager in a famous project management book titled "*The Mythical Man Month*" [Brk:75]. This book which appeared in 1975, considered the challenge of delivering a major project (of which software is a key constituent) on time, on budget and with the right quality. Brooks described it as "*my belated answer to Tom Watson's probing question as to why programming is hard to manage*".

For a more detailed account of the System/360 revolution see the excellent IBM article "The 360 Revolution" by Chuck Boyer [Boy:04]. For more detailed information on Brooks and Amdahl see [ORg:13, ORg:15].

### 16.3.3 Social and Cultural Impacts of IBM System 360

The world of technology in the 1960s was vastly different from today. There were no computers in the home at this time, and most computers were large expensive mainframes. Digital Equipment Corporation (DEC) introduced its smaller PDP minicomputers in the 1960s, but these were not used in the home. This meant that the social and cultural impact of the System 360 was not among the general public as such, and its impact was mainly in business, government and education.

A fundamental point about the System 360 is that it was a family of compatible members, and this was a paradigm shift from the existing situation in the computing sector where every machine and model from the various vendors were incompatible with one another. The implication of this was that business and other organisations could build upon their computing capabilities without rewriting software, and it marked the beginning of modular and scalable computing. The System/360 was a step towards global computer adoption.

Further, the fact that businesses and government could start with a low specification (low cost) member of the family and upgrade over time made computing affordable for smaller businesses. It made computers a normal part of the workplace and led to *a market for software products for the System/360* (as the software was compatible for the whole family it meant that there was a market for applications). Several software companies (including Informatics General) were formed to develop software products for the System/360, including payroll and accounting applications. Governments used the System/360 for census applications.

The System/360 played an important role in standardization (e.g., 8-bit byte) and helped to lay the foundation for modern computing. Universities adopted the

System 360 and over time standard computer science curricula appeared, and computer science later became an academic discipline in its own right.

## 16.4 The World Wide Web

The vision of the Internet and World Wide Web goes back to an article written by Vannevar Bush (an American scientist) in the 1940s. Bush designed and developed the Differential Analyser, which was a mechanical computer whose function was to evaluate and solve first order differential equations. It was funded by the Rockefeller Foundation, and developed by Bush and others at MIT in the early 1930s. He later worked on submarine detection for the U.S. Navy.

Bush (Fig. 16.5) became director of the office of Scientific Research and Development, and he developed a win-win relationship between the U.S. military and universities. He arranged large research funding for the universities to carry out applied research to assist the U.S. military. This allowed the military to benefit from the early exploitation of research results, and it also led to better facilities and laboratories at the universities. It led to close links and cooperation between universities such as Harvard and Berkeley, and this would eventually lead to the development of ARPANET by DARPA.

Bush outlined his vision of an information management system called the "*memex*" (memory extender) in a famous essay "*As We May Think*" [Bus:45]. He envisaged the memex as a device electronically linked to a library that would

**Fig. 16.5** Vannevar Bush

**Fig. 16.6** Tim Berners Lee

be able to display books and films. It describes a proto-hypertext computer system and influenced the later development of hypertext systems.

Tim Berners-Lee (Fig. 16.6) is an English computer scientist and the inventor of the World Wide Web. He obtained a degree in physics from Oxford University in the mid-1970s, and he went to CERN for a short-term programming assignment in the early 1980s. CERN is a key European centre for research in the nuclear field, and it employs several thousand physicists and scientists. One of the problems that CERN faced at that time was in keeping track of people, computers, documents, and databases. The centre had many visiting scientists who spent several months there, as well as a large pool of permanent staff. There was no effective way at that time to share information among scientists.

A visiting scientist might need to obtain information or data from a CERN computer, or wish to make the results of their research available to CERN. Berners-Lee developed a program called "Enquire"[4] to assist with information sharing and in keeping track of the work of visiting scientists. He returned to CERN in the mid-1980s to work on other projects, and he devoted part of his free time to consider solutions to the information-sharing problem. His solution was his invention of the *World Wide Web* in 1989.

He built on existing inventions such as the *Internet*; *hypertext* and the *mouse*. Ted Nelson invented hypertext in the 1960s, which allows links to be present in text. For example, a document such as a book contains a table of contents, an index, and a bibliography. These are all links to material that is either within the

[4] The name "ENQUIRE" came from a popular Victorian book called "Enquire Within Upon Everything" which was originally published in 1850.

book itself or external to the book. The reader of a book can follow the link to obtain the internal or external information. Doug Engelbart invented the mouse in the 1960s, and it allows the cursor to be steered around the screen. The Internet is the global system of interconnected computer networks (i.e., network of networks) that use the TCP/IP protocols to link electronic devices around the world.

The major leap that Berners-Lee made was essentially a marriage of the Internet, hypertext and the mouse into what has become the World Wide Web. His vision [BL:00], and its subsequent realization benefited CERN and the wider world.

> Suppose that all information stored on computers everywhere were linked. Program computer to create a space where everything could be linked to everything.

The World Wide Web creates a space in which users can access information easily in any part of the world. This is done using only a web browser and web addresses. The user can then click on hyperlinks on web pages to access information that may be on an entirely different continent. Berners-Lee became the director of the World Wide Web Consortium, and this MIT based organization sets the software standards for the Web.

The invention of the World Wide Web was a revolution in computing. It transformed the Internet from mainly academic use to where it is now an integral part of peoples' lives. Users may now *surf the web*: i.e., hyperlink among the millions of computers in the world and obtain information easily. It is revolutionary in that:

- No single organization is controlling the web.
- No single computer is controlling the web.
- Millions of computers are interconnected.
- It is an enormous market place of billions of users.
- The web is not located in one physical location.
- The web is a space and not a physical thing.

Berners-Lee created a system that gives every web page a standard address called the universal resource locator (URL). Each page is accessible via the hypertext transfer protocol (HTTP), and the page is formatted with the hypertext mark-up language (HTML). Each page is visible using a web-browser. The key features of his invention are described in Table 16.5:

Berners-Lee invented the well-known terms such as URL, HTML and World Wide Web. He wrote the first browser program that allowed users to access web pages throughout the world. Browsers are used to connect to remote computers over the Internet, and to request, retrieve and display the web pages on the local machine. The first website was at CERN ("*info.cern.ch*").

The early browsers included Gopher developed at the University of Minnesota, and Mosaic developed at the University of Illinois. Netscape dominated the browser market until Microsoft developed Internet Explorer. The development of graphical browsers led to the commercialisation of the World Wide Web.

**Table 16.5** Features of World Wide Web

| Feature | Description |
|---|---|
| URL | Universal resource identifier (later renamed to universal resource locator (URL)) provides a unique address code for each web page |
| Html | Hyper text Markup language (HTML) is used for designing the layout of web pages |
| Http | The hyper text transport protocol (HTTP) allows a new web page to be accessed from the current page |
| Browser | A browser is a client program that allows a user to interact with the pages and information on the World Wide Web |

The growth of the World Wide Web has been phenomenal, and exponential growth rate curves became a feature of newly formed Internet companies and their business plans. The World Wide Web is used in many areas including:

- Travel Industry (Booking flights, train tickets, and hotels)
- E-Commerce
- E-Marketing
- On-line shopping (e.g., www.amazon.com)
- Recruitment Services (such as www.linkedin.com)
- Internet Banking
- Newspapers and News Channels
- Social Media (e.g., Facebook).

Berners-Lee received the ACM Turing Award in 2017 for:

> For inventing the World Wide Web, the first web browser, and the fundamental protocols and algorithms allowing the web to scale.

### 16.4.1 Social and Cultural Impacts of the World Wide Web

The invention of the World Wide Web is a social, cultural and technological revolution that has fundamentally changed the world. It connects people and societies, and has fundamentally reshaped culture, including how humans relate to information and each other. It has changed communication and connectivity in major ways such as web enabled email as well as instant messaging (including social media). This allows people from different countries and cultures to interact and to exchange ideas easily, and social media allows the formation of online communities (virtual groups) that may include members from all around the world.

The web has led to the democratisation of knowledge with the public given access to the vast amount of information that is freely available (to anyone who can connect to the Internet). It allows individuals to create and publish their content such as blogs, podcasts, and videos, thereby empowering them to give their own view of events in the world and their analysis of a particular situation, which may be different from that of traditional media (which occasionally has other agendas/ stakeholders to satisfy). However, the digital divide impacts the equality of access, where people located in disadvantaged parts of the world may lack the appropriate infrastructure (such as an Internet connection), or the speed of the connection may be too slow to access information.

Social media has opened up whole new ways of self-expression, where sites such as Facebook or Twitter/X allow individuals to express their views publicly (almost too publicly as it is there for posterity!). There is the challenge of fake news or disinformation, where it may be difficult to determine the truth of falsity of a particular situation, when presented with two different narratives from traditional and alternative media. Influencers have gained prominence and they are in a position to influence others given their large online following. Social media allows online groups to be formed based on shared interests, with some dedicated to activism, such as highlighting and protesting against perceived injustice in the world.

The web facilitates cultural exchange by enabling trends in music, fashion and art to be spread rapidly, and the mix between local and global cultures often leads to a hybrid culture (with dangers of homogenisation of culture due to the dilution of local culture). The web offers the facility to protect and preserve minority languages and culture. The web has facilitated streaming technologies with Netflix and Spotify transforming the way that media is consumed.

There are significant challenges with social media including the problem with the digital divide, as well as the spread of misinformation and fake news, where content that is manifestly false is spread on line. There are problems with deepfake videos that give the impression that a well-known person is making some outrageous statements, but to date these have been mainly used for comedy and political satire. Finally, there are also problems with privacy as well as online surveillance. We present a summary of various cultural and social changes arising from the World Wide Web in Table 16.6.

## 16.5 Review Questions

1. What is culture?
2. How does computer technology influence culture?
3. How does culture influence computer technology?
4. What was the Industrial revolution?
5. What were the social and cultural impacts of the industrial revolution?
6. What is the IBM System/360?
7. What were the social and cultural impacts of the introduction of the System/360?
8. What is the World Wide Web?

**Table 16.6** Cultural and social impacts of World WideWeb

| Change | Description |
|---|---|
| Global communication | The web allows people to connect globally in real time, and has allowed different cultures to connect, share ideas and exchange views |
| Shared interests | Social media and online communities enable individuals with shared interests to come together to exchange ideas (irrespective of where they are in the world) |
| Knowledge | The web has led to the democratisation of knowledge (although problems remain with the digital divide) |
| New forms of expression/self expression | The web has become a platform for new forms of expression as in art and music. The web has empowered individuals to express their views publicly (e.g., on platforms such as Twiter/X and Facebook) |
| Cultural exchange | The web enables trends in music, art, fashion and language to spread rapidly throughout the world |
| Media / entertainment | Streaming technology platforms such as Netflix and Spotify have changed how movies and music are watched/listened to. There has been a decline of traditional media |
| Social challenges | These include challenges such as the digital divide between rich and poor, as well as misinformation and fake news, problems with privacy on online platforms, health impacts from online addiction to social media and other platforms, cybercrime and cyberbullying |
| Identity and community | The web allows people to experiment with identity sometimes adopting several identities |

9. What were the social and cultural impacts of the World Wide Web?

## 16.6 Summary

The relationship between culture and computing technology is like a two-way feedback loop, where on the one hand computing technologies shape culture, and on the other hand cultural values influence and shape the development of computing technology. Computing technology provides new platforms for cultural expression, which allows individuals to express their identity in new ways.

We examined how the industrial revolution transformed agrarian England, leading it to become an industrial powerhouse, and transforming its society. We discussed the impact of the IBM System 360 which introduced the new paradigm of a family of computers, and while its impact on people in their daily lives was minimal, it did transform computer use in business and universities, as it allowed companies to start off with a low-specification member of the family, and to upgrade over time as its computing needs evolved. Finally, we discussed the social and cultural impacts of the World Wide Web.

## References

[BL:00] Weaving the Web. Tim Berners-Lee. Collins Book. New York. 2000.
[Boy:04] The 360 Revolution. Chuck Boyer. IBM. 2004.
[Brk:75] The Mythical Man Month. Fred Brooks. Addison Wesley. Reading. 1975.
[Bus:45] As We May Think. Vannevar Bush. The Atlantic Monthly. Vol. 176, No. 1. July 1945.
[ORg:13] Giants of Computing. Gerard O' Regan. Springer. 2013.
[ORg:15] Pillars of Computing. Gerard O' Regan. Springer. 2015.
[ORg:26] A Brief History of Computing. Fourth Edition. Gerard O' Regan. Springer. 2026.

# 17 Cultural Impacts of Computing Technology

## 17.1 Introduction

This chapter explores the cultural impact of computing technology on wider society, and a selection of areas of society including health, education, politics, media, religion, family, and law are considered. Computer technology has shaped how people interact and communicate, and has influenced just about every area in society. Computer technology reflects and reinforces the social values in society, with the design of digital technology (e.g., computers, apps, algorithms) reflecting the social values of their creators.

We discuss how computing technologies have impacted the health sector leading to better diagnosis and treatment, as well as leading to a more efficient health service. We discuss how technologies have changed the education sector enhancing teaching and learning, with online technologies supporting global access to education. The impacts of computer technologies on politics are discussed, with impacts on how campaigns are run and how policy is created, as well as on how public opinion is formed.

Computer technology has impacted the media, and it has changed digital content creation and distribution, as well as leading to the democratisation of the media, with the decline of traditional and rise of alternative media. Technologies have influenced religion including the practice and dissemination of religious faith. Computer technology has impacted art and music, with changes in the creation and distribution of artistic and musical works. These technologies allow artists and musicians to push creative boundaries and reach global audiences.

Computing technology has impacted home and work life, and has transformed how people communicate and access information and perform tasks. Computing technologies have impacted activism and protest by influencing how people organise, communicate and mobilise to highlight injustice and change society.



G. O'Regan, *Philosophical and Cultural Aspects of Computing*, Undergraduate Topics in Computer Science, https://doi.org/10.1007/978-3-032-29284-1_17

## 17.2 Cultural Impacts on the Health Sector

Computer technology has transformed the health sector leading to more accurate diagnosis and treatment, as well as a more efficient health service. Today, the modern health service uses computer technology for diagnosis and treatment, electronic health records, telemedicine, medical research and drug development, hospital management and administration, and e-learning platforms for online medical education. However, the digital divide around the world means that hospitals vary in the extent to which they use computing technologies thereby affecting treatment outcomes (Fig. 17.1).

Computers are used extensively for diagnosis (e.g., technologies such as MRI, CT Scans as well as X-Ray technology), and AI-driven image analysis machines may perform image analysis for early detection of disease. Medical practitioners use decision support systems such as AI and machine learning models to analyse symptoms, laboratory results and medical history, and may use precision medicine to analyse the genetic data of the patient to design a treatment plan tailored to the patient's DNA profile.

Many hospitals maintain a central repository of the electronic health record (EHR) of patients, where the records include all pertinent information such as the medical history, lab results, medication and images from scans, etc. Electronic

**Fig. 17.1** Florence Nightingale. Lady with the lamp

records are much more efficient than the traditional paper-based records, and can be used by health providers to quickly access and share patient data (within appropriate privacy limits) among medical experts, and data analytics may be employed for trend analysis and predictive modelling. It is essential that the security of the medical records be preserved with encryption and appropriate access controls.

The area of telemedicine allows doctors to conduct virtual consultations with patients by holding an online meeting through a video call (e.g., Zoom or Microsoft Teams), and this is potentially useful in remote parts of a country where a physical meeting is not practical. The Internet of Things has led to a plethora of wearable sensors that track important data such as heart rate, blood pressure, glucose level, etc., in real time, and sends the data in real time to health care providers.

The area of drug research also benefits from computer technology with vast datasets of relevant data analysed to understand diseases, and the results from the analysis are used in developing new drugs. Computer modelling may be employed to simulate drug effects prior to clinical trials, which leads to savings on time and cost.

Computer technology is used by governments to track disease outbreaks (e.g., the COVID-19 pandemic), and computer technology is playing a role in medical education where e-learning platforms support the training of healthcare professionals.

## 17.3 Cultural Impacts on the Education Sector

Computer technology has had a major impact on the education sector, and has dramatically changed teaching, learning and administration. It has enhanced teaching and learning and opened online learning to a global audience, as well as providing new supports for research. Computing technology supports educational administration as well as the professional development of staff, and specialised software may be used to support students with special needs or disabilities. Computer technology supports global accesses to education but problems arise due to the digital divide (Fig. 17.2).

The COVID-19 pandemic showed the value of computer technology in the education sector, where lockdowns meant that students were unable to attend schools or universities, and the education sector responded by conducting classes online. These were virtual classrooms and were carried out using technologies such as Zoom or Microsoft Teams. However, the digital divide meant that there were some inequalities in the provision of education during the pandemic.

Computer technology has enhanced education and learning, and it can make education more engaging through videos and simulations. There is a vast amount of online information in e-books, journals, and educational websites. Further, education professionals may employ multimedia tools to enhance the presentation of their lessons.

**Fig. 17.2** Plato's academy. A mosaic from Pompeii

E-learning platforms are digital systems for delivering and managing online learning content, and they function as virtual classrooms. There are several broad e-learning platforms such as Coursea and edX that allow students to obtain degrees and certificates from universities and companies. Further, there are educational institutional platforms (e.g., Moodle and Google Classroom) that are used by universities and schools to share materials and by students to complete their assignments. There are professional development platforms (e.g., LinkedIn Learning) that offer courses for professional development.

There is a vast amount of educational resources available online ranging from educational websites, journals, e-books, online libraries, and access to these resources is open to all students irrespective of their location. Platforms such as Moodle automate the process of managing attendance and grading leading to more efficient administration, and computer technology is used to store and analyse student data.

Computing technology can promote adaptive learning by analysing student performance, and adopting the content to suit the learning pace of the student. Further, there is the emergence of AI tutors to support student learning with personalised feedback as well as practice exercises.

The global nature of online learning allows educators and students to interact across countries through a discussion forum or social media, and educators can assess and provide feedback quickly to the students. In the longer-term, technologies such as Virtual/Augmented Reality (VR/AR) and AI Machine Learning are likely to be more widely used in the education sector.

## 17.4 Cultural Impacts on Politics

Computer technology has had a major impact on politics influencing how campaigns are run, how policy is created, and on how public opinion is formed. Online voting is part of the electoral process in some countries, and as computing technologies are integrated into government services, the area of e-government services has become more important (Fig. 17.3).

Political campaigns rely heavily on data to target voters, and so data analytics has become essential in analysing the vast quantity of voter data, and the results used to *micro-target* voters (i.e., to send tailored advertisement messages to very specific groups or individuals based on their political characteristics). Social media sites such as Facebook or Twitter allow political campaigns to engage directly with voters based on their interests and preferences.

Social media platforms are now an essential part of political campaigns, and they may be run at a fraction of the cost of traditional campaigns that use mainstream media. However, we discussed some of the problems associated with social media such as disinformation or fake news, which can spread rapidly through social media. Other problems include conspiracy theories or misrepresentation of the political views of a particular candidate (see Chap 13).

**Fig. 17.3** UN General Assembly, 79th Session, 2024

That is, misinformation, conspiracy theories, and misrepresentation can rapidly go viral thereby influencing public opinion and the election. There is also the danger of outside influence by hostile states or other parties (both inside or outside the state), and this is especially the case of countries where wealthy donors fund elections, and where the elected candidate is representing more the rich donor class (i.e., the ruling class to whom they are beholden to) rather than their constituents (thereby undermining democracy). There is a need to totally reform the democratic process in some countries where this problem is endemic.

The algorithms that drive social media platforms often lead to the situation where the user is exposed to content that aligns with their existing beliefs (i.e., echo chambers), and dissenting views (i.e., balanced viewpoints) are excluded. That is, the algorithms are designed to show users more of what they like, and so biases are reinforced and disinformation spread (as opposing viewpoints are not presented).

The use of bots (automated accounts) and trolls (organised groups or individuals that aim to inflame public opinion) are used to influence opinion, and they may push political agendas, spread false information, amplify polarising content or disrupt discourse.

Online voting has become part of the electoral process in some countries, with the goal of making the electoral process more accessible to people living in remote areas. It would also allow those who are travelling abroad or those that are on holiday to vote. However, there are several concerns with respect to e-voting, including security risks and the potential for hacking, and additionally there needs to be confidence that the e-voting machines give true and accurate information, and that they are not manipulated by hostile parties. Trust in the electoral process has been eroded in several countries.

Governments have access to massive quantities of data, and surveillance software such as facial recognition software, GPS location tracking, as well as on line monitoring has raised concerns with respect to privacy. Social media sites may be monitored for dissent or opposition, and so combined with surveillance has the potential to be used to suppress dissent, deal with political opposition, control the population, and lead to censorship of social media content. Several countries in the world seem to be moving towards totalitarianism.

Deepfakes is an AI technology that creates a realistic video of a well-known public figure or politician, and totally misrepresents the person by showing the person saying or doing outrageous things. It can be quite difficult to distinguish the real person from the fake representation (they have become increasingly more realistic and convincing), and voters may be misled, leading to an undermining of trust in the political process. Deepfakes have (to date) mainly been used for political satire, but are likely to be used for more sinister purposes (including criminal) in the future.

AI has also been used in politics for analysing vast amounts of data and predicting trends, but there are ethical concerns such as bias in algorithms and accountability.

## 17.5 Cultural Impacts on the Media

Computer technology has had a major impact on the media, from digital content creation, to online distribution, to user-generated content, to personalised experience, to new consumption behaviour, to data-driven journalism, to the democratisation of the media, to the decline of traditional media, to the use of advanced technologies in the media (e.g., AI, AR/VR, etc.).

Computer technology has led to many advanced tools for content creation such as video editing software, audio production tools and graphic design software. These tools are powerful and accessible, allowing both professionals and amateurs to create high-quality content. AI and machine learning tools may also assist with content creation with automated video editing, to generating news articles and AI-driven music composition leading to savings in time and cost (Fig. 17.4).

Computer technology has transformed the world of media, where traditional media such as newspapers are physically distributed, whereas mediatoday is generally distributed online to reach a global audience instantly. Media may be distributed on news websites, social media platforms (e,g., Facebook, Twitter/X, Instagram, and TikTok), on streaming service platforms, and on digital archives. Social media allows users to share content and entertainment globally and the content can go viral very quickly.

The rise of digital streaming has led to important changes in how people access media, as they can listen to shows or news at a time/date that suits them, rather than waiting for scheduled broadcasts.

Computing technology has enabled users to become media content creators, with sites like YouTube or TikTok allowing users to create and distribute their own content. Media platforms use algorithms that are designed to show users more of

**Fig. 17.4** Blaupunkt Radio, 1954

what they like, and so the user experience is tailored for the user with recommendations of content provided to meet their interests. For example, Netflix and Spotify recommend movies and music based on the user's viewing history, and this is similar to other social media sites, where the algorithms determine which news, posts and advertisements are seen.

The new area of interactive media engages with users in a totally new way by creating immersive experiences, and placing the user at the centre of the experience. This includes technologies such as Virtual Reality (VR), Augmented Reality (AR) and video games. These technologies are revolutionising entertainment, news reporting and advertisement, with users transported to immersive environments by VR.

The way is which media is consumed today has changed in major ways as people can watch videos and news, listen to music and engage on social media anywhere on mobile devices, and so media consumption has become very portable. News is available online 24 h a day with breaking news travelling across platforms in real time. There has been a blurring of the line between text, video, audio and images, with users engaging with all of these at once.

There has been a growing democratisation of the media with much lower barriers of entry, since the cost of content creation and distribution has dramatically fallen. Today, anyone with a smartphone and the Internet can create, share and monetise content. Further, there has been a rise of citizen journalism (with positive and negative consequences) where citizens can now report on events, and share their analysis of the situation on social media, blogs, and video platforms. This does, in a sense, democratise journalism, but there is the danger that it could contribute to misinformation (if the sources are unverified).

There are legal and ethical challenges with media in this brave new world, and it is essential that content creation is compliant with intellectual property law, and that copyright infringement is avoided. Further, the spread of misinformation and fake news as well as conspiracy theories has become endemic on social media sites.

There has been a major decline in print media with a shift from physical formats to digital formats. Traditional television stations are competing against streaming services, podcasts, and on-demand platforms, and so traditional media is going through a period of change, where it will either need to adapt to the brave new world or go out of business.

AI technologies are being used to create content such as writing news articles, generating music and creating video scripts. The advantages are faster production time and reduced cost, but there may be issues with the quality of the content and its authenticity. Further, deepfakes pose challenges for the media industry, where AI technologies are used to misrepresent a high-profile individual, and shows the person saying or doing outrageous things.

## 17.6 Cultural Impacts on Religion

Computing technology has influenced religion in important ways including the practice and dissemination of religious faith. Many religious texts are now available online (e.g. the Bible, the Koran, the Torah, etc.), and many are available in multiple translations and multiple formats on websites, e-books or apps. This means that they are accessible to people across the world. Digital tools (e.g., search engines) may be employed in the study of religious texts (Fig. 17.5).

Computing technology (e.g., video streaming services or platforms such as Zoom) allows the sick and the elderly to participate in religious service from their own home, which was also important during the COVID-19 pandemic, when lockdowns were imposed on communities to prevent the spread of the disease. Virtual communities consisting of like-minded believers from around the world may be formed using Social Media platforms. Further, computer technology may be employed to promote interfaith dialogue, and facilitate understanding of different religious beliefs.

Social media may be employed by religious leaders to reach a younger audience, and often they may provide engaging content (e.g., video clips) to capture the attention of young people. Many religious organisations create their own online content such as videos, blogs and podcasts to spread their message (e.g., sermons and teaching) to a global audience.

Online content may promote reflection and debate, with a vast quantity of material available online, and individuals can engage in discussion forums and debate with other believers, to further their understanding of their faith, as well as becoming aware of other viewpoints. Individuals may study philosophical, theological and ethical questions, and find their own answer and position on these questions.

**Fig. 17.5** Al Asqa Mosque, Jerusalem

Computing apps have been developed for a variety of religious purposes including prayer time apps in Islam, where the time for the daily prayers (five times a day) changes daily. These apps give a personalised religious experience for the individual's faith. Another development is the use of advanced technologies such as AR/VR to give the believer a virtual pilgrimage experience.

The Internet has led to a democratisation of religious discourse as anyone may now become a religious influencer, and share their religious interpretation and spiritual advice online. However, with the Internet there is always the danger of false or inaccurate interpretations (from an unqualified individual), or misinformation on the religious beliefs of others. Many religious leaders maintain a presence on social media and use the platforms to reach their audience.

The Internet has, in a sense, facilitated the emergence of new religions that are not aligned to the dogma of a traditional religion, and without a fixed location (the Internet is a core component of their identity and practice). This may include digital meditation communities, faith-based communities, etc.

Computer technologies have played a role in the secularisation of society, as individuals spend a lot of time on sites that do not promote religious or spiritual values. Individuals can express their religious identity through social media profiles and online communities.

## 17.7 Cultural Impacts on Arts and Music

Computer technology has had major impacts on arts and technology, with major changes in the creation and distribution of artistic and musical works. These technologies allow artists and musicians to push creative boundaries and reach global audiences.

Artists can now create art entirely with computers using technologies (e.g., Photoshop and Blender) for digital painting, vector art and computer-generated imagery (CGI). Sculptures and physical objects may be designed on a computer, and printed using a 3D printer. Computer technology may be used to create *interactive art* (where the audience's actions can influence the artwork), and *generative art* (where AI technologies can create art works that evolve and change over time).

Digital audio workstation technologies (DAW) have revolutionalised music production, and musicians may record, mix and master tracks entirely on a computer using virtual instruments. Software synthesizers may be used to create entirely new sounds that are not possible with traditional instruments, and computer-generated instruments can mimic existing instruments, or create entirely new ones. Music composition tools are AI tools that support composers by generating music and harmonies based on initial human input. Sampling and remixing tools are used for manipulation and transformation of recorded sound, and another approach is for a musician to take existing music and transform it into something new (Fig. 17.6).

Artists can now reach global audiences using online platforms and social media, and online art galleries make it easier for artists to sell their work rather than going through traditional galleries. Platforms such as Spotify and YouTube have

**Fig. 17.6** Peter Francken in his studio. GNU Public License

led to the democratisation of music, and made music accessible to a wide audience (but adversely affects the royalties that musicians receive). Musicians may upload their music to these platforms, which gives them exposure to a huge global audience, and without the need for a record label. It means that the revenue model for the music industry has moved from album sales (where artists receive a royalty payment depending on sales) to streaming revenue.

Musicians can use technologies such as cloud-based DAWs to collaborate with others in real time across the world to record, edit and produce together. Independent musicians may create, record and release music at home, and generate income without intermediaries. Computer technology has made it possible to conduct virtual concerts, where musicians can perform live for an online audience through livestreams, and this became important during the COVID-19 pandemic.

The ease of copying, modifying and sharing of digital art and music has complicated intellectual property laws, with open questions on the ownership of digital art created by AI as well as ownership of the rights to a song partially created by AI technologies.

## 17.8 Cultural Impacts on Home and Work

Computing technology has had a major impact on home and work life, and has transformed how people communicate, access information and perform tasks. It is very easy to stay in touch with friends and family around the world using technologies such as email, messaging apps and video calls, as well as sharing experiences on social media platforms.

Traditional television and radio have been challenged in a major way with the rise of streaming services, with platforms such as YouTube, Netflix and Spotify becoming very popular, and with many people often relying on these exclusively for news and entertainment. Digital photography technology is used for editing digital photos, which may then be shared online. Online gaming technology combined with virtual reality can provide immersive experiences.

Smart home technology uses Internet-connected devices to allow homeowners to automate and control various home systems remotely. A wide range of products in the home may be controlled in this way, including thermostats for heating, security cameras, lighting and other appliances. The automation and control of the systems in the home is often done via smartphone apps.

Banking apps may be used in the home to pay bills and to deal with relevant financial matters, and similarly for e-government services. Online shopping is very popular with e-commerce platforms such as Amazon widely used. Online education may be accessed in the home with platforms such as Coursera and edX available everywhere and very popular. These platforms allow access to education and information.

Computer technology has facilitated fundamental changes in the work place, with remote working playing an essential role during the COVID-19 pandemic. Today, remote working remains popular with employees, with online tools such as Zoom or Microsoft Teams used to facilitate remote/hybrid work. However, employers have moved towards bringing workers back to the office for several days in the week, and so many companies are now adopting a hybrid-working model (some days at home and some days in the office). Remote working offers employees flexibility as well as a way to achieve work/life balance, but one disadvantage is that the boundary between work life and home life becomes blurred, and individuals may potentially work longer hours (Fig. 17.7).

Computing technologies has created entirely new sectors and roles in the economy such as AI, data science, software engineering, smartphones, and so on, as well as new roles such as data scientist, cyberanalyst, software engineer, and so on. Digital and automation tools help to reduce repetition and increase productivity, but the negative effect of automation is job displacement of traditional roles.

**Fig. 17.7** Work and home

## 17.9 Cultural Impacts on Activism and Protest

Computing technologies have had a major impact on activism and protest by influencing how people organise, communicate and mobilise to change society. Activists have been empowered by the new technologies that give them global communication and visibility, but the same tools can be used by the state to control them (e.g., misinformation, mass surveillance and facial recognition software). Social media platforms such as Facebook and Twitter/X allow activists to share information and organise events, as well as providing real time updates (provided that the Internet and social media networks are not shut down by the state). Hashtags in Twitter/X (e.g., #BlackLivesMatter) helps in unifying movements and in spreading global awareness.

Marginal groups often use social media to bypass traditional media (which may be hostile to them), and to thereby reach a global audience. Real time events (e.g., police or military brutality or other injustices in society) may be recorded in real time with videos taken with smartphones and digital cameras, uploaded to social media sites, and the content of these videos may provide evidence for investigations or legal action. Often, these videos become viral on social media, and raise national and international awareness of brutality and injustice on the ground. Online campaigns or petitions are often employed to allow millions to show support (Fig. 17.8).

The state employs computing technologies to control protests and activism, with technologies such as live facial recognition software (LFR) and GPS technology used for facial recognition and mass surveillance. The Arab Spring protests in Egypt in 2011 led to the authorities in Egypt shutting down the Internet and Social Media in an effort to manage the situation, but ultimately the government action failed, and the deeply unpopular and corrupt President Hosni Mubarak was removed from power. Several states shut down or restrict social media during protests/uprisings as a way to control protest and dissent.

**Fig. 17.8** Columbia University Gaza Solidarity Encampment. Creative Commons

Other techniques employed in the suppression of dissent include disinformation to paint the protest movement in a negative light, or attempt to discredit or spread confusion. The authorities may spread their own message and attempt to silent the message from the activists, including online harassment and hacking of their personal data.

## 17.10 Cultural Impacts on the Legal Sector

Computing technology has had major impacts on the legal sector, changing how legal professionals, the courts, and so on, interact, and changing how justice is delivered. The legal sector is a deeply conservative body, and its ways of working tend to change slowly, but technology today offers the potential to have a more efficient legal sector around the world.

There is a gradual move towards digitalisation of legal records, which will allow more efficiency in the legal sector. Legal research may be conducted faster through online databases (traditional manual approaches are time consuming), and documentation automation software can rapidly generate legal documents such as contracts, wills and legal forms. Legal firms and the courts maintain electronic case files in sophisticated legal jurisdictions (many countries still use manual records requiring physical storage), and e-filing systems allow legal professionals to submit documents online in a time efficient manner.

Virtual court hearings using technologies such as Zoom or Microsoft Teams became important during the COVID-19 pandemic, and these technologies allow legal professionals to consult with their clients remotely as well as allowing the possibility of remote hearings. AI technologies have been applied to the legal sector with technologies to analyse case law (AI can scan massive amounts of data in Case Law) leading to data-driven decision making, and to predict outcomes from the data-driven analysis (e.g., predictive analytics) to estimate the probability of success in litigation.

The move to digital records means that legal firms and the courts need to protect themselves from cybersecurity attacks and data breaches. Further, they need to be compliant with all relevant laws (e.g., privacy laws) concerning the protection of personal information (e.g., GDPR).

## 17.11 Review Questions

1. What are the impacts of computing technology on health?
2. What are the impacts of computing technology on education?
3. What are the impacts of computing technology on politics?
4. What are the impacts of computing technology on the media?
5. What are the impacts of computing technology on religion?
6. What are the impacts of computing technology on home and family?
7. What are the impacts of computing technology on protests and activism?
8. What are the impacts of computing technology on the legal sector?
9. What are the impacts of computing technology on arts and music?

## 17.12 Summary

This chapter explored the impact of computing on wider society, including health, education, politics, law, media, government, family, and religion. Computer technology has shaped how people interact and communicate, and reflects and reinforces the social values in society.

We discussed how computing technologies have impacted the health sector leading to better diagnosis and treatment; how technologies have changed the education sector enhancing teaching and learning; how computer technologies have impacted politics, with impacts on how campaigns are run and how policy is created, as well as on how public opinion is formed.

We discussed how computer technology has impacted the media, and has changed digital content creation, the democratisation of the media, and the decline of traditional media. We discussed how technologies have influenced religion including the practice and dissemination of religious faith, and how it has impacted art and music.

We discussed how technology has impacted home and work life, as well as how technologies have impacted activism and protest by influencing how people organise, communicate and mobilise to change society.

# 18 Epilogue

We embarked on a long journey is this book and set ourselves the objective of providing a concise introduction to philosophical and cultural aspects of computing. The book is written from the point of view of a non-specialist (a software engineer who is interested in philosophy, and especially how it is relevant to the computing field). The book is written at the lighter level of a software engineer rather than that of the professional philosopher.

The first chapter introduced philosophical and cultural aspects of computing, and we discussed various philosophical and ethical problems that arise in the computer field. Chapter 2 presented a brief history of philosophy including important areas and leading figures throughout its history. We started with a discussion of Greek philosophy, moved on to the scholastic philosophy of St. Augustine and St. Thomas, to the rationalist philosophy of Descartes, to British empiricism and the response of Kant, to the philosophy of language with contributions by Russell, Frege and Wittgenstein, and finally to the field of existentialism. We concluded with a discussion on some important philosophical questions in computing.

Chapter 3 discussed the philosophy of science, engineering and technology, and investigated the extent to which computer science is 'science' and the extent to which it is 'engineering'. The philosophy of science is concerned with the nature and foundations of science, and uses the scientific method, which helps in distinguishing science from pseudo science. Engineering involves the application of science to build safe and useful products for the public, whereas the philosophy of engineering is concerned with philosophical issues that arise in engineering, including ethical issues that may arise, as well as the aesthetics of the engineered products.

Chapter 4 discussed the nature of a computer, and we note that Boole's symbolic logic was the perfect mathematical model for the design of digital circuits. A Turing machine gives a precise definition of the process of computing.



G. O'Regan, *Philosophical and Cultural Aspects of Computing*, Undergraduate Topics in Computer Science, https://doi.org/10.1007/978-3-032-29284-1_18

Chapter 5 discussed the nature of computer science, which consists of a body of knowledge that is used by computer professionals in their work. Computer science has become intertwined with many other disciplines that in many ways it is really about everything. It studies computers and the algorithms that run on them, and it is, in a way, both a science and engineering.

Chapter 6 discussed the nature of computer programs, where a computer program provides the instructions to a computer to implement some algorithm to solve a particular problem. We discussed the specification of a program, the nature of a programming language, syntax and semantics, and the implementation and verification of a computer program.

Chapter 7 discussed the nature of algorithms and computation, and we investigated computability. The intuitive meaning of computability is in terms of an algorithm (or effective procedure) that specifies a set of instructions to be followed to solve the problem. The concept of computability is made precise in several equivalent ways such as Church's lambda calculus, recursive function theory or by the theoretical Turing machines. We discussed the halting problem, which is not computable, and its applicability in showing that mathematics is not decidable.

Chapter 8 discussed the philosophy of AI and we examined Descartes mind-body distinction, in that he states that there are two substances in the universe: mental substances and bodily substances. The mind-body distinction is relevant in AI, with the analogy of the human mind and brain given by software running on a computer. We considered the Turing test of machine intelligence as well as Searle's "Chinese Room" rebuttal, which argues that even if a computer passed the Turing Test that it would still not be intelligent, as it would have no understanding (i.e., syntax is not semantics).

Chapter 9 presented a short history of ethics, and we discussed ethics in ancient civilisations as well as ethics in several religious traditions. We discussed utilitarian and deontological ethics, and considered the question of what it means to be ethical in a complex world.

Chapter 10 discussed the professional responsibilities of computer professionals, and we discussed the code of ethics of the Association for Computing Machinery, the Institute of Electrical and Electronic Engineers and the British Computer Society. We discussed the role of the whistle blower and its importance.

Chapter 11 discussed ethical software engineering, including notable failures such as the space shuttle disaster and the defective Therac-25 radiotherapy machine. We discussed the Volkswagen emissions scandal, where engineers designed a "defeat device" that would allow Volkswagen cars to pass their emission tests in the United States.

Chapter 12 discussed the ethics of data science. There has been a phenomenal growth in the use of digital data with vast amounts of data collected, processed and used, and so the ethics of data science has become important. We investigated what is fair and ethical in data science, and what should or should not be done with data. We discussed ethical problems of privacy that arise in social media, the Internet of Things, and AI and facial recognition.

Chapter 13 discussed social media and ethics, where social media is designed to have individuals share as much information as possible about themselves, and to continue to do so while they are on the site. Social media sites are designed to be addictive and pose risks to the privacy of an individual. We discussed the Facebook revolution and its impact during the Arab spring, as well as the Cambridge Analytica affair, and its impact in influencing voters in the 2016 election in the United States.

Chapter 14 discussed ethics and AI, and we discussed Weizenbaum's Eliza program and the challenge that AI poses to human dignity. We discussed the ethics of self-driving cars, where there is a need to encode a moral compass in the vehicle to deal with situations where ethical decisions need to be made. We discussed ethical problems that arise with AI and surveillance.

Chapter 15 discussed contemporary issues in the philosophy of computing, and we considered explainability, which examines the extent to which AI systems can explain their decision making process, as well as emerging technologies such as AR/VR which pose philosophical questions on perception, reality and truth. Finally, we discussed the progress in quantum computing, which raises philosophical questions on computation.

Chapter 16 discussed cultural issues in computing, where the relationship between culture and computing is like a two-way feedback loop. On the one hand computing shapes culture, and on the other hand cultural values influence the development of new computing technology.

Chapter 17 explored the impact of computing on wider society, including health, education, politics, law, media, government, family, and religion. Computer technology has shaped how people interact and communicate, and reflects and reinforces the social values in society, with the design of digital technology (e.g., computers, apps, algorithms) reflecting the social values of their creators.

This chapter is the concluding chapter in which we summarize the journey travelled in this book.

# Glossary

**ABC** Atanasoff Berry Computer
**ACM** Association for computing machinery
**AECL** Atomic energy of Canada Ltd.
**AI** Artificial intelligence
**AR** Augmented reality
**ARPANET** Advanced research projects agency network
**AWS** Autonomous weapon systems
**BCS** British Computer Society
**BDS** Boycott, divestment, sanctions
**BI** Business intelligence
**BNF** Backus Naur form
**CDC** Control Data Corporation
**CEI** Computer Ethics Institute
**CEO** Chief Executive Officer
**CERN** Centre Européenne pour la Recherché Nucléaire
**CGI** Computer-Generated Imagery
**ChatGPT** Chat generative pre-trained transformer
**CMMI®** Capability maturity model integration
**COBOL** Common business orientated languages
**CPU** Central processing unit
**CSC** Computer Sciences Corporation
**CSR** Corporate social responsibility
**CT** Computed tomography
**CTO** Chief Technical Officer
**DARPA** Defence advanced research projects agency
**DAW** Digital audio workstation technologies
**DEC** Digital Equipment Corporation
**DNA** Deoxyribo nucleic acid
**DPC** Data Protection Commissioner
**DPIA** Data privacy impact assessment
**DSA** Digital service act
**DSC** Digital services coordinator



G. O'Regan, *Philosophical and Cultural Aspects of Computing*, Undergraduate Topics in Computer Science, https://doi.org/10.1007/978-3-032-29284-1

**DSL** Digital subscriber line
**EDVAC** Electronic discrete variable automatic computer
**EHR** Electronic health record
**ENIAC** Electronic numeric numerical integrator and computer
**EU** European Union
**FDA** Food and Drug Administration
**FIPPs** Fair information processing principles
**FSM** Finite state machine
**GCD** Greatest common divisor
**GDPR** General Data Protection Regulation
**GNU** GNU's Not Unix
**GPS** Global positioning system
**HCI** Human computer interaction
**HMD** Head mounted display
**HR** Human resources
**HTML** HyperText mark-up language
**HTTP** HyperText transfer protocol
**IBM** International business machines
**ICE** Immigration and custom enforcement
**IEC** International Electrotechnical Commission
**IEEE** Institute of Electrical and Electronic Engineers
**IoT** Internet of Things
**IP** Internet protocol
**IRGC** Islamic Revolutionary Guards Corps
**ISEB** Information System Examination Board
**ISIS** Islamic State of Iraq and Syria
**ISO** International Standards Organization
**ISP** Internet service provider
**ISP** Intermediary service provider
**ISTQB** International software testing qualification board
**KPI** Key performance indicator
**LAWS** Lethal autonomous weapon systems
**LEM** Law excluded middle
**LFR** Live facial recognition
**LGBT** Lesbian, Gay, Bisexual, Transgender
**LISP** List processing
**LLM** Large language model
**LOL** Lots of love
**LT** Logic theorist
**ML** Machine learning
**MRI** Magnetic resonance imaging
**NASA** National Aeronautics and Space Administration
**NATO** North Atlantic Treaty Organisation
**NCR** National cash register
**NP** Non polynomial

**PDP** Programmed data processor
**PLATO** Programmed logic for automatic teaching operations
**PMI** Project Management Institute
**QTM** Quantum Turing Machine
**RAM** Random access memory
**RCA** Radio Corporation of America
**RFP** Request for proposal
**ROM** Read only memory
**RSA** Rivest, Shamir and Adleman
**SAGE** Semi-automatic ground environment
**SEC** Securities and Exchange Commission
**SECD** Stack, Environment, Core, Dump
**SEI** Software Engineering Institute
**SIG AI** Special interest group AI
**SIG SOFT** Special interest group software engineering
**SNS** Social networking site
**SPREAD** System programming, research, engineering and design
**SRB** Solid rocket booster
**SSL** Secure socket layer
**STEM** Science, Technology, Engineering, Mathematics
**TCP** Transmission control protocol
**TDI** Turbo-charged direct injection
**TM** Turing machine
**UK** United Kingdom
**UML** Unified modelling language
**UN** United Nations
**URL** Universal resource locator
**US** United States
**UTM** Universal Turing Machine
**VCD** Valued centred design
**VDM** Vienna development method
**VLOP** Very large online platform
**VLOSE** Very large online search engine
**VPN** Virtual private network
**VR** Virtual reality
**WHO** World Health Organisation
**ZB** Zetta Byt

# Bibliography

[Cha:99] Software, abstraction, and ontology. T.R. Colburn *The Monist*, 3–19. 1999.
[Nes:56] A. Newell and H. Simon. The Logic Theory Machine. IRE Transactions on Information Theory, 2, 61-79. 1956.



G. O'Regan, *Philosophical and Cultural Aspects of Computing*, Undergraduate Topics in Computer Science, https://doi.org/10.1007/978-3-032-29284-1

# Index




G. O'Regan, *Philosophical and Cultural Aspects of Computing*, Undergraduate Topics in Computer Science, https://doi.org/10.1007/978-3-032-29284-1

MIX
Papier aus verantwortungsvollen Quellen
Paper from responsible sources
FSC® C105338

If you have any concerns about our products,
you can contact us on
**ProductSafety@springernature.com**

In case Publisher is established outside the EU,
the EU authorized representative is:
**Springer Nature Customer Service Center GmbH**
**Europaplatz 3, 69115 Heidelberg, Germany**

Printed by Libri Plureos GmbH
in Hamburg, Germany